CSI: THE FILES

An Unofficial and Unauthorised
Guide to the Hit Crime Scene
Investigation Shows

Paul Simpson

First published in Great Britain in 2003 by
Virgin Books Ltd
Thames Wharf Studios
Rainville Road
London
W6 9HA

A catalogue record for this book is available from the British Library.

ISBN 0 7535 0846 X

Typeset by TW Typesetting, Plymouth, Devon
Printed and bound in Great Britain by
Mackays of Chatham PLC

Dedication

This one's for Marc Shapiro

Thanks for all the tips – especially the one about this 'hot new crime show'

Acknowledgements

It would be practically impossible, and much less fun, to write a book like this without input from other people, and I am very grateful to everyone who gave their assistance. The Anglo-American Alliance – Katrina Gerhard, Jerry Boyajian, Jenn Fletcher, Kerry Glover and John Mosby – for the visual material; Andy and Helen Lane for spotting some of the less obvious fatal errors and explaining away some of the ones that weren't; Vince Cosgrove, Rod Edgar, Helen Grimmett, Gary Leigh and www.lifeormeth.com, Andrew Martin, Adam Newell, Carolyn Newman, Marc Shapiro and Keith Topping; the Sophie Brigade (Anali, Cherry, Clare and Sigrid) for keeping my one-year-old daughter out of trouble while I was engrossed in the Crime Lab; Kirstie Addis at Virgin for her never-failing patience; and especially my wife Alison for her love and support.

Contents

Introduction

The old family doctor comes in, takes one look at the body, and pronounces the time of death as 6.23 p.m. exactly . . .

That might have been permissible in the days of Agatha Christie, but if the old family doctor tried that trick in the presence of any of the criminalists that we've come to know during the four seasons that *CSI* and *CSI: Miami* have been on air, he would immediately be arrested as the prime suspect.

Crime investigation became more sophisticated as the twentieth century progressed, and the screen versions of it have had to keep up. In the late 60s and early 70s in Great Britain, viewers could follow the cases of Dr John Hardy, the forensic pathologist in the West Midlands, in the often gritty drama *The Expert*. The mid-70s saw the advent of *Quincy, M.E.*, the most popular pathologist, until Gil Grissom arrived on the scene. Quincy was a one-man investigative task force, getting his teeth into a problem and not letting go, no matter whether the case was within his jurisdiction or not. Forensics played their part in TV series after Quincy retired to his boat, but forensic pathologists didn't really come to the fore again until Amanda Burton took on the mantle of the *Silent Witness* in the mid-90s BBC TV series.

But none of those shows jumped to the top of the ratings in their home country in the way *CSI* has. Whether it is the novelty of seeing film actors William Petersen and Marg Helgenberger in regular TV roles, or prurient interest in the sort of crimes that might come to light in Sin City, something has clicked with audiences in America, and when *CSI* moved from Friday to Thursday evenings, it took off, becoming the most popular drama in the 2001/2 season, and the most popular programme in 2002/3, drawing audiences of over 25 million.

It's been as successful in Britain for Channel Five – its US crime drama imports, which also include *Law & Order* and *Boomtown*, have helped it to shed much of the channel's former reputation for sex and sleaze. The first season of *CSI* debuted in June 2001, shortly after the series started its summer break in America, and averaged 1.7 million viewers. That audience has steadily risen to an average of 2.9 million viewers for the third season, making it Five's number one series. Repeats on UK Living have also been highly successful for that cable channel.

In 2003 *CSI* was also nominated for six Emmys including Lead Actress in a Drama Series (Marg Helgenberger) and Best Drama Series. *CSI* is the brainchild of Anthony E. Zuiker, a former Las Vegas casino bellman and host for the parking lot tram. 'I knew I had too much talent to be working on a tram. I was literally seeing people making big decisions, doing really great things, with an eighth of my talent. I was on the brink of going insane,' he admitted in early 2003. At the suggestion of an agent who had seen a monologue he had written for an actor friend, Zuiker wrote a movie screenplay which went straight to video, and then worked on a script about The Harlem Globetrotters. That brought him to the attention of Hollywood super-producer Jerry Bruckheimer, who wanted to discuss television concepts with him.

Zuiker came up with the idea of a show that started with a body on the floor, a broken pot and an elephant standing in the corner, and the rest of the hour would explain how they got there. He spent weeks riding around with the Las Vegas Criminalistics operatives, listening to their stories, finding out how they operated, and coming to understand their mindset. From his research he came up with the team that appeared in the pilot episode – Captain Brass, in charge of the CSIs on the Graveyard Shift, with Gil Grissom, Catherine Willows, Warrick Brown and Nick Stokes working under him. Sara Sidle came on board in the first proper episode.

Gil Grissom was initially based on Vegas CSI Daniel Holstein, who continues to advise the series. Catherine had her roots in another criminalist, Yolanda McClary, as well as the former criminalist Elizabeth Devine, who is now the show's story editor. Of the original characters, Jim Brass has changed the most, now working as a homicide detective in one of the fastest career switches on record (quite literally overnight), and becoming a more likeable and approachable character than the overbearing tyrant seen in the Pilot.

Much of these changes came from the input of the actors. Star and producer William 'Billy' Petersen had played FBI profiler, Agent Will Graham in *Manhunter*, the first film to feature Hannibal Lecter (recently remade as *Red Dragon*), and in the late 90s was looking for a series that might expand on that role. *CSI* fitted the bill, and brought Petersen to television for his first regular series role.

Given the almost incestuous nature of popular culture at the start of the twenty-first century, with multiple versions of different series and old TV shows being remade as staple fodder for cinema audiences, a *CSI* spin-off was inevitable, but what surprised many people (including the *CSI* lead actors) was the speed with which it came to pass. By the start of 2002, *CSI: Miami* was in preparation, starting with what was originally planned as a two-part crossover episode between the criminalists of Las Vegas and Miami-Dade being used as a backdoor pilot for a new series. Former *NYPD Blue* star David Caruso was brought on board as the new team's leader, Horatio Caine, who established himself in many ways as the antithesis of Gil 'The case has no face' Grissom right from the start. No sooner were the ratings in than CBS commissioned the new show, which premiered with a run of ten new episodes and quickly aimed for the top ten shows.

CSI: Miami got off to a bit of a rocky start. In the crossover episode, the best scenes were between Caruso and Helgenberger, with an electric chemistry between the pair. There was no possibility of Helgenberger jumping ship to the new series so the producers tried to replicate it by casting another *NYPD Blue* alumna, Kim Delaney. For whatever reason, it simply didn't work, and Delaney slowly but surely began to sink from view. By the eleventh episode, she was history, and the hoped-for chemistry was sought elsewhere.

Shortly after the first spin-off came to the end of its first year, creator Anthony E. Zuiker revealed that he already knew where the next show could be set, and who he wanted to headline it. Lightning seems to have struck twice – can Zuiker make it three for three?

Reading The Files

CSI: The Files follows the regular pattern of these guides, dividing each episode up into, hopefully, easily manageable chunks.

US Air Date and **UK Air Date** refer to the first showing on CBS and Channel 5 respectively. The figures after the US date refer to the number of households, in millions, watching, and the percentage share (i.e. of all the people watching TV at the time, that percentage were watching CBS).

Teaser One-liner: Usually the last line before The Who crash in with the title music, but always an indicative line from the pre-credits sequence.

The Case(s): Follow each *CSI* case as it progresses, divided for the sake of convenience into each plot strand. If it looks as though there are two cases, but they're together, it's for a reason!

Personal Notes: No one could accuse the *CSI* shows of forgetting that their main purpose is to be about forensic science, but from time to time we do learn a few things about our central characters.

Techniques: A brief look at any new forensic techniques used in each episode. A lot of cases use previously seen techniques to examine new evidence, so don't get mentioned again. These are, of necessity, just an overview – there are whole books available on each and every one!

The Wit and Wisdom of Gil Grissom/Horatio Caine: Our team leaders are given some great comments by the writers.

Classic Dialogue: Some of the best of the rest.

Worst 'As You Know': Most of the time the *CSI* franchise is a great proponent of the principle of 'show, don't tell', but every so often something which our characters know very well has to be explained to the audience.

Fantastic Voyages: Titled in homage to the classic 1966 movie in which a wet-suited Raquel Welch was miniaturised and injected inside a human body, these are the CSI-camera trademarks – the close-ups within the body, and elsewhere, which visually set the shows apart.

The Usual Suspects: Many of the supporting cast and corpses have appeared elsewhere – here are some tips as to where you might have spotted them.

Pop Culture References: *CSI* isn't as blatant with these as some shows but here's a note of those that are there.

Real-life Inspirations: Many *CSI* cases are based on real incidents, suitably reworked for the necessities of a one-hour drama. Some of them are taken from the casebooks of the assorted criminalists who have offered their services over the years. Others come from very well known incidents.

Mistakes Really Can Be Fatal: Bearing in mind that the people convicted on the criminalists' evidence can be put to death, let's hope they don't screw up too often. What's not covered here is the time factor involved – of course DNA evidence and suchlike doesn't come back as quickly as is indicated by the show, and nó, the CSI criminalists wouldn't get as involved in each and every case as our heroes do – but this is a TV show, and dramatic licence is necessary. To get an idea of how long cases might really take, check out Max Allan Collins' novels based on the shows, which try to keep to a realistic timescale. Many episodes have been taken to task for the 'coincidences' which plague them, but often these are the way in which the real cases they are based on played out.

Notes: Any other observations of interest, particularly with regard to the dates of the episodes.

Overall: A personal note on each episode – feel free to disagree!

Full List of Episodes

CSI: Miami – Season One

M1 Golden Parachute
M2 Losing Face
M3 Wet Foot/Dry Foot
M4 Just One Kiss
M5 Ashes to Ashes
M6 Broken
M7 Breathless
M8 Slaughterhouse
M9 Kill Zone
M10 A Horrible Mind
M11 Camp Fear
M12 Entrance Wound
M13 Bunk
M14 Forced Entry
M15 Dead Woman Walking
M16 Evidence of Things Unseen
M17 Simple Man
M18 Dispo Day
M19 Double Cap
M20 Grave Young Men
M21 Spring Break
M22 Tinder Box
M23 Freaks and Tweaks
M24 Body Count

*'We scrutinise the crime scene, collect the evidence,
re-create what happened without actually
ever being there.'*

Season One

Regular Cast:

William Petersen (Gil Grissom)
Marg Helgenberger (Catherine Willows)
Gary Dourdan (Warrick Brown)
George Eads (Nick Stokes)
Jorja Fox (Sara Sidle 01–22)
Paul Guilfoyle (Captain Jim Brass)

Harrison Young (Judge Cohen 00, 01, 03)
Susan Gibney (Charlotte, Lab Technician 00)
Eric Szmanda (CSI DNA technician Greg Sanders 00, 01, 03–05, 07, 08,
10, 12–14, 16–22)
Skip O'Brien (Sgt O'Riley 00, 06, 11–13, 16, 17, 19–22)
Aasif Mandvi (Dr Leever 00, 06, 07)
Madison McReynolds (Lindsey Willows 00, 02, 05, 06, 15)
Judith Scott (Coroner Dr Jenna Williams 01–04, 08, 10)
Paul Terrell Clayton (Detective Kane 03, 04, 10)
David Berman (Deputy coroner David Phillips 04, 06, 08–11, 16, 17, 19,
20)
Mark Collver (Detective Evans 04, 05, 15)
Timothy Carhart (Eddie Willows 05, 06, 15)
Pamela Gidley (Teri Miller 05, 13, 16, 21)
Robert David Hall (Coroner Dr David Robbins 05–07, 09, 12–22)
Glenn Morshower (Sheriff Brian Mobley 06, 08, 09, 12, 14, 22)
Marc Vann (CSI daytime shift leader Conrad Ecklie 06, 09, 11, 12)
Greg Collins (Officer Arvington 00, 07, 12, 16)
Colette O'Connell (Detective Conroy 14)
Geoffrey Rivas (Detective Sam Vega 15)
Tom Gallop (Attorney Randy Painter 16, 19)
Brad Johnson (District Engineer Paul Newsome 17, 20)
Joseph Patrick Kelly (Officer Metcalf 19–21)

00
Pilot

US Air Date: 6 October 2000 11.8/21
UK Air Date: 9 June 2001

Written by: Anthony E. Zuiker
Directed by: Danny Cannon
Guest Cast: John Pyper-Ferguson (Husband),
Allan Rich (Dr Klausbach), Royce D. Applegate (Mr Laferty),
Barbara Tarbuck (Mrs Paige Harmon), Nancy Fish (Store Owner),
Cedrik Terrell (Boe Wilson), Chandra West (Holly Gribbs),
Matt O'Toole (Paul Millander), John Henry Whitaker (Jimmy),
Garland Whitt (Black Male aka Jerrod Cooper),
Ashley Holloway (Laura Scott), Jeff Snyder (Officer Smith),
Jane Leigh Connelley (Wife), Joseph Patrick Kelly (Hotel Security),
Terra Gold (Gina Harmon), Krista Allen (Kristy Hopkins),
Anthony E. Zuiker (Chip)

Teaser One-liner: 'My name is Royce Harmon . . . I am 41
years of age and I am going to kill myself . . .'
The Cases: Jim Brass summons Gil Grissom to a hotel
room, apparently the scene of a suicide. It seems a classic
case, but the suicide note itself is a little unusual: it's
recorded on a miniature dictaphone. However, when
Grissom plays the tape to the deceased's mother, she is
shocked – although the body is her son's, the voice on the
tape is not.

Dr Klausbach performs an autopsy on the late Royce
Harmon. The shape of the wound indicates that he was
killed from six to seven feet away.

The prints found at the scene of Royce Harmon's murder
are unusual. There are odd red flecks of latex inside, laced
with lecithin. These prints belong to Paul Millander, a
seemingly inoffensive citizen. Millander runs a business
creating Hallowe'en toys, including fake arms which carry
his fingerprints. Grissom realises that the murderer is
proficient in forensics. He visits Royce Harmon's mother,
who is relieved to know that her son didn't commit suicide.
Grissom promises that he will solve the case eventually.

* * *

New CSI recruit Holly Gribbs meets Grissom and is amazed to be asked for a pint of blood even before she's clocked in. Brass resents her being forced on the department simply because her mother is connected within the Police Department and tells Grissom to make her experience an autopsy. After Holly has to leave the autopsy because she's been sick, she visits a grocery store to dust it for prints after a robbery. The owner takes exception to her lack of progress and pulls a gun on her. Holly calls for back up and Catherine arrives to calm the situation down. Catherine gives Holly a backhanded pep talk before being called to another case.

Warrick is assigned to look after Holly. He leaves her at her next dusting job while he goes to place a bet. Holly is interrupted by a young black male while she's dusting the room. As the shift finishes Brass arrives with bad news. Holly Gribbs has been shot and is in surgery . . .

Warrick and Catherine are given a Home Invasion to investigate. The husband of the family claims that he shot his wife's drunk friend Jimmy, who had been staying with them, when Jimmy broke down the door after being thrown out. Catherine notices that the husband's little toe is injured, which he claims was done on a rattle. She and Warrick also discover that one of Jimmy's sneakers has been tied differently to the other but the husband denies doing anything to the body.

Warrick tests hair fibres found at the scene and realises that the hairs have been pulled out in a struggle, since he found seeds on the root. The husband amends his story to take this into account, but he knows that Warrick doesn't believe him. Warrick discusses his lack of progress with Grissom, who makes him focus on the central issue of the case – the shoe. Checking it carefully, Warrick discovers a piece of broken toenail inside.

He goes to Brass asking for a warrant against the husband, but Brass refuses to give it to him. He therefore goes to Judge Cohen, who gives him the warrant provided Warrick will lay a bet for him. Brass is furious that

Warrick went over his head and takes him off the case, telling him to look after Holly Gribbs.

Grissom takes over the home invasion case and serves the warrant for the husband's toenail clippings. The husband claims to have flushed them away, but Grissom searches the bathroom and comes up with a load of clippings. Taking them back to the lab, he compares the striation with the clipping that Warrick found in the sneaker – and they match. The husband is arrested for the murder.

Nick is assigned a robbery. He interviews Mr Laferty, a middle-aged businessman who was tricked by a hooker and woke up to find all his possessions gone. Nick notices an odd stain on his lips and gums. Unfortunately the swabs he takes don't show anything unusual.

At St Anthony's Hospital, Nick visits Kristy Hopkins, a girl who fell asleep while driving. She is a hooker, and Nick discovers the same discoloration on her nipples as was on Laferty's mouth. He persuades her to return Laferty's goods. Greg Sanders analyses the liquid Kristy uses and discovers it's scopolamine. Nick returns Mr Laferty's possessions and earns his promotion to CSI-3.

Catherine has to deal with an assaulted child.

Personal Notes: Grissom jokes around with the corpses in the mortuary. He took lab tech Charlotte out on a date that went spectacularly wrong. Catherine has a young daughter and, after seeing the assaulted girl, takes some time out to be with Lindsey when she wakes. Warrick has a gambling problem, and gets a warrant out of Judge Cohen by agreeing to place a bet on his behalf. The only problem is that he puts the bet on the wrong team. Nick and Warrick have a friendly wager on who will be promoted to CSI-3 first. Although Nick gets the case he doesn't really want, he's still successful. However, the celebrations are muted when they learn about Holly's shooting. Holly Gribbs doesn't really want to be a CSI, and is doing it only to please her mother. However, she starts to get an interest just in time to get shot.

Techniques: Let's start with the obvious one to get it out of the way – an autopsy is the procedure whereby the coroner examines the corpse, and endeavours to ascertain the cause of death. This usually involves making a Y-shaped incision down the torso to open up the interior and check the internal organs. Sometimes, as in this case, it's very obvious – there's a large bullet hole – but as *CSI* progresses, no one trusts the obvious.

ALS – the alternate light source (the blue light) – is one of the most common forms of detection used by the CSI team. By using different wavelengths of light, ALS shows up different fluids, such as blood and semen, and can reveal things that are totally invisible to the naked eye.

There is lots of dusting for fingerprints. These can then be scanned into AFIS, the Automated Fingerprint Identification System, a computer network that compares prints with the millions collected by law enforcement agencies around the world. Each feature of the print – the loops, whorls, arches and accidentals – are assigned values, and those values are compared. AFIS then provides a list of prints that have matching percentages, which can then be compared in microscopic detail with the new one.

Ink rolling: Warrick rolls ink on the underside of Jimmy's trainer to compare it with the marking on the door.

Larva metamorphosis is one of Gil Grissom's specialities. Grissom found a stage-three pupa on Royce Harmon's corpse which told him that Harmon had been dead for around seven days.

Toenails and fingernails come with stria, as do muscles. These are parallel grooves or lines and, if two pieces can be matched exactly, then they come from the same place.

The criminalists run swabs on suspect surfaces to get evidence; these might be items found at the scene, or from a suspect. These can then go for toxicology analysis (tox screen) to check for the presence or otherwise of drugs, chemicals, gases or metals, or for DNA analysis, depending on the case.

The Wit and Wisdom of Gil Grissom: 'Concentrate on what cannot lie: the evidence.'

'There is no room for subjectivity in this department.'

Classic Dialogue: Catherine to Holly: 'Stick with it, at least until you solve your first. And if after that you don't feel like King Kong on cocaine, then you can quit.'

Worst 'As You Know': Grissom: 'We scrutinise the crime scene, collect the evidence, re-create what happened without actually ever being there. Pretty cool, actually.' Grissom explains the concept of the series to Holly Gribbs, who points out, 'I just got out of the Academy – I know this.' She might, but the rest of us don't!

Fantastic Voyages: We travel with the bullet being fired into Royce Harmon as if he had fired it himself, and also if someone else had. We see the husband's toe-clipping inside Jimmy's shoe.

The Usual Suspects: William Petersen (Gil Grissom) has a distinguished film career behind him, with his work as Richard Chance in *To Live and Die in L.A.*, and as Will Graham in *Manhunter*, the vastly superior version of Thomas Harris' first Hannibal Lecter novel *Red Dragon*. Although *CSI* is the first series he's committed himself to, he has starred in a number of miniseries, notably *The Beast* by *Jaws* creator Peter Benchley.

Marg Helgenberger (Catherine Willows) has an equally distinguished career, with stints on everything from soap opera – *Ryan's Hope* – to the Vietnam series *China Beach*. She worked for *CSI* producer Jerry Bruckheimer on *Bad Boys*, and sci-fi fans will recognise her from the Stephen King miniseries *The Tommyknockers*, and the two *Species* movies with Michael Madsen.

Gary Dourdan (Warrick Brown) played Shazza Zulu on the comedy series *A Different World* before graduating to the big screen in the forgettable David Duchovny movie *Playing God*, and playing Christie in *Alien: Resurrection*. He's also played folk hero Malcolm X in the TV movie *King of the World* about Muhammad Ali.

Paul Guilfoyle (Captain Jim Brass) has one of those faces you know you've seen before, with over sixty credits in small–medium sized roles over the years – everything from *Howard The Duck* to *L.A. Confidential*, *Air Force One* and *Primary Colours*.

George Eads appeared in the 1996 TV series *Savannah*, as well as making small guest appearances on *ER* before graduating to the lead role of Nick Stokes in *CSI*.

Eric Szmanda played Jacob Resh in the short-lived TV version of the 1995 Sandra Bullock movie *The Net* before *CSI* shot him to fame as Greg Sanders.

Canadian actress Chandra West (Holly Gribbs) head-lined the two made-for-TV sequels to the Jean-Claude Van Damme thriller *Universal Soldier*, and joined *NYPD Blue* as Dr Devlin in its closing Season Ten episodes.

The craggy features of Matt O'Toole (Paul Millander) have livened up the 1994 feature *Wyatt Earp* and, in 1996, *Last Man Standing*; John Pyper-Ferguson (the murderous husband) has appeared in numerous TV series including *Star Trek: The Next Generation*. Royce D. Applegate (Mr Laferty) is another familiar face from large and small screen, playing Chief Crocker on *seaQuest DSV* and Stephen Segal's catering colleague in *Under Siege 2*. Harrison Young (Judge Cohen) played the old James Ryan in Spielberg's *Saving Private Ryan*, as well as portraying Palmer Harper in the long-running US soap *Passions*.

Pop Culture References: The Who's 'Who Are You' is a very appropriate choice of music for the series, as is their 'Won't Get Fooled Again' for *CSI: Miami*, although it might have been better if CBS had confirmed they had the right to use it worldwide straightaway. Nick Stokes and Greg Sanders are both computer game nerds, comparing notes on the latest Dreamcast games.

Mistakes Really Can Be Fatal: It seems more than a little odd that Holly Gribbs has been through the Academy and not seen an autopsy . . .

Notes: Series creator Anthony E. Zuiker appears as Chip, the ticket writer in a sports scene.

Real Vegas locations include XO Liquors, Bally's (Warrick was filmed in front of it), and the Fremont Street Experience. The aftermath of a traffic collision (Kristy Hopkins' accident) was filmed there.

The fake suicide that opens the show is re-examined in **07**, 'Anonymous'.

This episode was shown together with **01**, 'Cool Change' as a TV movie to launch the series in Britain on Channel 5. **Overall:** It's a pilot, and the whole function of a pilot is to try things out to see what works and what doesn't. The massive change that the characters go through between the Pilot and the next episode is nothing unusual in American television – but, slightly more unusual, is the fact that it happens literally overnight. Clearly at this stage Zuiker and his producing partners didn't know exactly what sort of show they wanted to create: a lot of the stylistic hallmarks of *CSI* are present and correct, as we follow the different paths of the bullet through Royce Harmon's body, but there's more material in this episode about the characters' private lives than appears in most of the second season!

01
Cool Change

US Air Date: 13 October 2000 10.9/19
UK Air Date: 9 June 2001 (with Pilot)

Written by: Anthony E. Zuiker
Directed by: Michael Watkins
Guest Cast: Tim DeZarn (Red Carlton), Johnny Messner (Ted Salinger), Timilee Romolini (Jamie Smith), Chandra West (Holly Gribbs), Zach Johnson (Detective Barns), Garland Whitt (Jerrod Cooper), M. Darnell Suttles (Elias Templeton), Rocky McMurray (Surveillance Director), Gerald McCullough (Bobby Dawson), Jeff Snyder (Uniformed Officer)

Teaser One-liner: 'Didn't you hear him? He just told me he didn't commit suicide.'
The Cases: Grissom visits the Hotel Monaco, from which Ted Salinger appears to have jumped, even though he's just won millions on the slot machines. He realises instantly that it's not a suicide – the man is still wearing his glasses. Nick assists him while Warrick is on suspension.

The autopsy on Ted Salinger shows tiny black glass shards in defensive wounds to his hands. Nick and

Grissom find a broken black champagne bottle and blood-soaked towels in the Presidential Suite. Salinger's girlfriend Jamie has stated that they had an argument when they reached the room because he told her to get lost now that he was a millionaire, and she cut him. When they interrogate her, she says he left the room after he was cut and didn't return. The records of the electronic keys back up her claim. Jamie, who has no claim on Ted's estate hence, apparently, no motive – is released. If Ted didn't fall from the room, the CSIs deduce that it must have been from the roof.

Grissom and Nick carry out tests with three dummies, one pushed, one jumping, and one falling. The evidence is conclusive: Ted was pushed. Ted's win on the slot machine came after someone else had been playing for over eleven hours. The casino tracks down Red Carlton, who has roof dust on his shoes. The CSIs arrest him for murder.

Carlton claims that he simply had a drink with Ted Salinger and then went up to the roof himself to jump – but chickened out. The evidence backs up his story – there was no roof dust on Ted's shoes. Only Carlton went up there. Ted must have departed from the room after all.

Grissom finds carpet fibres inside Ted's watch, indicating that he was dragged. Nick takes a pizza-box-sized sample of the Presidential Suite's carpet for comparison, while Dr Williams informs Grissom that Ted was hit over the head with a diamond-shaped object before he was pushed, the mark only coming to light when the corpse's head was shaved. Grissom discovers how Jamie got round the security lock, and faces her with the physical evidence that indicates she is the murderer. Coldly and remorselessly she confesses.

As a result of Holly's shooting (see **00**, 'Pilot'), Brass has been reassigned to Homicide, and the Sheriff has asked Grissom to take over the Graveyard Shift. He assigns Nick to investigate Holly's shooting but, when Catherine objects, passes it to her. He also reveals that he has invited Sara Sidle, a CSI from San Francisco, to come in to investigate the circumstances that led to Holly's shooting, rather than turn it over to the Internal Affairs Division.

Catherine discovers that Holly's weapon has been fired, and surmises that she got a chance to shoot back at her assailant. Sara arrives and sets to work to find out why Warrick left Holly's side. She meets Catherine who is working on a pager found at the scene, using a pager nest Grissom bought on Ebay. After some initial hostility they agree to co-operate. Sara then goes to find Warrick while Catherine discovers that the striations on the bullet taken from Holly match Holly's own gun.

Sara finds Warrick in a truck stop playing cards and doesn't accept his excuse that he left Holly to go for a coffee. He claims that he was regularly left when he was a rookie, but Sara points out it's different this time: Holly died twenty minutes earlier.

The pager Catherine is examining goes off, and she responds to it, making a date to meet its owner, Jerrod Cooper – Holly's killer. Cooper is arrested. He has a scratch on his face, and Catherine takes a DNA sample. She then matches it with a sample from Holly.

Personal Notes: According to Grissom, he and Sara are friends. She's 'someone I trust'. At the beginning of the episode, Warrick has been suspended from the department by Brass. Judge Cohen angrily demands a meeting with Warrick when he realises he's lost his bet. Warrick pays the money back to Judge Cohen and believes they're finished, but Cohen isn't going to let him off that easily. Grissom confronts Warrick, who admits that he went to lay a bet when he should have been with Holly, but Grissom refuses to fire him. They've lost one good person that day – he won't lose two.

Techniques: Grissom uses dummies to recreate Ted Salinger's fall. From what Sara says, this can just as easily be programmed into a computer.

Ballistics tests are carried out on Holly's gun, initially to eliminate it from consideration. The gun is test-fired in order that the test bullet's striations may be checked against the murder weapon.

DNA samples are taken from underneath Holly's finger-nails and from the wound on Jarrod's face. DNA is still not considered to be an exact science, although sometimes the odds against it being correct exceed the number of people on the planet. DNA comparisons on *CSI* are done very quickly; in real life these would take considerably longer than can be shown in a TV series. However, the actual processes that Greg Sanders uses are accurate.

The Wit and Wisdom of Gil Grissom: 'I'm a lot better scientist than a boss.'

'I'm a scientist. I like to see it. Newton dropped the apple. I drop dummies.'

Classic Dialogue: Cop: 'Do you want to talk to her?' Grissom: 'Not yet. Right now I want to talk to him.' (the deceased)

Worst 'As You Know': 'Just point the gun in the entry-hole to do a test-fire.' – Bobby Dawson to Catherine. She's been a CSI for how long?

Fantastic Voyages: We close in on the black glass shard in Ted's defence wounds. We follow the bullet being fired from Holly's gun. We get extreme detail of the injury on Jarrod's face.

The Usual Suspects: Jorja Fox (Sara Sidle) is probably best known now for her performance as Guy Pearce's wife in the thriller *Memento*, but prior to *CSI* she had long runs on *ER* as lesbian doctor Maggie Doyle, and on *The West Wing* as Gina Toscano.

Pop Culture References: The porter makes a sarcastic reference to Richard Gere, presumably to his millionaire character in *Pretty Woman*. Grissom and Sara swap references to *Three's Company*, and the Ropers. *Three's Company* was the longer-lasting US version of UK comedy *Man About the House*. Before they've met, Grissom refers to Red Carlton as Red Buttons, the dancer and singer from the 50s.

Mistakes Really Can Be Fatal: Why didn't Grissom and Nick check for dust on Ted's shoes as soon as they came up with their idea that he jumped off the roof? If they had found none, the time spent on the whole of the 'Red Buttons' investigation wouldn't have been wasted.

Notes: The episode is dedicated 'In Memory of Owen Wolf, 1971–2000'. Owen Alexander Wolf was a 29-year-old television production assistant who was shot in the head just as he was about to enter a supermarket in the Van Nuys suburb of Los Angeles. He had spent his summer working on *CSI*.
Overall: This is getting much closer to the normal pattern of *CSI* – a seemingly insoluble case with assorted red herrings getting in the way. Jorja Fox brings a new energy to the show and combines well with Marg Helgenberger. Only the 'soap opera' element of Judge Cohen's dealings with Warrick let this episode down.

02
Crate and Burial (aka Crate'n'Burial)

US Air Date: 20 October 2000 9.5/17
UK Air Date: 16 June 2001

Written by: Ann Donahue
Directed by: Danny Cannon
Guest Cast: John Beasley (Charles Moore), Erich Anderson (Jack Garris),
Jolene Blalock (Laura Garris), Hamilton Von Watts (Chip Rundle),
Samuel L. Jones III (James Moore), John Livingston (THD)

Teaser One-liner: 'Mr Garris, it's my experience in situations like this, if you want to go fast, go slow.'
The Cases: The CSI team has been called in to assist with the kidnap of Laura Garris. A ransom tape has been left, with an electronically altered voice demanding $2m. From noises on the tape, Grissom deduces that it was recorded in the desert, near power lines. There's only a three-hour window for delivery of the ransom, which means that it is likely that Laura will die if the ransom isn't paid. While Nick takes the tape back to the lab. Sara discovers that the security system in the Garris' house has been bypassed, and Laura was grabbed by an intruder.

Grissom finds some dirt inside the house which seems 'out of context'. He and Sara discover a rag on the patio with the anaesthetic drug halothane on it, and they surmise that the intruder tracked the dirt into the house.

Brass advises Garris not to pay the ransom but he won't listen. In the lab Grissom finds the dirt has cyanide and gold in it. He and Sara check for gold mines near power lines, within range of the ransom drop. There are only three. While they go up in a helicopter searching for Laura with a heat sensor, Nick joins Brass at the ransom drop. Sara and Grissom locate Laura alive but buried beneath the surface of the desert. Brass and the LVPD move in on the man who collected the ransom bag but who claims to have no knowledge of its contents. The suspect is Chip Rundle, Jack Garris' personal trainer.

The box in which Laura was found belongs to Garris Winery. Laura is shaken by her ordeal but is willing to do anything to catch her attacker. Brass interrogates Rundle, who knows that there is no evidence to hold him – he helped Jack move some boxes from the winery, explaining his prints on the crate. However, Rundle agreed to let Brass tape the interview, and Brass passes the tape to Grissom for comparison with the ransom demand.

Once the algorithms of the tape have been suitably adjusted, there's a perfect match – Rundle was the kidnapper. However, Grissom isn't finished yet. Sara and Nick check Rundle's van and can't understand why Laura would have been put in the front seat if she was unconscious. Sheepskin fibres found on the back of Laura's sleeve show that she was sitting in the seat normally. If she wasn't unconscious, that meant that the halothane-covered rag was a plant. Luckily, a blood sample was taken from Laura when she was recovered and there is no trace of halothane in the sample, but Sara can't understand why Laura ended up in the crate if she was Rundle's accomplice. Grissom confronts the Garrises, reconstructing the day's events. Laura was a willing accomplice, but Rundle double-crossed her after making the ransom call. When the tape is fully augmented, Laura's voice can clearly be heard in the background of the ransom call. She is arrested, leaving her husband devastated.

Catherine and Warrick are investigating a hit-and-run accident in which a young girl on a scooter was hit by a

car. Jenna Williams' autopsy of the accident victim,
Brenda Harris, reveals licence plate numbers on the skin,
forced in by the impact. Catherine and Warrick visit Mr
Charles Moore, an elderly black man who at first claims
that his car was stolen, but when they find it in his garage,
hastens to confess to the hit-and-run. Neither Catherine
nor Warrick believe him.

The radio in the car is set to a very loud rap station –
Moore can't have been the last driver, as he claimed. When
faced with the evidence, Moore says that his grandson
James was a passenger, and took over driving after the
accident. The CSIs bring James in, but the two Moores
maintain their story.

Warrick and Catherine find a tooth chip embedded in
the steering wheel which matches damage to James' teeth.
Faced with the evidence, the Moores confess that James
was driving. Mr Moore still wants to serve the sentence in
James' place, but it's not possible. James is taken into
custody; Warrick gives him some good advice, as well as
his cellphone number, in case he needs help.

Personal Notes: Nick outranks Sara, although she reminds
him that Grissom handpicked her for the team. It's taken
as read that she's decided to stay in Las Vegas rather than
return to San Francisco. She previously attended seminars
that Grissom gave. Lindsey Willows doesn't want to have
a birthday party; all the CSIs have bought her a present
except Sara. Warrick was brought up by his grandmother,
who referred to him as her 'work in progress'.

Techniques: The ransom tape is run through various audio
filters and 'reverse algorithms' (playing the tape at different
speeds and directions) to eliminate the background noises,
and to enhance otherwise inaudible items. Grissom ensures
that a control copy of the tape is recorded with a
spectrograph, which records the entire spectrum, to confirm that what they found was there originally.

The halothane-covered rag is run through a CG Mass
Spectrometer, which analyses complex organic substances
by sorting the gaseous ions into electric and magnetic fields
which can identify their molecular structure.

The Wit and Wisdom of Gil Grissom: 'Every case teaches me something about the next.'

'The thing is, Jack, I tend not to believe people. They lie. The evidence doesn't lie.'

'People leave us clues, Nick. They speak to us in thousands of different ways. It's our job to make sure we've heard everything they've said.'

Classic Dialogue: Sara: 'Gruesome, Grissom.'

Catherine: 'When you want evidence, you can't find it, when you don't want it it's as big as Dallas.'

Sara: 'Hey, Grissom! Could you come tape me up.' Grissom: 'I love my work.' Catherine: 'It shows.'

Fantastic Voyages: The licence plate numbers on Brenda Harris' thigh are highlighted, and we see James Moore's tooth chip off into the steering wheel.

The Usual Suspects: Jolene Blalock (Laura Garris) is now best known as the ultra-cool Vulcan science officer T'Pol on *Star Trek: Enterprise*. Samuel L. Jones III (James Moore) plays Pete Ross, Clark Kent's best buddy, on the Warner Brothers Superman prequel *Smallville*.

Pop Culture References: Brass calls Grissom 'Kreskin', a reference to the American psychic, The Amazing Kreskin, who has a high degree of success with his prophecies of future news headlines.

Overall: The series settles down with this episode – two investigations running in tandem, with a little bit of crossover between the characters when they're back at the lab. The subplot with Lindsey seems tacked on.

03
Pledging Mr Johnson

US Air Date: 27 October 2000 9.8/17
UK Air Date: 23 June 2001

Written by: Josh Berman & Anthony E. Zuiker
Directed by: R.J. Lewis
Guest Cast: Jim Ortlieb (Winston Barger), Vyto Ruginis (Phil Swelco), Mark Famiglietti (Matt Daniels), Craig Allen Wolf (Kyle Travis),

Grant Heslove (Dr Corbett), Robert Dolan (Hank),
Mark Daneri (George), Amy Collett (Martie),
Nicole Tarantini (Jill Wentworth), Elliott Grey (Barger's Attorney),
Chris Demetral (James Johnson)

Teaser One-liner: 'You don't wear flippers at a five-star restaurant. Why would you wear three-inch heels at a lake?'
The Cases: A human leg is found by two fishermen on Lake Mead when it tangles up their boat's engine. Grissom and Catherine find that the femur has been sliced clean through but coroner Jenna Williams explains that the leg was severed post-mortem. The rest of the body is found about half a mile east of the marina.

The floater is identified as Wendy Barger, a local woman who had not been reported missing by her husband. The rape kit carried out at the autopsy shows positive for semen, and there are signs of a struggle: Wendy's shoulder was dislocated and her skull was fractured. Her husband claims everyone loved her, and that she had gone away 'to get perspective'. They had not had sex for some months.

The husband's DNA doesn't match the sperm and, since there is no evidence against him, he is allowed to go. Barger says that when they find out what happened he wants to know everything, and though Grissom promises to let him know, Catherine isn't so sure that's a good idea, given that it's likely his wife was cheating on him.

None of Wendy's friends believes she had a lover, but Catherine is sure she did. Jenna reveals that Wendy Barger has a contusion on her right temple, embedded with lime green wood splinters. She also had no water in her lungs. She was possibly raped, killed and then dumped in the lake – after eating a nice dinner of calamari.

At the only restaurant near the lake that serves calamari, one of the waitresses says Wendy was there with one of the regulars. Restaurant regular Phil Swelco admits to his affair with Wendy. He thought she was filing for divorce but hadn't because she was scared of hurting her husband. On the night she died, they met at the restaurant, went to his house by boat, made love, and then she took the boat back to the marina.

As they are leaving Swelco's house, Catherine and Grissom realise that they have been followed by Wendy's husband, who assumes that Swelco was Wendy's murderer. The CSIs calm him down and Grissom promises that he'll tell him everything about his wife's death when he knows something for certain. Catherine believes that that will inevitably mean telling him that Wendy was having an affair, but Grissom still thinks not.

Swelco's boat isn't at the marina so Catherine and Grissom search for it in their own ways (see **Techniques**). It is found just south of Barring Point Bridge.

The two of them examine the boat and find blood – enough preliminary evidence to implicate Swelco. However, when Brass brings him in, Winston Barger is there. Catherine tells him that Swelco was Wendy's lover. Grissom is furious with her when he finds out.

Grissom realises that Wendy ran out of gas and dislocated her shoulder when she was pulling on the engine cord. She fell forward, hitting her head on the side of the boat, and then fell in the water. It was just an accident. However, Winston Barger isn't at home to hear the news – he's gone to Phil Swelco's house, where Catherine and Grisson find him sitting looking at Swelco's dead body . . .

Nick and Sara investigate a death at the Phi Alpha fraternity house. The body of a young man, James Johnson, has been found hanging in one of the upstairs rooms. No suicide note is found. The fraternity's leaders, Kyle Travis and Matt Daniels, give information that makes it seem likely that James Johnson committed suicide because he failed to get into the Phi Alpha house.

Dr Corbett carries out the autopsy on James, who has petechial haemorrhages, small spots on his eyes that are synonymous with asphyxia. But there are no bite marks on his tongue, so it's unlikely he died from hanging. Corbett has also discovered some writing on James' penis, and Nick realises that the chapter has been practising hazing – putting the new members through unpleasant forms of initiation. He challenges Kyle and Matt, who deny hazing, knowing it's illegal in Nevada, but admit that there is a form of initiation. The final test included getting parts of the anatomy signed, and Matt claims that James was found signing himself on his penis to get accepted. Sara and Nick don't believe them.

The preliminary findings on James indicate that he died from choking on a strip of raw calf's liver, which had some microscopic threads of fabric embedded in it. Nick won't accept Kyle's excuses that he knows nothing about it, and eventually Kyle admits that they challenged James to swallow raw liver, but he choked, and they weren't able to save him with the Heimlich manoeuvre. They then freaked and faked the suicide. Kyle doesn't think there'll be any major problems, as his father is a defence attorney. They'll plead guilty to manslaughter and get community service.

However, the coroner's evidence shows none of the bruising consistent with the Heimlich being tried. The signature on James' penis is traced to Kyle Travis' girlfriend Jill, and a search of the frat house uncovers the damning evidence – a piece of string with a loop on the end. Matt breaks down and confesses that Kyle challenged James to swallow the liver, which was on the loop, telling him that he must trust Kyle to pull it out. Angry at James getting his own girlfriend to sign his penis, Kyle didn't pull it back out until James had choked. Kyle now faces a charge of first degree murder. He's joining a new fraternity – in prison.

Personal Notes: Nick used to be a member of a Greek fraternity. When he was pledging for his fraternity, he wore a trout in his jeans pocket for a week till his leg went half numb. Judge Cohen (see **00**, 'Pilot', **01**, 'Cool Change') believes he still has Warrick under his thumb, and wants Warrick to tamper with evidence in a rape case. Warrick is nearly caught by Grissom. After asking Grissom for advice, Warrick calls the Judge and says that they need to meet. Judge Cohen is arrested by Jim Brass for obstruction of justice, tampering with state's evidence, 'and violating seven articles of scumbag.' Despite Warrick's errors of judgement, Grissom promotes him to CSI-3. Catherine wishes that Grissom had told her that her husband Eddie had been cheating on her during the marriage. She is also not overly happy about having the deceased's skin rolled over her hand for prints (see **Techniques**). Grissom keeps a pet tarantula – an African Red Baboon, the most feared of all arachnids.

Techniques: Wendy Barger is identified from her fingerprints, which are gained by rolling the skin from her hand over Catherine's hand.

Jenna Williams confirms that she will run a rape kit on Wendy Barger. This involves taking DNA samples for analysis from any clothing, particularly underwear, combing the head and pubic hair, checking fingernails for signs of struggle, vaginal, anal and oral swabs and saliva and blood samples. They also take note of any bruising, cuts, abrasions, concussion or evidence of penetration.

Grissom duplicates the weather conditions on the lake in the CSI garage to work out where Wendy Barger's boat would have ended up. Catherine follows clues around the lake.

The Wit and Wisdom of Gil Grissom: 'You know Grissom. Shortest distance between two points is science.' (Quoted by Warrick to Greg.)

'We're scientists, not psychiatrists or victim's rights advocates.'

Classic Dialogue: Grissom: 'May I take your hand?' to Catherine before peeling the deceased's skin over her so they can print it.

Catherine to Grissom: 'I should be just like you. Alone in my hermetically sealed condo watching Discovery on the big screen. Working genius level crossword puzzles, but no relationships. No chance any will slop over into a case.'

Grissom: 'I never screw up one of my cases with personal stuff.' Catherine: 'Grissom ... what personal stuff?'

Fantastic Voyages: We take a close look at James Johnson's eye, showing the hallmarks of strangulation, and also see the noose that held the liver in all its gory detail. Wendy Barger's green wood chipped forehead is examined in detail, and we also see how it looks inside a lung when you drown.

The Usual Suspects: Paul Terrell Clayton (Detective Kane) is best known as Eddie in the unusual Channel 4/HBO series *Six Feet Under*. Chris Demetral (James Johnson) was the title character in the short-lived *Secret Adventures of Jules Verne* in 1999. Jim Ortlieb (Winston Barger) played Professor Bill Hodges during *Felicity*'s fourth season.

Pop Culture References: Grissom makes a bad Sherlock Holmes pun regarding the severed appendage – 'Watson, the game's afoot!' Grissom quotes Robert Frost's poem 'Two roads diverged in a yellow wood' to Greg, who recognises it.

Real-life Inspirations: Grissom's request to use Catherine's hand can be traced back to accounts of a Florida criminalist who was trying to identify a hand that been washed up on the banks of the river Manatee. He was unable to get prints from the skin, because of the length of time it had been in the water, so peeled off the skin, and placed it over his own hand. He could then apply pressure to the ridges and get a print.

Mistakes Really Can Be Fatal: In this case, it's Catherine's: it's more than a little alarming that she seems to get away with effectively being the cause of Phil Swelco's murder!

Overall: Good to see the Judge Cohen plotline quickly resolved, so that we can get a chance to see Warrick in action without that hanging over him all the time. The two storylines hold up well on their own. Overall, a good early episode.

04
Friends and Lovers

US Air Date: 3 November 2000 10.1/17
UK Air Date: 30 June 2001

Written by: Andrew Lipsitz
Directed by: Lou Antonio

Guest Cast: Kelly Connell (Randy Gesek),
Milo Ventimiglia (Bobby Taylor), Amy Carlson (Kate Armstrong),
Elena Lyons (Julia Eastman), Jeff Parise (Ethan),
Timothy Landfield (Dean Vernon Woods), Tom Beyer (L. Collins),
Mike Graybeal (Eric R. Berkley), Susan Martino (Kimberly Cassano),
Elkin Antonio (Rave Girl)

Teaser One-liner: 'Someone chased this kid to death.'
The Cases: Grissom and Warrick are called to a young
man's body found in the desert. The maggots indicate that
he's been there for about three days, and the evidence
indicates that he was running, in fear for his life. Coroner
Jenna Williams' preliminary examination can't determine
whether the bruise marks on the boy's face were caused by
suffocation or impacting the ground. Warrick takes a
mouth swab, while Jenna shows Grissom that the boy's
interior was perfectly healthy, but his skin sample shows he
was very dry, possibly indicating a high temperature.
Although anything the boy ingested may have evaporated,
the maggots preserve the material for longer, so a toxicology scan is run on the maggots. The test shows positive for
Jimson weed.

Another teenage boy, Bobby, comes in to file a missing
person's report on his friend Eric. He was last seen at a
party out near Red Rock, although Bobby denies they
were doing drugs. Bobby identifies the desert corpse as
Eric. He says that he and Eric thought that Jimson weed
was a plant, not a drug, and they took it as a tea.

Warrick recognises the stamp identifying the rave and
there Grissom, Warrick and Brass find Ethan, the dealer
who sold the weed to Eric and Bobby. They find seeds
inside his car but unfortunately the tests show that the ones
Eric ingested were not toxic enough to kill him. The dealer
will walk.

When Grissom tells Bobby that the Jimson tea didn't kill
Eric, he notices that the boy is scratching his arm. Bobby
says a spider bit him, but Grissom knows that the mark
isn't from an insect. The mouth swab Warrick took shows
aluminium, found in fireworks – and Bobby works at a
fireworks factory. A mould is taken of Eric's teeth.

Bobby denies killing Eric, but the evidence shows that he did. Both men were affected by the Jimson weed and, between the confusion caused by Bobby's auditory hallucinations and Eric's high temperature and photophobia, they ended up in a position where Bobby desperately tried to shut Eric up – and ended up suffocating him. The bite mark on Bobby's arm was from Eric as he tried to escape. Bobby's attorney says they'll plead diminished responsibility, and Grissom hopes they win.

Catherine and Nick are sent to the Verbum Dei Charter School where the school dean has been found murdered. The prime suspect is the school's founder, Kate Armstrong, who called in the homicide.

Dean Vernon Woods was killed by multiple blunt force trauma wounds to the head. Kate says that he was molesting her. She grabbed the first thing that she could and hit him once. Catherine explains that they know she hit him more than once because of the bloodspatter. Armstrong agrees that maybe it was more than once. As Catherine realises she's being lied to, she and Nick decide to 'string it', checking out the blood sprays using pieces of string to mark where each drop came from. The evidence shows that the Dean received most of his blows lying on the ground, but a missing shape of blood indicates that there was someone standing between the Dean and the wall.

Kate Armstrong admits that her friend Julia Eastman was there. Eastman says that she agreed to be present to witness Woods harassing Armstrong and just stood by the door. However, she is shown the computerised version of the stringing, which indicates that Kate must have had help wrestling Woods to the floor.

Catherine and Nick realise that they haven't found blood on Julia's clothes, and she claims to have burned them. They therefore examine the Dean's shirt, and find the clear pattern of a hand, with an extended finger.

Julia Eastman is unable to move her hand properly and should be wearing a spraincast. That's what caused the shape of the extended finger. Julia held Woods down while Armstrong killed him but Catherine can't fathom why they went as far as they did. Detective Kane discovers that Armstrong was paying Woods regular cheques, which were apparently repaying loans. In fact he was blackmailing her because she and Julia Eastman were lovers. They killed him because he had decided to reveal their secret.

Sara is assigned to investigate a dead body found in a dumpster near Henderson. It has an unusual texture, and deputy coroner David Phillips confirms that she's been embalmed. She's identified as Stephanie Reyes, laid to rest at the Desert Haven Funeral Home the previous week. Sara visits the funeral home, and the creepy director, Randy Gesek, claims that the grave was robbed, but he didn't report it. However, Sara realises that not only was the body stolen – so was the casket. Sara examines one of Gesek's caskets, which he maintains are for one-time use only, and wants to know why there is so much evidence of other people in it.

Gesek confesses to getting rid of the body so he could reuse the casket, and Sara makes him pay for a proper burial for Stephanie Reyes. She then hands the case over to the District Attorney.

Personal Notes: David Phillips makes a pass at Sara who gives him some friendly advice, and tells him he's cute. Grissom reveals that there are certain things that make him annoyed. 'Guys that hit their wives; sexual assault on children, and the scum that deal death to kids.' He also rides the roller coaster when he is very stressed – as he is at the end of this episode.

Techniques: To determine what happened in the Dean's office, Nick and Catherine analyse the bloodspatters. The direction that the blood is travelling can be identified by looking at which way its tail is pointing. A cast-off pattern shows what happens when a bloody object is moved around the crime scene, while dripping blood can create secondary splatters. The source of the splattered blood can be determined by connecting stains created in the same way along a series of strings, which will converge to the source of the blood. In this case it indicates that the Dean was moved.

Grissom identifies Eric's bite on Bobby's arm by taking a mould of the wound and matching it with a cast of Eric's teeth. In fact, because of the nature of the struggle between them, it's unlikely to be the perfect match it seems in the episode.

The Wit and Wisdom of Gil Grissom: 'Entomology is our friend!' (Quoted by Warrick.)

'The evidence only knows one thing: the truth. It is what it is.'

'The more the why, the less the how. The less the how the more the why.' (Quoted by Nick – to which Catherine responds, 'Hey, Nick, Grissom's not always right.')

Classic Dialogue: Catherine: 'The walls in his office looks like the Dean went a couple rounds with Mike Tyson.'

Jenna Williams: 'Gruesome Grissom – tin man with a heart. Who knew?'

Worst 'As You Know': 'We've got bloodspatter and cast-off on the walls; Kate Armstrong's confession, her clothes. Three void areas and that's pretty much it. Anything else?' Catherine is telling Nick, who's been there all along! But it's after the advert break, so he might have forgotten.

Fantastic Voyages: We follow the Jimson weed seeds down Eric's throat to the intestinal tract.

The Usual Suspects: Amy Carlson (Kate Armstrong) played Alex Taylor on fire service series *Third Watch* from 2000–2003. Kelly Connell (Randy Gesek) played the creepy Norman Pfister in the *Buffy The Vampire Slayer* two-parter 'What's My Line?' and the White House press secretary in *13 Days*. Milo Ventimiglia (Bobby Taylor) has played Jess Mariano on drama series *The Gilmore Girls* since the second season.

Pop Culture References: Grissom tells Warrick to 'Benihana' the maggots – a reference to a chain of Chinese restaurants in the States where the food is chopped up and stir-fried at the table. Warrick and Greg Sanders exchange *Pulp Fiction* lines as they prepare the maggots. Grissom quotes from The Who's 'Baba O'Riley' when he arrives at the rave.

Overall: Some righteous anger from Grissom when he faces the pusher Ethan gives the series its first *Quincy* moment, as our placid lead suddenly becomes a crusading avenger – but as soon as the evidence points in a different direction, it's all over. Sara's case feels like padding, although the nefarious Mr Gesek appears again (see **20**, 'Justice Is Served').

05
Who Are You?

US Air Date: 10 November 2000 10.1/17
UK Air Date: 7 July 2001

Written by: Carol Mendelsohn & Josh Berman
Directed by: Danny Cannon
Guest Cast: Tony Crane (Officer Joe Tyner), K.K. Dodds (Amy Hendler), Andy Buckley (Jason Hendler), Anne E. Curry (Mrs Green), Michael Delano (Ted Beaton), Roxanne Day (April Lewis), Leonard Kelly-Young (Al), Phillip Jean Marie (Valet aka Jerrod), Brian LeBarron (Suspect)

Teaser One-liner: 'By law you have to declare everything. Three bedrooms, two baths and a skeleton!'

The Cases: A plumber investigating a leaky pipe finds a hand sticking out of the wall in the crawlspace underneath a house. The 'Jane Doe' is female, about twenty years old, and there are unusual gouges on her ribs, from a weapon with a serrated edge.

Grissom brings a section of the house foundations to the lab; it shows a partial impression of Jane Doe. The house was built five years earlier on the desert and sold, but the buyers are in the clear.

Forensic anthropologist Teri Miller comes to help Grissom identify the body. She rebuilds the head, eventually producing a face that is broadcast on the news. The TV appeal works, and the body is identified as Fay Green. Her mother tells Grissom that she was a scuba diver, and that she'd just moved in with her boyfriend, Jason Hendler.

Doc Robbins shows Grissom a hairline fracture on Fay's skull. He's also found sodium on the middle ear, and some earwax with grains of sand inside the skull. Greg Sanders finds that the sand is manmade rather than natural, so it isn't from a beach. Nick and Grissom visit Jason Hendler's home where they meet him and his wife Amy. Grissom notes that their fish tank seems to have been moved. They also find a warped floorboard, underneath which is some sand. Despite Hendler's denial, Grissom believes that the tank was in a different place formerly, and it broke there. Hendler asks them to leave.

Nick discovers that Hendler worked as a subcontractor on the estate where Fay's body was found and he and Grissom return to the Hendlers', to find the sand has been vacuumed up. They use luminol to search for blood but it won't work on the lacquered floor. However, the ALS, which is looking for protein molecules, finds blood. The CSIs accuse Hendler of killing Fay and dumping her at the site, although Amy Hendler says that Jason wasn't even in Vegas when Fay disappeared. But she is devastated when Hendler admits that he still loves Fay. Hendler is taken away while Nick starts to examine the crime scene. Unfortunately Amy Hendler is the murderer and she holds Nick at gunpoint as she confesses. Grissom arrives just in time to save Nick from being shot.

Sara and Warrick are assigned to investigate an Officer Involved Shooting at the Jockey Club. Officer Tyner says that he was pursuing a suspect who stopped, and then shot himself through the forehead. Tyner reluctantly hands over his weapon for checking, and even Brass seems to be reluctant to help the CSIs. Sara points out that gunshot residue would be on both people so it wouldn't help to show whether Tyner shot the man or he did it himself. Tyner's gun is missing a bullet, but suspecting Tyner could lead to major friction between the CSIs and the LVPD.

Tyner claims that he never 'tops off', leaving one bullet out so the gun won't jam. Tempers start to flare when the CSIs seem not to believe him, and Brass insists that they find the bullet that killed the suspect. Sara and Warrick search the parking lot without success. However, the valet in a neighbouring lot says he saw Tyner shoot the suspect.

Brass is furious that the DA is filing charges against Tyner based on the eyewitness and the missing bullet in Tyner's gun. Tyner starts a fight with Warrick, which Grissom breaks up.

Sara and Warrick find the bullet inside a spare tyre on the victim's car after taking the entire vehicle apart – and it matches the suspect's gun, not Tyner's. Tyner was telling the truth.

Grissom reluctantly assigns Catherine to an alleged rape – although there is a conflict of interest. The suspect is her ex-husband, Eddie. Eddie has asked for Catherine, but Grissom would prefer she didn't work the case, and if she does, she must pass it on after the preliminary phase. Eddie denies raping showgirl April Lewis, although he admits having sex with her. Catherine decides to pass on the case, but Eddie emotionally blackmails her with thoughts of Lindsey visiting him in prison. Grissom suspects that Catherine is still partly in love with Eddie, and insists that she hand the case over to Warrick as remaining on it she could compromise the investigation and hurt Eddie as much as help him. However she doesn't, so Grissom reminds her that she needs to look at the evidence if she's going to stay involved.

April Lewis claims that Eddie started kissing her and then slammed her against a wall before raping her. Catherine takes a sample from beneath her fingernails to prove the struggle. She then goes to the Paradise Garden where she used to work, and the owner, Ted, lets her look around, where she makes a surprising discovery in April's locker. The rape kit on April Lewis had shown chemicals indicating a contraceptive film. When Catherine finds the film, it had to be inserted between fifteen minutes and three hours before sex – April expected to have intercourse.

Catherine talks to April, and realises that she thought she could shake Eddie down for money to make the rape charge go away. The case is dropped.

Personal Notes: Eddie Willows is introduced for the first time, and we come to understand very quickly both why Catherine fell for him, and why she left him. Catherine's past as a pole dancer is also revealed. There's definite sexual tension between Teri Miller and Gil Grissom – before leaving she leaves her number on his notice board for him to call her. Grissom teases Nick about being a ladies' man.

Techniques: Teri Miller is a forensic anthropologist. Studying the skeletal remains can provide numerous clues, as they do here. Women have a broader pelvis than men; men have a larger jaw and forehead. Joints, bones and teeth all deteriorate as we grow older, so the state of them gives an indication of age. Height can be determined from the leg and arm joints, and the state of the knee and ankle joints can give an approximation of weight. Racial characteristics can be identified from the shape of the nose. Teri also doubles as a forensic artist, creating a two-dimensional blueprint for a guide, taking a cast of the skull, adding layers of 'skin' and then using modelling clay to create the features. There are various formulas that are used to sort out the size of the nose and the mouth, and then hair and eyes are added. The resulting 'person' can then be photographed.

The Wit and Wisdom of Gil Grissom: 'It's about the evidence, Catherine, and you may not like where it takes you.'

Classic Dialogue: Grissom: 'You know, for a ladies' man, you don't know much about bone structure.' Nick: 'I know all I need to know.'

Fantastic Voyages: More close-ups than moving shots – we look at the ribs of the skeleton and later at the hairline fracture on the skull; we also see the tiny bullet inside the tyre.

The Usual Suspects: Paraplegic actor Robert David Hall starred as the recruiting sergeant in *Starship Troopers*.

Timothy Carhart (Eddie Willows) is a regular on the second season of *24* as Eric Rayburn. Andrew Buckley (Jason Hendler) played JFK Jr in the TV miniseries *A*

Woman Named Jackie. Pamela Gidley (Teri Miller) is best known for playing Brigitte in *The Pretender* and has been cast in the Jerry Bruckheimer production *Skin* for the 2003/4 season.

Pop Culture References: Teri Miller jokes about Spider-Man, the Marvel comics and big-screen hero.

Real-life Inspirations: Grissom's case is inspired by a case from Los Angeles in 1987, when a woman's skeleton was found in the cement foundation of a house. The wet cement had created a 'death mask', which was used to identify her. The hand prints she left in the concrete were even sufficient to provide enough detail to confirm her fingerprints.

Forensic sculptures helped to identify the victims of serial killer John Wayne Gacy when there were only skeletal remains.

Notes: The real Vegas locations the Jockey Club parking lot, the Spearmint Rhino Strip Club and the Manhattan Express Rollercoaster all feature in this episode.

When faced with a gun in this episode, George Eads based his performance on his own reactions when he was mugged in Texas.

Overall: Although Warrick and Sara's case could have taken place anywhere in the USA, the other two are more Vegas-specific, making good use of the location both for filming and for its history. Director Danny Cannon is one of the best at making the town itself feel like a participant in the series.

06
Blood Drops (aka If These Walls Could Talk)

US Air Date: 17 November 2000 10.7/18
UK Air Date: 14 July 2001

Teleplay by: Ann Donahue
Story by: Tish McCarthy
Directed by: Kenneth Fink

Guest Cast: Allison Lange (Tina Collins), Eric Nenninger (Jesse Overton),
Dakota Fanning (Brenda Collins), Sean Smith (Ted Goggle),
Del Hunter-White (Family Services Rep), Jonathan T. Floyd (EMS #1),
Mike Bowman (Oliver), Paul Raci (Lie Detector Operator),
John Churchhill (Shibley), Traci Melchor (Reporter),
Drew Wood (Suburban Teen #2),
Morgan Lee Wojnowski (Young Tina – Age 6),
Jonathan Redford (Suburban Teen #1),

Teaser One-liner: 'What's the matter with your guys?'
'They've been inside . . .'

The Case: Distraught teenager Tina Collins races to her
next door neighbour, covered in blood. When the police
arrive, they discover a massacre. Her mother, father and
two teenage brothers are all murdered, and only Tina and
her younger sister have survived.

The father is lying in a blood pool, with multiple stab
wounds to his back and neck. There is a blood swirl on the
wall, and when Sara arrives, she wonders if it might be
connected to a Manson-like cult. Grissom and Sara find
the mother in bed in the master bedroom, with her throat
cut in her sleep. Grissom calls the entire Graveyard Shift
in. Sara photographs the corpses, and Grissom demands
magnified copies. He persuades Tina to let them have her
clothes, and she asks about her baby sister, Brenda.
Grissom talks gently to the little girl, but all she says is 'the
buffalo'.

When the team arrives, Grissom orders them not to talk
to the press or the sheriff about the case. Catherine works
on mapping the layout, and blood samples, while Nick and
Warrick work the perimeter to find out how the perpetrator arrived and left. In the kitchen, Grissom discovers that
there's a knife missing, but no other damage – the killer
knew where to go. He uses an Electrostatic Dust Print
Lifter to check for footprints. Unfortunately, the clean
prints match the EMS technicians.

Sheriff Mobley arrives, demanding answers which Grissom doesn't yet have. He assigns Sara to look after
Brenda, much to her annoyance.

Catherine and Grissom believe the swirls are a red
herring. They hypothesise that the mother was killed first,

and the father ran to protect the children and was killed in the hall. However, there should be more blood. They wonder about Tina, and Brenda's comment about a buffalo.

Brass questions Tina, who says she heard noises which sounded like footsteps coming from the kitchen, so she hid. She doesn't know anyone called Buffalo, and says she knows the difference between her family's footsteps and the ones she heard.

Warrick discovers a tyre track, which must have been made between 02.00 and 02.40, since the sprinkler didn't eliminate it. It looks like it comes from a scooter, which would match the age range of the bidi (handrolled) cigarette and match that Nick found. He checks with DMV, and a kid four blocks away owns a scooter of the same make.

Sara takes Brenda over to the hospital for a psychological evaluation. The doctors want Brenda to have a psychiatric examination, but Sara initially refuses to leave her with them.

Grissom checks Tina's clothing – there's no blood on it. She didn't even check her family before she ran from the house though her statement said that she hugged her mother, and tripped over her father's body. She holds to her story even though Grissom doesn't believe her.

Catherine realises she's forgotten to pick up Lindsey from school. The teachers therefore called Eddie, who brought her home. Before Catherine can catch her breath, Grissom calls, needing her back at base. Grissom has a brief run-in with his opposite number on day shift, Conrad Ecklie, who says that his team would do better.

Brass brings in the scooter's owner, Oliver, who points out that he owns the scooter with three other people. He also says that Tina is a 'freak'. The first two co-owners of the scooter have solid alibis, but the immediate reaction of the third one, Jesse Overton, is to call for a lawyer. Nick confiscates Jesse's pack of bidis and matchbook when he tries to light up. A broken match in his matchbook lines up with the piece of match Nick found earlier.

Tina is getting desperate to see Brenda, but Catherine and Grissom inform her that she's not going to get a chance to coach her sister.

Brass gets a warrant to search Jesse's home and finds massively bloodstained jeans and the scooter in the trash. Jesse admits that Tina asked him to kill her family because she was mad at her parents for keeping them apart, and so they could see each other, but the polygraph shows he is lying about the motive.

Grissom gets the Collins' effects from where Ecklie has been keeping them from him. He finds a buffalo medallion, and the pieces start to fall into place. He tells Sara to take some ultraviolet pictures of Brenda to see if there are signs of abuse.

Mapping out the murders, Catherine realises that the father wasn't entering Brenda's room when he was killed – he was leaving it. At that moment she is informed by a member of the Family Services Department that Eddie has filed a report of neglect against her because she didn't pick Lindsey up. According to him, that's just one instance of routine neglect.

Grissom and Catherine let Tina know that they've found sexual abuse evidence on Brenda, and that they know her father was leaving Brenda's room when he was killed. Inadvertently, Tina reveals that Brenda is her daughter, not her sister. She had been abused and then impregnated by her father and, when he started molesting Brenda, she determined to stop him. Her mother and brothers had to die because they should have protected Tina ...

Personal Notes: Eddie Willows seems to believe that Catherine is having an affair with Grissom, and files a neglect report against Catherine when she races back to the office.

Techniques: A polygraph machine is used on Jesse, which measures his galvanic skin response, his relative blood pressure and his respiration. Ordinary questions are asked to determine a baseline, and then if he lies, there's a clear movement.

Catherine determines that the blood on Mr Collins comes from both entrance and exit wounds because of the way the blood lies – it travels in the same direction as the bullet from the exit wound, but the opposite way from an entrance.

Warrick takes plastercasts of the tyre tracks found around the scene and compares them on the Tread Assistant, a CD ROM database of tread patterns.

An electrostatic dust print lifter creates an electrostatic field which can bring to the surface previously invisible prints in the dust.

Sara uses an ultraviolet camera which can identify bruising beneath the skin, and thus invisible to the naked eye.

The Wit and Wisdom of Gil Grissom: 'Air smells like copper. Lots of blood. Breathe through your mouth.'

Classic Dialogue: Sheriff Mobley: 'Why don't you be more like Ecklie?' Grissom: 'I could speak volumes about Conrad Ecklie, but right now I have a crime scene to process.'

Sara: '[I'm] going back to the girl. I left her in the car. But the windows are cracked.'

Ecklie: 'You kept the Sheriff out of the loop. That's a career killer, Gil.' Grissom: 'That's what's so sad, Conrad. You think of this as a career.'

The Usual Suspects: Despite her young years, Dakota Fanning (Brenda Collins) has an extensive resumé, including a lead role in the Steven Spielberg TV miniseries *Taken*. She also appears in *The Cat In The Hat*. Allison Lange (Tina Collins) went on to play Laurie Dupree in a four-episode arc of SF series *Roswell*. Marc Vann (Conrad Ecklie) has been seen in early episodes of *Early Edition*, as well as the offbeat vampire film *The Forsaken*.

Pop Culture References: Mass murderer Charles Manson was deemed responsible for the actions of his cult members when they butchered film director Roman Polanski's eight months pregnant wife Sharon Tate on 9 August 1969.

Grissom quotes Shakespeare's *Macbeth*: 'Who would have thought the old man would have so much blood in him.' And, 'Out, out damned spot.' Jesse refers to Sharon Stone's infamous interrogation sequence in *Basic Instinct*.

Real-life Inspirations: Catherine's suspicions that the swirl marks were deliberately daubed on the walls to make the Collins' murder look like a cult slaying echo the 1970 case of Jeffrey MacDonald, a US Captain who claimed that a hippie gang were responsible for the deaths of his wife and daughters. Investigators were suspicious, and found a book detailing the Manson murders openly displayed. Mac-Donald was convicted by a civilian court, even though a military court acquitted him.

Mistakes Really Can Be Fatal: If Grissom and the Graveyard Shift really had just come off duty at the start of the episode, presumably Ecklie has a point that the case should really have gone to the daytime team . . .

Notes: The original title of this episode is the same as a series of TV movies; subsequent US and all overseas airings have referred to it as 'Blood Drops'.

Although he's been mentioned as early as **01**, 'Cool Change', when he appoints Grissom as head of the Graveyard Shift, this is the first time we've met Sheriff Brian Mobley. It's also the debut of Grissom's counterpart on the daytime shift, the less than pleasant Conrad Ecklie.

Overall: At last the CSI unit feels like it's part of a whole, rather than Grissom's private little fiefdom. Although we've heard him complain about paperpushing, this is the first time we've seen any of the life that goes on in the building when the Graveyard Shift isn't there. Apart from the harrowing moment between Catherine and the little girl (see **00**, 'Pilot'), this is the first time that *CSI* has examined sexual areas involving children, something that it returns to perhaps too frequently. It's also the first 'one-case' episode which just about maintains the interest, although it's odd not to have any *CSI* trademark close-ups.

07
Anonymous

US Air Date: 24 November 2000 8.5
UK Air Date: 21 July 2001

Written by: Eli Talbert & Anthony E. Zuiker
Directed by: Danny Cannon
Guest Cast: Barbara Tarbuck (Mrs Harmon),
Matt O'Toole (Paul Millander), Tom McCleister (Walter Banglor),
Ricky Harris (Disco Placid), Sheeri Rappaport (Mandy),
Howard S. Miller (Bum), Jonathan T. Floyd (Paramedic/EMS #1),
Natasha Silver (Receptionist), James McPherson (Thug),
Doug Bennet (Stranded Motorist), John Churchill (Shibley),
Sewell Whitney (Stuart Rampler)

Teaser One-liner: 'Ring any bells? Rub-a-dub-dub. Dead man in a tub.'

The Cases: A man is found dead in a bathtub, apparently having shot himself – the same way as Royce Harmon was killed (see **00**, 'Pilot'). This man also has a tape recorder in his hands, although this time the recording is backwards. Played the right way around, Stuart Rampler's message is the same as Royce Harmon's. Sara is brought up to speed on the events (see **00**, 'Pilot'), and sent to dust the hotel bathroom using Red Creeper, Grissom's homemade concoction. However, it's not just clean of prints – it's completely sterile.

Doc Robbins compares his own autopsy of Rampler with Klausbach's notes of Harmon's death – while Harmon was shot from six or seven feet away, Stuart Rampler was forced into the tub at gunpoint, and there's muzzle stamp on him.

Grissom and Catherine visit Royce Harmon's mother, who still maintains that the voice on the tape isn't her son's. She has a talking Mother's Day card with his voice, which she lends them.

Sara takes some stamped envelopes found at the hotel for DNA analysis. All bar one bear Stuart Rampler's DNA – but one with the stamp on upside down is from someone else, who Sara dubs 'Anonymous'.

Grissom takes Catherine to meet Disco Placid, a DJ who specialises in audio and does voice comparisons for Grissom. Harmon's voice has been altered, and Disco confirms that the voice on the tape *is* Royce Harmon's. Played side by side, the two recordings are identical, save the names, addresses and ages. Clearly the killer is making the men read from a script.

Harmon and Rampler were born on 17 August, Harmon in 1958, Rampler in 1957. Sara checks for anything connected to the same date in 1956, as Mandy the print analyst shows that there are two prints on the tape recorder: on top is Paul Millander's, as expected from the fake hand, but the other belongs to Gil Grissom. Whoever is doing this is letting Grissom know he's under his thumb. Grissom goes back to visit Paul Millander to see if he has a list of buyers of the fake hand, but Millander says he doesn't.

Stuart Rampler's ATM card is being used and Grissom knows that there's a good chance Anonymous was photographed using it. Anonymous has left Grissom a clue on the ATM camera – a set of pictures which he deduces means that Anonymous will keep killing over and over again until he gets justice. The pictures are being shown by a tramp, who describes the man who paid him to flip the cards – Paul Millander.

Checking the databases, Sara discovers that when he was 10, Millander testified that he saw two hotel security guards force his father into a bathtub and shoot him. The official cause of death was suicide. John Millander died on 17 August 1959, and Paul is killing people born on the same day his father died, in preceding years. As they race to Millander's workplace, only to find it empty, Paul Millander makes a brief visit to CSI headquarters, leaving a message for Grissom saying 'a friend stopped by'.

Grissom gives Warrick and Nick a reckless driver case. A car has careered off the edge of the road, with a man strapped into the back seat. He's now in hospital, lucky to be alive.

The pair find a beer bottle by the side of the car, as well as tyre tracks and footprints. Nick believes a drunk driver baled out of the car just before it went over the cliff. The tyre tracks show another car as well, which Nick suggests belonged to someone who stopped and took the driver to the hospital. Warrick thinks otherwise – there are foot-marks leading to the edge. He thinks it was a crime scene. They bet each other $100 on the outcome.

At the hospital, the passenger is not going to be able to talk for at least twelve hours. He's got tan lines, but no ring or watch, which backs up Warrick's theory of foul play. Nick and Warrick double their bet.

Nick 'superglues' the entire car, checking for prints. Warrick has checked the hospitals and there's no phantom driver. The car was registered to the passenger, Walter Bangler. The print analysis on the car shows mostly Bangler's prints, although there is an odd blue dust in them.

Nick isn't having any luck with his phantom driver theory, and Warrick suggests upping the bet to $300. He still believes it was a robbery, and Bangler was forced into the back of the car. Warrick can't explain the blue dust in Bangler's prints, but his theory explains the footprints and tyre tracks.

Warrick finds that the prints come from Size 11 Converse All Stars, which are common, while Nick discovers that the tyres are high-performance Pirellis, only found on three cars in the Vegas area. Brass confirms that a Bentley using them was stolen recently, but unfortunately it has already been found after being thoroughly cleaned.

Nick checks Bangler's clothing for the blue dust, and Greg confirms it's pool cue chalk. Nick's theory is that Bangler was shooting pool with the phantom driver. They then drive off, but crash, and the driver gets out, leaving Bangler seesawing on the edge to take the fall. Warrick agrees that Bangler was shooting pool, but that he goes off on his own. The Bentley driver makes him crash, robs him, and then pushes him over the edge. Reluctantly, both men think the other's theory is plausible.

When Bangler wakes up, both men are proved wrong. Bangler explains that he was hustled at the pool hall, robbed, and he then went for a drive while still drunk. He careered to the edge of the dam, and got in the back seat himself, buckling up because he knew the fall would be dangerous. Nick and Warrick agree to drop the bet.

Personal Notes: Although Warrick appears to have his gambling under control, he's still happy to have a little bet on the side.

The Wit and Wisdom of Gil Grissom: 'I envy you, Mr Millander. I do. You can work by yourself. No one around to bother you. You just do what you do. I'd love to have that kind of autonomy.'

Classic Dialogue: Brass: 'Quincy wants to be alone.'

Nick: 'You look tired. Want me to fix you a bottle? Go ni-ni.' Warrick: 'You want me to clack that jaw? Put your ass ni-ni?'

Fantastic Voyages: There's a close-up of the muzzle stamp on Stuart's face, and we follow the bullet going into him.

The Usual Suspects: Matt O'Toole returns as Paul Millander, with Barbara Tarbuck reprising her role as Royce Harmon's mother, both from 00, 'Pilot'. Ricky Harris (Disco Placid) played J.W. on the long-running comedy *Moesha*.

Pop Culture References: Brass gently teases Grissom as Dr Livingstone, the nineteenth-century doctor and explorer, renowned for his humanitarian work in Africa. He also refers to Grissom as Quincy!

Mistakes Really Can Be Fatal: As 35, 'Identity Crisis' reveals, Grissom's birthday is 17 August 1956. When they start talking about possible murders of people born that day, don't you think Grissom just might have mentioned the fact?

Overall: *CSI*'s first returning villain wraps up a loose end from 00, 'Pilot' in a suitably satisfying way, but still leaving Paul Millander free to wreak havoc. The by-play between Warrick and Nick makes more of the B story than it warrants.

08
Unfriendly Skies

US Air Date: 8 December 2000 10.2
UK Air Date: 28 July 2001

Teleplay by: Andrew Lipsitz, Carol Mendelsohn, Anthony E. Zuiker
Story by: Andrew Lipsitz
Directed by: Michael Shapiro
Guest Cast: Christine Tucci (Dr Kiera Behrle),

James Avery (Preston Cash), Deidre Quinn (Shannon),
David Kaufman (Nate Metz), Lorry Goldman (Lou Everett),
Kevin Cooney (Captain Murdle), Douglas Roberts (Tony Candlewell),
Dyana Ortelli (Marlene Valdez), Gerald Castillo (Max Valdez),
Christina Chambers (Vicki Mercer), Joe Michael Burke (Carl Finn),
Channing Carson (Emily Behrle), Edmund Wyson (Co-Capt. Arrington)

Teaser One-liner: 'I got a dead body. And a crime scene
with wings. Something very wrong happened in this plane.'
The Case: A disturbance on board Las Vegas Air flight 909
brings the Graveyard Shift out to McCarran International
Airport. A first-class passenger apparently had a panic
attack and died before landing. Nine passengers and one
flight attendant saw him die. Grissom finds a hand and
shoe print on the cockpit door, and the body was found
lying between rows 1 and 2 with defensive wounds. He
orders the entire plane to be sealed off.

Since the Federal Aviation Administration has jurisdiction over incidents occurring on planes, Sheriff Mobley is
keen to be able to present results to the authorities when
they arrive to take over. Mobley can't believe that Grissom
would seal the plane off unless he was certain it was a
homicide. Grissom points out that he doesn't know
anything yet.

None of the passengers in coach class saw anything, so the
CSIs concentrate on the first-class passengers. The deceased
is Tony Candlewell, a 30-year-old married communications
manager. Sara thinks that one person could not have caused
so much damage inside the plane, but all the witnesses are
giving the same story. Warrick and Catherine interview the
passengers, while Nick goes to attend the autopsy.

The plane's captain recalls that he was called out by the
flight attendant Shannon because Candlewell was acting
oddly. He insisted on using the first-class toilet, and
wouldn't go back to the coach class. The captain doesn't
consider he was acting particularly oddly.

Coroner Jenna Williams discovers that Candlewell's
body temperature is still near normal, which is wrong given
that he died two hours earlier – he was therefore running
a fever. He has indications of suffocation, and contusions

on the side of his neck, possibly from the heel of a boot. There are multiple contusions on his front and back, and he has a broken hand – all in all, a mass of contradictions.

Nate Metz, who was sitting in front of Candlewell, recalls that Candlewell kept banging on his seat with his foot for a large part of the journey. Metz claims he ignored it, although he punched his seat in anger.

Sara and Grissom find blood spots away from the main area, near the seat belonging to Lou Everett. Everett says that Candlewell swung at him with a CD after he tried to stop Metz and Candlewell from arguing. Brass notices that Everett has had a few drinks.

Shannon, the flight attendant, recalls that Candlewell started pressing his call button over and over complaining of a headache, so she gave him some aspirin.

Grissom and Catherine compare notes and guess that the passengers are all hiding something. Jenna has confirmed that Candlewell, in addition to a fever, had internal bleeding, thoracic haemorrhaging and a ruptured spleen.

Marlene and Max Valdez's story is that they thought Candlewell was going to hijack the plane, so Marlene slashed him with a broken bottle. Figuring that Candlewell might go to the toilet to clean up, Grissom and Sara check it, but find no blood – although they find other proteins which indicate that two of the passengers were engaged in joining the Mile High Club. Carl Finn and Vicki Mercer are the obvious participants, but they tell Catherine they weren't together, and didn't hear anything. Finn even claims he fell asleep listening to air traffic control and missed all the commotion.

Catherine takes all the passengers' shoes so they can compare the contusions on Candlewell's body with the shape of the heels. Three of the passengers' shoes match – Lou Everett's, Max Valdez's and Dr Kiera Behrle's. Behrle is travelling with her daughter Emily. Behrle has a black eye which she says she got for being a Good Samaritan. She claims she tried to save Candlewell's life with CPR but couldn't. Brass offers her the possibility of a deal, pointing out that her daughter might need her to take one.

Sara and Grissom check the defibrillation paddles that every airline carries. They have not been used. Dr Behrle should have known about them, but even if she didn't, the flight attendant would. Shannon claims that it was all over by the time she thought of them.

Grissom and Warwick finally talk to Mr Cash, the man sitting in the front row. Unfortunately he can't tell them what he saw, since he is legally blind, but he has a good memory for voices, and he tells them what he heard, casting a new light on events.

Jenna Williams tells Grissom that Candlewell was suffering from undiagnosed encephalitis, which, when added to the altitude and the air pressure changes, explains all of Candlewell's symptoms. Any of the things he was suffering from could have killed him.

With time running out before the FAA arrive, Grissom carries out a reconstruction, with Brass playing Lou Everett, Sara as the flight attendant, Catherine as Kiera Behrle, and Nick and Warrick as Max and Marlene Valdez. Grissom himself plays Nate Metz. Candlewell calls for an aspirin which 'Shannon' takes over to him. 'Lou' is drunk and getting ticked off with Candlewell, but 'Nate' is feeling more aggravated, so gets up and breaks the seat. 'Lou' takes a swipe at Candlewell, but he's too drunk and misses, and gets a CD swipe across the face. He falls back and spills his own drink. 'Marlene' sends 'Max' out to try to calm things down but Candlewell pushes him into the food cart. 'Marlene' gets up and lashes out at Candlewell with a broken bottle, swiping him on the hands. Candlewell goes to the cockpit and bangs on the door, but it's locked. 'Shannon' is too scared to do anything, as Candlewell goes to the main door. Everyone gets scared then, and there's a free-for-all attacking Candlewell. Although the sick man tries to get away from them, the passengers become a mob – and all five who attacked him are liable for murder.

Grissom tells the Sheriff what the evidence shows, but admits he can't prove it. Mobley says that he's going to let the passengers go as no jury would convict.

The CSIs discuss the case, and Grissom points out that this is about how people behave under threat. Warrick thinks that if it came down to him or Candlewell, he could do the same as the passengers did; Sara says she couldn't; and Nick isn't sure. Catherine is positive – if Lindsey were on the plane, she would go all the way to protect her child. Grissom can't answer and points out that none of them put themselves in Tony Candlewell's position. Everyone assumed he was a jerk and then a threat – he became that, but he didn't have to be. It took five people to kill Tony Candlewell; it would only have taken one person to save his life.

Personal Notes: The CSIs' personal attitude to lifetaking is revealed. Sara admits to membership of the Mile High Club in a surprisingly flirtatious conversation with Grissom. Grissom's knowledge is apparently gained from a magazine!

Techniques: Because of the time factor involved in this episode, Grissom organises a reconstruction, using both dummies and the criminalists to recreate what happened on the plane.

The Wit and Wisdom of Gil Grissom: 'Having sex at this altitude is supposed to enhance the entire sexual experience. Increase the euphoria.'

'I put all their accounts in a mixing bowl, add eggs and some milk and stack it in the oven for thirty minutes and all I've got is a limp soufflé.'

Classic Dialogue: Flight attendant Shannon: 'Look. I've been flying for ten years. You know, I've seen it all. Ferrets in suitcases. Fellatio in First Class. Passengers stir-frying on their tray tables. I mean, who knows why anyone does anything?'

The Usual Suspects: Christine Tucci (Dr Behrle) is better known for playing another doctor, Rose Webber, on *Chicago Hope*. Lorry Goldman (Lou Everett) played the 'Gene Siskel' figure in Devlin & Emmerich's *Godzilla*. David Kaufman (Nate Metz) is more recognisable vocally following his role as Jimmy Olsen in the animated *Batman/Superman Adventures*.

Pop Culture References: Grissom mentions the 1999 movie *Run Lola Run*, in which Lola is racing against the clock to save her boyfriend's life. The title refers to United Airlines' slogan 'Fly The Friendly Skies'. Nate Metz refers to Candlewell as Pele, the world-famous Brazilian footballer. Brass mentions the police reality show *COPS*.

Real-life Inspirations: 'Unfriendly Skies' is heavily indebted to the case of Jonathan Burton, who travelled from Las Vegas to Salt Lake City in August 2000. Burton too began to act oddly, and kicked a hole in the cockpit door. He did sit down, but then exploded with violence shortly before touchdown, at which point the passengers overpowered him. When the police came on board, they found him beneath a melee of passengers, and Burton died within an hour. The US attorney decided that this was justifiable homicide, committed in self-defence, and declined to file charges.

Mistakes Really Can Be Fatal: Why does it take so long to get around to asking the passenger at the front of the plane about an incident that happened *at the front of the plane?*

Overall: *CSI* does Agatha Christie – it's *Murder on the Orient Express* with Grissom exercising his little grey cells to puzzle out how everyone did it! But did they run out of footage or something? The episode is very taut until the very talky last scene, which is completely out of place. It's American TV moralising at its worst – think *Clifford the Big Red Dog* times one thousand. Unfortunately it spoils an otherwise excellent episode with the various CSIs meshing together well. Nick and Warrick as a married couple are priceless.

09
Sex, Lies and Larvae

US Air Date: 22 December 2000 9.9/17
UK Air Date: 4 August 2001

Written by: Josh Berman & Ann Donahue
Directed by: Thomas J. Wright
Guest Cast: John Getz (Richard Zeigler), Mark Moses (Scott Shelton),

Jennifer Sommerfield (Detective Secula), Blake Lindsley (Jessica Lovett),
Lisa Arturo (Sheryl Applegate), Todd Sible (Jason Zeigler),
Jason Padgett (Troy Zeigler), John Bastien (Hiking Guy),
Alex Rice (Hiking Girl (Angie)), Will Potter (Michael),
Susan Martino (Public Defender), Jennifer Toffel (Lisa Zeigler),
Jody Lyn Wilson (Kaye Shelton)

Teaser One-liner: 'I want to keep these little fellows alive.
They're our first witness to the crime.'

The Cases: Hikers in the mountains find the body of a
woman, wrapped in a blanket, killed by a gunshot to the
head. It's surrounded by paper wasps, and Grissom
removes some beetles from the corpse.

Doc Robbins confirms that she was shot with a .38
calibre gun, flush to the scalp. Skull X-rays indicate that
the woman had been in a long-term abusive relationship.
Grissom realises that the insect found in the body is a
muscid fly, which typically only lives in urban areas –
although the woman was found in the mountains.

Grissom explains that the life cycle of the bugs will tell
him how long the woman has been there. Brass confirms
the woman's identity as Kaye Shelton; her husband Scott
claims he was out of town the previous week. He last saw
Kaye five days earlier. A neighbour heard a gunshot and a
scream in the apartment, which Shelton claims was probably on TV. He reluctantly admits to 'wrestling' his wife
off him in the past – there have been three complaints filed
for spousal abuse – but says he didn't lay a hand on her
this time, and agrees to let them search his apartment.

Grissom finds blanket fibres on the settee, and Brass
notes that Shelton has cleaned his gun recently. He's also
cleaned the back part of the apartment with bleach – but
the luminol still shows massive blood stains. Shelton's
attitude winds Sara up during the search. He gets aggressive with Sara and is taken away – and as Sara points out,
if he's like that with her, and she's armed, what would be
like with his wife?

Sara is being haunted by the case. Everything seems to
be pointing to Shelton killing Kaye five days ago, but the
bugs haven't spoken yet – and when they do, they reveal

that she's only been dead for three days. That seems to put Shelton in the clear. The blood could have come from one of the previous altercations between Kaye and her husband.

However, Grisson goes a stage further. Kaye's body was wrapped tightly in a blanket, and this might restrict the bugs' access to the body. Grissom experiments with a similarly wrapped pig – the closest he can get to human tissue – to see what happens. It was five days.

Grissom tells Sheriff Mobley that he has recomputed his calculations, but the Sheriff doesn't think a jury will understand what's happened. He needs something other than the bug evidence to arrest Shelton. Grissom gets Doc Robbins to re-examine Kaye's body and he finds some blue material embedded in her skin, formed from disintegrated Teflon – matching Shelton's ammunition. It's still circumstantial evidence, but that's more easily understood by a jury. Brass rearrests Shelton.

Catherine and Warrick are assigned to find a Paul Sorenson, last seen at the home of Richard Zeigler in a rich part of town. They discover that the Sorenson is a painting, not a person. Zeigler believes that he disturbed the burglar. The alarm had been disengaged, leading the CSIs to suspect an inside job.

Zeigler confirms that his wife, sons and daughter are the only ones with keys and security codes. Warrick finds an earprint beside the empty space where the painting sat, and takes a photograph and lift. The CSIs take earprints from the family, and they show that Zeigler's son Jason is responsible. Zeigler doesn't want to press charges, and as Jason hasn't sold the painting yet, he can't be held for selling stolen property.

Catherine, however, has the Sorenson recovered painting tested with an ElectroThermal atomiser which will show whether the paint used in the picture is of the right period. The presence of titanium is a clear indicator that Jason swapped a genuine picture for a forgery.

To Zeigler's horror, many of his paintings are forgeries, but he is relieved when Warrick tells him that they found the originals in Jason's dorm room. Jason did it to get his father's attention – and Zeigler tells him that he has got it. This time, he is pressing charges.

Sheryl Applegate's car was found at the bus station when her husband thought she was driving to LA. It seems obvious: she must have taken the bus, but since the husband notified the police, the car is a potential crime scene. At the Bus Station, Nick and Detective Secula compare notes – it seems like a waste of time until Nick finds hairs in the car indicating a possible struggle. They check the car for more evidence, and when they find blood, realise that this might be a homicide.

Sheryl Applegate's credit card is used at a motel, and Nick and Secula take some LVPD officers with them to check the room. They find Sheryl manacled voluntarily to a bed, and a boyfriend in the bathroom. She's not been abducted at all. She explains that the blood was from an injured dog.

Personal Notes: Warrick has been called by Child Services, who ask about Lindsey. He tells them that Catherine is a fantastic mother, and that Eddie is a messed up guy. Nick and Detective Secula had dinner the week before this episode. It looks as though Warrick is gambling again – he gets one of the day shift to cover a court appearance for him, and when Ecklie complains about this to Grissom, Gil asks Sara to investigate. Sure enough, the surveillance tape shows that Warrick was in the Monaco Casino. Sara is an inveterate muncher of beef jerky at the start of this episode, although we later learn that as a result of the experiment with the pig she becomes vegetarian.

Techniques: Identification can be made from an earprint, since it has distinct characteristics. Lotion is applied to a piece of glass and then pressed against the ear. The print is then dusted and has clear tape applied to it. However, at present, it's not sufficient evidence for a conviction (see **Real-life Inspirations** below).

The study of the bugs uses a speciality of The Body Farm at the University of Tennessee: to determine the PMI (post-mortem indication) – i.e. how long the body has been sitting there. Necrophagous species like flies and beetles feed directly off the body, and their stage of development indicates how long the body has been there. The Body Farm puts corpses into all sorts of different conditions to see how these affect the insects' actions. In this case, Shelton wrapped his wife in a blanket, which slowed down the insects getting to the body.

Catherine uses an ElectroThermal atomiser that determines the chemical composition of the substances it is checking.

The Wit and Wisdom of Gil Grissom: 'You're confused? . . . That's the best place for a scientist to be.'

'You're the one who's always saying you'd rather have ten pieces of forensic evidence than ten eyewitnesses.' (Quoted by Sara.)

Classic Dialogue: Sara: 'You want to sleep with me?' Grissom: 'Did you just say what I think you said?'

Fantastic Voyages: We follow the bullet from inside the muzzle of the gun into Kaye, both during the autopsy, and then in the flashback. We also travel with the bullet when Shelton's gun is test fired.

The Usual Suspects: Lisa Arturo (Sheryl Applegate) played one of the lesbians in *American Pie 2*. John Getz (Richard Ziegler) is one of the few actors to appear in both *The Fly* (1986) and its 1989 sequel. Jody Lyn Wilson (Kaye Shelton) was Neve Campbell's stunt double on *Wild Things*, and has worked on *Charmed* and *2 Fast 2 Furious*. Mark Moses (Scott Shelton) played Captain Archer's father Henry in the Pilot of *Enterprise*.

Pop Culture References: Grissom jokingly calls his beetles by the names of the Fab Four. Grissom is referred to as Dr Seuss, the American children's author, creator of The Grinch.

Grissom quotes Shakespeare: 'full of sound and fury signifying . . .?'

Real-life Inspirations: Identifying someone from an earprint is a recognised art, although at present it's not regarded as a science and thus not sufficient to gain a conviction in America. David Wayne Kunze's 1999 conviction in Washington State was overturned on appeal when the earprint evidence that convicted him was excluded, and the other evidence deemed insufficient to convict him again.

Mistakes Really Can Be Fatal: Only a few episodes ago, in **04**, 'Friends and Lovers', we were told that one of the few things that gets Grissom annoyed is people who beat up their wives, yet here it's not him getting annoyed at all – it's Sara!

Overall: A slightly frustrating episode that promises a lot and somehow fails to deliver. Nice to see something rattling Sara's cage, but it is, basically, a forgettable hour.

10
I-15 Murders

US Air Date: 12 January 2001 11.4
UK Air Date: 11 August 2001

Written by: Carol Mendelsohn
Directed by: Oz Scott
Guest Cast: Travis Fine (Kenny Berlin), Tony Amendola (Dr Rambar),
Krista Allen (Kristy Hopkins), Julie Ariola (Brenda Shorey),
Amanda Carlin (Margaret Shorey), Ray Proscia (John Himmel),
Kirk Trutner (Store Manager), Julius Ritter (Jason),
Mike Muscat (Security Guard), Jamie McShane (Jeff Berlin),
Sandy Martin (Female Trucker), Stacy Solodkin (Girlfriend),
Zylan Brooks (Dispatcher), David Paladino (Officer Pratt)

Teaser One-liner: 'Life holds no surprises.'
The Cases: Grissom goes to a supermarket from where a woman has gone missing. Margaret Shorey, who lives with her sister, went out for groceries and never came home. Her car is still in the parking lot, and her handbag is still in her shopping trolley. Grissom guesses that she broke a mustard jar, and went to the restroom. One of the cubicle doors has been cleaned up recently, and when it's taken back to the CSI lab, it reveals a chilling message: 'Iv'e Killed 5 women. Catch me iF you can?'

Forensic psychologist Dr Rambar tells Grissom that the writer of the note on the stall is left-handed, uneducated, has criminal tendencies and low impulse control. And it was written by a woman.

Catherine checks the database and finds four previous crime scenes – each with a stall door graffitied with a message showing how many women have been killed. Each represents a missing woman. There is no physical evidence to show the women were killed at the supermarkets where the stalls were graffitied. Grissom decides that this means the messages are intentions not facts. When they look at the locations of the crime scenes, they realise that they are all on Interstate 15 – from San Bernardino in California all the way to Salt Lake City, Utah.

A frozen body is found by the I 15. Jenna Williams confirms that it's Joan Sims, the victim from San Bernardino. She was strangled, and there are ligature marks around the wrists and ankles. What is unusual is that she has decomposed backwards – her organs are in better shape than her skin. She has ice crystals in her skin, which means she was kept frozen until about twelve hours earlier. They are looking for a refrigerated lorry.

Brass discovers that a woman trucker delivered to the Vegas crime scene the previous day. He finds her and Catherine gets her to write out phrases that include the incriminating words. Unfortunately, although she fits the rest of the pattern, she's not the culprit. Grissom wonders if they might be looking for a man with a woman who would do anything he asked.

Using satellite tracking technology, Grissom and Catherine are able to locate the only truck that fits all the parameters. They arrest the trucker and deduce that his girlfriend gained the confidence of the middle-aged women targets before he attacked them. Grissom and Catherine find Margaret Shorey in the cab of the truck, still alive.

Sara is assigned to investigate the dead body of Jeff Berlin. She goes to the townhouse where he died, and meets his brother Kenny, who found him. There are signs of a break-in, with a broken window and mess everywhere, but Sara is surprised that two \$20 bills weren't taken, nor any of the computer equipment. It's also unusual for the silverware to be taken in a bedsheet rather than a pillowcase. Sara tests Kenny for bloodspatter, and asks for his clothing for analysis. She also takes the window.

Sara is surprised to find that she's working with Warrick, and Grissom asks her to trust him. She tells Kenny that she found glass in his trousers, and he claims that it came from his car window which was broken the previous week. However, the glass in his trousers has the same density as the glass from his living room, not from his car. Kenny then claims that he thought that the burglars were returning, so he walked to the window to check. Without further evidence, the CSIs have to release Kenny, but Sara asks about his job and he reveals that he's a day trader. Sara guesses he's not very successful.

Sara and Warrick check the Haeckel marks on the glass which show that it was broken from the inside. They accuse Kenny of being responsible and he immediately demands a lawyer. The CSIs decide to get a warrant to check his computer for evidence.

When they do, they find the stolen jewellery inside it. They also find a torch which has numerous scratches on it – and a small piece of glass on a gun. The density tests confirm that the window was broken with the gun. Warrick has also discovered that with Jeff gone, Kenny is the sole beneficiary of their parents' estate.

Nick is assigned to investigate a fight at the Bellagio which involves a woman who says she's a friend of his. He discovers that his 'friend' is Kristy Hopkins, the hooker (see **00**, 'Pilot'). The security guard thinks she's cruising for business, but Kristy maintains that she was genuinely shopping until the guard started harassing her. She claims he spat on her so she slugged him. The security guard vehemently denies it and says he's pressing charges. Nick takes Kristy's shirt for testing, and Greg confirms it has been spat on. Nick needs a sample of the guard's saliva for comparison.

Brass tells Grissom that there's gossip going around about Nick and Kristy – a CSI doing favours for a hooker is not good news. Grissom questions Nick but Nick maintains that the relationship is purely platonic, before stalking away. He later apologises to Grissom, who suggests that someone else should handle the case. Nick doesn't want to let it go, but isn't sure how to get the evidence he needs. Grissom suggests that 'if Mohammed won't go to the mountain, then the mountain must go to Mohammed'. Nick befriends the security guard and gains a sample of his DNA on an envelope. Sure enough, it matches the saliva on Kristy's shirt. Nick tells Kristy that the case is being dropped, and they part company.

Personal Notes: Warrick tells Grissom that he wasn't gambling at the casino. He went there to collect a debt which he then used to help out a teenage friend. Warrick is teaching kids basketball after work. Grissom has acquired a singing Big Mouth Billy Bass, God help him, which he keeps above the office door. Grissom doesn't let Sara in on why he's not pursuing Warrick, and she is mistrustful of him throughout the episode – and is left pondering about him at the end when all is revealed.

Techniques: Handwriting analysis can reveal whether someone is right- or left-handed. A graphologist can determine more about the character, although whether sex can be identified is less certain.

Catherine checks for similar crimes in VICAP (Violent Crime Apprehension Program), which is a computerised database containing details about solved, unsolved and attempted homicides, as well as missing persons cases where foul play is suspected.

The glass fragments are subjected to density tests to see if they float in the same way. The glass is dropped into a mix of bromoform and bromobenzene, and the relative densities are then changed until the glass floats. When it does, the density of the glass is the same as the density of the chemical mix. A piece of glass from the same pane will float in the same density. The Haeckel marks indicate the stresses on the glass, which show whether it was broken from the inside or the outside. Concentric stress marks show on the side which was broken.

Nick uses HLA-DQA1 and STR-DNA tests to analyse the spittle from the guard.

The Wit and Wisdom of Gil Grissom: 'I see the whole puzzle, Sara. You're only seeing one piece.'

'Do you ever worry that technology's going to make us obsolete?'

Classic Dialogue: Kristy Hopkins: 'Why is it every time we meet, you're wanting me to take my clothes off?' Nick: 'Because, every time we meet, you put yourself in a position where you have to take them off.'

Catherine: 'What's his problem?' Grissom: 'Me, I guess.'

Fantastic Voyages: We follow the weapon breaking the window during the fake burglary, and close in on the piece of glass left in the base of the gun as a result.

The Usual Suspects: Krista Allen returns as Kristy Hopkins (see 00, 'Pilot'). Tony Amendola (Dr Rambar) is best known as Bra'tac on *Stargate SG*-1.

Pop Culture References: Brass asks Grissom where his E Street Band is – referring to Bruce Springsteen's band. Greg describes Kristy's top as 'very Jennifer Lopez'.

Grissom and Jenna exchange references to Kryptonite, the name of the surviving fragments from Superman's homeworld (now known as meteor rocks in the *Smallville* rendition of the myth). Nick dubs a pig foetus Miss Piggy, after the lovable porcine Muppet.

Real-life Inspirations: The communications from the serial killer to the police are reminiscent of the case of William Heirens, from the 1940s, who left a message on the bedroom wall of his second victim saying, 'For heaven's sake catch me before I kill more. I cannot control myself.' There are also numerous instances of a female accomplice helping a male murderer, with the Moors Murders in Britain being just one example.

Notes: Although broadcast quite late in the season, this was shot as the third episode, hence Brass and Grissom's otherwise inexplicable dialogue at the beginning. Kristy Hopkins' reappearance also fits in with the original placement. Unusually, there's a 'previously on *CSI*' recap, covering Nick's first meeting with Kristy, and the salient facts over Warrick's casino visit.

Overall: The explanation for Warrick's behaviour isn't really convincing, and Sara's suspicion of him is a bit out of place after the length of time they've been working together. Not one of the stronger episodes, and it was the right decision to delay its airing until later in the season.

11
Fahrenheit 932

US Air Date: 1 February 2001 14.0/21
UK Air Date: 18 August 2001

Written by: Jacqueline Zambrano
Directed by: Danny Cannon
Guest Cast: Sterling Macer Jr (Frank Damon),
Jarrad Paul (Tony/Teller 12), Fred Koehler (Danny Hillman),
Tamara Clatterbuck (Sandra Hillman), Chaka Forman (Runner 702),
Tom Beyer (Lt Collins), Meta Golding (Rachel),
Lucy Goncalves (Jeannie Damon), Robert D. Doqui (Inmate)

Teaser One-liner: 'An innocent man. Jail's full of them!'
The Cases: Grissom is sent a tape from Clark County Jail. It comes from Frank Damon, a convicted arsonist, who killed his wife and son in a fire. He claims that he is innocent and asks for Grissom's help.

They only have three days until the trial, at which the DA is going for the death penalty. Catherine recalls that Ecklie was the CSI on the case originally and fears trouble. Brass has done some preliminary legwork: Damon was seen running from the burning house while his wife and child were still inside. The wife was a big spender and they were regularly arguing about money. The evidence shows that there was gasoline in the master bedroom closet – and Damon bought a gallon of gasoline the week before. Brass thinks Grissom is wasting his time.

At the County Jail, Grissom meets Damon, who tells him that his wife sent him out for some ice-cream. Their son was in bed with them. He got back and saw smoke and heard the alarm. He checked the bedroom door for heat, but knew not to open it in case of flashover. (When a fire reaches 932°F, and oxygen is added, the smoke bursts into flames.) Damon reveals that he's a volunteer fireman. He says he ran out to call for a fire engine. Grissom asks him about the gasoline in the closet. Damon claims he knows nothing, and that the gasoline he bought was kept in the garage for the lawnmower. Grissom asks him how he burned his hand, but he claims not to know.

Sara, Warrick and Grissom examine the ruins of the house and find matches with the son's camping gear. The doorframe to the bedroom is severely charred. They inspect the closet, which shows a 'V' pattern, indicating a very intense, rapidly moving fire. They find shards of glass which have melted into the concrete – but don't know where they came from. Warrick and Sara think that the evidence only confirms Damon's guilt.

Ecklie and Grissom argue over the evidence. Ecklie thinks the case should now be left as he's done sufficient work on it. Grissom duplicates the conditions in Damon's bedroom in the lab, and confirms the flashover. The alligatoring on the wood of the bedroom frame confirms that the door must have been opened, so Damon lied. Grissom faces him with the fact that it was his bedroom door knob that burned his hand, which proves that he was outside the fire, but Damon can't face the fact that he forgot everything he had been trained in, and feels responsible for his wife and son's death. Grissom tells him bluntly that carbon monoxide would have killed them before the flames got them.

Grissom and Warrick make a further check of the Damon house. They find the remains of a space heater, which used high voltage. It could have overloaded the fuse box – and the box shows a circuit overload in the master bedroom.

Grissom and Ecklie have another run-in over the evidence when Grissom starts checking the electrical circuits. Ecklie still maintains that the only query is why there was gasoline in the closet. Even at this late stage before his trial, Damon still can't explain it.

Sara realises that Ecklie surmised that the gasoline was there from the burn pattern. However, there was no direct evidence that it was gasoline and not another hydrocarbon. Unfortunately there is no evidence left – the site has been swept clean. Ecklie and Grissom have another furious row, though Grissom suddenly calms down.

At the jail, Grissom asks Damon's sister Rachel about Damon's relationship with his wife and son. She confirms that Frank was a wonderful father, but says nothing about his wife. Damon admits to Grissom that he was leaving his wife and that she had thrown a kerosene lamp at him. Grissom tells him that the kerosene from the lamp was ignited by a spark coming from the storage heater when it overloaded the circuit.

When Damon leaves jail to be met by Rachel – who is in fact his lover, not his sister – Grissom is also there. Damon is surprised that he doesn't feel free now he's out – instead, as Grissom suggests, he feels responsible.

Nick and Catherine are assigned to investigate a Caucasian male found in the front seat of a car in the parking lot at the Monaco Hotel. They check the car. Nick takes a sample of some condensation they find on the back window. The deceased is only sixteen or so, and was killed by a gunshot to the back of the head at point-blank range. The teenager was wearing a hearing aid. Catherine finds a wad of about $15,000 with a note reading, 'Giants minus 9'. It's a Superbowl betting ticket. It's two days before the big game, and Catherine wonders why a youngster would be wandering around with that sort of money. They speak to Tony, the teller who wrote the ticket, and he tells them that the deceased was runner 517 for local bookmakers. Although the runners' activities are illegal, the house ignores it since they make a percentage on the bets.

The deceased runner is identified as Joey Hillman by his mother, who is furious to discover that her elder son

Danny involved Joey with the gambling racket. Unfortunately, Danny hasn't been around for a week either.

Catherine and Nick talk to the CSI's resident gambling expert Warrick about the runners. He advises them that the most likely suspect is another runner who wanted Joey's route. Tony points out another runner to Catherine and Nick, but he isn't particularly helpful.

The condensation on the back window is nasal mucus – the killer sneezed in the car. Joey's mum brings her other son Danny in. He admits that he lost some of his bosses' money on the gaming tables, and his bosses had Joey killed to teach Danny a lesson. Danny thinks it probable that another runner was responsible.

Nick and Catherine take swabs from all the runners who worked alongside Joey and Danny but none of them matches the DNA from the condensation. Nick goes back to the Monaco and becomes suspicious at the way that Tony is acting. When he sneezes, Nick is certain, and calls for the police.

Personal Notes: Warrick used to be a runner in order to work his way through college.

Techniques: Photographs of the fire damage indicate the speed and direction of the fire's movement. The remnants will also help indicate this, although a large part of the CSI's job is made harder because the fire-fighters' first priority is not one of preserving the crime scene. Hydrocarbon indicators, such as the J-W Automatic Hydrocarbon Indicator would probably have been used by Ecklie to confirm the presence of a hydrocarbon, correlating with Damon's purchase of gasoline.

The Wit and Wisdom of Gil Grissom: 'We chase the lie until it leads to the truth.'

Classic Dialogue: Sara: 'How did he find you? 1-800-GRISSOM?'

Grissom: 'What are you afraid of Conrad? We're just a couple of science geeks. Why can't we work together?'

Warrick: 'You ever worry about professional suicide?'
Grissom: 'Not while I'm committing it, no!'

The Usual Suspects: Tamara Clatterbuck (Mrs Hillman) is a regular face on US soap operas, with stints on *The Young and the Restless*, *General Hospital* and *Days of Our Lives*. Sterling Macer Jr, who bears a strong resemblance to a young Yaphet Kotto, appeared as Mike Newcombe alongside William Petersen in *The Beast*, as well as playing Colonel John Howard in *Tom Clancy's NetForce*. Jarrad Paul (Tony) is also a writer, responsible for the *Stargate SG-1* episodes 'Crystal Skull' and 'Message in a Bottle'.

Pop Culture References: The title is a loose reference to *Fahrenheit 451*, the famous book by Ray Bradbury, which refers to the temperature at which paper burns. Sara's 'Danger Will Robinson' is a quote from the TV series and film *Lost in Space*. Catherine refers to a 'bad moon rising' from the Creedence Clearwater Revival song.

Notes: This was the first episode broadcast by CBS on a Thursday evening in America, and the ratings skyrocketed, adding nearly 3 ratings points (well over four million viewers). It coincidentally also got the highest rating for a first-season episode on Channel 5 in the UK. The ending is very reminiscent of the conclusion of the wonderful heist movie *The Taking of Pelham 123*, when a sneeze alerts Walter Matthau's transit cop to the robber's identity.

Overall: Another overly drawn-out episode. The capture of Tony is more suited to an episode of *Quincy* than *CSI*, and it seems out of character for Grissom to go to the jail to offer Damon a ride. Basically missable.

12
Boom

US Air Date: 8 February 2001 13.8/20
UK Air Date: 25 August 2001

Written by: Josh Berman, Ann Donahue, Carol Mendelsohn
Directed by: Kenneth Fink
Guest Cast: Stephen Lee (Dominic Kretzker),
Krista Allen (Kristy Hopkins), Mark Valley (Jack Willman),
Gregory Itzin (Norman Stirling), Tim Redwine (Tyler Stirling),

J.D. Evermore (Eric), Kristin K. Ulrich (Nicole),
Jonathan Bray (Manager), Jeff Brockton (Jake Richards)

Teaser One-liner: 'Who? Why? Will he do it again? Time
will tell.'

The Cases: The end of the day at the Hansen Building, and
security guard Dominic Kretzker heads to collect the coffee
run. His partner, Jake Richards, spots a suspicious pack-
age – which blows up in his face. Grissom, Catherine,
Warrick and Sara find Richards with symmetrical amputa-
tion of his ears – he was looking directly at the bomb when
it exploded. They find some gunpowder, and their preliminary call is that the bomb was made with a low-velocity
propellant. They take everything that they can back to the
lab – bomb components survive the explosion – to piece
the bomb back together again.

Dominic, the surviving security guard, is a fount of
information about bombs. Grissom asks him if he'd be
interested in helping with the investigation but also tells the
police to keep an eye on him. Dominic reveals that he
experiments with bombs, but before he can say anything
incriminating, Public Defender Margaret Finn arrives at
the police station and tells him to stop co-operating.
Dominic wants to continue to help, but Warrick suggests
he should listen to his attorney.

Sara can't understand how the victim is intact, and
Catherine explains the vacuum effect: there's a calm at the
centre of the 'storm'. Catherine finds the initials FP
engraved on one of the fragments. The initials don't match
any profiles in the ATF's database. Grissom finds a clock
part which indicates that the bomb was time-delayed. It's
also covered in some orange material that Sara goes to
investigate.

Although Grissom is laboriously checking numerous
alarm clocks to identify the clock part, Sara discovers that
a TimeTell SnoozeWell is currently the most commonly
used timing device. The pair explode various versions of
the bomb, replicating the bits they do know: aluminium
briefcase, SnoozeWell clock and black gunpowder. All they
need to know is what sort of pipe was used. The tests prove

that the pipe was made of galvanised steel – like an exhaust silencer or tail pipe. Brass informs them that Dominic bought seven SnoozeWell clocks in the last three months, so they head out to see him at his ranch in the desert. Dominic listens to the police wavebands on a scanner so knows they're coming, and welcomes them with open arms. He freely admits using clocks to make bombs, but is surprised at their reaction when they find part of the Hansen Building bomb in his house. He has simply kept it as a souvenir. Brass arrests him.

Grissom visits Dominic in jail to see how he's holding up. Brass arrives with news of another bomb, at a Thrift Right car rental agency outlet. The bomb killed one of the check-in staff. This time the bomb has a motion sensor as well as a timer. Sara spots that the staff are wearing orange jackets, and takes one – it's the same colour and texture as the bomb covering. Since this bomb wasn't activated remotely, Dominic is released.

Sara confirms that the bomb wrappings did come from the Thrift Right jacket – and their headquarters are in the Hansen Building. She runs a Lexis database search and finds Norman Stirling, a former manager with a grievance. When she and Brass visit him, the letters FP clearly mean nothing to him, but he still has a Thrift Right jacket. Stirling is arrested and tells his teenage son Tyler to let his mother know what's happened

Warrick has discovered that the initials were engraved with an electric etcher. The particular version is only used for training purposes, and while Norman Stirling didn't have access to one, his son did at his high school. Tyler admits he was responsible. The FP stands for Fair Play – his father always used to yell that he was owed fair play. Tyler learned how to make the bombs from the internet, and is amazed that his father is angry, since he did it all for him. Tyler admits that there's one more bomb.

Dominic hears the police announcement of the bomb at Tyler's school on his scanner, but leaves before learning that it is trigger-activated and motion-delayed. He gets the bomb, activating it when he removes it from Tyler's locker.

Grissom arrives and tells Dominic to put it down, but the timer has counted down. The bomb explodes in Dominic's arms, killing him instantly.

Grissom places Dominic's obituary where he would have liked it: on the CSI board as one of their own missing.

Nick is enjoying some time off, but finds himself caught up with hooker Kristy Hopkins (see **00**, 'Pilot', **10**, 'I-15 Murders') again, when he interrupts an argument between her and a customer. Nick runs her home, and she tells him that she's planning on going back to school. She invites him in for a drink and, against his better judgement, he goes in.

The next morning Nick drives over to Kristy's place, trying to call her on the phone. To his horror, he sees her body being brought out of the house. Officer Arvington tells him that the day shift is covering the case, and Nick drives off.

Nick advises Grissom of his difficult situation. He was with Kristy till 4 a.m. Ecklie is working the case, and Catherine suggests that she should talk to him, rather than Grissom. Grissom suggests that Nick should look for Jack, the punter that Kristy was arguing with the previous evening, and after he's gone reminds Catherine that Nick will automatically be dismissed if he's arrested – even if he's cleared later.

Doc Robbins is conducting an autopsy on Kristy, and allows Catherine to watch, even though it's Ecklie's case. Kristy was strangled, but she put up a fight. Catherine asks if there are any fingerprints on the corpse, and Robbins points out that they might be Nick's. Catherine isn't concerned – the evidence is all they've got.

Catherine intercepts Ecklie before he can talk to Grissom. He says that Nick's fingerprints are everywhere. Nick interrupts them to confirm that he slept with Kristy, but also provides the surveillance tape from the Orpheus with Jack Willman's licence plate number. Ecklie doesn't want to believe a CSI could commit murder, but at the moment he has to follow protocol. Catherine asks O'Riley to track down Jack and tells Nick to go easy with Ecklie.

O'Riley brings Jack in and Catherine and Ecklie watch the interrogation. Jack claims he saw Nick kill Kristy. Unfortunately both Ecklie and Sheriff Mobley believe him. All Catherine can offer against that is her ten years of experience. Mobley grants her twelve hours to clear Nick. She checks Nick's semen from the discarded condom, which confirms that Nick ejaculated around 2 a.m. Unfortunately that doesn't disprove his presence at the scene of the homicide around 6 a.m.

Catherine returns to the scene and realises that the curtain sash was used to strangle Kristy. There are epithelials on it which Greg can match against Jack Willman's DNA, which is already on file because of his prior record of sexual assault. The DNA confirms that Willman is the killer.

After his arrest, Jack tells Nick that Kristy was lying to him. Jack was her pimp, and she was only going to college to recruit new hookers. Nick doesn't know what to believe . . .

Personal Notes: Doc Robbins' first name, David, is revealed in this episode. Catherine has been a CSI for ten years. Nick pays for Kristy's funeral since she has no one else left.

Techniques: Warrick identifies the tool responsible for etching the FP by duplicating the mark on the same sort of material with various tools until he finds the right one. Grissom intends to act similarly with the clock part that is found, until Sara 'spoils his fun' by checking with the ATF database, a record of all bombs and bomb parts maintained by the Alcohol, Tobacco and Firearms department of the FBI. She and Grissom carry out comparison tests to identify the sort of pipe used by the bomber.

Epithelials are fragments shed by the skin. They contain DNA, which can then be identified.

The Wit and Wisdom of Gil Grissom: 'The dirty little secret of bombs is how easy they are to make, and use.'

To Nick: 'When you're a suspect and you're innocent, you keep your mouth shut.'

To Dominic: 'Next time try not to be so trusting. You don't need to be a hero.'

Classic Dialogue: Grissom: 'What were you thinking, Nicky?' Nick: 'I wasn't.'

Worst 'As You Know': Catherine: 'If Nick's arrested, it's not going to matter that he's cleared later.' Grissom: 'No. It's an automatic dismissal.'

Fantastic Voyages: Each time that a bomb explodes, we are inside the workings watching it – which adds a frisson to the moments before Dominic's death.

The Usual Suspects: Krista Allen (Kristy Hopkins) makes her third and final appearance. Stephen Lee (Dominic Kretzker) has played numerous cops and army officers, but is best known for his role as Otto Blake on *The Sopranos*, and as Dan Vogelsang in the early episodes of *Dark Angel*. Gregory Itzin (Norman Stirling) played FBI Agent Joel Marks in the later episodes of *Profiler*.

Pop Culture References: Jack Willman points out to Nick that his relationship with Kristy isn't like *Pretty Woman*, the 1990 Richard Gere film about a 'tart with a heart'. Grissom misquotes *Hamlet* – 'Alas poor Warrick'.

Real-life Inspirations: 'Boom' is inspired by a number of separate incidents. The initials FP, standing for Fair Play, were used by the Mad Bomber, George Metesky, during his sixteen-year campaign against the city of New York, in communications with police. Metesky had also been fired from a job and felt he was treated unfairly. Initials also helped track down the Unabomber, Theodore John Kaczynski.

Dominic's willingness to help with the investigation brings to mind the case of Richard Jewell, who similarly was overly interested in bombs and bomb-making, and had a desire to be a hero. Like Dominic, Jewell was cleared.

Mistakes Really Can Be Fatal: Didn't anyone think to check for a murder weapon earlier? The markings around Kristy's neck aren't exactly normal.

Overall: Kristy Hopkins begins a trend for recurring guest stars on *CSI*, turning from being part of a case to being the reason for it. It's nice to see the attention on Nick Stokes for once – he was starting to become a little characterless, and his moment with Doc Robbins, when his feelings for Kristy are very clear, is a good piece of work from George Eads. The A plot has an air of inevitability about it – it would almost have been better if Dominic hadn't been killed, just as a surprise. But the show feels back on course after a few duff weeks.

13
To Halve and To Hold

US Air Date: 15 February 2001 14.1/21
UK Air Date: 1 September 2001

Written by: Andrew Lipsitz, Ann Donahue
Directed by: Lou Antonio
Guest Cast: Eileen Ryan (Rose Bennett), Dorie Barton (Meg Wheeler), Lisa Dean Ryan (Lynn Henry), Ele Keats (Joyce Lanier), Christopher Jacobs (Luke), Bobby G (Robb), Colby G (Matthew), Michael Vincent (Darren Pyne)

Teaser One-liner: 'I feel it in my two-hundred-and-six bones, that this was a murder.'

The Cases: A father and son find a human leg bone out on Mount Charleston. It's been picked clean, and there's no evidence left on it. Catherine suspects murder, but Grissom thinks it could be from a hiker who got lost. Catherine arranges for a class of cadets from the Police Academy to join them to search for the other 205 bones, and suggests that forensic anthropologist Teri Miller (see **05**, 'Who Are You?') would be helpful. Grissom is unsure.

With the cadets' help, they find around 100 bone fragments. Catherine, Nick and Grissom try to assemble the skeleton, who is male, roughly six feet tall, and around sixty to seventy years old. Grissom notices jagged marks on the leg bone which Catherine thinks indicates murder. Teri Miller, called in by Catherine – much to Grissom's discomfort – points out that they need to check for haemorrhagic tissue at the bone tool marks.

The dental records are put online and a local dentist recognises the skeleton as Mel Bennett, born in 1931. Teri Miller explains that a reciprocating electric saw was used to cut up Mel. His widow, Rose, claims that her husband is at the store, and Brass breaks the news to her that he's been dead for months. All the indications are that the Bennetts had a happy marriage, but Catherine, who isn't sure if Rose is distraught because of the news or because she got caught, finds blood in the drain, and Brass locates an electric saw in the widow's garage.

Teri confirms that it is the murder weapon, and that it was used by someone who was unfamiliar with how to operate it, and had a weakened musculature. Mrs Bennett can't understand why she's been questioned, and eventually asks for an attorney.

Nick checks the haemorrhagic tissue and there's no evidence of blood, so Mel Bennett was cut up after he was dead. Margaret Finn, the Public Defender who helped Dominic Kretzker (see **12**, 'Boom'), is representing Mrs Bennett, who admits disassembling her husband. She couldn't afford a burial so she cut him into manageable pieces to transport him to Mount Charleston. She didn't notify the social security authorities that he was dead, and continued to cash his cheques. There seems no evidence of murder, just fraud.

Greg Sanders finds evidence of a high amount of digoxin in the bones, and Mrs Bennett says that her husband deliberately took an overdose and asked her to leave him so he could commit suicide. He also made her promise to hide his body so she wouldn't lose her social security benefits. Since the CSIs can't prove either way what happened, Mrs Bennett has to be given the benefit of the doubt.

Sara and Warrick are assigned a 23-year-old male found dead at the Lucky 7 Motel and meet Sgt O'Riley at the scene. Darren Pyne was probably whacked over the head with a lamp. Although the room was registered to 'Celine Dion', it's been paid for by Lynn Henry of Eau Claire, Wisconsin. The CSIs go to meet her; her friend Meg is about to get married, and Lynn and her friend Joyce threw a bachelorette party the night before – Darren Pyne was the male stripper. They didn't want Meg's fiancé to find out, so they rented the room at the Lucky 7. According to Lynn, they left at 3 a.m. and Darren was alive and well. Darren asked if he could use the room, and they didn't mind. Sara spots bruises on Lynn's wrists, but she can't recall where she got them.

Doc Robbins confirms that Darren Pyne was killed by multiple blows to the head causing cranial bleeding. A penile swab shows vaginal cells – Darren slept with one of the women just before he died, around midnight. He could not have been alive at 3 a.m. as Lynn claimed.

When the three girls are brought in, Joyce says she can't get involved because she has a husband and small children, and Lynn tells her to shut up. Lynn claims that she went back to the room for her handbag, and Darren raped her. Sara sends her for a sexual assault examination.

Doc Robbins' final report shows that there are no traces of the lamp at the points of impact, which seems strange. Warrick also finds what seems to be a tiny diamond at the scene, but in fact is cubic zirconia.

The girls have gone off for Meg's wedding but Lynn's Sexual Assault Rape Test (SART) result shows that she wasn't raped. Sgt O'Riley stops the wedding and brings all three girls in for questioning.

Sara explains the 'clock test' to Lynn (see **Techniques**). The tests show Lynn hasn't had sex for 48 hours. Meg admits that she had consensual sex with Darren, but when she tried to get him to stop, he wouldn't, so she hit him. Meg's ring has a genuine diamond, but that of her fiancé Luke has zirconia. Luke is brought in, and he's missing a stone from his ring. It's clear that he caught Meg in bed with Darren and beat him up, killing him. Luke admits it, saying that they just wanted to get married and put it behind them. But as Warrick points out, laws don't end when you come to Vegas.

Personal Notes: Catherine has noticed the 'dopey look' in Grissom's eye when Teri is around. Grissom called her but Teri decided not to return the call. He then invites her for dinner but, unfortunately, their date isn't a great success, since Grissom's phone keeps going, and she eventually leaves to catch her flight home. Catherine didn't learn Latin. Sgt O'Riley can cope with all sorts of grisly murder scenes, but as soon as Sara starts discussing vaginal penetration and rape, he leaves the room!

Techniques: The CSIs employ a grid search on the mountain to look for bones, and place flags to indicate where bones are found. Grissom uses a non-scientific method – licking the piece of rock to see if it is bone or rock!

Sara explains the 'clock test' which shows whether sexual intercourse is voluntary or involuntary. Bruising around the 11–1 area of the vagina shows voluntary activity, while in the 5–7 area it is more indicative of involuntary intercourse.

The Wit and Wisdom of Gil Grissom: 'There's always a clue.' (Quoted by Catherine.)

Classic Dialogue: Grissom: 'It's interesting to me how you always expect the worst.' Catherine: 'You see, that way, I'm never disappointed. And sometimes I'm nicely surprised.'

Worst 'As You Know': Grissom: 'Did you know that there are two-hundred-and-six bones in the human body?' Catherine: 'Yes Professor, I too took Osteology.'

Fantastic Voyages: We see Catherine swabbing the plug from inside the drain, and then testing the swab for blood at close range. We also observe the saw cutting into the bone.

The Usual Suspects: Pamela Gidley returns as Teri Miller, and Palmer Davis makes her second appearance as Public Defender Margaret Finn. Eileen Ryan (Mrs Bennett) is the mother of actors Chris and Sean Penn – so she's Madonna's former mother-in-law. Dorie Barton (Meg Wheeler) played the young Martha Stewart in the 2003 biopic, *Martha, Inc.*

Pop Culture References: Grissom makes a reference to Alex Trebek, the host of the American game show *Jeopardy*. Singers Celine Dion and Elvis Presley and the play *The Vagina Monologues* all get namechecks.

Mistakes Really Can Be Fatal: Maths isn't Nick's strong suit. Since the episodes are dated roughly around the day of original transmission, if Mel Bennett was born in

September 1931, he's only 69 in February 2001, not 70 as Nick claims.

Notes: Scenes featuring the girls were shot at the Glass Pool Hotel and the Venetian Hotel.

Overall: There are some neat directorial touches in this episode, rescuing what is otherwise a not particularly inspired script. At least, though, this one tries to capture the Vegas mentality of visitors to Sin City.

14
Table Stakes

US Air Date: 22 February 2001 13.1/19
UK Air Date: 8 September 2001

Teleplay by: Carol Mendelsohn, Anthony E. Zuiker
Story by: Elizabeth Devine
Directed by: Danny Cannon
Guest Cast: Shawn Christian (Patrick Haynes aka Chad Matthews), Elizabeth Lackey (Amanda Haynes), Sheeri Rappaport (Mandy), Allison Dunbar (Rachel Carson), Joann Ritchter (Lacey Duvall), Nichole M. Hiltz (Dancer), Jack Wallace (Tony Mumms), Trey Alexander (Vincent Morgan), Lorraine Hunt (Mrs Burton), Robert Sutton (Stage Manager), John Churchill (Shibley), C.C. Carr (Guest), William Patrick Johnson (Tyson Green aka Dead Guy), Lloyd Kino (Gardner), Robert Iaquinto (Hit Man), Nick Trasente (Pit Boss), Kaye Wade (Portia Richmond ((stunts))

Teaser One-liner: 'Come for the hors d'oeuvres. Stay for the interrogation.'

The Cases: A party is in full swing at Vegas socialite Portia Richmond's house, organised by her house-sitters Patrick and Amanda Haynes in aid of her Burn Centre. It's attended by the Sheriff and many local dignitaries. It's spoiled by the discovery of the body of a girl in the pool.

Catherine finds a fingernail, while Warrick finds a cufflink, made from turquoise and silver, with the initials CM on it, in the pool. Doc Robbins discovers that the girl has had numerous body enhancements, including silicone breast implants. They all have serial numbers so she can be identified. The girl was strangled, and there's no water in her lungs, so she was dead before she hit the water. Grissom asks for a sexual assault kit to be run and for infrared photos to show up any subdermal bruising.

Most of the guests did not see or know anything about the dead girl. Portia Richmond herself is away with a toyboy, cruising on the Mediterranean. The Haynes have no idea who the dead girl is.

She is identified as Lacey Duvall, a showgirl at the Mediterranean Hotel. Catherine and Grissom meet her best friend, Rachel Carson, who tells them that Lacey was seeing a rich married man who wouldn't tell her anything about himself. Grissom discovers a music box engraved to Portia Richmond in Lacey's effects. The music box has the date March 7 1969 on it, and it turns out to be a regular tradition – an anniversary present. Grissom and Catherine find a collection of them when they return to the Richmond house, where they catch the Haynes in the middle of making love. The sexual assault kit test on Lacey Duvall comes back positive for semen, which matches the cold case of a dead cheerleader from Texas ten years earlier.

The Sheriff is hounding both Brass and Grissom for results. Grissom and Catherine check the rest of the house and find that Portia left her bathing suit, her lingerie and her jewels when she 'went away' – as well as a tiny piece of tooth. Greg can get the DNA from the tooth easily, but there's no remnant of Portia's DNA to compare it with – the hairbrush and toothbrush have been cleaned thoroughly. Catherine and Brass go to the Liberace Museum to see if there's any DNA on Portia Richmond's costume from the Folies Bergère that's kept there. The headdress that she had to wear was so heavy that it caused her hair to fall out – for the CSIs, it's DNA heaven.

Sara discovers that 'Patrick Haynes' died ten years ago aged eight months, according to his social security number. Greg compares the DNA from the tooth with the headdress (which he takes to wearing!) and it's a match.

Catherine and Grissom watch Amanda Haynes steal a fur coat in broad daylight and realise that they're on the right track with the Haynes. They're taken in for questioning, and Patrick Haynes admits that he had sex with Lacey before the party. He denies giving her the music box, and thinks that Lacey might have stolen it. Nick risks Grissom's wrath by interrupting the interrogation to tell him that the suspect in the Texas cheerleader case was one Chad Matthews – the CM from the cufflink.

The Sheriff pours the pressure on Grissom, telling him to either find Portia Richmond or a motive for her murder. Brass discovers that 'Patrick Haynes' is wanted in numerous jurisdictions, and that he kept a list of rich women as targets, including Portia Richmond. Checking her bank records, Catherine finds that Portia Richmond hasn't spent anything since she's been away. However, her signature has been copied from one of her cheques onto a blank sheet of paper, which the Haynes failed to destroy.

Grissom checks the Richmond mansion gardens, and is advised to keep his face away from the fishpond by the gardener. Returning to the lab, he asks Greg about the fingernail. Greg points out that it shares DNA markers with Haynes' semen, indicating a close family relative. Grissom asks Greg to check out the DNA from the lipstick on Amanda Haynes' straw.

Lack of direct evidence means that Patrick Haynes is freed from all charges filed in Nevada, but he is immediately rearrested for the murder of the cheerleader. He admits sleeping with her but not killing her – the same admission as he gave for Lacey. Grissom agrees – it's Haynes' sister Amanda who killed Lacey. The Haynes maintain that Portia is in Greece, but the piranha from the Richmond mansion indicate otherwise. They have too high a cholesterol level – acquired from eating Portia.

Warrick is taken off the body in the pool murder case to deal with a dead body found in one of the glass elevators at The Sphere. Detective Conroy and Warrick agree that it looks like a professional hit. The killer has even left a quarter in the wound – an old message to say 'call somebody who cares' – as well as the murder weapon.

Unfortunately, Warrick has to print the entire glass elevator.

Warrick discovers that the victim was being treated to Vegas hospitality – free food and encouragement to gamble. He's taken advantage of it: he has gambling markers everywhere. The gun is registered to Vincent Morgan, who lives on the Westside, but there are no prints from the quarter yet. Morgan, unfortunately, simply failed to report his gun stolen after a robbery, because he told his wife he had already got rid of it. Warrick's last lead dies when he learns that the only print on the quarter is the victim's. Warrick takes the victim's markers back to the casino and files the case under unsolved.

Personal notes: Doc Robbins has a personal coffee machine from which he shares a macchiato with Grissom. Eddie and Catherine Willows used to mark the anniversary of the day they first met with a lace teddy. Warrick has a crisis of conscience when he returns Green's markers to the casino, wanting to gamble but remembering his promise to Grissom.

Techniques: The DNA samples are matched in CODIS, the Combined DNA Index System, which is combining the State DNA Index Systems into one national database. All US states mandate the collection of DNA from convicted offenders.

The Wit and Wisdom of Gil Grissom: 'I think the Tooth Fairy might have left us a piece of Portia Richmond.'

'Sometimes in these interrogations, Nick, you get one chance, one answer. And while I'm out here screwing with you, he's in there thinking up the right answer that he didn't have before you walked in.'

'Evidence is like a fine wine, Brian. You can't just open the bottle and drink it. You've got to let it breathe.'

Classic Dialogue: Warrick: 'Whatever happened to "you cross the tape, you go the distance"?' Catherine: 'I was probably saying that to get you to service my needs at the time.'

Brass: 'Where you been?' Grissom: 'Proctologist.' Brass: 'Sheriff getting your ass, huh?'

Nick: 'I only go "Dutch" if girls ask the wrong question.' Catherine: 'And what question is that, Nick?' Nick: 'What do you drive?'

Worst 'As You Know': Grissom: 'Strangulation's a man's crime.' Doc Robbins: 'Preaching to the converted.'

Fantastic Voyages: The hyoid bone in the neck breaks in front of the camera, and the piranhas can be seen feasting on Portia.

The Usual Suspects: Shawn Christian (Patrick Haynes) was best known as Wayne on *Beverly Hills 90210* before his *CSI* performance, although he has gone on to play Wade Brixton in half the episodes of the short-lived *Birds of Prey* superhero show. Elizabeth Lackey (Amanda Haynes) played Roxanne Miller in Australian soap *Home and Away* before heading to America.

Pop Culture References: Nick and Catherine joke about a wrongly pricked piece of paper, referring to the controversial Presidential election result in Florida in 2000. Grissom refers to the biblical tale of Jonah and the whale.

Real-life Inspirations: The DNA linking Patrick Haynes to Chad Matthews has resonances of one of the first cases involving DNA evidence – Lynda Mann's murder in Narborough, England, where DNA strands from different crimes were used to prove the guilt or innocence of the suspects.

Mistakes Really Can Be Fatal: The credits refer to Detective Conroy as Detective Connors, although the script and Max Allan Collins' later official *CSI* novels refer to her as Conroy.

Notes: Lorraine Hunt, the Lt Governor of Nevada, appears as herself at the opening party.

Overall: A lot of intricate plotting in this one makes the hour move swiftly, and it's good to be reminded that the CSIs don't always win the day. It also has one of the laugh-out-loud highlights of the season, as Greg Sanders plays chorus girl with Portia Richmond's headdress!

15
Too Tough to Die

US Air Date: 1 March 2001 14.8/22
UK Air Date: 15 September 2001

Written by: Elizabeth Devine
Directed by: Richard J. Lewis
Guest Cast: Katy Boyer (Lauriane Hastings),
Ntare Mwine (Thomas Alder), Aldis Hodge (Tony Thorpe),
Andy Taylor (Sam), Michelle Anne Johnson (Pamela Adler),
Gary Bristow (Charles 'Chuckie' Hastings), Geoff Meed (Roy McCall),
Nefta Perry (Shandra Thorpe), Larry Bagby III (Hank Dudek),
Edi Patterson (Rosalyn Dudek)

Teaser One-liner: 'Locard's Principle – he took a piece of her with him, and left a piece of himself here. We get to find it.'

The Cases: A woman is carjacked and later abandoned at the side of the road after being shot in the head at point-blank range. Grissom sends Sara to accompany her to Cedar Palms Hospital and take a rape kit while Nick searches the scene. He finds a hat with a cobra emblem on it.

Sara is informed that the Jane Doe still has two bullets in her head, which can't be removed without killing her. Feeling odd that she's carrying out the tests on a live person, Sara performs the sexual assault kit.

While Nick is photographing the bullets at the crime scene, Grissom spots a belt loop which must belong to the attacker. He decides to use scent pads, and runs a machine over the loop, getting the scent onto the pad so that it can be used by the K-9 squad – sniffer dogs – once they have got a rough idea where the suspect lives.

Grissom visits the hospital where Sara is promising Jane Doe that she will find who did this to her. He tries to warn her not to get too involved.

The casings match a crime scene in North Vegas which was the site of a gangland shooting. The hat they found at the scene has the mark of the Snakeback gang on it. It also has sweat marks inside which Sara hopes could yield DNA matching the rape kit's. Detective Vega tells Grissom and Nick about the Snakebacks – they are unlikely to co-operate with any inquiries.

Grissom is increasingly concerned that Sara is becoming too involved and tries to persuade her to go home, but she continues to search through the missing persons database. She discovers Jane Doe is really Pamela Adler.

Grissom brings in the dogs. Although evidence found inside a house as a result of the K-9 unit isn't usable, what's outside is fair game. The dogs get the scent and find the young gang member, Tony, who is wearing the pair of jeans from which a belt loop is missing.

Grissom and Brass interrogate Tony, with his mother present. Sara is furious at Tony's uncaring attitude. She and Nick confirm that Tony's jeans match the belt loop

Sara visits Pamela and tells her that they have found her attacker. Her husband is there, and he tells Sara that Pamela is going to the Haven View Centre. Sara puts on a brave face for him but, when she sees Grissom, it's too much and she complains about the unfairness of it all. Pamela will always be in a vegetative state, whereas her attacker will be released in 48 months. Grissom tries to counsel her to let it go, but Sara leaves, telling him that she wishes she was like him, not feeling anything.

Catherine and Warrick are assigned an old case to sort out. The accused, Roy McCall, shot and killed his neighbour Chuckie Hastings over the loan of a motorcycle, but the CSI who had been handling it has quit. The DA can't sort out the evidence, and needs a CSI to do so. The trial is only four days away.

According to the evidence McCall claims that the killing was carried out in self-defence, after Hastings attacked him with a screwdriver, but Hastings' widow claims that McCall shot him in the back. The coroner's report confirms that Hastings was shot in the back. Unfortunately the screwdriver is missing.

Warrick and Catherine visit Mrs Hastings, who says that she heard noises, rushed outside and saw McCall shoot her husband. However, Catherine disbelieves this, since McCall was using a semi-automatic, and there would only be two-tenths of a second in-between the shots. There are therefore no witnesses.

Warrick and Catherine talk to McCall, who has a scar on his arm that fits the story about the screwdriver. He maintains that he and Hastings were facing each other, even if the evidence suggests otherwise, and his lawyer points out that once she tells the jury that the screwdriver has been lost, the forensic evidence probably won't be particularly well regarded.

The coroner confirms that the shots definitely entered Hastings' back, and Warrick realises that in the fight both men would have been ducking and weaving.

Catherine and Warrick check the victim's T-shirt and the gunpowder shows that the men were only three feet apart – not the five paces that Mrs Hastings and McCall had both claimed. After running some reconstruction tests, they deduce that the men were only two feet apart when the shooting began and even closer when it stopped. That doesn't fit with *any* of the stories.

Warrick and Catherine use a self-healing dummy to try to reconstruct what happened, and Warrick tries to wrestle the dummy into a bending position. Catherine jokingly tries to take a photo of Warrick's undignified position – and both realise what happened.

They explain to the DA that the two men were struggling. Hastings lunged forward with the screwdriver, and McCall shot him in self-defence, but then fired a second time when Hastings was on the ground. The second shot confirms McCall as a murderer.

Personal Notes: Grissom tells Catherine that Eddie has taken out a second mortgage on their house; since they're still married, although divorcing, it's legal. Sara Sidle has a very nice singing voice, and sings while she's working. Warrick is very good with Lindsey and takes her out of the way of the row between Eddie and Catherine. Eddie asks Catherine, 'Who paid to close up your nose?' which is the first hint of Catherine's former cocaine habit. Grissom breaks up the argument between them and bars Eddie from CSI headquarters.

Techniques: Grissom quotes Locard's Exchange Principle: 'Every contact leaves a trace'. Anyone who goes somewhere takes something of themselves with them and leaves it there, and/or brings back something from that place. The trace evidence is what the CSIs are searching for.

Scent pads were created by Niagara County Sheriff's Department dog-handler William Tolhurst. These operate on a vacuum principle to collect a scent into a sterile gauze pad, and then the scent can be blown to the dogs' noses by use of pressurised air flowing over the pad.

Catherine and Warrick use a self-healing dummy that allows them to experiment with varying angles to recreate the murders.

The Wit and Wisdom of Gil Grissom: 'If you don't find something, they'll all become special, and you'll burn out.'

Classic Dialogue: Grissom: 'What do you do for fun?' Sara: 'I chase rabbits and I read crime books and I listen to the scanner.'

Fantastic Voyages: We close in on Grissom sweeping up the crime scene; we see the cartridges ejecting from the gun. We also watch the screwdriver going into McCall's arm, and the trajectories of the two bullets he fires into Hastings. There are also extreme close-ups of the gunpowder stains from the bullets.

The Usual Suspects: Geoffrey Rivas (Detective Sam Vega) makes his debut, having played assorted Hispanic parts in everything from *Chicago Hope* to *NYPD Blue*.

Mistakes Really Can Be Fatal: In a desperate effort to give Sara a life outside the confines of the crime lab, this episode reveals that she sings. She hasn't done up till now, and she doesn't again!

Catherine automatically assumes that McCall would have fired off two shots quickly, and so discounts Mrs Hastings' story – but there's no reason to assume that at all.

Overall: Once again, this is a bit disappointing. It's good to see Sara getting heavily involved in a case, and venting her frustrations at the system, but the scenes between her and Grissom are starting to get moralistic again, and it's a heavy-handedness that shows.

16
Face Lift

US Air Date: 8 March 2001 14.4/22
UK Air Date: 22 September 2001

Written by: Josh Berman
Directed by: Lou Antonio
Guest Cast: Brigid Brannagh (Tammy Felton aka Melissa Marlowe),
Reginald VelJohnson (Dr Philip Kane),
James Eckhouse (Hank Marlowe), Joan McMurtrey (Mrs Marlowe),
Larry Holden (Darin Hanson), Brian Howe (Mr Winston),
James Wellington (Joseph Felton), Teddy Lane Jr (Uniform Officer),
Kathy Christopherson (Ann), Craig Wollson (Marc)

Teaser One-liner: 'Looks like our robbery suspect is a homicide victim.'

The Cases: The owners of a pottery store find that they've been burgled and the thieves have left something behind — a corpse, one Joseph Felton. Only a small amount of money was taken, and it looks as though Felton was surprised by something.

Doc Robbins discovers that he was hit on the head three times, causing trauma to the brain stem, and killing him instantaneously. The point of impact shows some yellow and glitter transferred. Catherine combs out some spores from Felton's hair.

The prints found at the crime scene match Melissa Marlowe — a kidnap victim from 21 years previously. However, they're old prints, so it looks as if there are two cases running side by side. Nick and Catherine deal with the homicide, while Grissom looks into the kidnapping.

Nick discovers that the safe was cracked with a plasma lance. Felton was once arrested for a robbery but granted immunity for testifying against his partner Darin Hanson, who used a plasma lance in that robbery. Hanson has just been released from jail. Nick thinks they might have teamed up, and then Hanson took his revenge. However, Hanson claims he has not seen Felton since the trial, and that it was Felton who was the lance expert, not him. He also has receipts showing that he was out of town at the time of the robbery.

Catherine meets Tammy Felton, Felton's daughter, and spots the same plant spores on her back as were on her father. She admits that she was at the robbery, and that she was trying to persuade her father not to do the job.

Grissom meets Mr and Mrs Marlowe, who have never given up hope that their daughter is still alive. He's called in Teri Miller to help to create a likeness of what Melissa might look like now. Teri uses computer software and pictures of Mrs Marlowe as a younger woman to create an image of the current Melissa – whom Catherine promptly recognises as Tammy Felton. Her prints are old and might be at the store from when she cased the place some weeks earlier.

Grissom and Catherine go to psychiatrist Dr Kane to get some insight into how much Tammy might remember of being Melissa. Kane believes she might have some small memory, which will lead to some frustration. Kidnapped children of that age exhibit sociopathy as adults, and have a very high survival instinct.

Nick chases up the sample from Felton's head wound, and Greg tells him that the glitter comes from tiny pieces of uranium, which will be on the murder weapon. Uranium used to be used as a colour enhancer in paints, dyes and glazes – and Felton was killed in a pottery store.

Grissom allows the Marlowes to see Tammy/Melissa being questioned by Catherine about her upbringing. Tammy refuses to answer and leaves. Mrs Marlowe desperately tries to connect with her, but Tammy cold-shoulders her away. Mrs Marlowe realises that Tammy was kidnapped by her babysitter, Mara Felton, whom Tammy had just referred to as her mother.

Tammy's apartment is searched, and the murder weapon found, as well as some gloves. Tammy claims she didn't kill

her father – it was Melissa Marlowe who did it! Dr Kane
thinks that it's possible there are two personalities within
Tammy. The Marlowes have hired Attorney Randy
Painter to defend their daughter. Tammy still denies that
she's their daughter, but seems to recognise a necklace Mrs
Marlowe is wearing. Mr Marlowe does his best to raise the
bail.

Tammy asks Catherine to visit her. She claims that now
she's the safe girl not the dangerous one, and she needs
Catherine to testify that she wasn't sane when she killed
Joe. Catherine points out that if she claims she can't
remember anything since being a child, she shouldn't be
able to remember her! Tammy's furious reaction confirms
to Catherine that it's all an act.

The following day Catherine learns that Tammy skipped
her bail, leaving the Marlowes ruined. They bailed her out
and bought her a load of bus tickets to cover her tracks.
The Marlowes refuse even now to believe the worst of their
daughter and would rather go to jail than help catch her.

Out in the desert, Tammy is picked up by her true
accomplice – Darin Hanson . . .

Sara and Warrick are dealing with a case of a woman who
fell asleep in her chair and incinerated. Sara believes that
it's a possible case of spontaneous human combustion, but
Warrick is sceptical. They find some cotton fibres, possibly
from her nightgown. The fire burned a hole in the roof
directly above Nadine Winston's chair. Her husband,
Larry, can't understand what happened. He left her asleep
in the chair, and ten hours later found a pile of ash.

All that Sara and Warrick have left of Nadine is her
foot, which David Phillips explains was burned off the
body. He sends a scraping to toxicology to check for
flammable compounds in the blood, although he warns
them that the heat may have compromised the sample.

Sara is still convinced that they are dealing with
spontaneous human combustion. The husband has no
motive, and there's no evidence of foul play. Even the ion
detector can find no trace of hydrocarbon fumes.

Warrick and Sara recreate Nadine Winston's death with the help of a pig. Nadine was smoking a cigarette, wearing a cotton nightgown, and had a high concentration of sleeping pills in her blood.

Grissom comes out to watch the end of the experiment. The pig's fat – and therefore Nadine's originally – acted like candle wax, and Grissom asks them if they've found the wick – a piece of fabric that's just scorched. Sara confirms that they have and asks Grissom why he didn't say anything earlier. Grissom points out that they needed to see it to believe it, and leaves them to clear up. Since Warrick covered for Sara, saying that neither of them had believed in spontaneous human combustion, she cleans up for him.

Personal Notes: Sara gave up meat following the pig experiment (see **09**, 'Sex, Lies and Larvae').

Techniques: The criminalists employ forensic palynology, studying the spores which, in this case, link the various parties to the scene of the crime.

Warrick uses an ion detector to test for hydrocarbon fumes that may have been used as an accelerant to burn Nadine.

Classic Dialogue: Warrick: 'You're siding with Sara because you have a crush on her.' David Phillips: 'No, that's why I wore a clean coat.'

Grissom: 'Since I screwed up our last date, will we ever have dinner again? Teri Miller: 'Oh we'll have dinner, just not together.'

Dr Kane: 'Be careful. Sociopaths are dangerous because they don't function by the same moral code as the rest of us.' Grissom: 'Welcome to my world.'

Fantastic Voyages: We see the ankle bone hollowed out by the effects of the fire.

The Usual Suspects: Brigid Brannagh (Tammy Felton) played Wesley's love interest Virginia Bryce on *Angel*. Larry Holden (Darin Hanson) appeared with Jorja Fox in the thriller *Memento*. Reginald VelJohnson (Dr Kane) appeared as Sgt Al Powell with Bruce Willis in *Die Hard* and *Die Hard 2: Die Harder*, recreating the role in various video spin-offs.

Pop Culture References: Miss Piggy gets another name check; Grissom makes a joking comment about Peter Parker, the alter ego of *The Amazing Spider-Man*.

Real-life Inspirations: Teri Miller's work recreating the 25-year-old Melissa Marlowe echoes the work done in the 1980s to age the appearance of killer John List, which led to his arrest.

The supposed Spontaneous Human Combustion (SHC) of Nadine combines the various pieces of research that have been done on SHC. In 1951, Mary Hardy Reeser died in similar circumstances, leading to rumours that she was a victim of SHC. The FBI's investigation into this developed the wick-effect theory that Grissom demonstrates. A 1991 case in Oregon provided photographic evidence.

Mistakes Really Can Be Fatal: Grissom thinks that Spider-Man is a creation of the 1950s; he's not. Stan Lee and Steve Ditko brought him to the world's attention in *Amazing Fantasy #15* in August 1962.

Overall: An intriguing episode that takes the CSIs into some different territory, as they explode one urban myth, and are caught up in a legal matter, which would normally be outside their scope, as Tammy Felton claims to be a dual personality.

17
$35K O.B.O.

US Air Date: 29 March 2001 13.8/21
UK Air Date: 29 September 2001

Written by: Eli Talbert
Directed by: Roy H. Wagner
Guest Cast: Reynaldo Christian (Justin Green),
Louis Mustillo (Allan Rich, the Knife Dealer),
Charley Rossman (Uniformed Officer),
Elizabeth Keener (Amy Shepherd), Jonathan Fraser (Kevin Shepherd),
Shelli Bergh (Jessica Hall)

Teaser One-liner: 'Our killer got lucky tonight.'
The Cases: A young couple celebrating their eighth wedding anniversary are killed in the street outside Andre's

Restaurant as they get to their SUV. The SUV is then stolen. As the CSI team start to make their preliminary assessment, finding some red hairs that don't match the victims', the heavens open, and they only have about three minutes before all their evidence is washed away. They bag what they can, but a lot of the investigation is compromised even before it can begin.

At least there is an eye witness, Justin Green, who says that he was crossing the street and a SUV came out of nowhere. It nearly hit him, and he turned and saw Kevin Shepherd's body lying in the street. Justin thinks that because he didn't perform CPR properly, he's responsible for the death, but Grissom reassures him he wasn't. Sara takes his clothes for examination.

Greg confirms that the red hairs are feline. Doc Robbins' autopsy reveals that Kevin was stabbed six times, once in the back, five times in the front, while Amy's neck was sliced from right to left. Robbins believes that Kevin was attacked with two different weapons, as there are two different sorts of wounds. One has a sharp double-edged blade, the other is blunt, and caused bruising around the entry points. Two weapons would suggest two attackers.

Sara discovers that the Shepherds seem to have normal lives, and there are plenty of eye witnesses confirming that Justin Green was trying CPR on Kevin. Everything points to a carjacking.

Warrick takes moulds of Kevin's stab wounds to try to identify the murder weapons. Brass locates the Shepherds' stolen SUV. Grissom opens the door, and a dead female falls out, much to his surprise. Jessica Hall has cat hairs on her similar to those on Kevin Shepherd, although there were none on Amy – but why is she in the SUV? Jessica's corpse sets off the metal detector at the coroner's, and inside her corpse they find the tip of a knife.

Sara and Brass take the knife tip to a dealer, Allan Rich, who runs an acid test on it to show that it's carbon steel, and uses basic geometry to work out the size of the knife. When the tip of the knife is added to the impression that Warrick has made of the blunt knife used on Kevin, it's a perfect fit. There was only one weapon. The killer started with Kevin, then went after Jessica, breaking off the tip, before going back to Kevin and finishing the job.

The prints on the Shepherds' SUV confirm that Jessica Hall was the last driver. Nick notices that there is blood flow on the left instep of Kevin's left shoe – because he curled up instinctively, it was protected from the rain. It's not his blood, and they deduce it must be Jessica's, which dripped on him when she was holding him down to assist the killer. It looks as though her stabbing was accidental.

The blood on Kevin's shoe is Jessica's and the Police Department have traced a call from Kevin Shepherd to Jessica from the restaurant. Checking her apartment, they find a red-haired tabby cat, indicating that Kevin was probably at the apartment without his wife. Brass goes to check both Kevin and Jessica's cellphone records. Nick accesses Jessica's ACHEX account on her computer – she conveniently leaves herself Post-its with useful information and reminders around the place. Jessica received $35,000 and paid it out the same day, although the recipient's name isn't posted yet. Kevin's records indicated that he paid out the same sum.

Technician Mark Bennett is able to bring up the print on Amy's notepad, which includes a note 'Andre's at 9 p.m. Green SUV. Corner of Sixth. Sunday K's office eight a.m.' The notepad message and Kevin's credit card receipt are in the same writing. It looks as if Kevin took out a hit on his wife, and paid Jessica to arrange it. But something went wrong.

Sara and Warrick check Justin Green's clothing, and find a handprint on it, which matches Kevin Shepherd. If Justin was performing CPR as he claimed, Kevin wouldn't have been able to grab his shirt. Justin is the killer.

A comparison of the phone and bank records confirms that Kevin transferred $35k to Jessica, who passed it to Justin. They used to have a joint account and the same surname – Jessica hired her ex-husband. Later that day, Justin called Amy and she offered to double the amount.

Justin therefore killed both of them, and got rid of Jessica to erase any loose ends.

Catherine is investigating three deaths at a collapsed building. O'Riley is surprised to see her there, but she points out that the building is a suspect in their deaths. She meets Paul Newsome, the City District Engineer, who irritates Catherine with his chauvinism from the moment they meet. Catherine spots that some of the wood is wet, and that there's some inferior drywall been used for repairs. Newsome tries to fob Catherine off with a copy of his report once it's compiled, but she refuses to leave, and wants to examine the scene of the collapse, in the laundry room.

Catherine crawls through the collapsed building, even though both Newsome and O'Riley try to persuade her otherwise. O'Riley admits that the mayor ran on a platform of urban renewal so any problems with city-maintained low-cost housing are going to look bad.

Catherine finds an insect down in the remains of the basement, which she bags ready to take to Grissom. The building starts to shake, and Newsome reassures her that the building is still secure. The shake is caused by the noise of an F-16 jet aircraft flying low overhead from Nellis Air Force Base. In the laundry room, Catherine discovers that someone has taken a sledgehammer or similar to one of the wooden support columns.

Grissom identifies the beetle as an Anobid Powder Post Beetle, which eats softwood. The Douglas Fir that the building was made of would be a delicacy. However, the damage to the support column is more likely to be the cause of the collapse.

Paul Newsome tells Catherine that five years ago a disgruntled tenant took a sledgehammer to the strut. He didn't indicate the damage in his inspection report because there wasn't enough to cause concern. Catherine suspects that the sound vibrations of the jets caused the collapse of the building and runs an experiment using some of Lindsey's rubber balls, and a very loud recording of

Beethoven's Ninth. The nails in the wood are worked loose by the sonic vibration. A combination of the noise from the jets, the dry rot, the earlier sabotage and the wood-chewing beetles caused the collapse. Newsome isn't very fulsome in his thanks, though thanks to Catherine he won't be facing charges of negligence.

Personal Notes: Greg checks out the DNA from some epithelials he took from his date the previous night. Warrick has been a CSI for six years by this stage and is still freaked out by the clothes drying room.

Techniques: David Phillips operates the fluoroscope, which uses X-rays to determine where the metal is in Jessica's body. Warrick makes a mould of the wounds in the bodies to identify the blade.

The Wit and Wisdom of Gil Grissom: 'They used to say never on Sunday, then Pearl Harbor happened. I never say never.'

'It's a scientist's right to re-examine your theory with each new piece of evidence, Nick.'

Grissom: 'You know what they say about looks.' Brass: 'They can be deceiving?' Grissom: 'They can kill.'

Classic Dialogue: Brass: 'You know, between you and me, as long as I've been on the job I still don't like touching dead bodies.' Warrick: 'Well, that's why you've got the badge, and I've got the syringe.'

Grissom: 'I haven't felt that in a while.' Brass: 'What's that?' Grissom: 'The element of surprise.'

Fantastic Voyages: We follow the blade of the knife entering and exiting the body, both with a tip and as a blunt weapon. We then see the syringe entering the wound and filling it with plaster to make the cast, from the wound's perspective, and finally see the tip breaking off the knife inside Jessica's body.

The Usual Suspects: Brad Johnson (Paul Newsome) has played Rayford Steele in the video versions of the best-selling Apocalypse series *Left Behind*.

Pop Culture References: There's a passing reference to the game show *Wheel of Fortune*.

Real-life Inspirations: This episode was adapted from the murders committed in Los Angeles on Mother's Day 1995.

A mother and grandmother were stabbed to death in their garage. CSI technical consultant Elizabeth Devine worked on the case for three years until there was sufficient scientific evidence to pin the crime on Paul Carasi and his girlfriend Donna Lee. A sudden rainstorm deluged the crime scene, washing away evidence, while Paul Carasi wore a bloody hand print on his shirt. He was sentenced to death in 1998.

The idea for the building collapse came from stories Anthony Zuiker heard while working on the Las Vegas trams.

Mistakes Really Can Be Fatal: Greg doesn't use a coverslip to prevent cross-contamination on the cat-hair sample Nick gives him.

Brass claims he doesn't like touching dead bodies, yet he was in charge of CSI when the show started, and makes a big deal about Holly Gribbs having to be at an autopsy on her first night . . .

Notes: O.B.O. stands for 'Or Best Offer', like the British Or Nearest Offer seen in the small ads pages. The first draft was entitled 'Four Square'.

Overall: Although the ending of the B plot is telegraphed from the moment that Paul Newsome mentions the Air Force Base, it's still fun to see how Catherine gets there. The twists and turns in the A plot also make this one of the better episodes of the season.

18
Gentle, Gentle

US Air Date: 12 April 2001 14.8/24
UK Air Date: 6 October 2001

Written by: Ann Donahue
Directed by: Danny Cannon
Guest Cast: Lisa Darr (Gwen Anderson),
Brian McNamara (Steven Anderson),

Reginald VelJohnson (Dr Philip Kane),
Jesse Littlejohn (Tyler Anderson), Natalie Zea (Needra Fenway),
Terry Bozeman (Brad Lewis), Wayne Thomas York (CSI Tech),
Kevin Will (Male Parent), Stewart Skelton (FBI Man),
Maureen Muldoon (Woman Reporter),
Tyler DeFrance (Robbie Anderson), Jim Jenkins (Media Person #2),
Kathrin Lautner (Female Parent-30s), Susan Grace (Female Parent-40s)

Teaser One-liner: 'The person who touched [this note] before you, has your son. And he's just left us the first piece of a puzzle.'

The Case: A ransom note has been found at the scene of the kidnapping of baby Zack Anderson from his parents' home. It doesn't say how much money the kidnappers want for his return, just that they'll call in six hours. From the neighbours' accounts, the Andersons are a regular family. Steve Anderson built his own business, and believes he can handle pressure, but he's very nervous with the FBI man preparing the phone for the kidnappers call. Grissom finds a Coke bottle which was apparently opened only a couple of hours earlier, and takes it and a fresh one from the fridge for examination.

Gwen Anderson says that she got up at 4.30 a.m. to breast feed Zack, but he was gone. Steve heard her scream, went to her, and then called 911. Grissom asks for a piece of the baby's clothing and also takes blood samples from each family member to use to eliminate them from the investigation. Catherine takes a Babygro for use for the dogs.

Grissom asks Sara to take the ransom note to Questioned Documents (QD), and tells her to take all the computers and printers from the house with her for comparison. He asks Nick to take both the used and unused bottles of Coke back to the lab to process. There's a ladder still outside the baby's open bedroom window, so Warrick is assigned to canvas the grounds from the outside in. He finds a footprint in the garden then comes up the ladder and surprises Grissom, who's working in the baby's room. There's a spider's web across the window which hasn't been disturbed. Grissom finds two distinct hairs in the room, and there's a very strong smell of cleansing fluid. There's blood present, and it's possible that Zack was killed even before he left the house.

In the QD lab, Ronnie Litre reveals that the note was on expensive paper, and there's a drum mark on the paper – three vertical dots that are specific to the printer with that error on it. The shoeprint that Warrick has found matches the gardener's boot although he's been away for three days. Grissom tells Sara to check all the printers at Steve Anderson's company.

The sniffer dogs find Zack's body wrapped up in a clean blanket and placed on some plastic beneath a statue on the neighbouring golf course. Grissom angrily keeps anyone else away and takes the pictures in situ himself.

Doc Robbins confirms that Zack was smothered: there are retinal haemorrhages as a result of intercranial pressure from an oedema, caused by lack of oxygen. There's a microscopic fibre in Zack's throat. However, Robbins doesn't think it was an accidental asphyxiation – the sternum is freshly cracked. Grissom takes the case personally and pressures his team for results. He even overrides an order from the Sheriff to Greg Sanders so Greg can process the blood comparison. Sara tries to reason with him, but he points out that he was the one who found the baby. He won't let the Andersons take Zack for burial, since he is still evidence, and the evidence including the fact that the kidnapper never rang, points to the fact that he wasn't taken by a stranger.

The blood in Zack's room is his brother Tyler's. He claims that he broke Zack's window playing ball and cut his finger on the glass. Tyler babysat for his two younger brothers during the previous evening while his parents were at a Home Owners' Meeting, and Brass points out that Tyler has a history of violence. Tyler reacts angrily at the possibility that he killed Zack, saying he misses him. But that doesn't mean he didn't kill him.

Grissom and Catherine make a further search of the house, and find a pair of nylon tights in Mr Anderson's closet, with a green mark on them. Nick believes that there's some alcohol in Steve's bottle of Coke, and is running a check.

There are three sets of prints on the ransom note – Steve's, Gwen's and those of Steve's secretary Needra Fenway. The note was printed on Needra's computer. And her hair was found in the cot. Needra comes in for questioning and is asked about her affair with Steve. Did the new baby screw up their relationship? Did Steve ask her to commit murder to get out of the obligation of a new-born?

Steve Anderson maintains that he broke up with Needra when he learned Gwen was pregnant with Zack, and he had sneaked her into the house to have a quick look at the new baby, hence the hair. The questioning is interrupted by the arrival of a reporter asking Steve about the photos of their affair that Needra has sold to a tabloid newspaper. Grissom notes that Gwen is having problems with Robbie, the now-youngest son.

Catherine, Grissom and Brass talk to Dr Kane about the possibility of Gwen killing Zack to get back at Steve over the affair. Catherine doesn't believe it, but her belief is knocked by news that Gwen was charged thirteen years earlier with shaking Tyler. Gwen is brought in for questioning, running a gamut of abuse. She claims that in that case Tyler had got a French fry stuck in his windpipe, and she realised that she'd hurt him getting it out, hence the 911 call. Unfortunately there was no proof that there was any food. Gwen categorically denies hurting him, or being involved in Zack's abduction and death. Grissom asks if she knew that the golf course on which Zack's body was found paints its grass. The paint matches the stain on the tights found in Steve's closet.

Gwen is released, and avoids contact with son Robbie. Doc Robbins has nailed the time of death to 9 p.m., and has identified the fabric as something designed to be near fire. At the Andersons' house, there is a potholder that fits the bill. Warrick analyses the 911 tape and Gwen's stress seems real. Catherine asks if he's checked whether Tyler made any calls on any other line.

The CSIs face the Andersons at their lawyers' office the next morning, where they lay out the evidence. The lack of a price on the ransom note indicates that the parents wrote it – in fact Steve did it at his office while Gwen wrapped Zack in a blanket and laid him to rest on the golf course, thus getting the green stains. Steve put the ladder up outside the window. The lawyers agree that the CSIs have proved there was a cover-up.

Steven and Gwen are arrested after she claims that she killed Zack because he was crying. She smothered him with the potholder and then came up with the kidnap story. But Warrick says that he's located a 911 call that Tyler made earlier in the evening after finding Robbie standing over Zack's body, having smothered him accidentally. The Andersons returned from their meeting and desperately tried to resuscitate Zack, then decided to cover up the death to prevent Robbie having the stigma of killing his brother. Grissom points out that since he's only three, he's clinically unaware of his actions. Gwen would rather go to prison than have anyone know what happened – but the CSIs can't allow that to happen.

Personal Notes: Warrick has become the audio analyst of the team.

The Wit and Wisdom of Gil Grissom: 'You told me a few weeks ago, nothing's personal. No victim should be special. Everyone follows your lead.' (Quoted by Sara.)

'Let me tell you something. People are presumed innocent. Innocent, until a court of law can examine the evidence. And until that happens, everything else is gossip.'

Fantastic Voyages: We focus on the interior of the swab as it reacts with the blood.

The Usual Suspects: Lisa Darr (Gwen Anderson) played Laurie Manning on the *Ellen* (DeGeneres) comedy show. Natalie Zea (Needra Fenway) is another soap opera veteran, playing Gwen Hotchkiss on *Passions* from 2000–2002. Terry Bozeman (Attorney Lewis) plays Richard Armus in the second season of *24*.

Real-life Inspirations: There are echoes in the circumstances surrounding events in this episode of the Jon Benét

Ramsay case in America, in which a child was found dead in her parents' basement.

Notes: This was the highest-rated first-run *CSI* first-season episode on CBS.

Overall: One of the most harrowing *CSI* episodes for any parent of young children, and a rare instance of one plotline fully sustaining the running time.

19
Sounds of Silence

US Air Date: 19 April 2001 14.8/22
UK Air Date: 13 October 2001

Written by: Josh Berman, Andrew Lipsitz
Directed by: Peter Markle
Guest Cast: Deanne Bray (Dr Jane Gilbert),
Mario Schugel (Brad Kendall), Elaine Kagen (Mrs Clemonds),
Jonah Rooney (Mark Rucker), Austin Nichols (Adam Walkey),
Arlene Malinowski (Halley), Greg Anderson (Brian Clemonds),
Scott 'Jesic' Caudill (Paul Arrington), Caroline Barba (Lisa),
Samantha Harris (Charlotte), Joannah Portman (Erin McCarty),
Mark Ginther (Al Robson), Kanan Howell (Roy Hinton),
Bonnie Morgan (Alice Neely), Jeff Podgurski (Frankie Flynn)

Teaser One-liner: 'I wouldn't book those suspects just yet. I think they ran over a corpse.'

The Cases: Two girls driving from a nightclub take a short cut and hit someone. When Grissom, Sara and Warrick investigate, they find that the vehicle that killed the man wasn't the girls' car at all. He was already dead. Warrick finds a pack of beer on the pavement. There's also a broken piece of tail light.

The victim is Brian Clemonds, a 22-year-old man who has been deaf since birth. Doc Robbins doesn't think it's as simple as him walking in front of an SUV. He has dried blood on his knuckles but no associated wounding, so he was in a fight. The blood is sent for DNA processing.

Sara and Warrick get off on the wrong foot with Dr Jane Gilbert, principal of the deaf school that Brian attended.

They bring an interpreter, who Dr Gilbert doesn't need, and ask to check the records. She kicks them out and asks them to send someone who has some more understanding of the deaf. Grissom takes over and surprises Dr Gilbert by using sign language to her, and looking closely at her as they speak. Dr Gilbert agrees to co-operate, and opens up Brian's records. He had problems with his room-mate, Paul, who only recently lost his hearing because of a tumour. Grissom explains to Sara that it's not a question of 'us' and 'them' when it comes to those who can hear and those who can't. They use a visual polygraph, which indicates when the user recognises a scene, to question Paul, but he has no recollection of the crime scene, and is allowed to go.

There are lice in Brian's clothes, and pyoverdin in the blood found on his fist. Sara matches the partial serial number from the tail light with the tyre tread mark, leading to the only Ford Explorer SUV registered in Vegas. Grissom invites Dr Gilbert to be present when its owner, Adam Walkey, comes in for questioning. Sara and Warrick find lice in the SUV. Walkey's attorney, Randy Painter, tells him to say nothing, but all Grissom wants is to comb his hair. Walkey doesn't have lice, but his blood does match the blood sample on Brian's knuckle.

Fabric on the SUV's exhaust matches Brian's sweater – but why was the SUV being driven backwards? Adam changes his story, now remembering hitting something – but he didn't look back. He says his friend Mark Rucker was with him. Jane Gilbert attacks Adam for what he did to Brian, and Grissom pulls her away, worried she'll compromise the investigation.

The headlice-ridden Mark Rucker comes in, and says that they hit something and kept going. Grissom points out that some of Mark's lice were on Brian, and he then admits that they got out but drove off to avoid trouble. Grissom tells him that he thinks that they tried to get Brian's attention but failed, so stopped and started taunting him. They beat him up, and then ran back over him. Rucker asks for a lawyer, and even though the interrogation is over, Grissom tells Rucker that Brian was deaf.

Grissom tells Dr Gilbert that they've found the killers, and she asks him how he learned to sign, making him use his hands.

Nick and Catherine investigate a multiple homicide at a coffee shop. One of the corpses is an innocent bystander who was listening to speed metal on his Walkman so would have heard nothing. There are four others dead, and loads of shell cases. One of the corpses is Frankie Flynn, a notorious villain; the second is Al Robson, his bodyguard; the other two are store employees. There's been no money taken from the till. The situation has all the hallmarks of a gangland hit.

Doc Robbins processes Frankie Flynn first. He has gunshot wounds to the head and abdomen, and Robbins gets one bullet out for comparisons. Flynn was dying of colon cancer, so if it was a hit, it was hardly necessary. One of the dead coffee shop employees, Erin McCarty, was six weeks pregnant. The manager Brad Kendall explains that Erin often locked up on her own, and was training Alice, the other dead girl, since she was moving on.

Brass discovers that Brad Kendall used to work for Frankie Flynn. He also has a concealed weapon's permit for a 9mm Glock – the same size as the casings found at the scene. Unfortunately, Kendall's gun isn't the murder weapon since the striations on the casings don't match. Nick and Catherine try to work out the pattern of events from the bullet casings, and deduce that the killer entered from the back of the store. He was after Erin, and everyone else was killed because they were potential witnesses.

Catherine is certain that Erin would know she was pregnant; since she lived at home and had no apparent boyfriend, she asks Doc Robbins to run a paternity test. Brad blusters that he's married and wouldn't get involved with one of his workers, but faced with a court order for DNA, he gives in and admits that he is the father.

Bobby Dawson discovers the murder weapon was Kendall's gun. He changed the barrel. They check the bunter marks – the casing information – to see if they can link the ammunition to the crime, and they prove that Kendall's ammunition was used. The manager finally admits responsibility.

Personal Notes: Grissom is notoriously bad at processing paperwork, so Catherine deliberately brings forward the date that she needs him to sign things by, so that she's got a grace period during which to harass him. Grissom knows how to use sign language, but won't reveal to his colleagues how he learned. He tells Dr Gilbert that his mother taught him. Warrick has been with the department at least since 1997, as he and Grissom used a visual polygraph to interview a rapist at that time.

Techniques: To question Brian's room-mate, the CSIs employ brain printing, which was developed by psychiatrist Lawrence Farwell. It shows MERMERs – memory and encoding related multifaceted electroencephalographic responses – to images that are recognised. All it shows is whether the person questioned was present at the scene, not whether they committed a crime or not.

Every bullet has a bunter mark, which displays information about the manufacturer and calibre of the projectile. These engravings are identical in each batch of ammunition so it's possible to prove that a bullet came from a certain batch. If the suspect has the remaining ammunition from that batch, it's a fair chance he used the bullet found at the scene.

The Wit and Wisdom of Gil Grissom: 'You don't need to hear or speak to communicate or commit murder.'

Classic Dialogue: Nick: 'One person dead, it's a shame. More than one, it's a party.'

Grissom: 'Would you like to talk to a family service counsellor?' Mrs Clemonds: 'Talking is over-rated, Mr Grissom. Just find out who did this to my boy, please.'

Doc Robbins: 'I deal with the pin cushions. Ballistics deals with the pins.'

Worst 'As You Know': This is possibly the classic example in the whole of *CSI*, between Nick Stokes, a CSI 3, and ballistics technician Bobby Dawson, as they explain bullet bunter marks – basically as described above in **Techniques**. Except that they're both professionals who know exactly what they're talking about. The scene should really go:

NICK:What about bunter marks?
BOBBY:Won't be as good, but let's try.
And off they should go ...

Fantastic Voyages: We travel inside a normal ear, and then see the malleus morph into Brian's affected one. The camera closes in on the louse in Brian's clothes, on the piece of fabric on the SUV exhaust, and then deep within the bunter marks on Kendall's gun.

The Usual Suspects: Deanne Bray (Dr Gilbert) is a genuinely deaf actor, who played the famous deaf cop Teddy Franklin from Ed McBain's *87th Precinct*, and headlined her own show *Sue Thomas, F.B. Eye*. Jeff Podgurski (Frankie Flynn) is a stuntman who has worked on *Eraser*, *Anaconda* and *Inspector Gadget*.

Notes: The producers are slightly sadistic, not providing any close captioning or subtitles for the sequence between Grissom and Dr Gilbert at the end. However, Grissom tells her that his mother lost her hearing when she was eight. One time, Grissom asked her what it was like to be deaf, and she told him to stick his head underwater to discover what it's like not being able to hear (to which Dr Gilbert agrees). She also taught him not to make fun of deaf people – they are like everyone else.

This is the first indication that Grissom potentially has hearing problems. Occasionally before this he has been lost in thought, but what becomes a key subplot in the third year starts here.

Overall: Marks down for the horrible Bobby Dawson/Nick Stokes infodump scene, but full marks for everything else. The special effects go up another notch, as we start seeing both normality and abnormality courtesy of morphing techniques.

20
Justice Is Served

US Air Date: 26 April 2001 14.4/22
UK Air Date: 20 October 2001

Written by: Jerry Stahl
Directed by: Tom Wright
Guest Cast: Kelly Connell (Randy Gesek),
W. Earl Brown (Thomas Pickens aka Roger Peet),
Kellie Waymire (Carla Dantini), Lee Arenberg (Joey),
Albie Selznick (Hugh Young), Alicia Coppola (Dr Susan Hillridge),
Steffani Brass (Sandy Dantini), Crawford James (Triathlete aka Edwin),
Jason Frudakis (Terry Manning)

Teaser One-liner: 'He picked the wrong time of day to be jogging alone.'

The Cases: Initial indications on the corpse of Terry Manning, a jogger found in Las Vegas' Sunset Park, are that he was mauled by a wild animal of some sort, possibly a mountain lion. But appearances are deceptive: Grissom immediately notices that there are scalpel marks as well. Doc Robbins thinks that the animal marks came from a canine, not a feline, but confirms Grissom's observation about the scalpel. Whoever used it to remove the jogger's organs knew how to handle one.

Nick and Warrick collect all the dog faeces they can find, and Warrick also brings in what looks like a piece of dirty ice. The mould of the dog's teeth pattern reveals that it's missing one of its 42 teeth and that it's a Great Dane/Mastiff mix. There are only forty registered in the Greater Las Vegas area.

Nick and Warrick are analysing the dog faeces without any success. O'Riley reveals that the dog they believe is responsible has already mauled a gasman checking the meter. He and Grissom visit Dr Susan Hillridge and her dog Simba. She denies that Simba is vicious, and that it was her old dog that attacked the gasman. Simba is taken into custody, although Hillridge maintains that they're making a mistake. Dr Hillridge is a nutrition expert, working with professional athletes, but she doesn't recognise Terry Manning's name.

Simba's teeth fit the mould on the jogger, but Nick and Warrick haven't yet found any human remains in the dog faeces though they have found one sample with high-quality food, including sirloin steak and rice. The ice that Warrick found at the scene didn't melt, but evaporated, indicating it was dry ice similar to that used to pack organs for transplant. They visit Dr Hillridge, who seems unperturbed by Simba's impending destruction, and makes a protein shake that includes raw meat. Warrick finds some antique surgical equipment from 1875 which is very well maintained, and kept near her front door.

Grissom visits Randy Gesek (see **04**, 'Friends and Lovers') to ask about organ theft. He knows a lot about it, including the going rates.

Nick matches the sirloin-filled faeces with faeces found at Dr Hillridge's house, except that the latter has human cell tissue in it. There's also blood on the scalpel which further tests reveal is antique, like the scalpel itself. Dr Hillridge gives Grissom some folic acid, and complains mildly about the police search of her house. He reminds her that she has three prior complaints for owning vicious dogs, each coming from a mountain state. Grissom asks her if she knows the going rate for organs, and Hillridge seems disappointed in him. When the CSIs check the material brought in from her kitchen, they find blood in the food blender that she was using the previous day. It looks as if Dr Hillridge is eating – or drinking – the victims.

Dr Hillridge is not surprised when Grissom tells her that the game is up. She says she has porphyria, and humans were the best source of haem that she could find. She also admits that she ground the organs up into protein powder, and offers Grissom the chance to try some from her fridge. Arresting her, O'Riley reckons she's mad; Grissom says otherwise.

Catherine assigns herself the case of Sandy Dantini, a six-year-old who died on the Tunnel of Love ride at a carnival that's currently in town. She starts taking the case personally from the start, insisting on a fresh body bag for the child. Sara talks to Sandy's mother, Carla, who was with her daughter on the ride and who says that one minute she was there, the next gone, fallen into the water over which the ride was travelling. She tried to find her but by the time she could get the operator to stop the ride, Sandy was dead.

The ride operator, Thomas Pickens, claims that he stopped the ride as soon as he heard Carla screaming, and that he checked the belts each day. They were always kept a little loose on the Tunnel of Love so people could snuggle closer – but might that let a six-year-old slip out? Catherine looks round the ride and finds a hammer in the water. She accuses Pickens of trying to tamper with the evidence, but he says the hammer's been lost since they arrived in Vegas. Catherine insists he gives a urine sample – she believes he's high on cocaine.

However, Pickens swaps samples: the one he gives Catherine shows he's on the contraceptive pill. Sara has spoken to the Health and Safety authorities, and the carnival has numerous violations; Pickens himself, under his real name Roger Peet, is a convicted sex offender on parole. He says it's irrelevant to Sandy's death. He claims he ran into the tunnel once the ride was stopped, and found Sandy lying face down in the water. Catherine promises him that if he's lying, she'll get him. Sara tries to get her to calm down, and Catherine points out that the Tunnel of Love is the only ride that's in the dark. Maybe Pickens pulled Sandy out.

Doc Robbins confirms that Sandy drowned. She wasn't concussed, so if she had been conscious she should have been able to get out of the 18-inch-deep water. Sandy had a spiral fracture on her forearm, indicating that somebody twisted it to break it only moments before she died. Catherine thinks that Pickens took her out of the ride car to take her somewhere else, but was trapped inside the ride because the doors were malfunctioning, so killed her to hide the evidence. Catherine meets Carla Dantini for the first time, and asks if she thinks someone pulled Sandy from the car.

Catherine and Sara tell Pickens that they're not going to let him leave town, and Brass provides a warrant. Catherine tries to duplicate Pickens taking Sandy out, and it's just not possible. She realises that Carla Dantini's reactions were wrong when they were talking – she was making something up rather than remembering.

Brass, Catherine and Sara visit Carla, whose boyfriend is an attorney. They check her clothes, and discover that, although her watch is waterlogged, her shoes are dry. She never went in the water. The nearest she came was when she pushed Sandy under until she drowned. She wanted her daughter out of the way, so she could run off with her boyfriend, and everyone knows that accidents happen at carnivals. Carla knows she now needs a new attorney . . .

Personal Notes: There's some tension between Grissom and Catherine at the start of the episode when Catherine assigns herself the carnival case. She recognises she may have overstepped the mark, but doesn't back down. She badgers Pickens, insisting he takes a urine sample and claiming it's mandatory. At the end of the case, she gets a call from District Engineer Paul Newsome (see **17**, '$35K O.B.O.'), and goes over to his house. Nick can tell the difference between cougar and dog faeces – the seminar at which he learned it sticks in his mind because of Julie, the attractive CSI who gave it. Grissom is still giving seminars. According to Dr Hillridge, Grissom's deficient in folic acid. Brass has a teenage daughter (see **32**, 'File').

The Wit and Wisdom of Gil Grissom: 'I'm wrong all the time. That's how I get to right.'

'It's interesting how we categorise evidence in terms of what it means to us, as opposed to what it might mean to the case.'

Classic Dialogue: Nick: 'Oh man, you turn it on like this at your seminars?' Grissom: 'People actually pay to go to my seminars, Nick.'

Dr Hillridge: 'Tell me, Mr Grissom, how does a man choose death as his profession? Grissom: 'It chose me, actually.'

Warrick: 'She gives me the willies.' Grissom: 'Can't arrest her for that.'

Worst 'As You Know': Nick: 'Weird, isn't it?'

Warrick: 'What's that?'

Nick: 'That to prove the presence of haem – the stuff that makes blood red – turns the swab blue.' How many times have they done that test?

Fantastic Voyages: The dog's jaws open onto the camera, and then we see them cut through the jugular vein. The camera closes in on the dry ice. We see the bone snapping in Sandy Dantini's forearm. Finally, in one of the best effects on the show in Season One, we see Grissom imagining Dr Hillridge being affected by porphyria, and morphing into a horror movie-esque figure.

The Usual Suspects: Unsurprisingly W. Earl Brown (Thomas Pickens) played rock star Meat Loaf in the 2000 TV movie of his life. Alicia Coppola (Dr Hillridge) played Karen Chandler in the US version of *Cold Feet*. Kellie Waymire (Carla Dantini) has recurring roles on *Six Feet Under* as Melissa, and *Enterprise* as Crewman Cutler. Albie Seznick (Hugh Young) played Ben Rubinstein in Brooke Shields' comedy series *Suddenly Susan*.

Pop Culture References: Pickens quotes from David Crosby's lyric 'If I'd have known I would have lived this long, I'd've taken better care of my teeth'. Greg makes a passing reference to Cujo, the titular canine from Stephen King's novel and movie. Catherine tells Pickens to stop the 'Hee Haw' routine, talking about the country folk seen in the 60s' US series *Hee Haw*. Greg's comment about dogs hearing 'blah blah blah' is reminiscent of one of Gary Larson's Far Side cartoons. Grissom and Dr Hillridge exchange quotations from Pascal and Buddha.

Real-life Inspirations: Carla Dantini's crime is reminiscent of the murders committed by Susan Smith in 1994, when she strapped her two young sons into the back seat of her car and pushed them into a lake to drown them.

Although Dr Hillridge's crimes seem to be nearer fiction than fact, Richard Trenton Chase was discovered with bones, body organs and a bloodstained blender in 1977. He claimed he drank the blood for therapeutic reasons.

Mistakes Really Can Be Fatal: When do the CSIs learn Terry Manning's name? The first time it's mentioned is when Grissom uses it to Dr Hillridge.

Overall: *CSI* seems to wander into horror film territory, but it's also closely based on fact. Alicia Coppola's resemblance to Marina Sirtis – *Star Trek: The Next*

Generation's Deanna Troi – is quite startling at times, and she makes a worthy opponent for Grissom.

21
Evaluation Day

US Air Date: 10 May 2001 12.3/19
UK Air Date: 27 October 2001

Written by: Anthony E. Zuiker
Directed by: Kenneth Fink
Guest Cast: John Beasley (Charles Moore), Sam Jones III (James Moore),
Ingo Neuhaus (Trent Calloway), Robb Deringer (Fred Applewhite),
Keri Lynn Pratt (Anna Leah), Shonda Farr (Lori),
Darren Kennedy (Victor Da Silva), Lee Cherry (Stranger),
Shirley Jordan (Deputy), Chet Grissom (Restaurant Manager),
DeJuan Guy (Black Detainee), Fred R. Ellis (Maintenance Engineer),
Kareen Grimes (Ronnie Connors)

Teaser One-liner: 'About six to eight hours ago, somebody lost their head. Then somebody lost their head.'
The Cases: Two joyriding teenage girls are stopped speeding down Interstate 15, and when they are arrested and the vehicle checked, there is a head in the car's trunk, but no torso. From the vitreous humour in the eye, Grissom can tell that the person died around six to eight hours before.

Nick and Sara are assigned to deal with a homicide forty miles outside Baker. Nick wants to handle it solo, but Grissom points out that he's not ready yet.

The head belonged to Victor Da Silva, the owner of the car. There are chopping wounds on the jawbone, and Catherine thinks it's a crime of passion, and leaves Grissom and Doc Robbins to boil the head to determine what tools were used to sever it.

The two girls, Anna Leah and Lori, had been at a bar, and left with no lift home. They went back to a stranger's van to play strip poker, but he then told them that someone had once asked him to help them commit suicide, so they got out, leaving their clothes in the van. Brass arrests them for evading arrest, grand theft auto and driving under the influence of alcohol, but doesn't think they knew anything about the head.

Nick and Sara's homicide is a headless corpse, who has also lost his skin and had his hands and feet amputated. There are no tracks on the surface at all, and the corpse is in a dent in the ground, as if it had fallen from the sky. Suspecting a connection between the cases, Nick and Sara check out the BMW that Da Silva's head was found in and find peanuts on the gas pedal.

Doc Robbins is conducting an autopsy on the torso, which is a puzzle. It has an enormous ribcage and larger shoulders than normal. Most of its bones are broken – it has been in a very steep fall. All Doc Robbins can confirm for certain is that it's not Da Silva – it's not even human.

Brass and Grissom go to Da Silva's house to find a casino bouncer, Trent Calloway, there, decorating the house, even though it's the middle of the night. Calloway hasn't seen Da Silva for a day or two; they're not particularly friendly, but Calloway wasn't going to turn down a job. He knows Da Silva worked for an advertising agency. Brass finds a mutilated photo of Da Silva with someone else, but only Da Silva can be seen properly. Grissom finds peanuts in the soles of a pair of size eleven shoes in the closet.

Nick and Catherine go to another headless body, which this time *is* Da Silva's – it's found wrapped in plastic sheeting in a footlocker in a shed registered to him. There are bloody sockprints going away from the shed. They find an axe and a clawhammer which match his head injuries – but why use the claw end of the hammer? Grissom and Catherine deduce that his head was removed so the rest of the body could fit in the locker.

The sock prints are size eleven, matching the shoes Grissom found. Da Silva was a size ten. Acting on their own initiative, Nick and Sara also find a peanut shell in the turned-up hem of a uniform from Spurs Corral, a restaurant which serves peanuts as a starter.

Doc Robbins confirms that the torso is Da Silva, and that he was shot through the heart. Catherine is surprised they didn't find a gun, but understands now why he was wrapped in plastic – Da Silva's house is encased in plastic to protect the furniture from paint damage. Calloway is brought in for questioning, but his feet are two sizes too big for the sock.

The manager of the Spurs Corral says Da Silva never worked there. However, he certainly had been there – it's the location of the photo that Brass found. All that can be seen of the other person who's been torn off is a pair of distinctive earrings. The manager recognises them as belonging to Fred Applewhite, one of the servers.

The CSIs paint the bottom of Applewhite's feet then ask him to walk, then run, along a strip of paper. The prints match those found at the scene of the crime. Applewhite says that he and Da Silva had been lovers, but Da Silva threw him out three months earlier. He had hoped for a reconciliation but when that wasn't going to happen, he killed Da Silva. After dismembering the body, and putting the head in the car trunk, he remembered that he had forgotten to lock the shed, so went back – during which time the car was stolen.

Teri Miller comes in to assist once Doc Robbins has determined that the original torso isn't human, and discovers that the torso is a gorilla. Grissom tells Sara that he doesn't think it's a case for CSI any more, to see whether she's getting too involved with it, and satisfied that she's not, allows her to continue trying to discover what happened to the gorilla.

Teri disassembles the gorilla as per instructions from the Centre for Disease Control. She explains to Sara why certain parts of the gorilla are missing, and Sara admits that she has no hope of finding the plane from which she believes the gorilla was dumped. There is something she can do, however – she scatters the gorilla's ashes on the mountain where it was found, and then meditates.

Warrick has been called for help by Charles Moore, the uncle of James Moore (see **02**, 'Crate and Burial'). At his detention centre, James, in the wrong place at the wrong time, witnessed a murder. If he talks, he'll be killed, and if he keeps quiet, the District Attorney will put pressure on to have him transferred to the state jail. James tells Warrick that he got caught between two gang kingpins. Everyone knows that James was a witness, and they're waiting to see what he does.

Warrick checks out the dorm area, then follows the sewerage pipes down to the cellars, where he finds the murder weapon – a toothbrush with a blade inserted at the end with a rubber band wrapped around it. He interrogates Ronnie Connors, one of the gang members. He bought the toothbrush and the rubber bands from the commissary, but stupidly shaved with the blade before he put it on the shank. The evidence alone is enough to convict him without James' testimony.

Personal Notes: Nick has been a CSI-3 for 9 months, but hasn't handled a dead body solo so far. Grissom doesn't think he's ready yet. Catherine has just filed for divorce, and is feeling almost overconfident. Grissom has a Komodo dragon on order as a pet. Warrick's evaluation takes the form of joining Grissom on a roller-coaster ride! Every nine years and 34 days, Grissom shares the experience with someone else. Sara's evaluation is outstanding overall, but she needs to improve her prioritisation.

Techniques: Grissom and Doc Robbins boil the head to get to the skull. Grissom and Catherine use computers to recreate the shape of the hammer and the marks in Da Silva's skull.

The Wit and Wisdom of Gil Grissom: Grissom: 'Repeat after me, silk, silk, silk.' Nick: 'Silk? Silk? Silk?' Grissom: 'What do cows drink?' Nick: 'Milk.' Grissom: 'Cows drink water. They give milk. A simple riddle. Common sense disguised in a puzzle of words.'

'Anybody who's great at anything, Nick, does it for their own approval. Not someone else's.'

Classic Dialogue: Catherine: 'Definitely a crime of passion.' Grissom: 'You think a female could have done this?' Catherine: 'I could have.' Grissom 'Scared of you.'

Warrick: 'Whose side am I on? Who reached out to you, man?' James Moore: 'Who put me in here?'

Fantastic Voyages: We take a close inspection of the wounds on Victor Da Silva's scalp and neck, then peer intently at the peanuts on the pedals. There's a microscope's view of Greg Sanders' eye as he looks down the lens, and we see a bullet hitting an apple and devastating it.

The Usual Suspects: John Beasley and Sam Jones III reprise their roles (see **02**, 'Crate and Burial'), and Pamela Gidley makes her final appearance of the first season as Teri Miller. Ingo Neuhaus (Trent Calloway) played the late Daryl Epps in *Buffy the Vampire Slayer*'s 'Some Assembly Required'. Shonda Farr (Lori) is another *Buffy* alumna – she played the psychotic robot April in 'I Was Made To Love You'.

Pop Culture References: Grissom calls Catherine 'Alice', a reference to the long-running American sitcom *The Honeymooners*. There are references to the Hannibal Lecter movie *The Silence of the Lambs*, and to the legend of Sleepy Hollow.

Mistakes Really Can Be Fatal: Grissom said that Howard Da Silva's vitreous humour had glazed over; however, the vitreous is located inside the posterior compartment of the eye, behind the lens. What we were looking at was the cornea, which does cloud over upon death.

If Victor Da Silva had been dead for six–eight hours, the blood surrounding the neck should have oxidised to a darker hue.

Notes: The working title of this episode was 'Sleepy Hollow'.

Series creator Anthony E. Zuiker makes his second on-screen appearance as a roller-coaster attendant in the final scenes.

Part of this episode was shot on location in Las Vegas, utilising Sahara's Speed – The Ride, for the roller coaster sequence.

Overall: Some nice character touches make this one of the best first-season episodes. The various strands combine and then separate to provide a pleasing hour. Try the silk/milk riddle on people – it's amazing how many don't get it!

22
Strip Strangler

US Air Date: 17 May, 2001 12.4/19
UK Air Date: 3 November 2001

Written by: Ann Donahue
Directed by: Danny Cannon
Guest Cast: Michael Cerveris (Syd Booth Goggle),
Rainn Wilson (Man in Supermarket),
Randall Slavin (Hunter F. Baumgartner),
Gregg Henry (Special Agent Rick Culpepper),
Todd McKee (Bradley Walden), Maureen Muldoon (Lynda Darby)

Teaser One-liner: 'Signature killers never want to get caught. And they won't stop till they do.'

The Case: The CSIs are called to the bedroom of Eileen Jane Snow, the third victim of a signature killer, who delivers three or four overpowering head blows from a weapon he finds at the scene, gives them a chemical restraint, ties them up, rapes them, and then strangles them. Afterwards he ejaculates on the bedsheets, and then poses the corpse like a pin-up.

Sara examines the latest scene and finds no prints. Grissom suggests that Brass check for Peeping Toms or sex offenders in the area. Warrick spots one hair.

To Grissom's surprise, because of the number of cases, the Sheriff insists on bringing in the FBI, and Special Agent Rick Culpepper arrives on the scene. Culpepper expects to be in charge, but Grissom makes it clear that he'll work *with* Culpepper, not for him. A security guard, Syd Goggle, says he saw someone speeding away the previous night but Grissom is preoccupied with the FBI's arrival.

Doc Robbins confirms that Eileen was hit over the head, and given sodium amytal, which allowed the Strangler to torture her for six hours. He choked her unconscious then

brought her around, and kept repeating the process.
Robbins finds a small piece of polymer, and Nick offers to
check the crime scene for a match. Robbins has also found
some fibres in her throat, which might be from white bath
towels.

Greg analyses the semen from Eileen's body, and finds
some mutated DNA in it. The hair at Eileen's crime scene
matches one from the previous victim, but there's no skin
on it to get a DNA match. The hairs are probably planted,
but without any DNA, they can't lead to the suspect's
intended decoy.

Culpepper calls a full meeting about the Strip Strangler
and doesn't notify Grissom. Culpepper plans to use Sara
as a human decoy; Grissom is furious.

Greg discovers that the mutated DNA is actually tomato
ketchup. Catherine tells Grissom that the Sheriff is preparing to remove Grissom from the case and put her in
charge.

Nick discovers that the killer was wearing thick latex
gloves. Brass wonders if Paul Millander (see **00**, 'Pilot' and
07, 'Anonymous') might be responsible, but the signature
is wrong. He inadvertently tells Grissom that Sara is still
going ahead with the operation.

The FBI stake out a grocery store that fits the pattern
for the Strangler, but end up getting a handbag thief
instead. Unfortunately while they're doing that, there's
another murder, at the Monaco Hotel.

Grissom is dubious that this is the work of the same
man. The lamp cord is still attached whereas, in all the
other cases, it was yanked off. The killer didn't come
through a window, and there's no ejaculate; it seems a golf
club was probably used for the object rape. Culpepper
thinks this means the killer's signature is evolving, but
Grissom suspects that this murder has been staged. The
woman's husband, Brad Walden, is brought in for questioning.

Doc Robbins confirms Grissom's suspicions that the
case is different from the others, and Grissom asks Walden
if he can look at his golf clubs. Walden says his case is

locked, but if that's so, how did the Strangler get at the clubs to use in the rape? Culpepper promptly arrests him for all the murders. Grissom is convinced he's wrong.

Culpepper calls a press conference to say that they've caught the Strangler, but when a reporter asks Grissom directly if they have the Strangler behind bars, he says they don't. The Sheriff removes Grissom from the case unless and until it can be proved that Walden isn't responsible for any death other than his wife. He's sent on a fortnight's leave. Catherine visits Grissom at home and tells him that she won't accept a promotion because he's politically tone-deaf. Everyone is ready to work the case in their own time.

Grissom sends his team out to re-examine the crime scenes. Greg gets a CODIS match on the sperm sample – it comes from Hunter F. Baumgartner, a bartender at the Dungeon Club. He's also a red herring – a male prostitute whose semen has been taken and deposited at the crime scenes, probably transported in little packets of ketchup.

Warrick and Sara come up with the theory that the towels may come from a gym club. All three victims tried out an introductory offer from Strong's Gym. Nick checks out the security guard Syd Goggle's story about someone burning rubber outside Eileen Snow's residence, but there is no evidence of that at all. Culpepper is aware that the CSIs are still working the case, and warns Nick not to let Grissom run him out of a job.

Grissom goes to Goggle's place, and finds him doing his laundry. Goggle is hairless – he has been deliberately ensuring there is no DNA evidence. Grissom has been snooping around Goggle's garbage and faces him with the evidence he's found, but Goggle attacks him. Grissom is saved by Catherine, who arrives in the nick of time, along with Culpepper – who then takes the credit for the case.

Personal Notes: Grissom still appears haunted by Dominic Kretzker's help (see **12**, 'Boom'); he refuses Syd Goggle's help so he avoids the same fate. Brass is equally haunted by sending Holly Gribbs out into the field on her first night (see **00**, 'Pilot'). Sara is trained in weaponless defence. We see inside Grissom's home: there are butterfly cases around, and a good hi-fi system. He suffers from migraines.

The Wit and Wisdom of Gil Grissom: 'A signature killer always knows his victim. But they don't know him. Until he tortures, rapes and kills them.'

'Listen Sara, if we study his past, we can predict his future.'

'Sometimes the hardest thing is to do nothing.'

'Occasionally I'm struck by the absence of evidence.'

Classic Dialogue: Sheriff Mobley to Grissom: 'Next time you want to play with my career, you'll think twice.'

Culpepper: 'We'll work the Strip Strangler case in conjunction.' Grissom: 'The what?' Culpepper 'He strangles them near Las Vegas Boulevard, then removes their clothes. Strip Strangler. Why, what've you been calling him?' Grissom: 'Unknown Signature Homicide, Metropolitan Las Vegas.'

Worst 'As You Know': 'MO's how he breaks in, signature's what he does once inside.' Brass explains for those of us who don't know. Except he's talking to Grissom.

Fantastic Voyages: We take a close look at the object that Doc Robbins found in the uterine wall, at the towel fibre embedded in Eileen's teeth and at the fragment of golf glove left after Brad Walden used it to kill his wife.

The Usual Suspects: Maureen Muldoon (Lynda Darby) returns as, presumably, the same pushy reporter who was asking questions in **18**, 'Gentle, Gentle'. Gregg Henry (Special Agent Rick Culpepper) plays Jonathan Wallace in the second season of *24*, and lit up the screen as Val Resnick in Mel Gibson's brutal thriller *Payback*. Rainn Wilson (the supermarket suspect) was the communications officer on *Galaxy Quest*, and is a regular as Arthur on *Six Feet Under*. Michael Cerveris (Syd Goggle) began his career as Ian Ware on the TV series of *Fame*.

Real-life Inspirations: This episode may have been based upon the Seattle-based signature killer George Russell. In a two-month span in 1990, he murdered three women, one in an alley, the following two in their homes. The *Seattle*

Times reported that 'The MO or modus operandi changed, but each woman's body was found grotesquely posed, an obvious and rare signature that revealed his distinct compulsion.' An additional inspiration may have been the San Diego killings carried out by Cleophus Prince Jr, the Clairemont Killer. It was believed that Prince identified his victims at a health club.

Mistakes Really Can Be Fatal: If Greg could easily discern that the 'red stuff' in the semen was ketchup, why couldn't it be recognised by whoever worked on it before him?

Notes: This episode was to have had a five-day shoot in Las Vegas, but script revisions changed it to one day.

Although Special Agent Rick Culpepper hasn't annoyed Grissom again in the series yet, he gets his comeuppance in the first official spin-off novel, *Double Dealer*.

Overall: The first season concludes with a very different sort of episode, in which Grissom gets a chance to play Quincy and carry on investigating even though he's been suspended. Gregg Henry slimes beautifully as Special Agent Rick Culpepper, and there are some great moments between William Petersen and Marg Helgenberger.

Season Two

Regular Cast:

William Petersen (Gil Grissom)
Marg Helgenberger (Catherine Willows)
Gary Dourdan (Warrick Brown) credited but does not appear in **29** 'Caged'
George Eads (Nick Stokes)
Jorja Fox (Sara Sidle)
Paul Guilfoyle (Jim Brass) credited but does not appear in **39** 'Felonious Monk'
Eric Szmanda (Greg Sanders)
Robert David Hall (Doc Robbins)

Geoffrey Rivas (Detective Sam Vega 23, 30, 32, 34)
Sheeri Rappaport (CSI technician Mandy 23)
Skip O'Brien (Sgt O'Riley 25–29, 39, 42)
Glenn Morshower (Sheriff Brian Mobley 25)
David Berman (Deputy coroner David Phillips 25–28, 30, 31, 34, 37, 39, 40, 42, 43)
Christopher Wiehl (Emergency medical technician Hank Peddigrew 26, 36)
Eric Stonestreet (CSI Questioned Documents technician Ronnie Litre 26, 27, 32, 43)
Brad Johnson (Paul Newsome 27)
Wayne Wilderson (CSI firearms technician 28, 29)
Gerald McCullouch (CSI firearms technician Bobby Dawson 28, 30, 31, 34)
Archie Kao (CSI audio/visual technician Archie Johnson 29, 31, 35, 41)
Tom Gallop (Attorney Randy Painter 31)
Susan Gibney (Charlotte, Lab Technician 31)
Marc Vann (CSI daytime shift leader Conrad Ecklie 32, 39)
Palmer Davis (Public defender Margaret Finn 34)
Madison McReynolds (Lindsey Willows 36)
Jeffrey D. Sams (Detective Lockwood 38, 43)
Joseph Patrick Kelley (Officer Metcalf 42, 43, 44)

23
Burked

US Air Date: 27 September 2001 14.2/21
UK Air Date: 2 February 2002

Written by: Carol Mendelsohn, Anthony E. Zuiker
Directed by: Danny Cannon
Guest Cast: Scott Wilson (Sam Braun), Melissa Crider (Janine Haywood),
Brenda Bakke (Bonnie Ritten), Fredric Lane (Curt Ritten),
Joseph Will (Walt Braun), Jeff Ricketts (Skinny),
Richard Ethan Courtney (Tony Braun), Hilary Crouse (Receptionist),
Tony Genaro (Gardener), Jeff Ricketts (Deliveryman)

Teaser One-liner: 'Blinds were drawn shut. Side gate unlocked. Dogs let out. "A" plus "B" plus "C" equals 911.'

The Case: A gardener arrives at work and is surprised to find the owner's dogs running free. Looking through the window, he can just see the legs of his employer, mobster Tony Braun, stretched out on the floor. The CSIs arrive to find Braun, an empty bottle of pills by his hand, an empty wine glass and some foil on the table beside him. It looks like a drug overdose, but Grissom is convinced otherwise.

Sara finds an earring near the body, while Grissom takes a sample of a sticky substance on Braun's wrists. Sara is surprised that there are none of the body fluids she'd expect to find after an overdose – maybe he has been cleaned up. There are also three spots on Braun's upper chest. He has been posed, and this is clearly a homicide.

The back gate has been left open, and was opened with a key, since there's no sign of forced entry. Also, a treasure trove of drugs is uncovered, including black tar heroin in balloons, and Sara finds some duct tape stuffed inside a cracker box in the rubbish in the kitchen. Nick notices that the dog flap in the back door is open, although the door is locked. On a hunch, he prints the area around the door.

Doc Robbins confirms that Tony was a heavy drug user, but can't explain the circular marks on his chest. He might have been suffocated. Grissom thinks he was restrained and forced to ingest lethal amounts of heroin and Xanax.

Janine Haywood, Braun's current girlfriend, who is very proprietorial about the house and its contents, claims that she left Tony alive and well when his drug dealer arrived the previous day.

Catherine visits Sam Braun, Tony's father, who has known her since she was a baby. His other son, Walt, is a pit boss at the Casino. Sam clearly adored Tony, but doesn't know who would kill him though he feels Janine Haywood is a gold digger. Grissom takes Janine's prints from the prescription bottle, as Warrick gets Tony's drug dealer's prints from one of the drug balloons. Nick is suffering from chigger bites on his leg, which Grissom deduces came from the ferns in Tony's backyard.

There are no undissolved Xanax pills in Tony's stomach, which is very unusual in an overdose case. The pills were probably dissolved in the red wine, but out of the hundred in the bottle, only fifty were used. Interrogating Tony's drug dealer, Warrick and Brass discover that Janine gave him thirty Xanax as a tip when he delivered the drugs the night before. Janine denies it and claims she was with a girlfriend, who's now out of town.

The mass spectrometer reading on Braun's blood reveals that the drugs in his system weren't enough to kill him, so, after Doc Robbins discovers that Tony's lungs had been compressed, Catherine and Grissom use Tony's shirt on a dummy to re-enact Braun's death. Grissom believes that Tony was 'burked' – someone knelt on his chest while covering his nose and made him drink the cocktail. The marks from the buttons on Tony's shirt match the marks on Tony's chest.

The CSIs are called out to Blue Diamond in the desert, where Brass has discovered Curt Ritten, a friend of Tony Braun's, digging furiously. Inside Ritten's truck are rolls of duct tape. The police carry on digging and discover an underground vault filled with silver bullion and silver items. The tape is taken back to the lab, where the end of one of the rolls is matched to the piece of tape Sara found in the rubbish. Catherine and Detective Vega get a warrant to check out Ritten's apartment, and discover Janine Haywood there.

However, the prints from the tape don't match either Ritten or Janine. The prints from the dog flap belong to Walt Braun, although the prints on the tape aren't his. Ritten's wife Bonnie comes to bail him out of jail, and Ritten has to choose between her and Janine. Janine loses.

Walt Braun claims that he had to use the dog flap a few weeks earlier to get into the house because Tony forgot his keys. He has a working back gate key, but not a front door key, because Tony changed the locks. Grissom notices that Walt is scratching his leg, and confirms that it's a chigger bite. Walt denies that he's been anywhere apart from the casino and his apartment, but the chigger marks are identical to those on Nick's leg, and show that he was at his brother's house recently.

Brass reveals that Sam Braun's will leaves everything to Tony, but Tony had agreed to split everything with Walt until very recently when he agreed to split his estate with Janine. The earring Sara found doesn't fit Janine, who doesn't wear studs. Janine doesn't think there could be another woman at the house, except the maid, who's old and heavyset, and comes in every day except her day off – the day Tony died.

Bonnie Ritten is brought in. It's her prints on the duct tape, and it's her earring. She refuses to talk, but Walt Braun confirms that they were responsible for the murder. They met at a party Tony threw where they were united by their mutual dislike of Janine.

Personal Notes: Sam Braun's introduction marks the start of the revelations about Catherine that will continue throughout the series. Braun has known Catherine since she was six months old and wishes he had married her mother. Catherine clearly regards him as a surrogate father. He refers to her affectionately as 'Mugs'. At some point in the past, Catherine bailed Eddie out of jail only to find him wanting to head off with some other female. Greg used to live in New York and knows some of the more arcane methods of taking drugs.

Techniques: Grissom gets prints off the prescription bottle by heating glue and exposing the bottle to the fumes in a sealed environment, which reveals what's there. Warrick uses the same procedure, cyanoacrylate fuming, to get a print from the balloon. Sara gets the prints from the duct tape by freezing it.

Grissom rubs carbon paper on Tony Braun's shirt buttons so they'll leave a mark on the dummy.

The Wit and Wisdom of Gil Grissom: 'Would you mind if I took a photograph for my bite collection?'

'Sometimes, doing the job that we do, our biggest break comes from the most innocent circumstance.'

Classic Dialogue: Warrick: 'I can get a print off air!'

Sam Braun: 'I remember the first time I saw you. You didn't have any clothes on . . . I would've taken you home right then . . .' Catherine: 'But you were married and I was a baby. It would've never worked.'

Fantastic Voyages: We look inside the balloon, showing the tar heroin on its interior. We travel towards the 'hamburger', which is all that's left of Tony Braun's nose. We also see the chigger at work ingesting blood.

The Usual Suspects: Melissa Crider (Janine Haywood) played William Petersen's daughter in *Peter Benchley's The Beast* miniseries, and was Sharon Rooney in the second year of *Murder One*. Scott Wilson (Sam Braun) played General George C. Marshall in *Pearl Harbor*. Joseph Will (Walt Braun) makes semi-regular appearances as Crewman Michael Rostov on *Enterprise*.

Pop Culture References: Catherine makes a sarcastic reference to Sherlock Holmes. Grissom quotes from John Milton's poem *Comus*.

Real-life Inspirations: The episode has strong resemblances to the September 1998 murder by Sandy Murphy and Rick Tabish of Ted Binion, a casino executive with a heroin addiction. It was initially thought to be an overdose, but turned out to be a case of 'burking' – deliberate suffocation after taking heroin and Xanax. The evidence is strikingly similar to the evidence found at Tony Braun's house.

Mistakes Really Can Be Fatal: Grissom's knowledge of Burke and Hare seems to derive from the 1959 movie *The Flesh and The Fiends*, in which Peter Cushing discovers his fiancée's body is one of the graverobbers' victims.

The half-life of heroin is only three minutes, according to the American National Institute on Drug Abuse, not nine.

Notes: Although this was the first episode of Season Two to be aired, it was shot second. Sections of B roll footage, showing the actors at work in the casino and out in the desert, are contained on the UK DVD box set of Season One, indicating that the script was revised on 25 July 2001.

The episode itself is set on 26 September 2001 (Tony Braun's pills issued 'yesterday' were dated 25 September). It was originally going to air on 20 September, but was pushed back a week because of the ongoing alterations to the schedules after the attack on the World Trade Center on 11 September 2001.

Early versions of the script had the characters named Ben Gochner (Sam Braun), Ted Gochner (Tony Braun), Steven Gochner (Walter Braun) and Janine Harlow (Janine Haywood).

Overall: A strong start to the season, eliminating all the politics that was cluttering up the end of the previous year, and giving us a 'straightforward' case for the CSIs to investigate.

24
Chaos Theory

US Air Date: 4 October 2001 12.6/19
UK Air Date: 9 February 2002

Written by: Eli Talbert, Josh Berman
Directed by: Ken Fink
Guest Cast: Dale Midkiff (Robert Woodbury),
Clayne Crawford (Henry McFadden), Garrett M. Brown (Mr Rycoff),
Sherry Hursey (Mrs Rycoff), Danielle Nicolet (Jennifer Riggs),
Shelby Fenner (Paige Rycoff), Kate McNeil (Sharon Woodbury),
Grant Garrison (Kevin Watson), Paula Francis (Herself),
Jon Herschfield (N.D. Student), Archie Kao (Campus Security Tech),
Brent Sexton (Mark Doyle)

Teaser One-liner: 'People don't vanish, Jim. It's a molecular impossibility.'

The Case: The CSI team are called in to investigate the disappearance of student Paige Rycoff from her dorm room at Las Vegas University. She seemed set to drop out of college and return to her parents in Boulder, Colorado, even going so far as to confirm to the taxi driver that she was about to come downstairs to go to the airport. But she never arrived. Grissom checks the room, and finds her plane ticket still inside her handbag, and her suitcase still there. There's no sign of a struggle, and there are no keys in her bag, so Grissom can't understand why she didn't just walk back into her room.

There are turnstiles to prevent unauthorised entry and security cameras everywhere. Nick checks the video from the cameras. Sara discovers that Paige asked for all her mail, including her security deposit, to be forwarded and that Paige's room-mate, Jennifer Riggs, left school two weeks into the term. Grissom notices that something has been removed from the room, possibly a rug.

Warrick and Catherine examine the garbage chute, which has a broken spring, but there's nothing down it. The sniffer dogs are having as little luck. Sara looks for DNA evidence in Paige's room and finds blood and semen. Nick checks the tapes and discovers someone reaching up to block off one of the cameras. He gets a print from the wall where the camera blocker supported himself and it leads them to student Henry McFadden, who admits that he stole rugs from the floor that Paige was living on as a prank, but denies having anything to do with her death. They had dated but she broke it off, and was now dating 'someone more mature'.

Greg checks out the samples Sara found against the DNA from the items in Paige's handbag. The blood isn't Paige's, but it contains the date-rape drug Rohypnol and matches the vaginal contribution to the semen stain. Paige's former room-mate confirms that she was date-raped by someone from her own floor but doesn't know who. The CSIs take DNA from the students and the semen matches Kevin Watson. Although they can get him for Jennifer's rape, he has a confirmed alibi for Paige's disappearance.

Nick and Catherine check the video and spot a car repeatedly circling the building around the time of Paige's disappearance. Close examination reveals an LVU parking permit, which belongs to Professor Robert Woodbury. When questioned he admits that he had an affair with Paige. He was going to try to persuade Paige not to leave but she never came downstairs. He said nothing previously because he's married. He says Paige never went to his house or got in his car, but Nick finds light hairs in the car, which match Paige's. Woodbury still denies that Paige was in the car, and says he knows nothing about a phone call from his home to Paige as he was at a faculty lunch at the time. Mrs Woodbury admits that she met Paige, but says that she caught her hair in the headrest accidentally. The interrogation is stopped by the news that Paige's body has been found crushed in the dumpster at the bottom of the garbage chute.

Doc Robbins confirms that she was dead before she was crushed. She died as a result of massive internal bleeding from a ruptured spleen caused by blunt force trauma. Nick finds some paint specks on the dumpster, and they theorise that Paige might have been hit by a car which also hit the dumpster, and the driver then dumped Paige's body inside. The car is identified as an 89 or 90 Cherokee, which is traced to faculty member Mark Doyle. He admits cutting through the alleyway and hitting the dumpster, but analysis confirms there's no human DNA on his car.

Trying to recreate Paige's last moments, Sara and Grissom realise that just before leaving, she would have taken out the rubbish. They theorise that Paige dropped the whole can down the chute (breaking the spring), and therefore had to go down to get the can out of the dumpster. It was her bad luck that at that moment Mark Doyle drove through the alleyway, hitting the dumpster, catching Paige between it and the wall. She was knocked unconscious and fell into the dumpster where she bled to death internally. It was an accident – even if Paige's parents refuse to believe it.

Personal Notes: The first clear hints of Grissom's deafness are shown when he can't quite hear what the Rycoffs are saying to him. Warrick attended Las Vegas University. Doc Robbins used to work in Arlington, Virginia.

Techniques: Sara uses an argon-ion laser to trace DNA. (The props man spent a day learning how to use it from Lt Charles Illsey of the West Valley Police before instructing Jorja Fox for the scene.)

Greg uses computer databases CO-Filer and Profiler Plus to check the DNA.

The paint found at the dumpster is analysed to check its light absorption rate – every paint has a different rate so it can be identified.

The Wit and Wisdom of Gil Grissom: 'In this case, more is less – the more time goes by the less chance we have of finding this girl.'

'This is the worst place you can be on a missing person – a dead end.'

'You know, when a tree falls in the forest even if no one's there to hear it, it does, in fact, make a sound.'

'I can't be everywhere, Warrick. And they banned human cloning.'

Classic Dialogue: Grissom: 'What does that look like?' Catherine: 'A five-foot-eleven workaholic.'

Fantastic Voyages: Pulling a hair out at the roots. Paige's rib cracking and spleen rupturing causing blood to spout out.

The Usual Suspects: Dale Midkiff (Professor Woodbury) played the lead character, Darien Lambert, on the sci-fi show *Time Trax*, and was Louis Creed in the underrated film of Stephen King's *Pet Sematary*. Sherry Hursey (Mrs Rycoff) played regular guest star Ilene Markham in the comedy series *Home Improvement*. Garrett M. Brown (Mr Rycoff) played Philip in the final season of *Roswell*.

Pop Culture References: Brass mentions that Kevin Watson also plays as number 25, like top baseball player Mark McGwire. Grissom quotes from Henry David Thoreau and misquotes from H.L. Mencken. Warrick jokingly refers to Nick as Nostradamus, the sixteenth-century astrologer.

Real-life Inspirations: At the time of transmission, a number of US magazines drew parallels between this episode and the case of the missing Washington intern Chandra Levy, whose murder has still, at the time of writing, not been solved.

Overall: A slightly weak episode, it feels as if new red herrings are thrown in just to fill in the second act. Could have done with a separate B plot to involve the rest of the team more.

25
Overload

US Air Date: 11 October 2001 13.8/21
UK Air Date: 16 February 2002

Written by: Josh Berman
Directed by: Richard J. Lewis
Guest Cast: Brenda Strong (Dr Leigh Sapien),
Harold Thomas Wright (Robert Harris), David Sutcliffe (Ian Wolf),
Gina Hecht (Mrs Buckley), Kelly Connell (Randy Gesek),
Marc Christie (Driver), Zane B. Holtz (Dylan Buckley),
Rocky McMurray (Construction Worker)

Teaser One-liner: 'On the day you decide to end your life, why would you go to work?'

The Cases: A hard hat falls from high up on a construction building, closely followed by its owner, Roger Valenti. The Sheriff is surprised to find Grissom at the scene, since he's been told by the site manager, Robert Harris, that it's a clear-cut case of suicide. Grissom disagrees.

The building is going to be a desperately needed, new county jail, and there's a lot of pressure on Harris to get it completed. Grissom discovers that Valenti's drill has shorted out. The circuit interrupter should have ensured that he didn't get a massive shock, but the third prong on the plug has been cut short.

Virtually every bone in Valenti's body is fractured or broken. Doc Robbins can find no physical evidence of electrocution, but Grissom is convinced it wasn't an accident, and unusually wants to work backwards from the conclusion to the evidence. There is no trace of melting on Valenti's boots, but the wires inside the drill have been tampered with. Sara believes that Valenti should have been safe from the shock anyway because of his boots, so looks for a conductor – and finds a nail in his boot.

The print on the cutters belongs to Robert Harris, who claims that he regularly checks the tools on the site. Brass tells Grissom that Valenti was the new union representative, looking for increased overtime pay, and that Bob Harris was the Sheriff's Best Man. Both the Sheriff and Harris are still convinced that Valenti was not electrocuted and that it was suicide.

Grissom is approached by Ian Wolf, Roger Valenti's predecessor as union rep. He says his family was threatened if he didn't cave in to the company's terms, so he resigned. Grissom wants to look at the body again, but it's been released for disposal. He takes Robbins through his notes, and discovers that Valenti's skin was yellow and there was a high concentration of iron in his blood. He asks about his testicles, but Robbins didn't notice anything unusual. Funeral Director Randy Gesek agrees to allow Valenti's corpse to be viewed – his testicles are atrophied and Grissom gets Gesek to pull a pint of Valenti's blood. He asks Sara to dust the nail found in Valenti's boot, and test the metal cutters found at the scene to see if they cut the drill's grounding prong. She gets a print off the nail, but the metal cutters weren't used on the drill. Grissom checks Valenti's blood and finds that it was capable of conducting electricity.

Grissom borrows a dill pickle from Sara and electrocutes it – but there are no signs of electrocution on it, because it is high in sodium, another electricity conductor, like iron. However, Greg has bad news: the print on the nail doesn't belong to Bob Harris, and the Sheriff wants Grissom to make a full public apology. Grissom is determined to prove it's murder and gets Brass to talk to Ian Wolf. Before he does so, Brass discovers that Wolf attacked Valenti four days before the murder, and there's a possibility he's trying to get Harris framed for the murder he committed. When they discover that the print on the nail matches Wolf's and his tool cutters fit the marks on the drill, Brass arrests him. The Sheriff admits that Grissom might not need to make a public apology after all.

Catherine and Nick investigate the death of a 14-year-old boy, Dylan Buckley. He died in the middle of a session with his psychiatrist, Dr Leigh Sapien. She says that he suffered from Reactive Attachment Disorder. He was an epileptic, and she believed that he was having a grand mal seizure. Nick notices a fibre on Sapien's sweater, and they tape lift it. He then checks through Dylan's clothes and finds the same tan-coloured fibres on his white boxer shorts. Doc Robbins tells him that Dylan died of cranial-cerebral injuries, which at first glance appear consistent with a grand mal seizure. But Dylan is covered in bruises and tan fibres, like the ones on his underwear. Why would he be with his psychiatrist dressed only in his underwear?

Sergeant O'Riley tells Nick and Catherine that Dr Sabien has had her licence suspended in the past for sex with a minor. Greg identifies the fibres as goat hairs. The CSIs search Dr Sabien's house and find a blanket that matches the fibres. Sabien is still adamant that she did nothing to Dylan.

The lab tests show that Dylan's blood didn't have the elevated levels of creatine kinase, which it should have after a seizure. Catherine feels that Nick is competing with her to solve the case and confronts him, and he admits that he was assaulted when he was nine years old.

Greg checks out the blanket from Dr Sapien's house, and finds DNA from Dylan, Sapien and Dylan's mother on it. Doc Robbins discovers that the blanket fibres were inside Dylan's body as well – he was wrapped inside the blanket from head to toe. Mrs Buckley finally admits that they were trying a re-birthing experience, which went

disastrously wrong. Dylan struggled to get free, but she and Dr Sapien wouldn't let him loose, and he died of suffocation.
Personal Notes: Nick was assaulted by his babysitter when he was nine years old, and becomes very engrossed with Dylan's case when it appears there might be similar aspects. Doc Robbins' youngest child has just turned 14 years old; it's also his wedding anniversary.

Techniques: Grissom superglues the prints to the metal cutters to ensure they're secure.
The Wit and Wisdom of Gil Grissom: 'Man versus Gravity. Man lost.'

'Every now and then we have to break the rules. Start with the conclusion and work our way backwards.'

'Bodies tell a story because we interpret them the way our predecessors taught us to. Just because we don't see something we're supposed to see doesn't mean that it's not there.'
Classic Dialogue: Grissom: 'I need to see his testicles.' Randy Gesek: 'I always thought there was something weird about you.'

Sheriff Mobley: 'Actions have consequences, Gil. Even yours.'
Fantastic Voyages: We watch a burn mark that would have appeared on Roger Valenti's arm if he had been electrocuted, then we see what would have happened to his chest. We take a close look at the nail in his boot. The pattern of electricity going through the body is charted. We see the inside of Valenti's drill when the current meets the crossed wires and goes back out to him. We also see the pressure cracking Dylan Buckley's skull, and the fibres from the blanket going into his throat.
The Usual Suspects: Kelly Connell returns as Randy Gesek. Brenda Strong (Dr Sapien) played Kathleen Isley on *Party of Five*. Tom Wright (Robert Harris) was Lt Benjamin Winship on martial arts cop show *Martial Law*. Canadian actor David Sutcliffe (Ian Wolf) plays Christopher Hayden on *The Gilmore Girls*, and was Adam in the US version of *Cold Feet*.

Real-life Inspirations: Nick and Catherine's case is based on the April 2000 case of ten-year-old Candace Newmaker who was suffocated in a rebirthing therapy session held in Colorado.

Mistakes Really Can Be Fatal: Grissom talks about terminal velocity when he means the gravity acceleration.

Notes: This episode was nominated for an Emmy for Outstanding Make-Up for a Series (Prosthetic). Its first US transmission was delayed for President Bush's speech against terrorism in the wake of 11 September.

Overall: The various theories that are put forward by Grissom, Sara and Warrick have come in for considerable criticism from experts for being far-fetched, and it's one of the few times that the show really bends credibility. Nick and Catherine's case is depressingly realistic, although I'm not sure whether we needed to see a re-enactment of the supposed sexual abuse between Dr Sabien and Dylan, particularly with Nick standing there in a rather chilling Peeping-Tom way.

26
Bully for You

US Air Date: 18 October 2001 14.1/12
UK Air Date: 23 February 2002

Written by: Ann Donahue
Directed by: Thomas J. Wright
Guest Cast: Dublin James (Dennis Fram), Lisa Brenner (Kelsey Fram),
Joseph Kell (Peter Dram), Jamie Martz (Aaron Schragen),
Tess Harper (Julia Barrett), Jameson Baltes (Bram aka 'Flinch'),
Brady Bluhm (Alan), Thomas Crawford (Janitor), Josh Gilman (Dylan),
Michael Krawic (Moses/William Cartsen),
Randy Lowell (Principal Perrin)

Teaser One-liner: 'People usually aren't scared of class clowns.'

The Cases: High school student Barry Schickle confidently spray paints some graffiti onto a locker at school before going into the bathroom – where he is shot in the back.

Catherine and Warrick join Grissom at the scene, and prevent the janitor from removing Schickle's handiwork from the locker. Principal Perrin confirms that it isn't unusual for a student to still be in school that late in the evening.

Grissom starts stringing the bullet holes as Catherine spots an orange-smudged thumbprint on the inside of one of the bathroom stalls. From the stringing Warrick and Grissom deduce that the shooter was quite short, maybe five foot three or four tall. Warrick takes a sample of the air.

School Counsellor Julia Barrett tells Catherine that Barry had graffitied Dennis Fram's locker many times before, with comments about his slight build. Dennis is the right height for the shooter, and Grissom runs tests on his shirt where gunshot residue is found. Dennis claims it's from target practice at a shooting range – a story his sister can corroborate. At that moment his older sister Kelsey bursts into the room and accuses Brass of harassing her brother.

Doc Robbins shows Grissom the path of the bullets. The second one punctured his lung and the third hit his heart, which is opposite the normal place, as Barry had dextrocardia – his organs are on opposite sides. Robbins also discovers that someone tried to stab Barry six months earlier and only his dextrocardia saved him.

Barry's parents don't know he was stabbed, and Julia Barrett points out that Barry was a bully so there were probably a dozen kids who wanted him dead. Dylan, one of the students questioned, however, admits that he did try to kill him using a fork, but he has an alibi for the shooting.

Catherine checks how long it takes the paint to dry, Warrick runs the test on the air sample and Grissom works on the angles of the bullets. Catherine can place Dennis Fram at the scene and she and Brass go to confront him. It was Dennis' print smudged in the orange paint on the bathroom wall and, because the paint doesn't take long to dry, he had to be there at the time of the murder. Dennis gets a panic attack and Catherine watches as his sister feeds him ulcer medicine. Kelsey is five foot four in heels.

Grissom and Warrick find something unusual in the air sample – a perfume. Using the software from an expensive electronic nose, Grissom finds that it's Chanteuse – a perfume which Kelsey uses. She is questioned but says she was out driving around.

Dennis eventually admits he was at the school, but was hiding in the bathroom when the shots were fired. Brass discovers that Kelsey got a parking ticket at the time of the shooting, as did the high school coach, who admits that Kelsey slept with him to try to get him to intercede with Barry. Dennis thinks Kelsey was the murderer because he smelt her perfume, but it wasn't her. It was counsellor Julia Barrett, who also wore Chanteuse. She killed Barry to prevent another Columbine-type massacre carried out by one of his victims. As a result of its efficacy, Grissom orders the expensive electronic nose for the department.

Nick and Sara are taken by helicopter to Red Rock where a large leather bag containing the skeleton of a hand has been found. The bag is taken back to the lab, where it is X-rayed, showing up a silver dollar, a four-inch medical implanted pin, and a plate that has come from a skull. Inside the bag, they also find an army jacket and a gaming chip. All that's left otherwise is human soup, which is washed down the drain.

Sara finds a nametag: W Cartsen, and Nick finds a matchbook in the jacket pocket, which he takes to Questioned Documents. Ronnie Litre is able to read some writing on the cover: Romanini's, the name of a nightclub. The body is identified from his dog tags: former Lt William Cartsen, who left hospital 31 years ago and hasn't been heard of since.

Aaron Schragen, the manager of Romanini's, recognises Cartsen as 'Moses', a drifter who was causing problems two months earlier outside the club. He claims he gave him a gaming chip and sent him on his way. This tallies with the time that Cartsen died, so Schragen is arrested. He then claims he left Cartsen out by Red Rock. However, he gets nervous when he's told there are prints on the bag Cartsen was found in. He then admits that Cartsen was drunk, so he put him in the bag and rolled him down the hill. He figured that Cartsen would be able to free himself – but he didn't, and died.

Personal Notes: Catherine admits that she was a bit of a bully at school, while Nick was 'dependable'. Sara was a science nerd. Warrick was short, had big feet and thick glasses, and got bullied. Sara meets Hank Peddigrew for the first time, and there's a spark between them. However, when he comes to visit her, she stinks of Liquid Man's remains. She also develops more respect for David Phillips after his calm way of handling the liquid corpse. Warrick likes using the cool toys – and admits it!

Techniques: Warrick uses a Polymer Sensor Proboscis, the Cyranose 320, which is effectively an electronic nose using polymer plastics, painted with conductive material to absorb and identify odorants. Grissom hands him a flask and an air pump to do the same thing, to which Warrick adds some crushed chalk to act as an absorbent. However, the software in the Cyranose 320 can break down the components of a perfume into its constituent parts.

The Wit and Wisdom of Gil Grissom: 'If that thing ran out of here and bit the shooter in the ass, the county would not approve a $10,000 purchase order.'

'Our job is to think, Warrick. Machinery should never matter more than our mind.'

'Do you ever smell a fart and end up blaming the wrong guy?'

Classic Dialogue: Brass: 'Well, the nerd squad is off and running. I'm going to burn a little shoe leather.'

Warrick: 'What were you? A jock or a brain?' Grissom: 'I was a ghost.'

Grissom: 'Scent triggers memory more acutely than any of the five senses.' Catherine: 'Yeah? Well, I smell a rat in the Fram family.'

Nick: 'Treating another human being like garbage is not a job. It's a choice.'

Fantastic Voyages: We take a close look at the thumbprint on the bathroom wall, and watch gunshot residue being created as a handgun is fired. The operation of the airflask is shown in detail as the chalk absorbs the air. We see the bullets going into Barry's body, and also the fork trying to puncture his heart. We also watch paint dry in extreme detail!

The Usual Suspects: Tess Harper (Ms Barrett) played Lois Hobson throughout the fantasy series *Early Edition*.

Pop Culture References: When Grissom mentions Doctor No, it is the character from the Ian Fleming novel, in which the villain suffers from dextrocardia, to which he refers, rather than the 1962 movie.

Real-life Inspirations: The bodies of the 1993 Waco victims liquified in the heat when the cooler at the county morgue failed. The actual case is based on an unsolved murder where the victim liquified in a canvas bag.

Mistakes Really Can Be Fatal: Why don't they take tox screens of Cartsen's remains?

The envelope going to the Federal Grant Department has differing numbers of address lines in different shots.

The timeline has gone a little screwy, assuming that we're seeing the cases in the order they happen. **23**, 'Burked' took place on 26 September 2001; however, this episode takes place on 18 September, according to the date that Cartsen is logged into the coroner's system.

Notes: Initially there was going to be a separate nightclub bouncer, Roger, who was responsible for the dirty work, rather than Schragen himself.

Overall: Only *CSI* could make you watch paint dry and make it interesting! Julia Barrett's motivation – she witnessed a Columbine-type massacre – is a bit 'out there', and detracts from the overall effect of the A story. The B plot once again gives some much needed focus on Nick Stokes, probably the most underdeveloped character in the first season.

27
Scuba Doobie-Doo

US Air Date: 25 October 2001 15.7/23
UK Air Date: 2 March 2002

Written by: Andrew Lipsitz and Elizabeth Devine
Directed by: Jefery Levy
Guest Cast: Mark Tymchyshyn (Stu Evans),
David DeLuise (Cliff Renteria), Rick Peters (Jerry Walden),
Jenna Gering (Alison Scott),
Terry Bozeman (Attorney), Marci Brickhouse (Nancy),
Terry Simpson (Steve)

Teaser One-liner: 'A human has only eight pints of blood.
So, whoever the victim is . . . is now dead.'
The Cases: Landlord Stuart Evans is showing two prospec-
tive tenants an apartment until they open the door to find
an empty room with blood everywhere. Grissom tests the
blood – it's human, and from the volume of it, whoever it
comes from must now be dead. Sara and Grissom examine
the bloodspatter while Warrick covers the room with
luminol, which shows up the voids where the blood isn't.
The gaps indicate a couch, a television, a magazine, a coat
rack and possibly an electric saw – which would have made
the bloodspatter found. The apartment's previous tenants
were Cliff Renteria and his girlfriend Alison, but the
landlord says he hasn't seen Alison in over a month.

Brass tracks down Renteria, who says Alison is visiting
her parents in Canada. He says the landlord 'had it
coming' so he trashed the place with his blood – he gets
nosebleeds from hepatitis C. Grissom doesn't believe him
– the patterns are wrong, V-shaped rather than ovals.
Renteria is living out of a truck, inside which Grissom sees
an electric saw and a lamp with some blood on it. Renteria
gives a blood sample, which matches the blood in the
apartment. However, the blood from the lamp is from a
female. Sara and Warrick test different electric saws to see
which ones would make the spatter patterns found.

Alison's parents have said that she never went
to Canada. Both Grissom and Sara notice a high

preponderance of flies, which only feed on fresh blood. Searching through the vent in Renteria's apartment, Grissom finds a Silphid beetle, which feeds on decomposing flesh, and the CSIs ask permission to break into the walls. The landlord refuses. Sara and Warrick extract a sample from the beetle and Greg confirms that the beetle is feeding on human remains, allowing the CSIs to get a warrant.

Grissom, Warrick and Sara go off to knock down the walls until they are surprised by Brass who introduces them to Alison Scott. She stubbed her toe on the lamp, causing the blood, and had gone back to an old boyfriend.

Undeterred, the CSIs move next door to Stuart Evans' apartment. Brass gets a warrant to knock down the walls in Evans' apartment, since his wife is missing. There's clear evidence of recent work on the walls, and when Grissom looks into the heating vent, there are masses of Silphid beetles.

Evans refuses to admit where his wife's body is, so the CSIs tear the building apart. When Grissom tries the hot water, there's no pressure. Checking the filtration tank, they find Evans' wife. All he can say is 'she nagged me'.

There's a major fire in the hills near Lake Mead, and a most unusual dead body: a scuba diver found up a tree. Nick believes it might be a real-life version of the urban myth of a diver caught up in a water bucket. The diver's pressure gauge is frozen stuck. There is an odd spot of unburned vegetation, which Catherine thinks might be from shifting winds, but Nick spots a cigarette butt and a matchbook which indicate arson.

Doc Robbins confirms that the scuba diver didn't die in the fire, but he wasn't dropped from a helicopter either. He had cardiac concussion – he was hit on the chest and it made his heart start fibrillating. Robbins also finds soap residue between his toes, which, Greg says, is probably liquid soap to help get the suit on.

Nick realises there's been an explosion in the diver's tank, and checks the serial number on the tank, which might tell them its user's identity. It leads them to Jerry Walden, who says he lent his business partner, experienced diver Bruce Skeller, a spare tank. Catherine notices the gap where a coffee table has been and finds splinters of wood on the floor, although Walden claims he sent the table away for refinishing.

Catherine gets District Engineer Paul Newsome (see **17**, '$35K O.B.O.') to check out the deeds regarding the land that Skeller and Walden owned together. It was sold a week earlier to Adventures Development, but from all accounts Skeller seemed unwilling to sell. Ronnie Litre at QD checks the original deed, and it all seems legitimate, albeit signed with two separate pens.

Greg gets DNA evidence from the cigarette butt to discover the smoker. Robbins combs Skeller's body and finds wood chips which match the pieces Catherine found at Walden's apartment.

Walden's lawyer doesn't think they've got a case, but Nick and Catherine explain that Walden killed Skeller, took the body out to the lake, dumped it there, set the fire, and expected the body to be burned in the fire. However, the gas tank exploded, sending Skeller into the tree.

Personal Notes: There's a tender moment between Grissom and Sara when she cleans some chalk off his face as he's outside trying to calm down (see **47**, 'The Accused is Entitled'). Paul Newsome isn't overly pleased with Catherine just using him. Catherine doesn't appreciate being called 'Cat'. Jim Brass worked in a slaughterhouse one summer, presumably during his college days. Greg used to do some diving, although he exaggerates the places he's been to.

Techniques: Greg runs a test to determine the amelogenin in the blood sample from the apartment. This shows the sex of the donor. Nick uses acid to get the serial number off the diver's tank.

Ronnie Litre uses a VSC-4 machine to check the wavelengths of the inks used on the land document.

The Wit and Wisdom of Gil Grissom: 'You never get a second chance to make a first impression.'

Classic Dialogue: Brass: 'I thought you said the blood on the wall couldn't be his.' Grissom: 'I also thought the metric system would catch on.'

Catherine: 'Hey, coffee boy. Where's my DNA? Cigarette butt? Matchbook time-delay device? Hair spray? Any of this sound familiar?' Greg: 'Bags under the eyes, coffee cups, stress face. Any of this look familiar?'

Fantastic Voyages: A voyage through a magnifying lens up to Grissom's eye. A version of the diver being caught up in the bucket. The hair spray, used to preserve the cigarette, coating the burned matchbook sticks, and the arson being set with the cigarette and the matchbook. A baseball hitting the centre of a player's chest then following the impact through to the now irregularly beating heart.

The Usual Suspects: Terry Bozeman returns as Attorney Lewis (see **18**, 'Gentle, Gentle'). Brad Johnson makes his final appearance to date as Paul Newsome before heading to New Zealand to film the TV pilot of *Riverworld*. David DeLuise (Cliff Renteria) played Bug on *3rd Rock From The Sun*. Jenna Gering (Alison Scott) played Kristen Moore on *NYPD Blue*.

Pop Culture References: Doc Robbins makes a joking reference to world-famous French underwater explorer Jacques Cousteau, and the title is of course a pun on the infamous children's cartoon series *Scooby-Doo*.

Real-life Inspirations: The idea of a diver caught up in an aircraft's water scoop and dumped in a tree is one of the most common American urban legends. Someone really did defile their apartment by spraying their blood around.

Mistakes Really Can Be Fatal: The CSIs should really have been wearing face masks when they were ripping out the fibreglass filters in the walls of the apartment.

Notes: Actor Matt Battaglia was supposed to be in this episode as a fire chief who becomes a love interest for Catherine, but that failed to materialise.

This episode is set around 9 October 2001 (the land deed from a week earlier is dated 2 October).

Overall: Some very nice touches make this episode one of the stronger contributions to the first half of the season. Eric Szmanda is starting to get more airtime, and there are the first hints that he might like to get out of the lab from time to time and contribute more fully to cases.

28
Alter Boys

US Air Date: 1 November 2001 14.5/21
UK Air Date: 9 March 2002

Written by: Ann Donahue
Directed by: Danny Cannon
Guest Cast: Dylan Baker (Father Powell),
Corbin Allred (Benjamin Jennings), Jeremy Renner (Roger Jennings),
Sasha Alexander (Robin Childs),
Lindsay Price (Kim Marita), Nicole DeHuff (Tina Kolas),
Craig Cady (Cell Cop), Tara D'Agostino (Shelley Danvers),
Paula Francis (Herself), Noel Guglielmi (David Ramirez),
Bill Kalmenson (Oliver Dunne), Ori Pfeffer (Kirk)

Teaser One-liner: 'You don't have to talk to us. He'll talk to us.'
The Cases: Simple-minded Benjamin Jennings is interrupted by a Park Ranger in the middle of burying a body. Preliminary examination indicates that the body has been moved from the murder scene, so Jennings' car is impounded. The CSIs process the suspect, finding a strand of hair on his back, and some red fibres. There are no wounds on him. Sara finds some flour on the corpse, and some fibres in the wound on his neck. He's wearing a dress shirt, but doesn't have a tie.

The body is identified as Oliver Dunne, a corporate lawyer, by his widow. Doc Robbins finds three .380 bullets in him, but it seems that he was actually asphyxiated. The flour is identified as coming from a pizza manufacturing company. Jennings owns a Lorcin 380 but claims he lost it. He admits he works at a pizza place, but won't say anything else although he inadvertently reveals there is more than one corpse. Returning to the site and using georadar, they find another body. As it is excavated, Grissom is approached by Father Powell, who wants to comfort Jennings, who is one of his parishioners. The second body is identified as Kenny Ramirez. O'Riley announces that Dunne's car has been found abandoned at a gas station, along with another car registered to Ramirez.

The gas station attendant admits leaving his post for a few minutes. When he returned, the cars were there. He also admits hosing down the blood that was on the forecourt.

Grissom is visited at the CSI garage by Father Powell, who is shocked by the blood that Grissom finds in the back of Jennings' car. Nick and Sara think they've nailed Jennings for murder – the bullets came from a gun similar to that registered to him, he used the gas station they were killed at, and there's blood in his car. There are also fibres from his car on the bodies. Grissom is dubious, but agrees to let them run the evidence past the DA.

Grissom does some background checking on Ben and discovers he has a record for non-violent crime, but his brother Roger is an armed robber. If he offends for a third time, he will face a major jail term. Ben refuses to admit that he only buried the bodies for his brother. Grissom and O'Riley visit the pizza parlour where Roger is working, and he claims that Ben told him that he did it. Grissom thinks otherwise, and the flour evidence supports his view. Nick and Sara check out Roger's trailer, and find dry-cleaned clothes – but dry-cleaning bakes blood in. They also find blood, and the murder weapon thrown in the rubbish.

Grissom checks the gun, but it jams after three tries. He realises that the reason Dunne was strangled was because the gun jammed. Unfortunately dry-cleaning the blood degraded the DNA too far, and the bullets don't match the test-fires from Jennings' gun. They don't have enough to hold Roger.

Grissom tries to persuade the DA not to pursue the case, but she tells him that Roger brought in the murder tie. It's got Ben's epithelials all over it – which, Ben tells Grissom, was from when his brother told him to pick it up. He believed his brother when he said that it would all blow over, and is horrified when he realises the reality of the situation. The DA pursues the case, but Ben Jennings kills himself rather than go to jail.

Catherine and Warrick are working a dead body at the Mediterranean Casino Women's Spa. First indications are that Shelley Danvers was sitting reading and just died.

However the CSIs believe she may have been moved. The maid, Kim Marita, admits that she covered the corpse with a robe but denies moving her into the sauna. Catherine suspects Shelley may have drowned in the Jacuzzi but Marita claims that Shelley didn't use it. Doc Robbins discovers that Shelley didn't drown, and there's bright red lividity down the body, possibly caused by heat stroke.

Shelley's best friend, Tina Kolas, with whom she travelled to Las Vegas, confirms that Shelley was heading off to the sauna. She says she can prove it – she rang down for an appointment from the room phone. Warrick takes the notepad from by the phone for checking by QD.

Marita says there is no record that Shelley used the sauna, but the notepad is clear that she wrote an appointment time down. The temperature is ideal for causing heatstroke, although a hotel employee should have checked everything was OK every fifteen minutes. However, the records show that no one came in between 7.30 p.m. and when Marita found Shelley around 10 p.m.

Catherine and Warrick are about to go off-shift when Brass tells them that he now knows that Shelley and Tina were arguing over a man named Jeremy on the day Shelley died. Checking the room service order against Shelley's medical records reveals the truth: she was allergic to shellfish. Tina had given her a bowl of soup which had some in, in order to make her mildly ill so she would miss her date with Jeremy, little realising what effect the combination of the sauna and the allergic reaction would have on her friend.

Personal Notes: Grissom is a lapsed Catholic.

Techniques: Nick uses a georadar machine that takes a radar picture underneath the soil.

Lividity is how blood shows on the surface of a body. At death gravity pulls the blood to the lowest part of the body; if a body's moved there will be marks from where the blood arrived the first time and from its second port of call – known as double lividity.

The Wit and Wisdom of Gil Grissom: 'How many crusades were fought in the name of God? How many people died because of someone's religion?'

Classic Dialogue: Grissom: 'We both have jobs that begin after the crime.' Powell: 'After the sin.' Grissom: 'Some people would call that a career in futility.' Powell: 'Some call it a vocation.'

Fantastic Voyages: We see the bullet entering Dunne's body, and also a graphic reconstruction from the inside of what it's like to be choked. We follow a bullet emerging from the barrel of the gun, catching the sides and causing the striations on the way out, and then a tool altering the shape of the barrel from the barrel's perspective.

The Usual Suspects: Sasha Alexander (DA Childs) played Gretchen Witter on *Dawson's Creek*; Corbin Allred (Ben Jennings) played the title character in the video series *Josh Kirby, Time Warrior*. Dylan Baker (Father Powell) played Senator Keith Ellison on *The Practice* and Dr Curt Connors, aka The Lizard, in *Spider-Man 2*. Jeremy Renner (Roger Jennings) played serial killer Jeffrey Dahmer in the 2002 biopic, *Dahmer*.

Pop Culture References: Sara references to Doubting Thomas, the apostle St Thomas who refused to believe in the Resurrection. Father Powell quotes from St Luke 12: 48.

Mistakes Really Can Be Fatal: The character of Kenny Ramirez is listed as David Ramirez in the end credits.

Why aren't the medics wearing gloves to deal with the bleeding Ben Jennings at the end?

Shouldn't one of the people who followed Shelley into the sauna have noticed a dead body there?

Notes: This episode begins on 24/25 October 2001 (Catherine's evidence bag note).

Overall: There's a lot of talk about religion that barely scratches the surface of what someone like Gil Grissom probably believes. For a series that prides itself on obeying the cardinal dramatic rule of 'show, don't tell', it's a shame that there are such talky scenes in this. The B plot feels like it's from an early draft – there are gaping plot holes that escape everyone's attention. A definite curate's egg!

29
Caged

US Air Date: 8 November 2001 15.1/23
UK Air Date: 16 March 2002

Written by: Elizabeth Devine and Carol Mendelsohn
Directed by: Richard J. Lewis
Guest Cast: Currie Graham (Stanley Hunter), David Dunard (Engineer),
John Duerler (Croft), Tsianina Joelson (Megan Treadwell),
Maria Celedonio (Melanie), Michael Goorjian (Aaron Pratt),
Faline England (Wendy), Nicole Freeman (Veronica Bradley)

Teaser One-liner: 'One-on-one with a train. Did she think
that she could beat it?'
The Cases: Megan Treadwell is racing down the road in
her SUV. She reaches the railway crossing, but despite
pushing hard on the brakes, she is unable to prevent the
car from going through the guard rail onto the tracks –
where she is killed. Grissom and Catherine examine the
scene and find the door handle of the passenger side door
embedded in the front of the train. Because the train is on
the main railroad route through Vegas, the Sheriff tells
Grissom that he has only two hours.

Neither Sara nor Catherine like working against the clock.
A small dog, Maverick, runs towards them, and Sara decides
to get it home. The train driver tells Brass that he thought the
SUV was stopping, but then, suddenly, it was in the middle of
the tracks. Brass confirms that Megan's address was the same
as the dog's. Catherine and Sara find some glass filament from
a vehicle light, and some contradictory treadmarks that make
it appear as though someone was rushing towards the gate,
skidded, but then had the tyres spinning in place, in reverse.

Sara discovers that the SUV's filament is intact, so the
one they found must come from another car. Catherine
finds black paint transfer on the back bumper. And the
handbrake is on as well. The train driver might not have
seen the second car. Megan's cellphone battery is dead.
There's no glass on the filament they found, which
indicates the driver was driving with no lights on.

Archie Johnson, the audio specialist, breaks down the 911 call that Megan made from her phone. She claims she was being followed. Breaking down the sound, there's clear evidence of another car – a turbo motor, possibly a diesel engine.

Sara and Brass trace Megan's movements. After work, she bought some dog treats for Maverick which are only made at one store, The Pet Place. One of the workers there confirms that Megan upset one of the regulars, Mr Croft, by nearly hitting him. Megan left, and Croft followed.

Brass brings Croft in, and he denies everything. However, he has a rental car, and claims he sold his car, although he has no receipts. But they find the car being worked on at a garage, and it matches the physical evidence on Megan's. There's also an empty coffee cup and coffee stains on the window. They realise that Croft chased Megan, and Megan threw her coffee at Croft after he swore at her. He then chased her and pushed her onto the line. She wouldn't get out and leave her dog – so she died.

Grissom meets O'Riley at the Western State Historical Society Library. The police received a 'burglary in progress' call. When they entered the library lower level, they called the CSIs – there's a dead woman locked in the secured cage. She has foam on her mouth, and her skin is cyanotic. The only witness is Aaron Pratt, an autistic assistant at the library. His memory of details is very acute: a uniball pen fell from Veronica Bradley's hand, then she sweated heavily, grabbed her stomach, 'put on her new face – Shelley's Frankenstein', then had a lot of seizures.

Doc Robbins confirms that Veronica was cyanosed, but she wasn't asphyxiated. He's waiting for blood tests. Grissom suspects murder. The curator, Stanley Hunter, tries to stop Nick from using a flashlight or the fingerprint dust because of the damage it might do to the books, but Grissom tells Nick that they effectively had a camera in there anyway – Aaron Pratt.

Hunter explains what Veronica was working on – restoring an old eighteenth-century British botanical book

– and their security measures to prevent theft. They don't seem to be too effective, as O'Riley has found a copy of *Othello* in Aaron's briefcase. Aaron says that Hunter breaks the rules too – he eats 'lunch and Veronica' in his office.

The bottles of restoration fluid are all what they say they are. Nick and Grissom inspect Aaron's apartment, where there are numerous books from the library. Aaron says Veronica brought them – they were dating. Nick finds some of Veronica's items in Aaron's bedroom dresser: lipstick, earrings, photos and a hairbrush.

Greg discovers a protein in Veronica's blood and narrows it down to ricin, a biotoxin. The symptoms match what Aaron said Veronica was suffering from. Doc Robbins says that it made contact with her tongue, so it's probably a powder. Nick checks out the cage for anything powdery, and also checks Veronica's compact.

Grissom has found a book about ricin among Aaron's stash, and Nick points out that that would be enough for anyone else to be arrested. Grissom takes the point, and Aaron is brought in. He says he doesn't touch the book any more because it doesn't feel right. Veronica told him that's because of the restoration work. He tried to tell Hunter about the book and he didn't want to know. At the time, Aaron witnessed an argument between Hunter and Veronica in which he hit her and told her that he wasn't going to let her ruin his reputation. Nick checks out Hunter's office, including his salt shaker.

Hunter says that he knew Veronica was forging copies of the books and reselling them. He was furious at her but, now she is dead, he hopes things are sorted. Aaron walks Grissom through what happened on the night, and now remembers that Veronica was chewing her pen as she tried to decide something. Nick finds numerous pens of the same sort at Veronica's house, as well as a great deal of forgery equipment. He also discovers a castor bean, source of the ricin, under her fridge. She presumably prepared the ricin to use on Hunter, but spilled some on her own notebook, which got on to the pen that she chewed. She killed herself.

* * *

Offscreen throughout the episode, Warrick is working on three residential burglaries.

Personal Notes: Nick is still panicky about getting infected. Greg was a Phi Beta Kappa at Stanford University. (Nick asks which one of his relatives got him in!)

Techniques: Archie Johnson breaks down the 911 call into its constituent components, so that they can hear all the parts of the ambient noise.

Classic Dialogue: Grissom: 'Aaron Pratt is a high-functioning autistic man with superior right brain abilities.' Nick: 'Kind of sounds like you.'

Stanley Hunter: 'These are masterpieces. One of a kind.' Grissom: 'They're evidence in an active criminal investigation – also one of a kind.'

Greg: 'I know what you all think of me – I'm just another pretty face who got to where I am by sleeping with Catherine.'

Fantastic Voyages: We watch Veronica suffocating from cyanosis, and the effect of ricin on her tongue. We see a light filament fusing the glass when it touches it in an accident.

The Usual Suspects: Michael Goorjian (Aaron Pratt) played Justin Thompson on *Party of Five*. Tsianina Joelson (Megan Treadwell) was Varia in the final season of *Xena: Warrior Princess*. Currie Graham (Stanley Hunter) played Ted Cofell during the first year of *24*. Archie Kao joins the show as semi-regular audio technician Archie Johnson, after playing the campus security guard in **24**, 'Chaos Theory'.

Pop Culture References: Greg talks about the cult classic *Attack of the Killer Tomatoes*. Grissom talks about Shakespeare's plays *King Lear* and *Othello*. There are references to *Rain Man*, the Tom Cruise/Dustin Hoffman film about an autistic man, and *Shakespeare in Love*.

Real-life Inspirations: Maverick is the name of George Eads' golden retriever.

Mistakes Really Can Be Fatal: One minute Sara is bitching that they've only got two hours to process the crime scene, the next she's rushing to take a stray dog home!

Ricin doesn't act that fast – death can take up to three days (as Greg points out earlier in the episode to calm Nick down!).

Notes: In the original script, Warrick solved his cases and assisted in checking out the books and, at the end of the episode, Grissom admitted to Aaron that he had never been in love.

Overall: A taut episode and you don't actually notice that Warrick is missing. Michael Goorjian's performance sells the rather outlandish Grissom story, while Sara and Catherine prove that they're once again an excellent partnership.

30
Slaves of Las Vegas

US Air Date: 15 November 2001 15.7/24
UK Air Date: 23 March 2002

Written by: Jerry Stahl
Directed by: Peter Markle
Guest Cast: Melinda Clarke (Lady Heather),
Kelly Rowan (Eileen Nelson), Mitchell Whitfield (Cameron Nelson),
Tracy Vilar (Carla Delgado), Amaury Nolasco (Hector),
Perry Anzilotti (Marvin Fortay),
John Benjamin Hickey (Dr Sidney Cornfeld), Stacey Dash (Amy Young),
Manuel Suarez, Dennis Bertsch (Randolph), Suyun Kim (Headmistress),
Danica Stewart (Girl), Nicola Hindshaw (Mona Taylor),
Keilana Smith (Dealer)

Teaser One-liner: 'The only person who knows where the crime scene is has her mouth full of sand.'

The Cases: A young couple find a dead female body in a sandbox. The CSIs find no sign of struggle. Back at the lab, Grissom examines the body, noticing restraint marks on the ankle. He finds a silver sliver on her back, and the ALS reveals a sticky substance on the back of her calf. Once he's washed the body down, Grissom also finds multiple bruises on her back and thighs, and restraint marks on her wrist, of which he makes a mould.

Doc Robbins reports that the woman died between two and four hours before she was found. It was almost certainly a violent death. There are many old and new scars on her, but this wasn't rape: the victim had not had sex for months. She's kept good care of herself, and had a top of the line breast augmentation. The silver sliver Grissom found on her back is tempered steel with an aluminium coating, and the sticky substance is liquid latex.

Catherine visits the surgeon who supplied the implants, and he identifies the woman from the serial number as Mona Taylor. The bill was paid by a third party, whom the CSIs visit. It's a fetish club run by 'Lady Heather'. They find Mona's car and some liquid latex with an impression in it inside a trashcan. Lady Heather confirms that Mona worked till around midnight in the pool house. She's surprised to learn that the whipmarks on Mona were fresh, since Mona had been a Dominant with her clients though it might have come from a private client. Grissom borrows a leather mask for testing. In Mona's work room, there's a large silver chain, and Nick finds some liquid latex.

Doc Robbins confirms that Mona died from asphyxiation, and there are odd red marks in her nose. Grissom believes these could be from straws for air. Greg finds Mona's DNA on the mask and the straws. There's also some other DNA on the straw, which was probably blocked once it was up Mona's nose so she couldn't breathe.

The combination of the impression in the latex that Nick found and the mould from Mona's wrist shows a man's watch. The purchaser was Cameron Nelson, but he denies murder or going to her. Grissom and Catherine visit his wife, who admits she bought it, but lost it. She's having an affair with her boss, but denies anything else.

Grissom and Catherine get a warrant for Eileen Nelson's watchbox. Inside it they find some liquid latex. Lady Heather recognises a photo of Cameron Nelson who, she explains to Grissom, is definitely the submissive in his marriage. Catherine finds sand in a jacket in the Nelsons' car. Cameron is arrested and Eileen insists on being his lawyer. She then hears the evidence – Cameron made Mona wear liquid latex as well as Eileen's watch every time that he humiliated her. But the session went too far and Mona died.

An employee at a cheque-cashing facility is shot in the leg during a robbery. It's not surprising he's been hit, since he makes the money deposit at the same time every night. Sara finds the money bag, which still has the cheques inside, and a deposit slip for $22,500. The store owner, Carla Delgado, confirms that she and her brother (the victim) are insured. Possibly it's a scam by the brother to get the money and the insurance money.

From the presence of flyers still on the neighbouring cars, Warrick deduces that whoever put them there hadn't left long before the shooting. The man putting the flyers out confirms that he saw a couple of lowlifes in baseball caps who threatened him.

New technician Amy Young gets a match off a tyre track at the mall; she also finds that the tyre had gone over a bottle cap at some point leaving a distinctive mark in the tread. Bobby Dawson finds that the bullet in the victim's leg was from a Colt .38 – the same gun that Santee Cherna, the victim, owns himself.

Sara and Vega visit Santee, who says his gun is at the shop. Amy Young finds fibreglass fibres transferred into the bag from the knife used to slice it open. Warrick and Sara go to one of the fibreglass manufacturers – and see Carla Delgado's husband Hector there. He hands over his knife, but then makes a mistake about the car he owns, and runs. Warrick catches him and he admits that the Honda in the parking lot belonged to a friend of his, and that he stole Santee's gun and borrowed a friend's car to do the hold-up. He goes to jail, to his wife's pleasure. Santee is also arrested for stealing $5,000 that the CSIs found in his jeans.

Personal Notes: According to Lady Heather, Grissom's greatest fear is being known. 'You can't accept that I might know what you really desire because that would mean that I know you, something, for whatever reason, you spend your entire life making sure no one else does.' And the show fades to black at the end of the episode just as Grissom is about to reveal something! According to Catherine, the only advice her mother gave her was 'Cash up front'. Lindsey is now seven.

Techniques: Greg uses the Avatar E.S.P. FT-IR (Fourier Transform Infrared) Spectrometer to analyse samples for Nick. This measures how different materials absorb various infrared light wavelengths, from which their molecular structure can be worked out.

The Wit and Wisdom of Gil Grissom: 'I find all deviant behaviour fascinating, in that to understand human nature we have to understand our aberrations.'

Classic Dialogue: Warrick: 'He's either stupid or suicidal.'
Vega: 'We can't arrest people for that, unfortunately.'

Businessman: 'I don't know what city you live in, Missy, but, in Las Vegas, unusual is what happens when you leave the house.'

Catherine (to Grissom): 'Do you get these haikus out of a book, or do they just come to you?'

Catherine: 'If there's one thing you learn on this job is that human beings are capable of *anything*.'

Lady Heather: 'Sex pays a lot better than death.'
Catherine: 'Plus, the outfits are cooler.'

Fantastic Voyages: We travel inside the fake breasts to see the serial numbers on the saline bags and see Greg's machine processing the fragment. We travel inside Mona's nose to examine the red mark. We follow a car tyre running over a bottle cap, leaving a mark in the tread.

The Usual Suspects: Melinda Clarke (Lady Heather) played Sarin in the pilot of *Enterprise*, and is one of the voices in *The Animatrix*. Kelly Rowan (Eileen Nelson) went on to play Marian McNorris on *Boomtown*.

Pop Culture References: Catherine mentions the fairytale of Hansel and Gretel. Grissom quotes from Edgar Allen Poe's poem 'A Dream Within A Dream'; he also quotes from Marcel Proust.

Mistakes Really Can Be Fatal: The writers assume that the violence in the S&M is theatrical, but according to dominatrix Mistress Juliana who acted as technical consultant, this isn't the case.

Notes: This was the first episode to be prefaced with the warning: 'Due to brief nudity and adult themes, viewer discretion is advised.' It was nominated for an Emmy for Outstanding Make-Up for a Series (Non-Prosthetic).

Overall: A foil for Grissom at long last – after a false start with the vampire doctor in the first season (**20**, 'Justice Is Served'), the producers get it right with Melinda Clarke's scene-stealing performance as Lady Heather. Little surprise that she returns the following season as the centrepiece of *CSI*'s first extended episode.

31
And Then There Were None

US Air Date: 22 November 2001 12.4/22
UK Air Date: 30 March 2002

Teleplay by: Eli Talbert, Carol Mendelsohn
Story by: Josh Berman
Directed by: John Patterson
Guest Cast: Michael Cudlitz (Officer William Spencer),
Tom O'Brien (Max Duncan), Brigid Brannagh (Tammy Felton),
Larry Holden (Darin Hanson), Joe Sabatino (Security Officer),
Marc Valera (Valet), Chris Grillo (Fraternity Guy),
Bobbie Norman (Elderly Woman), Keilana Smith (Dealer),
Amy Weber (Cocktail Waitress)

Teaser One-liner: 'Dangerous, yes. Ladies, no.'
The Case: A casino is raided by three women – a blonde, a brunette and a redhead – who shoot the security officers escorting the takings, but then get into a firefight. At the end the blonde and the brunette escape, but the redhead lies on the ground dead. They only managed to get a quarter of a million dollars. But these were no ladies – the redhead is a man wearing a wig. The raiders were using .45 calibre ammunition. The pit boss, Max Duncan, says that

the chandelier came down first, which distracted the guards and made them easy targets. Brass points out that the raiders have hit before, at a casino in Laughlin.

Meanwhile, Catherine and Sara are attending a homicide in Calnevari, a tiny town of only twenty people. The store clerk, Dustin Bale, has been shot through the heart, and the cash register emptied. The state trooper, Spencer, who found him, covers a very large area and is anxious to leave. The CSIs find potato on the floor, a poor man's silencer. The last customer was there eight hours previously and Sara deduces that the assailant flipped the store sign to Closed to delay pursuit. Sara prints the store counter, while Catherine checks the sign. There are shoe prints on the counter, but they are small.

Back in Vegas, none of the eye witness statements correlates. The valet says that the driver left in a hurry, but there was no screech of tyres. There's an odd substance on the floor. Greg confirms the substance is transmission fluid, and also its type, which backs up Nick's theory that it was the wrong colour for that type of car – this would cause the gears to go.

Robbins tells Grissom that the redhead, Adam Brower, was shot in the back by one of his own people – the bullet is a .45 calibre, and the security guards had 9 mm ammunition. Warrick checks the video surveillance footage from the casino, and confirms that one of the others – the one who shot Adam – was a man, but the third 'lady' was female. Brower has a record for grand larceny. Warrick takes clothing from his apartment for checking for trace elements.

The shoe print that Sara and Catherine found is from a shoe for an adult female. Fingerprints show that the State Trooper had touched the sign, despite the fact he had told the CSIs that he knew what he was doing, and the register shows Tammy Felton's print. Catherine brings Sara up to speed on Tammy and tells Grissom that Tammy is back.

Greg informs Grissom that there was potato on the bullet used to kill Brower, which means that the two cases might be linked. Another print from the convenience store is that of Darin Hanson, the partner of Tammy's father. Catherine and Grissom realise that Darin and Tammy were working together. The bullets from Adam Brower and the convenience store clerk, Dustin Bale, match.

The getaway car is found, and the treadmarks indicate that whoever left it disappeared on a motorcycle. Inside the trunk of the car is the late Tammy Felton. Doc Robbins confirms that she was strangled and didn't put up any resistance – indicating that it was probably by Hanson, the one person she trusted, and later DNA evidence from her neck proves this.

Nick and Warrick find dust in the car which matches the dust that Warrick found on Brower's clothes. It's silica – and Grissom knows that there's an abandoned silica mine outside Calnevari. There they find a motorcycle, and the late Darin Hanson, shot with a .45 in the head.

The CSIs are baffled, until they are told that there were four gunmen at the Laughlin robbery. Warrick checks the video footage again and they realise that the pit boss, Max Duncan, ducked for cover before the gunfire started. He also used to work at Laughlin. He's arrested, and silica dust is found on his car. He claims that Darin was already dead when he got there. Brass believes him.

Archie Johnson checks the Laughlin footage, and the fourth robber there turns out to be Dustin Bale, the convenience store clerk. Bobby Dawson runs a test on the bullet that killed Darin, and narrows it down to a Heckler and Koch. One of the registered owners is Officer Spencer. Catherine deduces that he interrupted the murder of Bale, and Tammy bribed him with some of the proceeds of the robbery in Vegas that they were on the way to commit. But he saw a chance of easy money, and killed Darin, the last survivor. The money is found in Spencer's locker.

Personal Notes: Catherine complains about being stuck with this case, given that she has the right to pick her cases. Sara gives her a candy bar to shut her up! Greg claims to be a surfer, even though they're 300 miles from the beach. Doc Robbins' first name is now given as Albert (see **Mistakes**).

Techniques: Catherine uses a fumette to get prints off the cardboard (an old-fashioned technique that is still the best, according to her).

The Wit and Wisdom of Gil Grissom: 'Dressed as a woman, among men dressed as women. Now see, that's a disguise.'

Fantastic Voyages: We follow the bullet going through the 'redhead's' body. We see how a potato can be used as a silencer, and how the film Sara uses collects the prints. We then see bits of potato adhering to the gun and zoom in on the dust found in the car.

The Usual Suspects: Brigid Brannagh and Larry Holden reprise their roles (see **16**, 'Face Lift'). Susan Gibney returns as the lab tech, Charlotte, who went on a date with Grissom just before **00**, 'Pilot'. Tom O'Brien (Max Duncan) played the unpleasant reporter Roger Nixon on *Smallville*. Michael Cudlitz (Officer Spencer) played agent Rick Phillips in the second season of *24*, and Sgt Denver 'Bull' Randleman on *Band of Brothers*.

Mistakes Really Can Be Fatal: It's pushing credibility that Sara didn't hear anything about Tammy Felton during the events of **16**, 'Face Lift' – even if she was obsessing about Spontaneous Human Combustion.

Doc Robbins was very definitely called David in **12**, 'Boom' not Albert. It seems likely that when David Phillips was pushed up into a recurring role, where he would be seen working with Robbins, the producers decided to change Robbins' forename to avoid confusion.

Spot the moving gloves. When Bobby Dawson goes to get the gun, he's wearing gloves, but they're off when he takes it down off the rack, and back on when he's in the other room a few seconds later.

Notes: The title derives from the American title of Agatha Christie's murder mystery published in the UK as *Ten Little Niggers/Indians*.

Overall: All a bit contrived (which could mean it's based beat for beat on one of Elizabeth Devine's real cases!) and Brigid Brannagh is wasted in Tammy's brief return. There's some nice attention to continuity detail with a brief mention of Tammy's real parents, the Marlowes.

32
Ellie

US Air Date: 6 December 2001 14.9/23
UK Air Date: 6 April 2002

Written by: Anthony E. Zuiker
Directed by: Charlie Correll
Guest Cast: Nicki Aycox (Ellie Brass), Geoffrey Blake (Matthew Orton),
Nancy Everhard (Cindy Orton),
Daniel Dae Kim (Special Agent Beckman),
Rodney Eastman (Keith Driscoll), Sandra Thigpen (Attorney),
John Fugelsang (Victor Avery), Liesl Lombardo (X-Ray Technician),
Joel Stoffer (Marty Gillmore), Anthony Zuiker (Cashier)

Teaser One-liner: 'Guy was running one of the oldest scams in Vegas . . .'

The Case: A young couple, the Ortons, decide to help someone in distress outside the Tropicana Casino. He needs someone to cash in his $10k worth of chips, but he's barred. They give him $2k to prove their honesty – but of course it's a scam. The chips are worthless, and the man has vanished. They hear a gunshot followed by a car disappearing rapidly – he's been shot. Grissom arrives, and takes the Ortons' genuine money as evidence. Grissom has to leave, as he's giving a tutorial in preserving mass crime scenes in Duluth. Since Catherine is also going out of town, Grissom decides to leave Warrick in charge, even though Nick is his superior.

Nick and Sara are at the scene and photograph oil spots, and the tyre treadmarks. Sara finds a film container under a car, containing black pill capsules. Warrick arrives and starts pushing them.

Doc Robbins tells Warrick that the deceased is Vincent Thomas Avery who died from a gunshot to the outer ear. X-rays also show something in his stomach. Opening him up, they find around fifty balloons filled with a white substance (later proved to be cocaine), covered in a green dye, probably lime-flavoured gelatine. Why is a drug runner bothering with a cheap con?

Nick identifies a nail in the tyre tread. Greg analyses the pills, and they're an antacid, something a drug mule would need. Sara also finds two airline tickets – for Vincent Avery and Ellie Rebecca; Warrick is annoyed that she jumped the gun and checked the evidence – it's his job. The stub for Ellie Rebecca reveals her surname – Brass. It is Jim's daughter. Sam Vega brings her in, and when she sees her father, she spits on his badge.

Ellie is carrying one of the fake chips Avery was using, but she denies any knowledge of the drug running. She says she lent her car to her boyfriend, Keith Driscoll. Her X-ray comes back clean – she has already passed the drugs on. Warrick considers calling Grissom, but decides against it.

Brass spots Ellie's Camero, and stops Driscoll. A hitchhiker gets out of the way of the angry Brass, who starts to interrogate Driscoll. He, however, claims Ellie is the boss. Sam Vega arrives in time to stop Brass doing anything stupid even though he's already pulled his gun.

Sara discovers that the money Avery had was fake, and notifies the Treasury. Warrick is surprised by the arrival of Special Agent Beckman to deal with the counterfeiting case, and reluctantly lets Sara run with it, as he and Nick need to check out Ellie's car. It's got the 'nail' mark – a tyre plug. It's the getaway car. However, the evidence isn't strong enough to hold Driscoll and Brass' gun play works against them.

Beckman tells Sara that the Ortons, aka the Duffys, are major counterfeiters. However, Sara has really been taken in by a Treasury operation set up to see what happens to counterfeit money once it's in law enforcement's hands. She's passed the test but isn't too happy.

Brass bails Ellie out and she says she's heading to Driscoll's place. A bit later that night, Warrick is called to an officer-involved shooting. Brass appears to have shot and killed Driscoll. He claims that he went to look for Ellie. She wasn't there, and Driscoll knocked him out. He doesn't recall pulling his gun.

Nick and Warrick find blood on the slide – the mark of a novice shooter. Warrick checks Brass' hands, and takes his badge from him. The blood on the gun doesn't belong to Brass, Ellie or Driscoll.

Warrick matches up the credit card numbers on the plane manifest, and discovers that Vincent and Ellie's tickets were paid for by one Marty Gillmore – who turns out to be the hitchhiker with Driscoll. He has slide bite on his hand. Gillmore starts to overdose from the drugs in his system, and Brass eventually calls for a medic.

Personal Notes: Grissom races cockroaches in his spare time at conventions. Catherine is going to Reno with Sam Braun (see **23**, 'Burked'), as his date. Jim Brass and his daughter Ellie Rebecca do not get along – to put it mildly. Greg discovers that they don't share DNA. Brass knows; Ellie doesn't. There's a mild thawing of their relationship by the end of the episode. Brass' ex-wife lives in New Jersey.

Techniques: Greg uses a Spectratech machine to check the chemical analysis of the pills.

The Wit and Wisdom of Gil Grissom: 'When I leave CSI, there won't be any cake in the break room. I'll just be gone.'

Classic Dialogue: Sara: 'Who died and made you boss?' Warrick: 'He's not exactly dead.'

Worst 'As You Know': Sara: 'Did you know that ninety-seven per cent of all $100 bills have traces of cocaine on them?' Ronnie Litre: 'I was the one that told you that.'

Fantastic Voyages: A close-up on the entry wound in Avery's head, and then of the bullet going in. We see what an autopsy looks like from the inside, and the balloons burst inside Avery's stomach. The light working on the Spectratech machine. The balloons being swallowed and causing gastric acid to appear. We go inside the X-ray of Ellie Brass. We see Brass' gun firing and the slide catching.

The Usual Suspects: Nicki Aycox (Ellie Brass) played Lily Gallagher on the superior soap opera *Providence*. Daniel Dae Kim (Agent Beckman) played Gavin Park on *Angel*, and Agent Tom Baker (who's the *Doctor Who* fan?) on the second year of *24*. Nancy Everhard (Mrs Orton) plays Sharon Hart on *Everwood*. Creator Anthony E. Zuiker makes another brief cameo.

Pop Culture References: A famous cockroach is known as Cocky Balboa, a riff on the *Rocky* movies; another is

Priscilla, Queen of the Gutters. Grissom quotes from the *Peanuts* character Linus.

Mistakes Really Can Be Fatal: Sara tells the Ortons the penalty for passing counterfeit money is fifteen years imprisonment; under the US Penal Code in force at the time – 2002 – it was ten.

Ellie's car is meant to be a 1976 Camero, licence plate QLF 084; but the one spotted is a 1978 model, licence 428 RQW.

Car 574 6ZI is seen in two simultaneous scenes at different locations – one of them being driven by Detective Vega.

If he's in charge, why isn't Warrick carrying a cellphone?

Notes: A number of names changed from the original script: the Ortons began life as the Olsons, and their codename was Detweiler (after the special effects supervisor) rather than Duffy. Keith Driscoll was Keith Drezden, and Special Agent Tessari was Special Agent Petullo.

Overall: Another contrived episode that at least focuses on the younger members of the team and gives a little bit of an insight into Jim Brass. It still seems unrealistic though that Avery would bother with the small con at the same time as running the drugs.

33
Organ Grinder

US Air Date: 13 December 2001 11.2/18
UK Air Date: 13 April 2002

Written by: Ann Donahue and Elizabeth Devine
Directed by: Allison Liddi
Guest Cast: Marcia Cross (Julia Fairmont),
Anne Ramsay (Claudia Gideon), Kelly Connell (Randy Gesek),
John F. O'Donohue (Carl Mercer), Spencer Garrett (Bob Fairmont),
Erinn Bartlett (Cindy), Dax Griffin (Chuck), Rene Ashton (Receptionist)

Teaser One-liner: 'It's impossible to re-dress an unconscious person to make it look like they dressed themselves.'

The Case: Two lovers find a body in an elevator at the Devon Hotel, and a mysterious male voice calls 911 to say someone has collapsed at the hotel.

The victim, housing developer Bob Fairmont is taken to Desert Palms Hospital since he's still breathing. The photos taken at the scene show that he has been posed – whatever happened to him occurred elsewhere. Brass talks to Fairmont's wife Julia as her husband is undergoing surgery, but she doesn't know who could have been responsible. He had affairs with younger women, but she chose not to know about them.

There are two champagne glasses in his hotel room, neither with lipstick. There's a hint of bleach, and evidence of sexual intercourse – with the curtains left open. Sara finds a 34C bra, so if Fairmont was one party, and a woman was the other, who was the man who placed the 911 call?

Nick and Catherine find some white powder in the elevator where Fairmont was found, which turns out to be dandruff. The room is checked for stains: Grissom leaves Sara and Nick to process the multitude that they find – from champagne to semen. They find a recently used condom. Brass tells Grissom that the tape of the 911 call has been lost but the dispatcher who took it thinks it could have been a woman whispering.

One of Warrick's first cases was at the Fairmont house when the housing mogul shot himself while cleaning his gun. In light of the new events, Warrick decides to check the records.

Fairmont dies at the hospital, but according to Doc Robbins he was effectively dead from the moment he collapsed with an aneurysm at the hotel. Because Fairmont was only 38, he was quickly stripped of all his useable organs for transplant, at his wife's request.

Sara spots stripes on Fairmont's fingernails in the autopsy photos, which indicate an onset of toxicity, but they can't tell what sort without the body. Unfortunately it has already been released for disposal, and sent to Desert Haven, Randy Gesek's mortuary. When Nick and Sara get there, it has already been cremated. Julia Fairmont approved a rapid cremation.

Sara analyses Fairmont's ashes and finds traces of selenium. Julia says she knows nothing about any poisoning, didn't notice any garlicky breath (a sign of selenium), or the striations on his fingernails. She has dealt with her husband as he wished, and now wants to get on with his memorial service. She does, however, want to be told what they discover about the poisoning.

Nick visits Carl Mercer, who received Fairmont's kidney, but he's not willing to undergo further surgery so Nick takes a biopsy. Sara gets similar news from other donees.

Catherine is processing Fairmont's items at the hospital when his secretary Claudia Gideon comes to collect his property. Catherine notices that she has dandruff. Also, she was working for the Fairmonts at the time of the original shooting accident, although she was off sick that day. She's taken in for questioning and eventually admits that she had been told to meet Fairmont at the hotel at 9 p.m., found him naked and unconscious, so remembering his order to her to maintain his reputation, dressed him and put him in the elevator. She doesn't know who was in the room with Fairmont though.

Warrick has reprocessed the evidence from three years earlier, and it shows that someone shot Fairmont. Claudia Gideon went with Fairmont to the hospital, but she maintains that it was nothing to do with her. She doesn't know where Julia was at the time. Julia admits that she shot Fairmont after he came home at 2 a.m., trying to scare him. They covered it up to maintain his reputation.

Grissom points out that selenium is the primary ingredient of anti-dandruff medication. Brass and Catherine go to the Fairmonts' house and find the medication in Claudia's cabinet, as well as garlicky cream cheese in the fridge, which they deduce would be used to hide the aftertaste of the selenium. Julia and Gideon get into a slanging match.

Carl Mercer has a change of heart, after his body rejects Fairmont's kidney, but Nick feels uneasy about asking him to proceed. Sara identifies the champagne bottle print – it's from Julia Fairmont. She admits that she was there, but says that she was never asked about the sex in the room before, only the re-dressing. According to her, Fairmont was alive and well when she left. Sara discovers that Julia arranged for her husband's gold teeth to be extracted prior to cremation, as Nick finds Julia herself collapsing in the parking lot. She's suffering from metal poisoning.

Claudia Gideon denies it all again, and claims that Julia was trying to frame her with the medication. Julia, however, says that Fairmont refused to leave her for Claudia. Claudia says she didn't want to marry him.

Greg does an internet search on the two women, and comes up blank for Julia, but Claudia had a rich husband who died when he was young. His organs were also donated, and the liver was rejected by the donee, who subsequently died. He's exhumed, and there's selenium in his liver. The Gideons owned a dairy farm – and their secretary was Julia Fairmont.

Sara and Catherine face the two women with their suspicions that they teamed up to murder first Gideon then Fairmont, but the DA thinks that each will merely implicate the other, making it impossible to get a conviction. Much to Sara's disgust, the two women get away with it but, as Grissom reminds her, there's no statute of limitation for murder.

Personal Notes: Catherine is able to recognise cocaine just by looking. Greg asks Catherine whether she thinks Sara would go on a date with him ('only as long as she doesn't know it's a date,' is the reply). He's quite surprised when Sara agrees to take their break together. A shooting at the Fairmont house was one of Warrick's first calls 'three years ago' – i.e. 1998. He fell for Fairmont's claim that it was accidental because he was new and didn't want to press another man about almost shooting his manhood off.

The Wit and Wisdom of Gil Grissom: 'This is as phoney as a Chappaquidick neck brace.'

'Why do they think they can fool us?'

Classic Dialogue: Grissom: 'What's the most important component in a poisoning?' Sara: 'Poison.' Grissom: 'Patience.'

Fantastic Voyages: We look at the white specks of dandruff found in the elevator then travel up the microscope to Catherine's eye. We travel inside Bob Fairmont's head to see the blood leaking out of his brain.

The Usual Suspects: Marcia Cross (Julia Fairmont) was a regular on both *Melrose Place* as Dr Kimberly Shaw Mancini and *Knots Landing* as Victoria Broyelard. Spencer Garrett (Bob Fairmont) played Jarod Stark on the most recent version of *The Invisible Man*. Anne Ramsay (Claudia Gideon) was Lt Col. Grace Alexander in the reinvention of *Planet of the Apes*. John F. O'Donohue (Mr Mercer) is Detective Eddie Gibson on *NYPD Blue*.

Pop Culture References: There's references to Chappaquidick, and the death of Mary Jo Kopechne in 1969, which put paid to Teddy Kennedy's presidential aspirations.

Real-life Inspirations: A case of murder by selenium was the true story at the heart of the 1999 TV movie *Lethal Vows*, which starred Marg Helgenberger as the woman convinced her ex-husband killed his new wife.

Mistakes Really Can Be Fatal: Warrick's experience seems to be changing. According to **19**, 'Sounds of Silence', he and Grissom interrogated a rapist in 1997, yet here he says that autumn 1998 saw one of his earliest cases.

Aldrich Mees lines show arsenic, not selenium, poisoning.

Julia refers to Claudia Gideon as Claudia Richards – her name in an earlier draft of the script.

How much selenium was in Gideon's liver? Nick says 280 mg, but Catherine later says 240 mg.

Notes: This episode is set on and after 12 December 2001 (Fairmont dies at 4 a.m. on 13 December).

The ratings dip reflects the fact that CBS placed this episode an hour later than normal in an attempt to spoil *ER's* ratings for the key episode in which Dr Benton left.

Overall: It feels like an unsatisfactory ending, but that's the effect that the producers want – the audience shares Sara's frustration that the two women have succeeded in their plans. Some nice character moments, especially for Nick.

34
You've Got Male

US Air Date: 20 December 2001 15.0/24
UK Air Date: 20 April 2002

Written by: Marc Dube and Corey Miller
Directed by: Charlie Correll
Guest Cast: Amanda Wyss (Donna Marks), Holly Fulger (Linda Jasper),
Clayton Rohner (Park Ranger), Rod Rowland (Gavin Pallard),
Kirk B.R. Woller (Warden Mather), Robia La Morte (Joan Marks),
Thomas Kopache (James Jasper), Nick Chinlund (Mickey Rutledge),
Simon Brooke (Inmate #1), Palmer Davis (Margaret Finn),
Amanda Righetti (Young Teen), Todd Sandler (Probation Officer),
Edmund Wyson (Inmate #2)

Teaser One-liner: 'A girl in a culvert pipe at a highway construction site in the middle of an alfalfa field.'

The Cases: A woman's body, stuffed into a large drainpipe at a highway construction site, is found by a woman out riding. When the CSIs arrive, they find a second woman also dead. Doc Robbins determines that both died approximately two hours earlier, around 4 a.m. One died from a snapped neck, while the other had cuts to her forehead and arm, and there is glass in her wounds. She also has scratches on her neck. The cut on her arm caused her to bleed to death.

The two girls couldn't be more different: the girl with the broken neck has multiple body piercings and tattoos, while the bleeder doesn't even have pierced ears, or shaved legs. Sara has no luck processing the crime scene, but prints identify the tattooed girl as Joan Marks, who has a felony record. At the registered address, Sara and Grissom check the car they find, which has hardly been used. It's registered to Donna Marks, Joan's older sister, and their other corpse.

Warrick found the remnants of a glass door at the house, which Donna had gone through. There's a partial shoe print in the blood outside, which might fit with blood found on Joan's shoe. Grissom and Sara find family-sized portions of fresh Chinese takeaway food at the front of the fridge, and single, old servings at the back. They also find piles of catalogues and deduce from that that Donna spent a lot of her time inside. Sara also notices that the toilet seat is up – there's been a man in the house very recently.

Greg determines that the scratches on Donna's neck were caused by her sister. Brass and Sara discover that Joan Marks and her boyfriend Gavin Pallard had Restraining Orders against each other. Brought in for questioning, Pallard says that they fought regularly, most recently the day before, when she took his car. He's surprised that Joan went to Donna's as they were like oil and water. Gavin happily shows Sara the bottom of his shoes – and there are bloodstains.

Sara goes through Donna's email and finds that she did a lot of mail order over the phone but there are private emails from 'Apollo'. They trace the email from the IP address to the Western Nevada Correctional Facility. Grissom visits the prison, and finds that the inmates are working for catalogue companies. Apollo, aka Mickey Rutledge, was released from the private prison three days earlier.

Warrick finds some fibres on Donna's clothing that may be car upholstery. This could match the upholstery in Gavin Pallard's car – the car that Joan allegedly borrowed. DNA has confirmed that the blood on his shoe is from Donna, as is the blood from Joan's. Pallard admits he went to the house, but didn't call 911 because he was scared.

Grissom matches prints from the upright toilet seat to Mickey Rutledge. The convict says that he and Donna got on well over the Internet, so he went to visit her. All was going well until Joan turned up and started a fight with her sister. He then got out of there, leaving them to it.

Warrick pieces together the fragments of the glass door and finds the point of impact. From this Grissom deduces that Donna walked through it. Pallard's car is found with a cracked radiator. Someone used water to refill it, so Sara prints the cap while Grissom takes a sample of the water, which turns out to have a high sodium count. The fertiliser at the construction site at which the sisters' bodies were found matches the water in the radiator.

Donna died accidentally, walking into the glass door. Joan was going to blame Rutledge for it, so he killed her. He then took the bodies and hid them at the construction site, using the fertiliser from there to refill the car's cracked radiator. Rutledge killed Joan because he didn't think anyone would believe him if he said Donna's death was an accident.

Catherine, Nick and David Phillips attend a shooting out in the National Park. The park ranger found an SUV after closing, so checked the scene. The deceased had a hunting rifle that wasn't fired. From his temperature, it seems that James Jasper died around 2 p.m. (ten hours earlier). The ranger tells them that it's deer season, and Jasper should have been wearing his orange safety vest. But Nick and Catherine can't find a bullet in the body, or in the tree he's found against. Nick uses a night scope, and finds a bullet embedded in a nearby tree.

The coroner reports that the bullet severed an abdominal artery. Jasper's widow says that he had gone hunting – they were both recently laid off from work and were finding it difficult to cope. She can't understand why he wasn't wearing a safety vest.

Bobby Dawson tells them that, from the oxidation, the bullet Nick found is older than the crime scene. Catherine and Nick are about to write the case off as an accident when Detective Vega tells them that Mrs Jasper is about to get a million dollars from a two-month-old insurance policy.

Nick and Catherine search once more for the missing bullet, this time with metal detectors, but with no luck. The park ranger is surprised to see them there, and tells them that James Jasper didn't have a hunting permit. And why would he be trying to hunt deer at 2 p.m., when they're normally hunted at dawn and dusk?

Nick finds gunshot residue on James' clothing – he was killed by someone very close whom he didn't struggle against. It can't be his wife – Mrs Jasper apparently was at work and ate lunch at her desk. It appears that Jasper was shot and then just sat down to die. Catherine wonders if it might be suicide, and he brought another weapon which he threw in the nearby lake. They find the gun, confirming the theory.

Mrs Jasper says she knew nothing about the insurance policy – and QD confirms that the policy was forged by her husband. He killed himself so she would benefit.

Personal Notes: Sara cooks by ringing for takeaway meals. She's also a catalogue junkie. At the end of the episode she recognises that she's getting too insular, and throws out the old takeaway boxes, and the menus, calling someone (Nick in the original script) to ask them out.

Techniques: Warrick uses ALS to determine which side up the pieces of glass go.

The Wit and Wisdom of Gil Grissom: 'When they cool sheet glass, they lay it out on tin.'

To the prison warden: 'As long as I'm in business, you're in business.'

Classic Dialogue: Grissom: 'Who found the body?' Brass: 'Our friend Flicka.' Grissom: 'Well, there goes that theory.' Brass: 'What's that?' Grissom: 'Whoever finds the body is the first suspect.'

Fantastic Voyages: We watch Joan's neck snap and the glass cutting through Donna's artery. We follow the path of the bullet chasing after a deer but hitting something brown instead, and what happens to it after that.

The Usual Suspects: Nick Chinlund (Mickey Rutledge) played another con, William 'Billy Bedlam' Bedford in *Con Air*. Clayton Rohner (the park ranger) played Chandler Smythe on *G vs E* (aka *Good vs Evil*). Robia La Morte (Joan Marks) was the ill-fated Jenny Calendar on *Buffy the Vampire Slayer*. Amanda Wyss (Donna Marks) was Bridget Cagney on *Cagney and Lacey*. Rodney Rowland (Gavin Pallard) played Lt Cooper Hawkes on *Space: Above and Beyond*, but is probably best known for dating *X-Files* star Gillian Anderson.

Pop Culture References: The horse stories *My Friend Flicka* and its sequels.

Mistakes Really Can Be Fatal: It seems unusual to give the time so specifically in the episode – Grissom and Robbins are carrying out an autopsy at 6 a.m. which we are led to believe is simultaneous with Nick and Catherine at the scene of the other death at midnight . . .

Why is O'Riley checking Mrs Jasper's alibi, when it's Vega's case? And anyway, whoever did it made an error. If Mrs Jasper really was laid off as she claimed, how could her alibi of being at work be verified?

Overall: Too many plotholes and continuity errors spoil this episode which was quite rightly placed in the run up to Christmas when there were plenty of other things to watch. Its high rating shows just how strong a hold *CSI* had in America by then.

35
Identity Crisis

US Air Date: 17 January 2002 14.9/22
UK Air Date: 27 April 2002

Written by: Anthony E. Zuiker and Ann Donahue
Directed by: Ken Fink
Guest Cast: Matt O'Toole (Paul Millander aka Judge Mason),
Micole Mercurio (Isabelle Millander), Neil Flynn (Officer Kevin Yarnell),
Cheryl White (Isabelle Mason), Steve Witting (Pete Walker),
Rob Roy Fitzgerald, Jason Azikiwe, Devon Alan (Craig Mason),
Steven M. Gagnon (Bailiff), Ryan James (Young Paul Millander),
Frank Novak (Clark County Judge)

Teaser One-liner: 'Isn't your birthday in August?'
The Case: A driver comes to regret picking up a hitchhiker in the pouring rain – it's Paul Millander, the serial killer seen in **00**, 'Pilot' and **07**, 'Anonymous'. Pete Walker becomes his next victim, and the tape left at the site is marked for Grissom's attention. Walker was born on 17 August 1957, and leaves an identical suicide note to Millander's earlier victims, Royce Harmon and Stuart Rampler. If Millander is working backwards, his next victim will be someone born on 17 August 1956 – such as Gil Grissom. Grissom dismisses this as coincidence, but is clearly unnerved.

Warrick and Sara check the perimeter of the warehouse where Walker was found. Unfortunately, the mud has washed virtually everything away. Warrick finds a mud print indicative of someone carrying something heavy. Grissom notices stippling on the side of Walker's face, as Catherine finds a long, probably female, dark hair by the body.

Nick and Archie Johnson deduce that the tape was probably recorded in a car. The recorder was only an inch from Walker's mouth when he was speaking. Archie extracts a whirring sound from the background, as well as a country and western song. The way in which the song sounds indicates that Walker was in the passenger seat, and Millander was driving.

Doc Robbins confirms that Walker died from a gunshot to the chest, and Grissom believes that the stippling is just a message to him from Millander that he's going to show both sides of something.

Brass finds the car, and Warrick wonders how Millander knew that its owner had the correct date of birth for his plans. He and Sara examine the car, and find gunshot residue. They believe that the bullet went out of the window: the whirring sound was the window opening. Greg's analysis of the hair from the scene confirms that it is female, and from an older person. They believe that it's been kept in a freezer, because of the good condition it's in. Greg finds endogenous testosterone in the hair, which might mean the woman was trying to enhance her athletic performance, or increase her sex drive. Nick finds an eight-digit number with a dash paper-burned into the front seat of the car.

The CSIs pool their evidence but Grissom thinks Millander is actually staging everything. Brass tells them that Pete Walker travelled the same route every week. The paper burn is from a speeding ticket. The CSIs pull Walker's record and compare it with Royce Harmon and Stuart Rampler – all of them were given a speeding ticket by the same policeman, Kevin Yarnell. Yarnell is a zealous cop who defends his cases in front of the traffic court judges.

Grissom and Catherine go in with him to Judge Mason's courtroom – Mason is Paul Millander. Grissom tries to get the court officer to arrest the judge but is taken away for contempt. Judge Mason goes to visit Grissom in the cells and maintains that he is Millander's doppelgänger. He then invites Grissom to come over for dinner, leaving his fingerprints on the cell bars.

Grissom meets Mrs Mason and their adopted son, Craig. They've lived in the same house since 1992. Mason apparently spends some of his private time driving around the state looking for bargains. Catherine rings to confirm that Mason's prints belong to Judge Mason.

Grissom is still unconvinced. Mason has no birth certificate as the hall of records where it was kept burned down. However, the current hall of records gives a property record for Paul and Isabelle Millander. Grissom and Catherine visit Isabelle Millander. She tells them about her husband, who started the Halloweird store that Grissom went to with Paul Millander. Catherine has a little snoop around and finds a girl's bedroom with the nameplate Pauline Millander. Isabelle shows Grissom an ashtray her child made, which has an odd green substance on it. Catherine is caught in the daughter's room, just after finding a hair. Isabelle says her daughter died a long time ago, and gets upset when she's asked about her son Paul. The CSIs leave, and Catherine wonders if Paul killed his sister.

The green substance is from old-style mould-making equipment. Grissom realises that the hand that was causing all the problems was that of Paul Millander's father. Catherine brought a baseball card back from Pauline's room with a print on which matches Judge Mason's. The hairs from the bedroom and the warehouse are identical. They realise that Pauline underwent a sex change to become Paul. Isabelle Millander agrees to let them take proper evidence, and Judge Mason is brought in. He admits that he was Pauline until his father's death, when he thought that a boy could have saved him. Millander asks Grissom if he wonders if he's the next victim, and then tells him he's chosen his next victim.

Millander escapes from jail using a fake CSI ID that he made up.

Catherine tells Grissom she believes that Millander slipped up with Pete Walker – although the 'suicide' message says he'd like to say 'I love you' to his mother, his mother in fact died in childbirth. Grissom knows that Millander wouldn't have made a mistake like that and rushes to the Millanders' house where he finds Isabelle dead from a knife to the stomach, and Paul in the bathtub, in the same way as his victims. Beside him is his birth certificate – date of birth 17 August 1956 . . .

Personal Notes: Grissom's birthday is given as 17 August 1956. His slight deafness shows again – possibly in one of the conference scenes.

Techniques: Grissom borrows Catherine's mentholatum to produce fumes to reveal the fingerprints on the cell bars.

The Wit and Wisdom of Gil Grissom: 'It's one of those few cases where physical evidence isn't helping us much.'

Classic Dialogue: Greg: 'The guy's pretty shrewd. Every murder comes back to a dead man.' Grissom: 'Greg, if I refer to Millander as smart, that's one thing, but I mind if other people do it, OK?' Greg: 'Got it.'

Fantastic Voyages: We see Walker being shot in the chest, and the gunpowder moving away from the bullet hole.

The Usual Suspects: Matt O'Toole makes his third and final appearance as Paul Millander. Neil Flynn (Officer Yarnell) is the voice of XR on *Buzz Lightyear of Star Command*.

Pop Culture References: There's a baseball card for legendary baseball player Tom Seaver at the Millanders' house.

Real-life Inspirations: It's doubtful there are any judges out there who are secretly serial killers – but you never know!

Mistakes Really Can Be Fatal: This episode contradicts a lot of the facts established in **07**, 'Anonymous'. According to that episode, the first victim was born in 1958; here Grissom says it was 1959. In **07**, 'Anonymous', Paul was ten when his father died in 1959; here he was born on 17 August 1956, so he would have been three. But even that episode gets it wrong – according to the database that Sara checks in **07**, 'Anonymous', Millander was 42 years old at the time (which would mean he was born in 1959!)

Millander was brought in for questioning in **00**, 'Pilot' because the print found was his! Not his father's!

Grissom's date of birth was apparently changed on the official site shortly before this episode aired, to match the information given here. As mentioned earlier, no one comments on 17 August 1956 being an important date in Grissom's life during **07**, 'Anonymous'!

Notes: This episode was nominated for an Emmy for Outstanding Cinematography for a Single-Camera series.

Overall: Horrible. Horrible. Horrible. One of the few episodes of *CSI* that should never have been made. Not only is it the weakest part of the Millander trilogy, it also contradicts virtually everything established in the first two episodes. If this was the best they could think of to do with Paul Millander, they should not have bothered. Try to imagine that this is just a Grissom cheese nightmare.

36
The Finger

US Air Date: 31 January 2002 14.8/22
UK Air Date: 4 May 2002

Written by: Danny Cannon and Carol Mendelsohn
Directed by: Richard J. Lewis
Guest Cast: Tom Irwin (Roy Logan),
Al Sapienza (Paul, Logan's Attorney), Barbara Williams (Diane Logan),
J. Robin Miller (Amanda Freeman), Gigi Bermingham (Waitress),
Stan Sellers (Bank Manager), Ty Upshaw (Police Officer),
Rachel Dara Wolfe (Female Teller)

Teaser One-liner: 'I'm not saying anything without my lawyer.'
The Case: Roy Logan enters his bank at 4.50 p.m. to make a withdrawal of $1million from his account. There's blood on the slip and the teller asks to see some identification, then says she needs to clear it with the manager. It takes an hour for the money to be assembled and placed in the metal briefcase Logan has brought with him. He leaves the

bank, but is intercepted by the police. As they question him, his cellphone rings but he ignores it. The Police Officer sees blood on his hands and arrests him.

He refuses to say anything without his lawyer, but the CSIs can still get the physical evidence from him. Catherine swabs his blood-covered hand and photographs him, while Grissom checks his clothes. Logan is constantly looking at the time – it's 6.30 as his attorney arrives to free him. Catherine asks Grissom to drop the samples in the lab as she's late for Lindsey's nursery rhyme recital. As she leaves, she notices Logan's sunglasses, and picks them up. She takes them out to him, but he tells her to get away from him. She puts them in his pocket and goes to leave, but his cellphone rings and the electronically altered voice at the other end wants to speak to Catherine. The voice tells her that it's good she's not a cop, otherwise 'she' would already be dead. The voice tells Catherine to dump her gun, her pager, her phone and her briefcase on the ground. She has to follow instructions or 'Amanda' will be killed. She is ordered to drive Logan's car; Grissom comes out, surprised to see her disappearing with Logan. He calls her cellphone – which is on the ground beside him.

Greg confirms that the blood on Logan's hand is female. Brass tells Grissom that Logan has no criminal record or warrants. He's married with a seven-year-old son. The police are now looking out for the car. Logan tells Catherine that 'Amanda' is his girlfriend. He claims that he went to her house and found a small container in which lay a severed index finger. Then he got the first call from the kidnapper, demanding a million dollars or Amanda would be killed. Catherine says she needs a drink, and stops at a diner. Sara and Hank Peddigrew are on a date there but Catherine ignores them. She puts the finger into a glass of ice, as the kidnapper calls with instructions to go south on Boulder Highway and then east on Yucca to the Horseshoe Tavern. As they leave the diner, Catherine puts the glass containing the finger in front of Sara.

Brass tells Grissom that Mrs Logan is alive and well. Sara brings the finger back to the lab, but Robbins is away at a wedding. The CSIs deduce that this is still a kidnapping case, but Sara is surprised that Catherine knew where she would be.

Catherine gets Logan to mark the money and, when they arrive at the Horseshoe Tavern, she deliberately brakes to leave a skidmark. She then drags her feet as she walks to leave a clear trail. They walk on until they see a figure wearing a rabbit mask and carrying a rifle. He demands the money, but Catherine insists they need to see Amanda. The kidnapper says he'll provide evidence at their next stopping point, and although Catherine wants to dig her heels in, Logan hands over the money. At the old gas station they've been sent to, Catherine finds a map showing where Amanda Freeman can be found, near the Easelwood Reservoir.

Mrs Logan won't co-operate with questions about her husband. The blood from the finger matches the blood on Logan's hands, and Nick points out that Logan had another property. A police car has spotted Logan and Catherine, and Grissom, Warrick and Sara head out to the Horseshoe Tavern where they find the clues Catherine left, and a second set of treadmarks.

Nick goes to Logan's other property, Amanda Freeman's home. He finds her handbag, and two wine glasses, both with lipstick stains. The answer machine shows she's missed calls from Logan and from her gym. Her pet cockatoo has blood on its feathers.

Catherine and Logan go to the Reservoir, where they find Amanda's dead body.

Doc Robbins comes back from a family wedding in Kansas City to check the finger, and tells Grissom that it was severed post-mortem, as Catherine finally gets a chance to call. When she gets back to CSI, Warrick and Greg have been looking after Lindsey for her.

Amanda has been in the water about 24 hours. There are blowfly eggs under her tongue, and in her nose and trachea, indicating she was killed 24 hours before that by a blunt force trauma. Robbins finds a small piece of stone in her scalp. Logan wants to see her one last time, and then goes to stay in a hotel.

Nick processes Amanda's house and deduces that there was a struggle. Amanda fell to the floor, hitting her head on a marble table as she fell, with the bloodspattering as far as her cockatoo's cage. All the knives have been run through the dishwasher, but the glasses are still there. He and Catherine work out that Amanda was removed from the room in some form of plastic, and discover that the shower curtain is missing. Warrick and Sara find it in the storm drain in which her body was placed. There's a small tear in the shower curtain which might have been done at the same time as the finger slicing. Warrick and Sara also discover a grease stain on the outside of the curtain, which turns out to be peanut butter. Nick recalls that Mrs Logan was scolding her son for eating peanut butter sandwiches in his father's car. Checking out Logan's car, the CSIs find a matching stain.

Amanda's phone records show that the last call made from the house was to Mrs Logan. The DNA from saliva in the glasses match Amanda and another woman. Grissom and Catherine tell Mrs Logan that they think that a civilised drink between her and Amanda turned nasty. Mrs Logan maintains that Amanda claimed Logan was going to marry her, and Mrs Logan put her straight. Logan arrived and she left them to it. The CSIs check her hands, and they're clean, but Logan's lawyer, who is with her, has glow marks from the money on his hands. The lawyer admits that he made the phone calls, and wore the rabbit mask, but he denies that he killed Amanda. He just did what his client instructed. The money is at Logan's country club. Catherine goes to the hotel to see Logan, but the room is unused. The locker also is empty.

Logan has just about got away with murder – until he's picked up for speeding and arrested.

Personal Notes: Sara and Hank Peddigrew (see **26**, 'Bully for You') go on a date which is interrupted by Catherine and Logan's arrival. This could be the person that she rang at the end of **35**, 'Identity Crisis' (which would explain why the reference to Nick in the script was excised). Doc Robbins has a brother in Kansas City who gets married on 31 January. Nick enjoys the Discovery Channel.

Techniques: Greg uses an Agilent Technologies machine to identify the grease on the shower curtain.

Classic Dialogue: Catherine: 'Didn't Shakespeare say, "Let's kill all the lawyers."' Grissom: 'Yeah. *Henry VI*. Where is he when we need him?'

Catherine: 'So, let's get to know each other. You first. You were born; you came home from the hospital. Then what?'

Fantastic Voyages: We look closely at the oil in the skidmarks that Catherine left outside the Horseshoe Tavern. We then examine Amanda Freeman's scalp at close range, and get an idea of what a finger looks like when it's being sliced off the hand. Less gorily, there's a shot of a carpet being thoroughly cleaned.

The Usual Suspects: Tom Irwin (Roy Logan) played Lou in the remake of *The Haunting*. Al Sapienza (Paul, the attorney), was Mikey Palmice on *The Sopranos*, and Paul Koplin in the second season of *24*.

Pop Culture References: Nick is an avid watcher of the Discovery Channel, which focuses on natural wildlife. Catherine quotes from Shakespeare's *Henry VI*.

Notes: The episode is set on 30/31 January 2002 (Roy Logan's withdrawal slip).

Overall: You almost expect Roy Logan to snarl 'I'd've got away with it if it wasn't for these meddling criminalists' in best *Scooby-Doo* fashion at the end of this. Coincidences do happen in real life, and Catherine's arrival at the same diner that Sara is at is a bit implausible, but acceptable. There's a little bit of the 'Scully in Jeopardy' syndrome that affected middle seasons of *The X-Files*, but thankfully, this isn't the start of a trend.

37
Burden of Proof

US Air Date: 7 February 2002 15.8/23
UK Air Date: 11 May 2002

Written by: Ann Donahue
Directed by: Kenneth Fink

Guest Cast: Janet Gunn (Jane Bradley), Sara Paxton (Jody Bradley),
Dan Byrd (Jake Bradley), Terry Bozeman (Brad Gottleib),
Nancy Valen (Mike's Neighbour),
Monnae Michaell (Doctor at Hospital), Jason Beghe (Russ Bradley),
Patrick Thomas O'Brien (Edward Cormier),
John Rosenfeld (Child Advocate), David Sobel (Mike Kimble),
Roger Hamilton (Dog Handler)

Teaser One-liner: 'A Body Farm is not creepy. It's a controlled study of situational decomposition. All in all, a very healthy place.'

The Case: The CSIs are called in to investigate the discovery of an unknown body at the University of Western Nevada Body Farm, where pathologists study dead bodies which have been donated to science to see how outside factors affect their decay. The deceased has no identification, and apparently died of a gunshot wound to the chest. Catherine spots a carpet beetle on the body and Grissom realises that they're getting cross contamination from the other bodies at the farm.

Doc Robbins agrees that the deceased sustained a projectile, but there's no evidence of a bullet. He and Grissom decide to excise the wound tract. The victim is identified from his fingerprints as Mike Kimble. Robbins finds a piece of titanium in the body, but it's part of Kimble's ribs. Grissom discovers a bovine maggot that has been feeding on something inside the wound. Catherine and Warrick head out to Kimble's house. However, it's on fire when they get there. The next door neighbour says Kimble's only regular visitor was his fiancée Jane.

Nick and Warrick check out the house once the fire has been extinguished. The patterns show the fire moved downwards, which is very unusual. They believe it was chasing an accelerant, possibly furniture polish. Upstairs, Nick discovers a large bloodstain under the carpet.

Brass and Catherine break the news of Kimble's death to his fiancée Jane Bradley, who tells them they were going to be married a week later. Her kids apparently loved Kimble, who was a photographer. They're interrupted by Jane Bradley's ex-husband Russ, who points out that he has no reason to murder Kimble: he stops paying alimony when his wife remarries.

At Kimble's house there is a room that was untouched by the fire. Hidden inside it are photos of Jane Bradley's daughter Jody in provocative poses. Jody claims that Mike loved her, and she loved him. Catherine thinks she is just protecting her abuser. The photos were taken by a camera similar to Kimble's. Warrick examines the photo closely, and discovers a finger obscuring part of it.

Grissom is checking raw beef to see if he can duplicate what the maggot was eating in Kimble's body. Jody's father is furious about the photos of his daughter, and says that he never liked the way Kimble looked at her. Russ Bradley is the registered owner of a handgun, which has recently been cleaned.

The accelerant for the fire is identified as nail polish. Jody is given a sexual abuse and rape test, during which a burn is found on her body; she says it's from a curling iron, but Catherine suspects it might be from setting the fire with nail polish.

There's definite evidence of chronic sexual abuse on Jody. Nick and Catherine search the house using an ALS to look for body fluids, and find some on Jody's nightgown. Brass has discovered that Jane had cancelled her wedding to Kimble. She says it's because she got cold feet, but Catherine and Brass think it's because she sensed what was going on. However, the DNA tests reveal that neither Kimble nor Bradley put the semen on the nightgown – it was Jody's brother Jake. Nick thinks that Jake had simply masturbated on the nightgown. The teenager admits it, and says that Jody was weird around Mike Kimble.

Grissom deduces that the bullet might have been embedded in ice – and possibly made from ground beef. Doc Robbins comes in on his day off to see Grissom demonstrate his frozen meat bullet. It fits the evidence they found. Brass finds evidence that Bradley packs his own bullets, and there's ground beef in his reloader. Bradley admits that he shot Kimble and then set fire to the house. Grissom isn't so sure he's responsible for the fire, but Bradley's case for murder is expedited.

The police find the nail polish accelerant in Jody's locker, but Jody's curling iron story proves true.

Grissom suggests to Warrick that he look closely at Jody's eyes in the photo to see if they reflect the photographer; he thinks that he can see a porthole reflected in Jody's eye. Jane Bradley says that Kimble didn't have a boat, but her ex-husband did. Warrick goes to visit it.

Catherine tells Jody they know that her father was abusing her. She says she told Kimble, but Bradley killed him. Warrick discovers evidence that Bradley was having sex with Jody, a twelve year old, which leaves him in prison for a mandatory life sentence with no possibility of parole.

Personal Notes: Grissom has a bad habit of putting his experiments in the communal fridge – bugs and blood! He's also failed to notice that Sara has become a vegetarian (see **09**, 'Sex, Lies and Larvae'). Sara becomes so exasperated by him that she decides she wants a long leave of absence, or to leave altogether, because of Grissom's failure to communicate properly. Catherine manages to explain to Grissom where he's gone wrong – and he orders a plant to be sent to Sara 'from Grissom'. Lindsey Willows has turned eight.

Techniques: Warrick uses a lot of computer techniques to isolate the images also captured in the photo of Jody.

The Wit and Wisdom of Gil Grissom: 'What I think and what the evidence proves are possibly two different things.'

Classic Dialogue: Catherine to Grissom: 'You have responsibilities, and people are making a family around you whether you like it or not, whether you give them permission or not.'

Fantastic Voyages: We watch exactly what happens to a bullet when it enters the body and splinters fall away from it as it hits the bone; and the same thing happening a second time, except this time the bullet is embedded in ice, which melts and, finally, with the bullet made of meat.

The Usual Suspects: Dan Byrd (Jake Bradley) has an affinity for Stephen King-related projects – he's Paul in *Firestarter 2*, and Mark Petrie, the central figure in the remake of *Salem's Lot*. Janet Gunn (Jane Bradley) graduated from being Susan Howard's stunt double on *Dallas* to playing Sgt Cassy St John on *Silk Stalkings*.

Overall: Another case of incest and child abuse for *CSI*. There's not enough in the A story to justify not having a second case running in parallel, and the Grissom/Sara relationship problems only just about work. The internet fans who think the pair should get together were in heaven; the rest of us just want another case.

38
Primum Non Nocere

US Air Date: 28 February 2002 17.1/26
UK Air Date: 18 May 2002

Written by: Andrew Lipsitz
Directed by: Danny Cannon
Guest Cast: Nicole Ari Parker (Lillie Ivers),
Jeremy Ratchford (Tommy Sconzo), Abby Brammell (Jane Gallagher),
Peter MacKenzie (Doctor), David Andriole (Terry Rivers),
Anthony DiMaria (Bartender), Dig Wayne (Joe Baker)

Teaser One-liner: 'Looks like that other team worked him over pretty good.'

The Cases: Hockey player Terry Rivers sustains a cut during a match between his team, the Rat Pack, and Area 51 and, against the team doctor's advice, returns to the game after being stitched up and taking a couple of pills. A few minutes later he slams into the opposing goalie, and finishes beneath a melee of players. He is helped back to the bench, and dies. Grissom and Catherine find a recent gash on his cheek and a large gash in the side of his neck. Grissom works the scene with Sara, finding some small off-white slivers and some blood on the safety glass, before the Zamboni, the ice cleaning machine, arrives.

Catherine talks to the doctor, who says he brought Rivers back to the bench to work on him, giving him CPR. One of Rivers' team-mates, Tommy Sconzo, gives Catherine a hard time and explains that the physical nature of the game is the attraction. Grissom finds part of a tooth in the Zamboni and he and Sara melt the compacted ice to look for the remainder, without any luck.

Doc Robbins performs an autopsy on Rivers, and finds quinine in his body. He had a lot of old injuries but Robbins isn't sure of the cause of death. The cut to his neck nicked the carotid artery, which might have caused him to black out – but they can't be sure if the death caused his fall, or the fall caused his death.

Catherine talks to Area 51 player Jane Gallagher, who says that other teams may have disliked Rivers, but his own team-mates disliked him a lot more. There is blood-spatter on Jane Gallagher's highly sharpened skates. She used to be part of the Rat Pack, and like most of Rivers' team-mates, had lost heavily through deals that Rivers did in his 'real' job as a stockbroker. She denies doing anything to him deliberately, and then throws up, claiming it's from bad shellfish eaten twelve hours earlier. But Grissom gathers the vomit up as evidence since that sort of reaction should have happened much earlier. Greg checks the sample, and there's no shellfish in it – but it does show that Jane is pregnant.

Sara and Grissom check Jane's bed sheets and find a lot of semen stains and a male toenail. The toenail DNA matches the piece of tooth found on the ice, and both match Tommy Sconzo's. He also had no love for Rivers, who had lost $12,000 for him.

Doc Robbins discovers that Rivers had a coronary anomaly which interfered with his heart's electrical system. The quinine in his system would have been lethal. Jane Gallagher admits she knew about Rivers' problem and that she was sleeping with both Rivers and Tommy; Tommy was the father of the baby.

However, Jane had no access to quinine, and there wasn't any in Rivers' apartment. Someone with access to Rivers' medical records knew about his heart problem – which leads the CSIs to the doctor, who filled a large prescription for quinine a month earlier. They also find a photo of him with Jane Gallagher, and deduce that he killed Rivers because he thought he was the father of Jane's baby. With Rivers out of the way, Jane would come back to him.

Nick and Warrick meet Homicide Detective Lockwood at a hotel, where Warrick is very taken with the lounge singer, Lillie Ivers. The corpse is Stan Grevey, a sax player, found with white powder on his mouth, and needle marks on his arms. The scene has all the hallmarks of an overdose without any of the necessary paraphernalia. There are two coasters on the table, but only one glass. The CSIs spot a contact lens.

Greg discovers that Grevey died from taking 91 per cent pure heroin – most West Coast heroin is 20–30 per cent. Nick notices that Warrick is interested in Lillie and offers to go through the rubbish while Warrick interviews her. Warrick is grateful, but refuses. In the rubbish Nick finds the drug paraphernalia wrapped in a black scarf, which Lillie admits is hers.

The two CSIs question Bill, Stan's friend who got him the job. He admits he got rid of the drug gear, because he didn't want Stan's eight-year-old son to know his father died with a needle in his arm. He says Lillie's scarf was the first thing he found. He doesn't wear contact lenses.

Warrick talks to Lillie, who's more interested in persuading him to turn pro as a musician. She's having a good career. When she goes back on stage, Warrick notices the bartender slip something between two coasters. Back at the lab, the two coasters found at the scene test positive for heroin. Nick points out to Warrick that Lillie was also using a drink with two coasters.

The bartender claims he didn't know what he was doing when he was cutting the heroin, which is why it was so strong, but is arrested for supplying it. Knowing she is involved with the drugs, Warrick says goodbye to Lillie.

Personal Notes: Grissom claims to have been a baseball fan his entire life. He makes a deadpan comment to Sara about his interest in beauty since he met her. Warrick is a good pianist, but doesn't like playing in front of strangers. The friendship between Nick and Warrick is strong at this point – at the end of the episode, Nick joins Warrick as he plays cards to try to forget Lillie. Greg was captain of the high school chess squad. (Sara points out that that isn't a sport and tells him she doesn't think sex is either.)

The Wit and Wisdom of Gil Grissom: 'Sounds like these boys went to a fight and a hockey game broke out.'

'There are three things in life that people like to stare at. A rippling stream, a fire in a fireplace and a Zamboni going round and round.' (Quoting Charlie Brown)

'Organised sports is the paradigmatic model of a just society. Everyone knows the same language, everyone knows the rules. And there's a specific punishment handed out the moment someone tries to cheat. Instant morality.'

'One hundred and twenty-three goldsmiths took a bite out of the victim insuring that no one individual could be blamed for the murder. For who would know which one administered the lethal bite.'

Classic Dialogue: Brass: 'Hockey, rough game.' Grissom: 'Yeah, it's murder.'

Catherine: 'It's never a good sign when the number of women a guy sleeps with is more than the number of chairs he owns.'

Grissom: 'What is Victoria's Secret, I wonder?' Sara: 'Beauty, Grissom. Remember?'

Fantastic Voyages: We see the hockey skate cut Rivers' neck, and a close up of Terry Rivers' heart atrium.

The Usual Suspects: Jeremy Ratchford (Tommy Sconzo) played badass vampire Lyle Gorch on *Buffy the Vampire Slayer*. Nicole Ari Parker (Lillie Ivers) is best known for her role on *Soul Food*.

Pop Culture References: Grissom quotes from Charles Schulz' 'Peanuts' cartoon.

Mistakes Really Can Be Fatal: If you read Latin, the title's a bit of a giveaway! It's taken from the Hippocratic Oath (it means, 'first, do no harm'), and is the bit about doctors not being allowed to hurt patients. So we have a case where there's someone who's been harmed, and a doctor involved . . . Hmmm . . .

Notes: This episode was nominated for an Emmy for Outstanding Single-Camera Sound Mixing for a Series. A number of scenes were filmed on location in Vegas, along the Strip and in the House of Blues.

Overall: A mediocre plot immeasurably improved by some choice dialogue, a totally unexpected declaration about beauty from Grissom, and further insight into both Warrick and Nick. In fact, all the CSIs have a moment in the sun in this episode.

39
Felonious Monk

US Air Date: 7 March 2002 16.2/24
UK Air Date: 25 May 2002

Written by: Jerry Stahl
Directed by: Kenneth Fink
Guest Cast: Bruce McGill (Detective Jimmy Tadero),
Marshall Bell (Peter Hutchins Sr), Aaron Paul (Pete Hutchins),
Nicholas Sadler (Kelso), Randy Thompson, Mark Dacascos (Ananda),
Jusak Yang Bernhard (David Suddahara), Michael Delano (Ted Benton),
Koji Kataoka (Monk #2), Steve Kozlowski (Tommy),
Kimberly Lyon (Stephanie Watson), Gregory Onga (Monk #3),
Woon Young Park (Monk #1), Eck Stone (Monk #4)

Teaser One-liner: 'How do you get one vic, let alone four, to lie still while you put a bullet between their eyes?'

The Cases: Grissom, Sara and Nick are called to a shooting at a Buddhist temple. Four monks have been killed, and placed in a neat formation. There's a gang marking from the Snakebacks chalked on the walls. There's also a lot of expensive items still around, and it's clear that it's a hit, not a robbery. Grissom searches the temple's Zen garden, and finds a rifle. The monk who notified the police about the deaths, Ananda, says he was making a deposit at the bank during the murders.

O'Brien talks to David Suddahara, the part-time cook at the temple, who says the monks are too trusting, and that he saw some gang signs a few weeks earlier, but the monks asked him not to report them. Sara finds a boot print in one of the rugs, while Nick searches through the monks' belongings, finding a stack of CDs and some pornography. Sara finds a blue smear on one of the golden statues of Buddha, and a piece of chewing gum where the third eye should be. She thinks that this is probably an outside job.

Doc Robbins explains to Grissom that all the monks were shot in the 'third eye', the sixth chakra and he thinks that the killer is a Buddhist. Ballistics prove that the rifle was the murder weapon, and that the prints are Ananda's. The monk admits that he moved the gun – it was on his desk when he returned, he went to ask the other monks about it, found them dead, then placed it outside. He also claims that someone left the pornography at the temple, and he was simply looking after it. However, the prints on the rifle are only on the stock, not on the trigger. Ananda isn't the killer.

Nick is puzzled by the Snakeback graffiti since the gang was virtually eliminated by the police after they attacked some German tourists. He and Grissom deduce that the graffiti was a plant. Grissom asks for help from the Air Force: since 11 September, military installations have been kept under surveillance, and Grissom wonders if the temple might have been picked up since it's so close to Nellis AFB. It has, and the Air Force provide a licence plate of the only vehicle that went through the temple gates at the time of the murders, which turns out to belong to a Peter Hutchins.

Hutchins runs a coffee shop. He says that business is difficult because of the monks, and his aged and rather bigoted father adds that the monks have caused a real problem. Sara finds some prayer beads in the truck, which belongs to Hutchins Sr. He denies going near the temple and his alibi checks out.

Greg identifies the blue substance as paintball paint. Hutchins Jr is found at a paintball emporium, and Sara notices his boots, which appear to match the print she found. He denies ever going to the temple, but confronted with the evidence, admits that he went a week earlier with some friends, one of whom stole a statue. Hutchins went back to replace it, and saw the bodies as he was taking off his boots. Grissom wonders why he was taking off his boots unless he had been there before. Hutchins Jr then admits, much to his father's amazement, that the monks were his friends.

Grissom asks Greg to isolate food samples within the chewing gum and this clears both Hutchins. Grissom asks Amanda about the curry and saffron that Greg has found. As he's doing so, O'Brien arrives and accuses Ananda of embezzling money. Although the monks raised $13,000, only $12,000 was banked. Ananda explains that the money was kept in a box in his office, inside which there's a small pile of curry powder. Ananda admits that he caught Suddahara, and subsequently dismissed him. Suddahara confesses to the murders – he shot the monks between the eyes.

Catherine goes to visit her old friend, policeman Jimmy Tadero, who's nearing retirement. They've both seen a disturbing newscast – Dwight Kelso, a convicted murderer, gave a deathbed confession to one of the murders he's served a life sentence for, but denied killing Stephanie Watson, who was Catherine's best friend. Jimmy worked on the case, and he is still certain that Kelso was responsible. There were witnesses to Kelso harassing Stephanie, and he had a knife cut. Jimmy points out that the evidence never lies. Catherine and Warrick check out the evidence in the cold-storage room, and decide to start with the knife. Greg finds three blood samples on it: Stephanie Watson's, Dwight Kelso's and a very weak third that, fifteen years ago, couldn't be processed. Catherine asks him to check it out as his top priority.

Ecklie is surprised at Catherine's excavation of the past, but they are both surprised by Warrick's discovery that the glove found at the scene of the crime isn't in the on-scene photographs, but was only logged by Jimmy a few days later.

Jimmy and Catherine meet at Catherine's old workplace, where Stephanie was killed. He points out that it was the worst day of his life when Stephanie died – they were close

– and he's not happy when Catherine effectively accuses
him of planting Kelso's glove. There's saliva in the blood
sample on the glove so it's from a different injury. The
glove must have been planted. Jimmy finally admits
'helping the evidence along', and is horrified when
Catherine asks for a blood sample to compare with the
third trace.

However, Jimmy's blood sample doesn't match the third
trace, and CODIS reveals that there's no match anywhere.
Stephanie's killer has got away with murder. Catherine has
no option but to reveal her findings and turn Jimmy in,
even if, for framing someone who has since died, he faces
life imprisonment or, possibly, the death penalty. Sadly,
Catherine returns the evidence from Stephanie's murder to
the cold storage, marking the box 'case unsolved'.

Personal Notes: Catherine became a CSI as a result of her
friendship with Jimmy Tadero, and the way in which
Stephanie Watson's murder was 'solved' by the CSI's
work. We see her in flashback working with Stephanie at
the club. Nick hates taking his shoes off to process the
crime scene in the temple. After he lost his legs, Doc
Robbins started to study the chakras. Ecklie was working
as a CSI fifteen years earlier (1987) when Stephanie
Watson was killed.

Techniques: Sara uses an Electrostatic Dust Print Lifter,
which uses an electrostatic field to lift the prints from the
surface and enhance their visibility.

The Wit and Wisdom of Gil Grissom: 'Sometimes [the past]
leaves its fingerprints on the future.'

'It's got to be a lot easier to be a monk in a monastery
on a mountaintop than one on Las Vegas Boulevard.'

'What we've got here is a Warhol: it's not a real soup
can, it's a painting of a soup can.'

Classic Dialogue: Grissom: 'One survivor, one suspect.'
Nick: 'And a whole lot of bad karma.'

Jimmy: 'I can't believe you're doing this to me. I gave
you your career.' Catherine: 'I earned my career.'

Fantastic Voyages: We go right down into the rug with the
Electrostatic Dust Lifter to pick up the boot print.

The Usual Suspects: Michael Delano returns as Catherine's ex-boss Ted Beaton (here called Benton) (see 05, 'Who Are You?'). Mark Dacascos (Ananda) played Eric Draven in *The Crow: Stairway to Heaven* TV series, as well as Dr Ash Mattley in the appropriately named TV movie *DNA*. Bruce McGill (Jimmy Tadero) played Jack Dalton on *McGyver*, and Captain Braxton in *Star Trek: Voyager*'s timetravel story 'Relativity'.

Pop Culture References: *Good Morning, Vietnam*.

Real-life Inspirations: This is loosely based on the murder of some Buddhist monks in Arizona some years ago.

Mistakes Really Can Be Fatal: Why doesn't Sara react more strongly to mention of the Snakebacks? She got so involved in the 'Jane Doe' case (see 15, 'Too Tough To Die') that you'd think she'd still be sensitive on the subject.

Suddahara is caught by Ananda, but kills the other monks, not him. Odd, to say the least . . .

Notes: The title is a pun on Thelonious Monk – the highly regarded jazz musician, who otherwise has no connection to the episode.

Overall: Apart from the annoying incidental music used during the scenes set in the temple, this is a very strong episode. It's intriguing to learn that Ecklie, for all the hassle he gets from the Graveyard Shift, is an extremely experienced CSI, and Marg Helgenberger gets a chance to shine in some powerful scenes.

40
Chasing the Bus

US Air Date: 28 March 2002 15.4/25
UK Air Date: 1 June 2002

Written by: Eli Talbert
Directed by: Richard J. Lewis
Guest Cast: Denis Arndt (Larry Maddox),
Joseph D. Reitman (Sean Nolan), Scott Plank (Eric Kevlin),
Eric Matheny (Dr Hawkins), Lauren Hodges (Young Female Passenger),
Kris Iyer (ER Surgeon), Christopher Caso (Ryan Hyde),

Stephon Fuller (Gas Station Attendant), Monica Garcia (Mrs Parker),
Stuart Gold (John Cooper), Jim Hanna (Jack), Jerry Hauck (Mr Parker),
Revital Krawetz (Diane Cooper), Mark Lentry (Calvin McBride),
Billy Mayo (Fire Chief James Walker), Julie Mintz (Sabrina Wright),
Kate Orsini (Mini-Mart Clerk), Todd Slayton (Paramedic),
Mona Wyatt (Gwen Murray), Cara Buono (Eric's Girlfriend)

Teaser One-liner: 'We're not running this show.'

The Case: A tour bus runs off the road out in the desert
near Las Vegas, and ends up on its side, on top of a car.
The CSIs arrive as the rescue operations are still going on,
and once the passengers are taken to hospital, Grissom sets
everyone to work processing the scene, calling in every
spare Las Vegas CSI and cadets. Greg arrives at the scene,
eager to help out, and Grissom tells Nick to look after him
and ensure he doesn't contaminate the scene. There are six
fatalities. The bus driver was the only one wearing a
seatbelt.

The bus company owner Larry Maddox hurries to the
scene, and gives Brass the passenger list. There were
twenty-four passengers, and one Parolee at large – Calvin
McBride.

Grissom finds shredded rubber and deduces that a radius
rod connecting the axle to the frame has snapped, which
would lead to the blow-out. Catherine examines the car
underneath the bus, and the driver grabs her arm, still alive.

Nick and Greg talk to the bus driver, who's getting
increasingly confused, and is sweating. Nick tries to get
him to take a breathalyser test, but he ends up coughing
up blood.

McBride has vanished. Nick checks through the bus,
finding a bottle of booze that someone offered the driver
before the crash. McBride's seat would have given him an
unobstructed path through the windscreen. Nick and
Grissom find his body near part of the windscreen.

Catherine accompanies the car driver to the hospital; he
says his name is Eric, and he just wanted to 'surprise her'.
At the same time, a girl who's clearly been in the accident
is still hanging around at the scene, but can't explain to
Grissom why she's still there.

Warrick and Sara process the road. Sara finds numerous shreds of rubber, while Warrick examines the roadside rail. They deduce that the bus crossed four lanes of traffic and only hit one car.

The whiskey bottle has McBride's DNA on it but Doc Robbins confirms to Nick that the bus driver's symptoms were not caused by drink – he was hungry. He suffered from Type II diabetes. He has now died from massive injuries and internal bleeding.

Warrick and Sara find a sheared bolt on the road, and tests show that it's not the type that should have been fitted. Nick tells Grissom that the bus was allegedly in perfect working order, but it's clear that's not the case.

Eric Kevlin, the car driver, dies; he was heading to Vegas to see his girlfriend. Brass is surprised that he signed a 'Do Not Resuscitate' order. But, it transpires, the order was because he was a doctor and didn't want anyone else to have to make the decision on his behalf.

The bus company owner Maddox says the company had a perfect record until this accident. He is perturbed by accusations against the company, but admits that he started buying bolts from a cheaper supplier, and the accident may have been the consequence.

Sara checks the rubber samples against the car and bus tyres, while Brass checks out anything unusual happening at the bus' last regular stop where, he learns, a couple were seen arguing. Catherine and Nick check out the car, and find the driver's wallet, with photos of the girl that Grissom saw at the accident scene. They visit the girl, who says that Eric had met up with her at the rest stop, following her around during a girls' weekend.

Grissom examines the accident scene photos for signs of when the rod snapped, while Greg checks swabs from the tyres. Grissom deduces that the right tyre blew, the driver overcorrected, and the rod then broke. The tyre blew because of the presence of chloroform, which destroys the elasticity of rubber inside it – it was sabotage.

Sara asks Vincent, a new lab tech, how chloroform could have got inside the tyre, and he explains that you can urinate against a rope, and the urine will dribble down. A bus is set up on a treadmill to duplicate the accident conditions. Sara adds chloroform via a rope, leaning on her left hand to stay steady as she does so.

A print on the tyre matches that of Sean Nolan, a former driver. Nolan was fired for having marijuana in his locker, and is now working in Barstow. The tyre blows exactly when they expect provided the chloroform was added at the last rest stop in Barstow. Three of Maddox's buses have had blow-outs, but only one had the faulty bolts fitted. Nolan admits putting the chloroform on the tyres, but he assumed that the suspension system would hold, as it did on the first two occasions, but this time the cheap bolt sheared and led to the deaths.

Personal Notes: Grissom found a head in a bucket of paint once. Nick's first case as a CSI-1 was a triple homicide of a mother and two kids; he thought he was going to a robbery. Greg finds that seeing blood all over someone in the field is very different from seeing samples of it in the lab.

Classic Dialogue: Maddox: 'Accidents are inevitable.' Grissom: 'Criminal acts, however, are not.'

The Usual Suspects: Denis Arndt (Larry Maddox) appeared with William Petersen in *Peter Benchley's The Beast*, as Osborne Manning. Scott Plank (Eric Kevlin) was a regular on *Melrose Place* as Nick Reardon.

Mistakes Really Can Be Fatal: Maddox claims that his buses have a great safety record, but we learn at the end that there have been two other tyre blow-outs in the short time that Nolan was working in Barstow. Surely you'd think that that might have been relevant?

Notes: This episode was nominated for an Emmy for Outstanding Sound-Editing for a Series.

Overall: Nice to see the CSI team working as a team and pulling all the evidence together from the different areas – plus some good character development for both Greg and Nick. A good solid episode.

41
Stalker

US Air Date: 4 April 2002 16.1/25
UK Air Date: 8 June 2002

Written by: Anthony E. Zuiker & Danny Cannon
Directed by: Peter Markle
Guest Cast: Doug Hutchison (Nigel Crane),
Bryan Kirkwood (Adam Piorio), Shelley Robertson (Doctor),
Leland Orser (Morris Pearson), Brianna Lynn Brown (Jane Galloway)

Teaser One-liner: 'As far as we know her place was perfectly hermetically sealed until the cops batter-rammed their way in.'

The Case: Jane Galloway becomes frightened when she receives an obscene answerphone message. The caller tells her not to bite her nails, and she realises that he can see her. She can't get out of her bathroom window, because it's covered and nailed shut, so she hides in her closet. Her dog scratches at the door, so she brings him in with her and keeps the door tightly shut. But then two hands grab her.

When the CSI team arrives, Jane is dead, and posed hugging her toilet. Her hair is still wet with hair dye. Grissom and Catherine can't find the dog, or explain how the killer got out. The place is completely sealed. It even has aluminium foil on the insides of the windows.

Something about the position Jane is in disturbs Nick. Catherine finds a hair which is thick, but might still be human, on Jane's bed. Sara checks Jane's phone records.

Doc Robbins confirms Jane was suffocated, but not raped. Greg informs Warrick that the hair isn't human. Nick fumes a plastic bag found at the crime scene – and Greg sees Jane's face imprinted inside it. Brass finds that there was a restraining order against Jane's boyfriend but he rang her thirteen times that day. Warrick realises the 'hair' is not refracting light, so it's artificial.

Brass and Sara go to the house of Jane's boyfriend, Adam Piorio, and find him with a bloody face sitting in his car. He says he can't remember how he got it. Under questioning he says that Jane started to act weirdly. He admits that he called her a lot of times, because he was high on Ecstasy. However, the blood on his face isn't from Jane – Piorio's alibi is that he was in a fight elsewhere.

Nick receives an email from his old prom date containing three pictures, one of which is the identical set-up to Jane's murder scene. Nick calls his date; she now lives in Maine. He can't understand how anyone could have seen it unless they'd accessed his email.

Morris Pearson, a psychic, says he foresaw Jane's murder and has details that he shouldn't have known. He saw a screaming face in a plastic womb, a blood shower and three hearts beating fast – one of them small. He informs Grissom that the dog didn't make it.

Sara has checked out Jane's movements. She started to act scared about three weeks earlier, took a leave of absence, but then quit her job, before buying a number of locks. She checked into the Monaco Hotel for a couple of nights. Her phone records, however, indicate that most of her incoming calls came from inside her own house.

Pearson was staying at the Monaco in the room next to Jane Galloway on the night of her murder. He says he didn't realise that she was the murder victim, and that he had tried to talk to her that night because he felt negative energy, and was trying to heal her. He checked out shortly after Jane left. He's had another vision, of three locks and of frames. All the items he saw check out in Jane's apartment, but the angle feels wrong to Pearson – it's as if he was looking at them from above. Grissom finds a hole in the ceiling of the closet and goes up to the attic, where he finds corked holes with markings indicating what can be seen through them. The attic is filled with fibreglass insulation, and there's a phone ready to plug into the system. Grissom uses it to ring Warrick, who confirms that the 'hair' was fibreglass. He and Catherine find a collection of electronic gadgets including a fibre-optic camera, night-vision goggles and a digital recorder. But how did the voyeur get in? They deduce it was probably someone in a uniform, so they check with the various utility companies.

Nick and Warrick go to Jane's cable installer's house – it's the same company that installed Nick's own system. While Warrick takes a call on his cellphone outside, a man stealthily drops from the ceiling and throws Nick out of a window. Nick sustains concussion, cracked ribs, and a sprained wrist. Grissom and Catherine discover that Nigel Crane, the cable installer, lives in his attic, rather than in the house. Catherine finds the hair dye in the rubbish, and Grissom finds a library of tapes of Crane's surveillances. Warrick and Sara take Nick home, then return to the lab. As they arrive, Catherine spots a copy of the article about Nick on one of the video tapes. They go to the last tape and realise that Nick is Crane's current subject.

At 1 a.m. Nick is roused by Morris Pearson, who's had a vision of something dreadful happening. As Grissom rings Nick to warn him, Crane grabs Pearson, kills him and drops him through the ceiling. He gets Nick's gun and holds him at gunpoint. Nick doesn't recognise him until Crane tells him he installed the cable. He killed Jane as a present for Nick, and even dyed her hair to make it the same colour as Nick's prom date from the photo that was emailed to him. Nick realises that Crane intends to commit suicide so that Nick will have to remember his name, but the police arrive just in time. Crane's mind is completely broken as he sits in the interrogation room.

Personal Notes: Nick is featured in the departmental newsletter as a result of a letter of commendation, but he's not happy about his privacy being invaded.

The Wit and Wisdom of Gil Grissom: 'I don't think this thing was about sex at all. I think it was about control, voyeurism. Jane was like his little goldfish.'

'In Nigel's mind, Jane Galloway was someone he could control, which was OK for a while, but you were someone he could actually become. See, Maslow's Fifth Tier of the Hierarchy is Self-Actualisation.'

Classic Dialogue: Robbins: 'We know two things for certain. Jane Galloway died from a lack of O_2 and she is a natural blonde.' Catherine: 'What are you looking at me for?'

Grissom: 'Mr Pearson, I'm a scientist.' Morris Pearson: 'And I am a clairvoyant. You see science without abstractions. I see visions with abstractions. Am I less credible than you Mr Grissom?'

Fantastic Voyages: Watching the effects of suffocation, as the eyes redden, the skin turns blue round the eyes and the fingertips, and then going inside the skull to see the effects on the brain.

The Usual Suspects: Major reunion time here: Leland Orser (Morris Pearson) worked with Gary Dourdan on *Alien Resurrection*. Orser also appeared as the killer in *The Bone Collector*. Doug Hutchison (Nigel Crane) was the eponymous Tooms in some of *The X-Files'* creepiest episodes, and worked with George Eads on the pilot *Skip Chasers*. Bryan Kirkwood (Adam Piorio) played Derek on *Sabrina The Teenage Witch*.

Pop Culture References: *A Man Called Ironside*.

Notes: This episode is set on 17 April 2002 (as indicated by the phone records and Nick's prescription).

Overall: Creepy and stylish, it's a relief that it's not Catherine or Sara being stalked. Good to see Nick coping with the situation using his brain, and credit is due to George Eads for his performance.

42
Cats in the Cradle

US Air Date: 25 April 2002 14.5/22
UK Air Date: 15 June 2002

Written by: Kris Dobkin
Directed by: Richard J. Lewis
Guest Cast: Ed Lauter (Barclay Tobin), Diane Farr (Marcie Tobin),
Tuck Watkins (Marcus Remmick), Megan Gallagher (Mrs Trent),
Steve Hytner (Jonathan Claddon), Ellen Geer (Ruth Elliott),
Frank Military (Tyler Elliott), Larissa Laskin (Debbie Stein),
Courtney Jines (Jessica Rachel Trent), Mary Jo Mrochinski (Advocate),
Jeannette McCurdy (Jackie Trent)

Teaser One-liner: 'This woman was stabbed. I guess the cats are off the hook.'

The Cases: Sgt O'Riley calls Catherine and Grissom to the house of Mrs Ruth Elliott, which is overrun with cats. Their smell even masks the stench of the elderly lady's decomposing body – David Phillips estimates she's been dead for three or four days. They wonder if the cats were feeding on her or turned on her. However, Grissom finds a deep wound track – Mrs Elliott was stabbed. Catherine finds a single footprint that is unlikely to be the victim's, since it's from a high-heeled shoe. Warrick finds an empty safe in the bedroom closet with a large scorch mark on the front; dusting it for prints, he finds a set. The knives, however, don't have traces of blood on them.

Doc Robbins confirms that the wound was from the fatal blow, and that the cat damage was post-mortem. He's found foreign substances in the wound track which he's sent for analysis. Mrs Elliott had a bad infection and her lungs were full of fluid. O'Riley rings to say there's a witness – the daughter of Janet Trent, the woman who lives across the street. Eight-year-old Jessica and her sister Jackie say they heard Mrs Elliott's neighbour, Mrs Stein, have an argument with Mrs Elliott and then leave. O'Riley confirms that Mrs Stein had filed a nuisance complaint against Mrs Elliott. The girls whisper to Catherine that Mrs Stein hates cats. Catherine gets Mrs Stein's shoes, prints them and gets a match. Mrs Stein says that she went to Mrs Elliott's house to give her one last chance before she called the Humane Society.

Mrs Stein's alibi holds up, but a new suspect appears – Mrs Elliott's son Tyler, whose print was on the safe. He's brought in for questioning and shows little remorse at his mother's death. He says he had to bust open the safe because one of the cats got stuck inside. His mother had no money, and the house was going to a cat sanctuary.

The substance in Mrs Elliott's wound was mineral oil, used to sharpen knives. Grissom and Catherine go through the house without success. They are surprised to find a cat still on the premises and follow it to the Trents' house. Rascal has a sore on its leg. Catherine swabs it as the open sore and missing fur are signs of a possible staph infection, similar to Mrs Elliott's.

Rascal tests positive for staph, but the Trents are fine. Grissom and Catherine deduce that one of the Trents adopted the cat. Checking the Trent household, they find a pen that tests positive for blood. The girls initially claim that their mother went to ask if they could keep Rascal and then attacked Mrs Elliott when she said no. When Catherine points out that the fingerprints on the pen belong to a child, not an adult, Jessica then admits that she did it. Janet Trent had promised them that they could have a cat if Mrs Elliott gave it to them, knowing she never would – but Jessica wouldn't take no for an answer.

A BMW belonging to housewife Marcie Tobin has been blown up; there's one eyewitness, mechanic Marcus Remmick. Marcie says she was heading to her father's office when she heard a strange noise, so pulled into a garage. Remmick agreed to look at it, but when he opened the hood, he told her to run just before the car exploded. Marcie says her car was last parked in her garage at home and only her husband had access. Nick finds that the explosion was rigged to kill the driver.

Nick and Sara analyse the remains of the car, finding a number of springs, and two end caps, signifying a pipe bomb. Sara finds a grommet, which indicates that there was a timing device – the wire threads through the grommet when it's embedded in the end cap. Marcie's husband, Jonathan Claddon, is a foreman at Tobin C & D Incorporated (Construction and Demolition). Nick and Sara visit Claddon who admits he knows how to make a bomb, he denies being involved. Marcie's father, Barclay Tobin, comes over and sends him on an errand so he can talk to the CSIs. He doesn't like his son-in-law, and believes he's having an affair.

Greg confirms that the explosive was dynamite, made from sawdust rather than silica. The print on the cap matches the print of Claddon's that Tobin has provided. Claddon claims that his print is there because he logs inventory. Brass asks him about a missing stick of dynamite, which Claddon himself reported stolen. He denies Tobin's accusation that he has a girlfriend, and points out that since Marcie does the payroll, and has a reputation for short-changing overtime, any number of people could be annoyed at her.

Nick identifies the striations on the end cap as a vice grip, but none of the vices from the Claddons' house and C & D Inc. matches. Examining the car again, he and Sara realise that the mechanic must have been lying, as the car hood was down when the bomb exploded.

Remmick says he must have shut it wearing gloves, hence the lack of prints. The CSIs see a vice grip on the bench and take a print of it. The striae are identical, and the prints on the grip match Marcie Tobin's. Faced with the evidence, she admits she needed to have her husband arrested so that he couldn't benefit from a divorce. Her, and her father's, bank records show a payment between them of $50,000, supposedly for car repairs. She admits making the bomb, but since no one was hurt, she wonders why it can't all be forgotten. Brass arrests her for conspiracy to frame her husband for attempted murder.

Personal Notes: David Phillips is allergic to cats; Doc Robbins is a dog person.

Techniques: Nick and Sara use a sandwich to take an impression of the vice grip.

The Wit and Wisdom of Gil Grissom: 'Male cat urine . . . to us, smelly. To a female cat, it must be like aftershave.'

'House cats have only been domesticated for 4,000 years. They still have predatory instincts.'

'Mineral oil fluoresces at 525 nanometers when filtered through a kv590. A little more absorbing . . . a little less rock and roll.'

Classic Dialogue: Warrick: 'Phew. Eau de cat.' Catherine: 'Eau de match.'

Greg: 'I'm like a sponge. I just absorb information.' Grissom: 'I thought that was my line.' Greg: 'Yeah, and I absorbed it.'

Worst 'As You Know': Sara: 'Did you know there's a dozen moving parts inside a ticking clock?' Nick: 'I do now.'

Brass: 'As you know, per the ATF every stick of dynamite is catalogued.'

Fantastic Voyages: An interesting view of Gil Grissom as seen from the inside of a flowing wound that he's opening. The explosion inside the BMW from the driver's seat perspective as it's blown up. We see the murder weapon going into Mrs Elliott. We follow her wound down to the heart. The workings of the bomb that exploded inside the BMW as they prepare to go boom. We also see the BMW return to its pre-explosion state as Nick and Sara examine it.

The Usual Suspects: Diane Farr (Marcie Tobin) played Amy DeLuca on *Roswell*. Ed Lauter (Barclay Tobin) played Joe Camber in the film of Stephen King's *Cujo*, and Sheriff Cain in the *Any Which Way But Loose* TV homage, *BJ And The Bear*. Megan Gallagher (Janet Trent) was Catherine Black in Chris Carter's *Millennium*, and appeared with Marg Helgenberger in both *China Beach* and the TV movie *Lethal Vows*.

Real-life Inspirations: A man really was found in the shower with just his cats around him – the internet report of this inspired the producers to create the episode.

Overall: Another day, another child who kills, but once again good to see the two teams analysing the evidence and applying it to the case, rather than waiting for a deus ex machina to appear from Brass or O'Riley.

43
Anatomy of a Lye

US Air Date: 2 May 2002 15.9/24
UK Air Date: 22 June 2002

Written by: Josh Berman and Andrew Lipsitz
Directed by: Ken Fink
Guest Cast: Gabriel Olds (Ben Weston), Anthony Starke (Matt Hudson), Zachary Quinto (Mitchell Sullivan), Adam Nelson (Reed Collins), Paul Schackman (Bob Martin), J. Marvin Campbell (Hazmat Guy), Cathy Herd (Stacy Warner), Lyndon Smith (Graham), James Coffey (Peter Tobin)

Teaser One-liner: 'Ashes to ashes, dust to dust. Without the wait.'

The Cases: A body is found underneath some toxic material in Sunset Park. The clothing has been reduced to shreds, and the skin has virtually gone. Sara finds what's left of the victim's wallet, identifying him as Bob Martin. There are shiny white flecks around the grave site, which might be paint flecks or metal chips. The body was covered in lye, which the killer hoped would destroy the body, and Martin died about 24 hours previously. Doc Robbins points out the damage to Martin's legs – he was hit by a car. There's bruising, which indicates he wasn't killed immediately and there are multiple incised wounds containing slivers of glass. From the lack of arterial damage, he deduces that Martin was hit 48 hours before he died.

Sara and Brass meet Martin's room-mate, Reed Collins. Martin's wife had kicked him out, so he moved in with Collins, who has little interest in Martin's life. He knows that on a Monday Martin went to the university as he was an amateur photographer. Grissom and Sara go there, and collect the photos Martin was working on. The roads round the university are very busy and they're nearly knocked over as they cross the road. Grissom looks down at the road, and sees silver flecks like those found near Martin's body, and pieces of plastic. But there's no sign of blood. The paint and the plastic both correlate to an S-Class Mercedes. There's only one viable suspect in Vegas, lawyer Ben Weston, who claims his car was stolen. Grissom and Sara ask to see the clothes he was wearing the previous day, and he's had them dry-cleaned but, even so, there's evidence of damage to the shirt.

Brass discovers Weston's Mercedes at a salvage yard, but Mitchell Sullivan, the owner, has already dismantled the car since he claims it was totalled. Grissom demands all the parts, and when they're back at CSI, they're tested for blood – it's found in abundance on the passenger seat and the dashboard.

The blood is Martin's. Grissom finds some drops under the seat, formed when the bloodspattered in a pool on the floor. Although she can't work the case because she's on call at court, Catherine idly wonders whether the ignition lock has been punched, and Grissom and Sara realise that the car wasn't stolen. Weston now claims that he left his $80,000 Mercedes idling outside a restaurant, and someone stole it. The CSIs don't believe him, and have a warrant for his shirt. When he removes it, they see the bruise from the seatbelt's impact when he braked suddenly. He claims he hit something, stopped, couldn't see anything, so thought it might be a dog, and then went on to his restaurant from where the car was stolen.

In Weston's garage the CSIs find a large bleached area underneath the rental car Weston is using to replace his Mercedes, which has previously been outside. Grissom can't understand why he didn't use the garage all the time.

Grissom, Sara and Doc Robbins reconstruct the crime, and reckon that Bob Martin came crashing through Weston's windscreen. They realise that Sullivan must have been lying – the only damage would have been to the bumper and the windscreen. Sullivan admits that he was called by Weston, who asked him to dispose of the car.

There's no trace left of blood in the garage floor stain. Sara finds some white powder in Weston's rental car. Weston is brought in and is dismissive of the evidence until Grissom and Sara play him a call from his cellphone, which he had left in the car. It's the injured Bob Martin calling for help as he lies dying. Weston hit Martin, and left him unconscious in his garage while Weston sobered up; however, Martin woke up. Before they can proceed, Reed Collins brings in a suicide note he found in Martin's material. Martin wanted to be hit: Weston wouldn't have faced charges if he hadn't let Martin die.

A routine helicopter check of Diablo Canyon reveals the dead body of Stacy Warner. The only footmarks are from the paramedics and Detective Lockwood. Nick sees wounds on Stacy's right cheek, and notes that her orbital bone is fractured. He finds some down feathers in the corner of her mouth, although she's not wearing a jacket, and a larva in her ear. He leaves Lockwood to collect a sample of the ground under her once the coroner has moved her.

Stacy drowned, even though she was miles from water. It was a dry drowning – her windpipe closed up to prevent water entering the lungs. Her fiancé, Matt Hudson, says that Stacy was doing a solo trek for her Extreme Sports Trainer Finals, so he didn't expect her back. Nick spots some blood on a pool tile, but Hudson says he'd never hurt Stacy. The reports of domestic disturbance that were called in were from his over-zealous training methods.

Nick tests water from Hudson's pool, his bathroom, Lake Mead and Clark County Reservoir, but none match the water found in Stacy's stomach. Warrick is also on court call, but recognises the rock underneath Stacy's body as basalt, which is found only at an altitude of about 4,000 feet, 2,500 feet higher than the place where Stacy was found.

Nick and Lockwood retrace Stacy's steps and find the coat from which the down probably came – it's a man's extra large jacket with an emailed map to Matt Hudson in its pocket. Hudson claims that Stacy borrowed his jacket. He asks if he can have the map back, but Nick points out that it's evidence now. He's so keen on having it back that it makes Nick suspicious.

Nick gets Ronnie Litre in QD to check the map, and asks Grissom about the maggot. Grissom informs him it's dead, its development stunted, probably by frozen air. Nick and Greg deduce that Diablo Canyon was suffering the Mountain Shadow Effect – although it was fine weather in Vegas, it was completely different in Diablo Canyon.

Nick believes that Stacy got caught in a flash flood, hit her head and drowned in the flood water which carried her body to the bottom of the canyon. But Ronnie Litre calls Nick to let him know that the map has been altered. Stacy wasn't where she thought she was, and that's why she got caught in the rain. Hudson can't be arrested – all he wanted was for his girlfriend to be delayed so she wouldn't beat his time; he didn't make it rain.

Personal Notes: Grissom sold Ecklie his Mercedes five years earlier. Catherine and Eddie used to test drive

Mercedes for fun (although she conspicuously refers to him as 'my ex', rather than 'Eddie'). Warrick went on a field trip to Table Mountain during his senior year at university. Greg knows quite a bit about meteorology.

The Wit and Wisdom of Gil Grissom: 'Aristotle said something about the whole being more than the sum of its parts. Of course, he never worked in a chop shop. We want all of the parts.'

'Fifteen years to build your dream and a fifteen-second phone call destroys it.'

Classic Dialogue: Grissom: 'You've already shared this information with Sara?' Greg: 'Yeah . . . And she was way more fascinated than you are.' Grissom: 'Well, I'm somewhat fascinated by the fact that I'm your boss, but you talked to her first.'

Nick: 'You should try describing a scuba diver up in a tree, man. This is nothing.'

Doc Robbins: 'Sometimes I'm glad I only deal with dead people.'

Fantastic Voyages: We see the effects of lye on the body. We see the difference between wet drowning and dry drowning from the inside of the throat.

The Usual Suspects: Anthony Starke (Matt Hudson) played David Chandler in the US version of *Cold Feet*, and was Sanchez' gofer Truman-Lodge in *Licence to Kill*.

Real-life Influences: The death of Bob Martin is based on the case of Gregory Glenn Biggs, a 37-year-old homeless man who begged driver Charlie Mallard to get him aid. She hid him in her garage until he bled to death. She was only caught because she laughed about the case at a party. She was charged with murder.

Notes: This episode takes place on and around 29 April 2002 (from the evidence bag with the rock in).

Overall: A bit too much reliance on deus ex machina in this – both Warrick and Catherine appear for one scene and give the vital piece of information. Nice to see Nick dealing with a dead body on his own without any fuss.

44
Cross-Jurisdictions

US Air Date: 9 May 2002 16.5/25
UK Air Date: 29 June 2002

Written by: Carol Mendelsohn, Ann Donahue and Anthony E. Zuiker
Directed by: Danny Cannon
Guest Cast: David Caruso (Horatio Caine),
Adam Rodriguez (Eric Delko), Emily Procter (Calleigh Duquesne),
Khandi Alexander (Alexx Woods), Rory Cochrane (Tim Speedle),
Jenna Boyd (Sasha Rittle), Tom Hillman (Agent Dennis Sackheim),
Darlene Vogel (Mina Rittle),
David Alan Basche (Gordon Daimler/Adam van der Welk),
John Kapelos (Duke Rittle), Kari Wurher (Tiffany Langer),
Jackson Rose (Dylan Corwin), Kerry Nicholson,
Andre Blake (Composite Artist), Kim Delgado (Security Guard),
Todd Felix (Safe-Cracking Tech), Monika Kramlik (Honey Girl),
Marc Macaulay (Florida State Trooper),
Patrick Mickler (Patrol Captain), Ralph Navarro (Doorman)

Teaser One-liner: 'There's only one interpretation for this:
"Kill the pig." '
The Cases: Police Chief Rittle is holding a party after
which his young daughter is woken by two gunshots. Two
days later, the housekeeper arrives to find the Chief naked
on the dining table, with an apple stuffed in his mouth. His
wife Mina and daughter Sasha are missing, as is his car.
Doc Robbins examines the body where it lies, and believes
it was an execution: the Chief was shot in the back of the
head, and there's bruising around the handcuffs on his
wrists. Catherine finds a 9 mm shell casing. Inside the
chief's gun safe they find a .38, and a .25, but a gun given
to him for special services has gone. The gate guard says
he saw the Chief leaving with his wife and daughter at
5.14 a.m. after the party – but admits that what he really
saw was a baseball cap and sunglasses rather than being
able to positively identify the Chief.

The Chief's car is found in a garage, and in the trunk
there's a dead body wearing the Chief's baseball cap. Brass
receives a call from Miami-Dade County in Florida: a girl
matching Sasha's description has been seen walking down

a side road. Grissom sends Catherine and Warrick to Florida to process Sasha once she's found.

In Miami-Dade County, CSI chief Horatio Caine watches as search parties are sent out looking for Sasha. He walks down the road and finds a pink hair clip, which leads him to Sasha, still carrying a shell casing in her hand. Miami CSI Calleigh Duquesne believes the bullet is from a Taurus 9, which is common in Miami. The shooter wasn't fleeing from Las Vegas, he was coming home to Miami.

Back in Vegas, Doc Robbins performs an autopsy on the trunk corpse, Jason Doyle. He was shot in the head, although a fragment of the bullet found its way down his back. He too was shot with a 9 mm bullet. Nick and Sara are checking fingerprints from the party, and identify showgirl Tiffany Langer. Langer is reluctant to identify her date at the party – he was just someone showing her a good time, but eventually says his name was Adam van der Welk. About the only useful thing she remembers is that he wore really cheap cologne, or used a cheap mouthwash – he smelled sickly sweet.

Warrick finds a diazepam at the scene where Sasha escaped from the car. Horatio deduces that the driver stopped to urinate, and they find the spot. With any luck they can get DNA from urethral cells sloughed off with the urine. The FBI call Miami CSI Tim Speedle for a meeting – the Vegas case matches a serial killer the FBI has been tracking. Wealthy couples are targeted, the husband is killed, the wife is raped and then killed 48 hours after the husband. Horatio buttonholes FBI Agent Dennis Sackheim, who admits that all the victims used the Shore Club.

Warrick joins Miami CSI Eric Delko at a canal, in which a coastguard helicopter has spotted a car matching the description. When it's brought out, they find the naked body of Mina Rittle, wrapped in plastic wrap. Miami coroner Alexx Woods examines the body and finds two gunshot wounds. Mina was alive when she was put in the canal. Her eyes are glued shut with a gold crusty substance, which Alexx subsequently finds in every orifice. Delko finds the gun in the water.

In Vegas Tiffany Langer works with a composite artist to create an image of van der Welk, while Sasha works with another one in Miami. The two pictures are of differing views of the same person. Horatio discovers that the substance was honey. Plastic wrap and honey are used together at Hives, a new Miami nightclub where honey is poured over a naked woman wrapped in plastic and then eaten by the patrons. Horatio takes Catherine there to get a sample, which matches the honey found on Mina Rittle.

Grissom and Robbins work their way through textbooks to try to identify the smell that Tiffany mentioned.

Catherine, Calleigh, Warrick and Horatio return to Hives to identify who bought the honey, and find a recent receipt for honey bought by a limo driver for a high roller from Vegas. They find the driver, Gordon Daimler, who admits that he bought the honey. He doesn't remember a sweet smell. Catherine and Horatio check the bottles of alcohol in his limo, but nothing matches. On a hunch, Horatio starts the engine and turns on the air conditioner – releasing the smell into the car.

Grissom gets Tiffany to smell the baseball cap found on Jason Doyle, and she says that it's Adam's. She also says he only ever drank champagne. Grissom contacts Catherine and tells her that van der Welk is a diabetic, and needs novalin insulin. Luckily there's blood in the urine sample found at Sasha's getaway scene, and it confirms that the perpetrator is diabetic. Checking a database for prescriptions brings up Daimler's name and an address that is far too high class for a limo driver. It's registered to the Corwins, the couple Gordon said he was late collecting when he was pulled over.

They go to the Corwins' house and find evidence of a struggle, and some plastic wrap. There's also a 9 mm shell case, and a bullet mark with dry scalp and blood around it. Tim Speedle notices that the Corwins' boat is missing. It's found at the docks, and the FBI prepare to take out the one sign of life on the boat. Horatio realises that Daimler may not have used the same pattern, and is preparing to use the Corwins' plane. He persuades the FBI sharpshooter not to shoot, which is a relief, as it's Corwin, who is still alive.

Gordon Daimler is ready to leave on board the Corwins' jet when Horatio and Catherine arrive and arrest him. He tries to bluster that the Corwins lent him the plane, thinking that the husband is dead, and is shocked when he's told that Dylan Corwin is still alive.

Personal Notes: CSI Vegas team: Grissom, unusually, wears a suit into the office – initially he claims it's because Catherine's returning, but she doesn't believe him, so he admits it's because he attended the Chief's funeral. There's an element of flirting between Catherine and Horatio Caine, which would be good to see again. Warrick has never been to Florida. At frat parties, Nick got into situations with multiple sex partners. Sara seems unimpressed.

CSI Miami-Dade team: Horatio Caine was named after writer Horatio Alger. He is good with children: he has an empathy that Grissom completely lacks. He attended the opening night of nightclub Hives as a VIP. He lost someone close to him, but no other details are given. Not much is seen of the rest of the Miami team.

Techniques: Speedle uses liquid chromatography to identify the type of honey that was found at Hives and on the body of Mina Rittle.

The Wit and Wisdom of Gil Grissom: 'Hey, guess what? This isn't about you. This is about a missing seven-year-old girl.'

The Wit and Wisdom of Horatio Caine: 'Our guy's still in the wind, folks. Still in the wind.'

'Now, if you take this shot I'm going to be in your grille for the rest of your natural life. I want you to think about what that might be like.'

Classic Dialogue: Sasha: 'You're tricking me.' Horatio: 'You're too smart for that.'

Catherine: 'We don't really work theories. Do we, Warrick?' Warrick: 'No, just evidence.' Calleigh: 'We're much more fanciful down here. Aren't we, Horatio?'

Catherine: 'Adam van der Welk. Little girl saw a monster. Showgirl saw a husband. So this guy could be anybody.'

Worst 'As You Know': Speedle: 'Delko, you've been down there for 45 minutes. Do you know the level of bacteria in the water? You can get all kinds of infections.' (He may know, but we don't!)

Fantastic Voyages: We follow the progress of the safe cracking, travel with the bullet on its long passage from its entrance to the trunk guy's lower back, and enter the ear of Mina Rittle to examine the honey that's found there.

The Usual Suspects: Kari Wuhrer (Tiffany Langer) played Maggie Beckett on sci-fi series *Sliders*. Darlene Vogel (Mina Rittle) was Chris Kelly on *Pacific Blue*, and John Crichton's fiancée Alex on *Farscape*. (The *CSI: Miami* team's past is investigated at the start of its own section.)

Mistakes Really Can Be Fatal: There must be hundreds of limo drivers in Miami – how come Tim Speedle gets lucky so quickly and finds Gordon?

Overall: Definitely more a *CSI: Miami* episode than a standard issue *Vegas* one; we hardly see anything of Brass, Nick and Sara, and even Warrick, although he's present in a number of the Florida-based scenes, doesn't get a lot to do. It's a two-hander for Marg Helgenberger and David Caruso, and establishes that the new series is going to have enough differences to make it stand alone. There's a weird moment as Helgenberger stands next to Emily Proctor: the two extremely undumb – and very similar – blondes together. Speedle, Delko and Alexx Woods are hardly established as characters, and you can understand the producers wanting someone else in the mix before the show hit the airwaves.

45
The Hunger Artist

US Air Date: 16 May 2002 16.3/25
UK Air Date: 6 July 2002

Written by: Jerry Stahl
Directed by: Richard J. Lewis
Guest Cast: Susan Misner (Cassie James),

Bill Sage (Bruce Justin/Frank McBride),
Mark A. Sheppard (Rod Darling), Tricia Helfer (Ashleigh James),
Catherine MacNeal (Doctor),
Jimmie F. Skaggs (Tookie the Homeless Guy),
Bonnie Burroughs (Dusty), Keith Allan (Fashion Photographer),
Erin Guzowski (Lola), Nicole Randall Johnson (Nurse)

Teaser One-liner: 'I think she just ratted herself out.'
The Case: Grissom is called by Brass to a disfigured and
naked dead body found wrapped in a blanket in a
shopping trolley near some homeless people. As Grissom
examines the corpse, a rat crawls out of her mouth.
Grissom finds a small pool of liquid on the ground. There's
a handbag in the cart, containing a day planner, and six
syringes. Doc Robbins' autopsy reveals no visible track
marks from drug addiction, and the tox screen only shows
botulin. There are puncture wounds in her forehead, which
Robbins believes come from beauty treatments – and the
doctor missed with one of his injections, getting botulin
into the victim's blood stream. There's a crater in her
cheek, and it's clear that a blade was inserted more than
once. However, there are no ligature marks.

Sara examines the day planner, which appears to be in
code. Warrick wonders what a homeless woman is doing
with a day planner and a $300 handbag. The audio visual
technician Dusty makes a more attractive version of the
woman's face and realises she knows her from somewhere.
It's the cover girl from the most recent issue of *Vegas.com*,
Ashleigh James, although someone obviously wanted her
looking ugly.

Brass takes Grissom and Catherine to Ashleigh's apartment, where an officer found the bathtub overflowing.
There are numerous pictures of Ashleigh around the walls,
but also some rag dolls. There is a white minty-smelling
substance on a table, and a man's toiletry kit.

Catherine finds blood in the sink, but none on the floor.
There are enema boxes, and some of the waste product
kept in plastic bags. Ashleigh's car is full of junk food
wrappers and rubbish. Nick and Warrick find a note in the
car, presumably from a spurned lover, saying that 'he' isn't

good enough for Ashleigh, doesn't have their 'history', and that she'll live to regret the decision. In Ashleigh's closet Catherine finds a heavy black coat that seems out of place. Grissom finds a hand-sized blood smudge on the wall, and botox in the fridge. He then walks outside to the place where Ashleigh was found in the cart. Sara is trying to contexualise the scene. They look up and see a huge billboard of Ashleigh James looking down on them.

Back at the lab, Sara continues to study the day planner. Grissom is interested in who used to inhabit the trolley before Ashleigh was put in it. There are numerous pieces of paper and articles relating to Ashleigh in it. Nick and Warrick go to Ashleigh's boyfriend's apartment, but he's out. In the rubbish can, they find a torn-up photo of Ashleigh. Catherine and Brass visit her agent, Rod Darling, who says that he dropped her a couple of months earlier, although his shaving gear was still at her place. Before they can continue, Darling is attacked by Frank McBride, Ashleigh's boyfriend. He claims Darling made her dependent on him. Darling tells Catherine that he wasn't sleeping with Ashleigh – she was an asset that needed protecting.

Sara and Grissom find crabs in the coat Catherine found and deduce that it probably came from a homeless person who visited Ashleigh regularly and is now missing the coat. Grissom goes among the homeless people around Ashleigh's apartment, and trades his jacket for a scarf one of them is wearing, with a red stain on it. A homeless woman starts to take exception, but quietens down when Grissom trades his torch for her ring and cosmetics kit.

The blood on the scarf is Ashleigh's but McBride's knife isn't the murder weapon. The epithelials on the ring prove that the homeless woman, Cassie, is Ashleigh's sister. Grissom talks to Cassie, who says that Ashleigh didn't have a sister. She claims Ashleigh stole her life from her. Rod Darling admits that he had given up on Cassie. She used to be a model but started freebasing cocaine so Rod started using Ashleigh as the model instead.

Sara is getting obsessed with the day planner and has started cracking bits of the code. With help from

Ashleigh's schedule, she discovers the names of photographers, but finds she had packed up working two months previously.

Brass believes that Cassie killed Ashleigh but, in her confused state, Cassie seems to indicate that she tried to stop her sister. Doc Robbins discovers blisters in the back of Ashleigh's throat, indicative of an eating disorder rather than forced oral sex. Ashleigh was bulimic and anorexic. Her system was shutting down – the cause of death was a failed kidney, fuelled by septicaemia.

The psychiatric report on Cassie shows she's a classic paranoid schizophrenic, and Grissom doesn't think she inflicted the wounds that made Ashleigh ugly. However, prints confirm that Cassie had been in her sister's apartment. Oddly, the scrapings from underneath Ashleigh's fingernails are from her own skin.

Sara cracks Ashleigh's code – it relates to the calorific content of the food she was eating. She was desperate to balance her intake and output, so checked her food, weighed her excretions and cut at herself to make them balance. The CSIs pool the evidence and deduce that Cassie found her sister in a desperate state, so took her out in the shopping trolley to a place where she could see the billboard and realise that she really was beautiful, before her system finally gave up.

Personal Notes: Grissom starts the episode at the doctor's but leaves before he is seen. It concludes with him visiting the doctor after having an episode where he finds himself with no hearing. He knows that he needs to be able to hear in order to do his job properly. However, he is diagnosed with otosclerosis, the same disease that his mother has. The doctor cannot tell him how long he's got before it affects him seriously.

Techniques: Dusty reconstructs Ashleigh's face on the computer.

The Wit and Wisdom of Gil Grissom: 'Sometimes I'm not sure of anything.'

'Aren't you putting the shopping cart before the horse? In order to decipher a code you need to know the alphabet for the code. In order to know the alphabet, you need to know the author.'

'All animals prefer symmetry in their mates. The male Japanese scorpion flies with the most symmetrical wings gets the most mates.'

'The very nature of addiction – whether it be self-medicating herself or self-mutilating – is that the very behaviour we use to survive it becomes a behaviour that ends up killing us.'

Classic Dialogue: Grissom: 'Enema. The secret life of women.' Catherine: 'Don't generalise. It's not very scientific of you.' Grissom: 'You're right. I'm sorry.'

Cassie: 'Now I can see what the dark looks like.' Grissom: 'I've been trying to do that for years.'

Cassie: 'You can pick through a million lives and never have one of your own.' Grissom: 'Looking for things, analysing them ... trying to figure out the world – that's a life.'

Fantastic Voyages: We see a botox injection as it enters the forehead. We look at the actions of the pthirus pubis crab as it goes up a hair. We follow the progress of the vomit as Ashleigh sticks her finger down her throat.

The Usual Suspects: Tricia Helfer (Ashleigh James) is the new face of the Cylons on the reinvention of *Battlestar Galactica*. Ironically, she also was a cover star for *Health* magazine a few weeks after this episode first aired. Mark Sheppard (Rod Darling) played Paddy Armstrong in *In the Name of the Father*, and is a familiar face from sci-fi shows including *Star Trek*, *The X-Files* and *Firefly*. Catherine MacNeal (Grissom's doctor) was Pat Hamilton on the soap opera *Days of Our Lives*.

Real-life Inspirations: The rat coming out of Ashleigh's mouth is based on one of the cases that Elizabeth Devine recalled for the production team.

Mistakes Really Can Be Fatal: Grissom asks Sara why Ashleigh stopped working, but we already know that Rod Darling dropped her.

Overall: Another Grissom-centric episode to finish the season, with Nick and Warrick hardly getting a look in.

Odd to see Grissom being the person who can connect with a witness, but it neatly counterpoints the increasing isolation that he's feeling in his own life as his hearing problem is finally recognised. It feels like a cliff-hanger ending, but it isn't.

Season Three

Regular Cast:

William Petersen (Gil Grissom)
Marg Helgenberger (Catherine Willows) credited but does not appear in **58**, 'Random Acts of Violence'
Gary Dourdan (Warrick Brown)
George Eads (Nick Stokes) credited but does not appear in **54**, 'Blood Lust'
Jorja Fox (Sara Sidle) credited but does not appear in **58**, 'Random Acts of Violence'
Paul Guilfoyle (Jim Brass)
Eric Szmanda (Greg Sanders)
Robert David Hall (Doc Robbins)

Christopher Wiehl (Hank Peddigrew 46, 47, 52, 56, 62)
Eric Stonestreet (Ronnie Litre 46)
Gerald McCullouch (Bobby Dawson 46, 52, 54, 55, 58, 59, 68)
Jeffrey D. Sams (Detective Cyrus Lockwood 46, 48, 61, 62, 66, 68)
David Berman (David Phillips 46–49, 51, 53–55, 57, 58, 62, 65, 67, 68)
Archie Kao (Archie Johnson 48–50, 53, 58, 60, 64, 67)
Skip O'Brien (Sgt O'Riley 51, 52, 55, 64)
Romy Rosemont (CSI technician Jacqui Franco 51, 58, 59, 64, 67, 68)
Joseph Patrick Kelly (Officer Metcalf 52, 54, 61, 62)
Pamela Gidley (Teri Miller 52)
Larry Clarke (Detective Sulik 53, 56)
Palmer Davis (Public defender Margaret Finn 54, 58)
Leslie Bega (CSI technician Leah 55, 60, 65)
Wallace Langham (CSI technician David Hodges 56, 62, 64, 65, 67)
Doan Ly (Veterinarian Jessie Menken 57, 66)
Geoffrey Rivas (Detective Sam Vega 58, 60, 63)
Timothy Carhart (Eddie Willows 60)
Madison McReynolds (Lindsey Willows 60)

46
Revenge Is Best Served Cold

US Air Date: 26 September 2002 18.2/27
UK Air Date: 28 January 2003

Written by: Anthony E. Zuiker & Carol Mendelsohn
Directed by: Danny Cannon
Guest Cast: Ian Somerhalder (Tony Del Nagro),
Cliff De Young (Mr Del Nagro), Carmine Giovionazzo,
Madison Mason (Card Players), J. P. Pitoc (Michelangelo),
Todd Stashwick (Mark Bunin), Donna Scott, Brent Hinkley,
Walter Emmanuel Jones (Street Racers), Mike Bunin (Bartender),
Andrea DeOliveira (Nadine), Christopher Gehrman (Steven Masters),
Doug Jones (Grinder), Damara Reilly (Lita Gibbons),
Hillary Shepard Turner (Mrs Del Nagro)

Teaser One-liner: 'This is high stakes. We're treating it like a murder.'
The Cases: A card game between high stakes poker players comes to a sudden halt when Doyle Pfeiffer collapses, and dies. The game has been running for eighteen hours before Pfeiffer's death and Mark Bunin, the player who was about to win, is furious that the game has been halted.

Sara finds a green piece of chocolate. Warrick finds urine on the chairs – players won't leave a game like this. Doc Robbins carries out an autopsy on Pfeiffer and finds all the symptoms of lead poisoning. He has a bullet in his thigh that has probably been leeching lead into his system. Grissom examines the video of the game, looking for clues about the players, and notices that Lita Gibbons uses eyedrops. Greg discovers there was tetrahydrozoline in Pfeiffer's drink – which is contained in eyedrops. But Lita was the last one to sit down at the table and never left her chair – how could she have got the drops into the drink? Brass and Grissom talk to Lita Gibbons and wonder why she only has one tinted contact lens.

Robbins deduces that lead from the bullet made Pfeiffer's brain swell up, which gave him a stroke. If his blood pressure had been OK, he would have been fine, but the tetrahydrozoline raised his blood pressure.

Ronnie Litre prepares a large version of Lita's tinted lens. She was marking the deck and then was able to read it with her tinted lens. However, her eyedrops are a different formula to the one that killed Pfeiffer.

Warrick talks to Nadine, the waitress who was serving the table, and wonders why she was attentive to Pfeiffer when he hadn't given her anything. Brass asks Mark why he tipped her so much, but he says it was just to get good service – he wanted to beat Pfeiffer not kill him. The bartender explains that everything is computerised now – the girls have to order the drinks in the right order: soft drinks, then mixers, then beers. Grissom also discovers that the alcohol is stored well away from the bar.

Warrick finds a bottle of 'fast-acting' eyedrops in Nadine's handbag, which now contains some of the drink. Grissom notices that one of Nadine's orders was made in the wrong way. She admits that she did that to get time to spike Pfeiffer's drink, but she was trying to give him diarrhoea, not kill him.

However, the lead from the bullet doesn't account for the amount of lead in Pfeiffer's body. The CSIs reconstruct the poker game.

As Grissom duplicates Pfeiffer's chocolate-eating, a thought occurs to him. He checks the chocolate: it was grown in a place with heavy lead content in the rain. Eating so much chocolate gave Pfeiffer lead poisoning, which ended up killing him.

Catherine and Nick are called by Detective Lockwood to Frenchman airfield, an old landing strip, where a body has been dumped. The deceased died somewhere else from a gunshot wound to the cheek.

AFIS identifies the corpse as Jace Felder, a methadone seller. Robbins confirms that he was killed by the gunshot, and notes that his eardrum was blown out shortly before he died. There's a smell of gasoline on his clothing, and two symmetrical lines on his torso. Nick discovers some tyre tread marks at the airfield, and finding a smashed rear-view mirror confirms his theory that the airfield was used for 'street racing' between two powerful cars. Lockwood takes Nick and Catherine to where the racers hang out, and they see harnesses that would have caused the bruising to the victim, as well as learning about different fuels, such as nitrous oxide, used to give a burst of speed. They talk to Thumpy G, one of the racers, who has his sound system at a high enough level to burst eardrums.

Thumpy directs Catherine and Nick to Michelangelo, who prepared the car that Felder was racing against the night he died. Michelangelo says he sold the car to some kid who paid by insurance company cheque.

LVPD find Felder's car up for sale. It's been cleaned, but there's a 9 mm round still in it, and a large amount of blood trace, with a void in the driver's seat. The man selling it, Steven Masters, says that he and his brother found the car abandoned, with Felder's body in it. They wanted the car, so dumped the body.

The insurance cheque was made out to Tony Del Nagro, who admits he raced Jace. Nick finds a fresh window in the passenger door of Del Nagro's car as well as gunshot residue. Del Nagro's father gets angry that Catherine and Nick might be accusing Tony of murder, and tells them that the gun that Tony admits firing in the car was his, and that the police never helped when his wife was murdered, so why are they here now? He throws them out.

Bobby Dawson finds tinted glass on the tip of the round Nick found in the car and Catherine discovers that Mrs Del Nagro was allegedly killed by Jace Felder. Nick and Catherine duplicate the race between Del Nagro and Felder and realise that he could have shot Felder, and then fired up the acceleration. Tony Del Nagro confesses that he learned to street race just so that he could bring Felder down for the death of his mother.

Personal Notes: Grissom is surprised when Hank Peddigrew asks Warrick to tell Sara he said hi. Grissom financed his first body farm when he was in college by playing poker. He hasn't discussed it with Warrick before, despite their many conversations about gambling, because he doesn't like to reveal his hand. Sara doesn't want to discuss her relationship with Hank with Greg. Nick's brother used to rebuild and race cars.

Techniques: Robbins starts using a new turbo handsaw for cutting into bone.

The Wit and Wisdom of Gil Grissom: 'E-C-G . . . C major chord. All the slots play the same notes – perfect harmony. Makes people happy.'

'Poker's not a game of interaction. It's a game of observation. I used to study people. And then I guess I, uh . . . got bored. Now I study evidence.'

'Did you guys know that seventy per cent of the world's chocolate is produced in West Africa?'

Classic Dialogue: Grissom: 'I did not know that.' Doc Robbins: 'Stop the world.'

Grissom: 'All right, stick around. I need your eyes.' Ronnie Litre: 'As long as they stay in my head.'

Fantastic Voyages: We watch how eyedrops work in the eye. We see the bullet enter Jace Felder's cheek and the effects on the other side of his face. We also take a close-up of his inner ear. We see how the drink is brought from the vats beneath the casino up to the bar, and how some of the drink gets into the eyedrop bottle.

The Usual Suspects: Cliff De Young (Mr Del Nagro) played Joe Paulson on *The Tommyknockers* alongside Marg Helgenberger. J.P. (Jean-Paul) Pitoc (Michelangelo) now plays Phil on *Six Feet Under*.

Pop Culture References: Greg tries to pretend he likes Tupac (but can't pronounce it right!).

Notes: There's a nice reference back to 00, 'Pilot' and the eyedrops on Kristy Hopkins' nipples.

Overall: There has to be a better explanation for Pfeiffer's death – the death by chocolate idea is horrible, and feels forced into the episode. It's an odd season-opener in other ways as well, with Catherine and Nick doing their *Fast and the Furious* routine. With *CSI: Miami* possibly competing for viewers, you'd have expected something better.

47
The Accused Is Entitled

US Air Date: 3 October 2002 17.4/26
UK Air Date: 4 February 2003

Written by: Elizabeth Devine & Ann Donahue
Directed by: Kenneth Fink
Guest Cast: Chad Michael Murray (Tom Haviland),
Michael B. Silver (Prosecutor), Michael Ensign (the Judge),
Marta Martin (Suzi Bergh), David Purdham (Raymond Lester),
Lindsay Frost (Marjorie Wescott), Raymond J. Barry (Dr Philip Gerard),
Linda Kim (Tonya), Tom Kuehl (Raymond Lester),
J. Antonion Moon (Bailiff), Nancy Yoon (Kim Hsu),
Shahid Ali (Craps Player/Fan), Nate Bynum (Black Media),
C.C. Carr (Female Media), Jamal Clark (Security Guard),
Justin Cooper (Caucasian Media),
Corinna Harney-Jones (Girl Gone Wild), Don Mirault (Ken Murdock),
Frank Patton (Stick Player), Max Shippee (Fan)

Teaser One-liner: 'Clark Gable was a movie star.'

The Case: Film star Tom Haviland claims that he returned to his hotel room to find Kim, one of two women whom he had recently slept with, lying dead in the bed, and the other girl, Tonya, vanished. Haviland's assistant, Raymond Lester, called security, and 911, and then left for an LA meeting. Grissom immediately believes that the crime occurred earlier than Haviland claims. Haviland also says that Kim told him before she died that the other girl was responsible. There's blood on Haviland's hands, despite the fact that he claims he never touched the body. He's arrested and hires one of the top attorneys, Marjorie Westcott, to defend him.

Nick processes the table where Haviland was playing craps, but Grissom's decided to supervise this case. Sara goes up to the room, where Hank is waiting for her. He tells her that he had to reposition the victim's bra when he tried to revive her. Catherine can't find any blood in the bathroom so investigates the other rooms on the same floor, and finds a utility room. There's blood in the sink and she gets a bare footprint from the floor. Nick asks for the dice from the table. He finds blood on one set of dice. Warrick is taking the blood evidence to the lab, but gets caught in a traffic accident, and leaves his car to help the victim.

Doc Robbins says that a corkscrew would be consistent with the tissue damage he finds in Kim's throat and there is no possibility that she could have spoken to Haviland. The CSIs believe that their case is secure, but Haviland's attorney claims on live TV that their evidence is irretrievably contaminated. The DA explains that the chain of custody was broken when Warrick stopped at the accident. She's also pushing for a speedy trial, and has appointed a forensic scientist – Dr Philip Gerard, Grissom's mentor – to oversee all of the CSI's work.

Greg confirms Kim's blood was on the dice. Haviland wiped his mouth with his arm and then spat the blood over the dice when he blew on them. Grissom and Sara check the bloodspatter pattern on the sheet; he thinks that Kim was collateral damage, her throat slashed to silence her, and that the majority of the blood comes from the other girl. Gerard talks to them, and comments on Sara's relationship with Hank.

Westcott asks for all of the CSI proficiency tests by midnight, which worries Catherine, because hers is still on appeal. She's also asked for Warrick's shirt, which he's thrown out because the road accident victim bled on it. The video reveals Raymond Lester leaving with a set of golf clubs over his left shoulder and pulling a hard bag. The distribution of clubs could leave room for a body in the hard bag. Gerard sees this as enough to provide reasonable doubt that Haviland committed the murder.

Lester claims that Haviland called while he was playing craps so he could hear Haviland with the girls. He's brought the golf bag in with him, but it's already been cleaned. When it's tested for blood, the bleach cross-reacts with the luminol, destroying the evidence. Nick reacts angrily and Gerard warns Grissom that Westcott will destroy Nick on the stand. Gerard tries to persuade Grissom to drop the case for the moment, and Grissom realises that his mentor has sold out. He's no longer just following the evidence.

Greg finds evidence of male blood on the bed sheet – not Lester's or Haviland's. Tonya is found at Briarway Golf Course – and she's a he. The CSIs surmise that Haviland would have lost his temper when he discovered that Tonya wasn't who she claimed to be. Gerard informs Grissom that he's aware of his hearing problem.

As the court case starts, neither Grissom nor Sara can find anything that matches one of the blood patterns on the sheet. The case doesn't start well – Nick forgot to put case identifiers on his dice photos because the casino manager was pushing to get them out; Warrick can't find his discarded shirt and gets questioned about his gambling habit; Sara is asked about Hank, and also about the time she wiped chalk dust off Grissom's face (see 27, 'Scuba Doobie-Doo'). Westcott infers that Sara will do anything to get Grissom's attention. Catherine is asked about her dancing past, and about her failed exam – there's the truth, and her interpretation of it, according to Westcott. Catherine believes the case is about to be dismissed, until Grissom asks where he can get full body shots of Haviland.

Grissom shows the image of the bed sheet to the court, and the unidentified blood pattern. Westcott tries to trap him by whispering so he can't hear, but he answers that he's confident that the blood pattern is from Haviland because it matches a scar he got on his last film. Grissom proves that it's from a time when Haviland tripped on a step. Haviland is remanded for trial, without bail.

Personal Notes: Grissom has no knowledge of modern films – he doesn't recognise Haviland, who's one of the hottest properties in the business. His deafness is having one of its bad periods – he struggles to hear certain conversations.

The Wit and Wisdom of Gil Grissom: 'CSI's always on trial, Warrick. You know this. Burden of proof is on us.'

'Looks like that old Hollywood saying, never get caught with a dead girl or a live boy.'

Classic Dialogue: Gerard: 'A jury believes me because of my reputation just like they do you.' Grissom: 'The difference is, Philip, I get the same paycheque regardless of what I testify to.'

Catherine: 'Did the judge exclude the dice?' Nick: 'No. No, just my credibility.'

Catherine: 'I'm up there front and centre taking hits along with the rest of CSI. You know, you've turned into a really lousy leader. I need your help, and you're on the sidelines.'

Fantastic Voyages: We see Kim screaming then zoom in through her mouth, and through the larynx as a corkscrew pierces the muscles, and then see Haviland's saliva with Kim's blood in it going onto the die.

The Usual Suspects: Raymond J. Barry (Philip Gerard) played Senator Richard Matheson on *The X-Files*. Lindsay Frost (Marjorie Westcott) played Marilyn Sheppard in the TV biopic about Sam Sheppard, the inspiration for *The Fugitive*. Chad Murray (Tom Haviland) played *The Lone Ranger* in the TV Movie. Michael B. Silver (The DA) was Dr Paul Myers on *ER* for six years.

Pop Culture References: Film director Roman Polanski's flight from US justice after he raped a 13-year-old girl.

Overall: A very different episode, which perhaps should have been the season premiere. Grissom's anger at his mentor's selling out is palpable, and it's good to see the team working as a team even when things are going wrong.

48
Let The Seller Beware

US Air Date: 10 October 2002 19.4/29
UK Air Date: 11 February 2003

Written by: Andrew Lipsitz & Anthony E. Zuiker
Directed by: Richard J. Lewis
Guest Cast: Chris Payne Gilbert (Peter Berglund),
Mary-Margaret Humes (Jeri Newman),
Taylor Handley (Max Newman), Nicole Paggi (Nicole Exmoor),
Laurie Fortier (Janine Wood), Monique Demers,
Edward Edwards (Mr Darwell), Peter Asle Holden (Augie Heitz),
Chris Johnson (Chuck Darwell), Michael Rafferty (Poolman Jack Jarvis),
Rachel Schumate (Mandy Kirk), Kendra D. Smith (Nurse)

Teaser One-liner: 'You do the math: Dead female spouse plus missing husband equals murder.'

The Cases: A young couple, Peter Berglund and Janine Wood, are looking round a house without the estate agent present. They have a good search round, and make love in one of the bedrooms. Going outside, they get a shock as blood drips down on them from the body of the property's owner, Monica Newman. She's on a canopy awning, dressed only in her underwear and a short robe.

Catherine finds a .380 calibre shell casing. There's a gun by Monica's hand, but neither Grissom nor Catherine believe she shot herself. Nick and Warrick find evidence of extensive bruising on her body while Grissom discovers cigarette ends in the flower pot and wonders if they were thrown from the upstairs window. The Newmans have a son Max, aged fifteen, who's missing.

Estate agent Augie Heitz arrives, and explains that his clients never have to see him. He admits that he gave out the combination for the lockbox so Berglund and Wood could enter. Nick finds red dye on the ground and then processes the area round the pool with ALS, finding two sets of prints. Warrick finds Cal Newman's clothes and, when they realise that the pool is clogged, Nick goes in and finds Newman's body, his hand caught in the filter. Max Newman and his mother Jeri, Cal Newman's ex-wife, turn up, and Jeri is asked to identify the body. Grissom notices that the anti-vortex filter is missing some screws.

Archie Johnson recognises a Peter Croft sculpture from the 'before' photos of the crime scene, but it has now vanished.

Doc Robbins confirms that Cal Newman drowned, but he caught his hand in the filter after he died. He has some abrasion or friction marks on his chest, and he has several broken ribs and a forehead bruise. Monica Newman was shot, and there's no evidence of rape. She didn't shoot herself; she had help.

Nick, Catherine, Brass and Archie review a video of a sales pitch made by Monica Newman that becomes overtly sexual. The video was apparently taken by Augie Heitz, who has suffered thefts at the houses he's been selling.

Augie admits lusting after Monica, but no more than that. He says that there's someone else who spent a lot of time with her – Jack Jarvis, the poolman. Jarvis recalls an argument between Cal and his son. Warrick finds the three missing screws from the filter in Jarvis' van, which he claims were an excuse so he could go back and see Mrs Newman again.

The chemicals in Cal's lungs match those in the pool water, while the head wound matches the side of the pool. Nick finds hairs and a tooth filling in the water while Grissom discovers mildew in the print. Monica's sexual test kit reveals two sets of sperm – her husband's and one that is unidentified, but not Jack Jarvis'.

Nick tries to recreate the video, with Warrick's aid, and they find a cardboard cut-out of Augie Heitz where 'he' appeared to be on the video. With further technical trickery, Archie reveals the real cameraman: Max.

The CSIs believe Max drowned his father so he could have his stepmother, and then killed her when she refused to stay with him. But his mother says that Max can't swim, therefore he can't be the double killer.

There's a blond hair, tooth filling, and some detritus from the bottom of the pool, including some white neoprene, which might come from a wet suit. Peter Berglund is brought in: he's a Scandinavian ex-navy SEAL. As Greg is of Scandinavian descent, Grissom infects his left foot with mildew. He then gets a warrant to see Berglund's feet. He too is suffering from the infection, which works on Scandinavian people. Investigating Berglund's background, they find a link to Jeri Newman – she and Berglund got a loan together three weeks earlier. She hired him to kill her ex-husband.

Sara is sent solo to deal with a dead body at Tuscadero High School: seventeen-year-old Mandy Kirk, a cheerleader seems to have been eviscerated – but nobody heard her scream. She was found by the janitor. David Phillips carries out the autopsy and says Mandy died of exsanguination. There's trauma to all her internal organs and the bite marks on her ribs are human. She also had an e-coli infection, which will have been passed to her attacker.

Mandy was the 'soccer bunny' for Chuck Darwell: she gave him gifts before the game. Chuck claims not to have seen her the previous night, but he's been rushed to hospital. Although Chuck's father won't let them take a cast of his teeth, Chuck has already thrown up – and his vomit is in the public domain. Sara goes through the stomach contents and finds human skin. The coroner has found the hallucinogenic drug PCP in there.

Chuck is arrested. He may not remember killing Mandy but he definitely remembers eating something. However, the teeth marks on Mandy's ribs don't match Chuck's and when Sara and Detective Lockwood discover that fellow cheerleader Nicole Exmoor can't stop vomiting, she admits that she killed and started to eat Mandy under the PCP influence, also passing some to Chuck to enjoy.

Personal Notes: Grissom knows enough Latin to be able to translate 'let the seller beware'. Sara comes in on her day off but doesn't get much sympathy. Warrick and Nick play scissors-paper-stone to decide things. Greg's mother's maiden name was Hojem – her father came from Norway.

The Wit and Wisdom of Gil Grissom: 'Aureobasidium pullulans is a mildew. We found it around the Newmans' pool. It induces rashes in people of Scandinavian descent – and it does so in a predictable progression which provides us with a valuable timeline.'

Classic Dialogue: Brass: 'My guess, second marriage.' Catherine: 'Cos she's a babe and he's . . .' Brass: 'He's, um . . . got a good sense of humour.'

Augie Heitz: 'Someone died, I know . . . But you got people knocking down awnings, stomping through the flower beds. How am I supposed to sell this house?' Grissom: 'You're not. It's a crime scene.'

Brass: 'So you must've thought you won the lottery. And the only thing standing between you and the winning ticket was your father.'

Greg: 'See, now we're getting into this whole strip

forensics thing and I'm not so sure I can hang with that even if you are my boss.'

Fantastic Voyages: We go inside Mandy Kirk to see the human teethmarks and through the Fire Department nozzle with the water. We also see Cal Newman's hand getting trapped in the filter and the brain being affected by PCP.

The Usual Suspects: Mary-Margaret Humes (Jeri Newman) played Gail Leary on *Dawson's Creek*.

Pop Culture References: Warrick refers to Newman 'pulling a Clark Kent' – leaving everything behind as Clark Kent does when he turns into Superman. Archie Johnson imitates Elvis Presley. Lockwood talks about *Rocky* as an example of an inspirational video. Warrick refers to Nick as tennis player John McEnroe when he exclaims, 'You cannot be serious!' Grissom refers to the play *Six Degrees of Separation*.

Mistakes Really Can Be Fatal: Sara is only a CSI-2 (unless she's been promoted and nobody's mentioned it). Why doesn't Grissom take one of the others off the Newman case and send them over rather than bring Sara in on her day off?

Notes: This episode occurs about 7 October 2002, according to the evidence bag with the filling in. The title refers to the old Latin tag 'caveat emptor' – let the buyer beware.

The episode was altered after initial transmission: real estate company Re/Max International sued CBS because the boards used by Augie were suspiciously like their signs. The red, white and blue bars have now been changed.

Overall: Only three episodes into the season, and already it feels like they're reaching too far for explanations. It feels as if someone heard about the Scandinavian-affecting disease and worked backwards.

49
A Little Murder

US Air Date: 17 October 2002 18.3/29
UK Air Date: 18 February 2003

Written by: Naren Shankar & Ann Donahue
Directed by: Tucker Gates
Guest Cast: Phil Fondacaro (Kevin Marcus),
Meredith Eaton (Melanie Grace), Danny Woodburn (Max),
Linden Ashby (Detective Wolf), Kaarina Aufranc (Jessica Marcus),
Michael Gilden (Lawrence Ames), Greg Dohanic (Young Man),
Jack Galle (Dwayne Gallo), Matthew Lang (1st Officer Clark),
Andy MacKenzie (Teddy Henders),
Arlene Malinowski (Signing Student)

Teaser One-liner: 'I think we've got a little murder.'
The Cases: At a convention of Little People, Lawrence
Ames, a clothing salesman, is found hanging from the
rafters above the stage by Melanie Grace, one of the event
co-ordinators. Sara finds some fibres on Ames. The
handrail rope provided for the convention is the same sort
as the suicide rope. Grissom finds a hair caught in the knot.

Robbins carries out an autopsy on Ames and finds that
he underwent bone-lengthening surgery. He died of asphyxiation due to strangulation and, although preliminary
signs are of hanging, there is a bruise that is the result of
a blow that paralysed him – something that can only
happen to dwarves with pseudoachondroplasia.

Melanie Grace tells them that Ames was a 'pseudo' and
looked like normal people, so he had little difficulty getting
attention. Grissom and Sara then go to Ames' room and
are surprised to find Jessica Marcus there. She's five feet
seven and claims she's Ames' fiancée. Ames has a broken
reaching tool by his laptop, and there's a gouge in the wall,
deeper at the bottom than the top. There's a piece of
plastic on the floor which fits the reaching tool. They ask
Jessica if she and Ames argued, and she denies it. There's
a champagne glass with lipstick on it which Jessica says
isn't hers, as she's seven weeks pregnant. Grissom and Sara
take the laptop for investigation.

Greg finds a skin tag on one of the hairs from the rope,
and the fibres on the body came from cheap rugs. Grissom
takes the hairs. Greg is ready to compare the DNA when
he has a comparison sample.

Sara finds emails on the laptop from a woman, Danielle,
to Ames. The email records show that Jessica was aware of

this. She says she wasn't worried, but the CSIs think she was, because Danielle was the same size as Ames. Jessica can't explain how her skin cells came to be on the rope.

Grissom tests the hair and proves that it came from a dwarf, so Jessica is clear of the murder. The suspect had Cartilage Hair Hypoplasia (CHH).

Archie Johnson looks at the photo of Danielle that she sent to Ames, and points out it's a composite, created to lure Ames away from his fiancée. Brass tells them that Ames had had to get call blocking against Melanie two months earlier – the same time that 'Danielle' started emailing him. Melanie denies that she killed him.

Nick gets some hassle from one of the dwarfs, who has a wheelchair that can lift him up to Nick's eye level.

The DNA on the hair does have a connection to Jessica – the alleles indicate that they are related. Grissom, Brass and Nick visit Kevin Marcus, a salesman at the convention, who has the same sort of rope available at his stall. He's Jessica's father and suffers from CHH. Jessica admits that she and Ames had a fight over 'Danielle', she rushed back to her father, and then she and Ames made up the next night before he left for the convention. Kevin Marcus says he didn't like Ames, but didn't kill him. And he's not capable of getting him as high as needed.

Nick remembers the man in the special wheelchair, which would explain how Marcus could lift him. Faced with this, Marcus admits what he did. He was trying to prevent Ames and Jessica from procreating – and the CSIs point out that it's too late. She's already pregnant.

Detective Drew Wolf briefs Catherine about a male body found at the site of a probable home invasion. He goes to interview a neighbour, and Catherine gets rid of the rather bilious young cop on body watch. As she's working, a figure comes from inside a cabinet and attacks her. She ends up falling into the blood from the body. The police chase the suspect outside, and Warrick then berates the cop for not clearing the scene properly. He goes to help

Catherine, but she's now evidence. She swabs her own wound and removes all her clothing for trace to check.

Catherine recalls that her attacker had been drinking. She finds a denim fibre on the cabinet but no prints. Warrick gets footprints from the suspect's escape. The photos of the property's owners don't match the deceased so chances are that both suspect and victim were burglars.

The deceased, Teddy Henders, died from blunt force trauma. There's a letter Z imprinted on his scalp, and Catherine recalls seeing a Z-mover video game box at the scene. They surmise that two burglars came in, had a fight and one killed the other. Warrick finds cooking grease both on the dead man's skin, and on the denim found on the cabinet. The owner of the house ran a fast food franchise, and gives Wolf the addresses of the outlets.

Catherine, Warrick and Wolf visit the outlet where Dwayne Gallo works. The other workers agree to provide evidence, but Gallo refuses. However, Catherine finds the fingerprint powder up his nose. He admits the murder but says it was an accident.

Personal Notes: Grissom says he gets the Little People newsletter, and from his knowledge of them, it seems like he's telling the truth. He decides at the end of the episode to take a class in lip reading. Catherine is scared by the attack, and Warrick is a good shoulder for her.

Techniques: Grissom uses a Tinius Olsen machine to test the strength of the hair.

The Wit and Wisdom of Gil Grissom: 'Being a dwarf doesn't mean you're disabled, Nick. It means you're . . . short.'

'Discrimination isn't just for tall people.'

'I think we look for the differences in each other to prove that we're not alone.'

Classic Dialogue: Catherine: 'Well . . . alive . . . it's inside your bowels. Dead, it ends up on the floor.'

Melanie: 'Does he ever talk?' Sara: 'Yeah. At, uh, random intervals.'

Melanie: 'Eventually, I guess I realised it's nice to see eye-to-eye with someone.' Grissom: 'Mm.' Melanie: 'I get the impression that's a little tough for you.:

Fantastic Voyages: We look at the small hair within the knot. We see the process of bone lengthening from inside the bone, and the skeleton being snapped between the first and second vertebrae. We go inside Gallo's nose to see the fingerprint dust.

The Usual Suspects: Linden Ashby (Detective Wolf) was the star of the sadly short-lived series *Spy Game*. Phil Fondacaro and Michael Gilden were both Ewoks in *Return of the Jedi*. Danny Woodburn (the man in the wheelchair) was Carl the Gnome on *Special Unit 2*, and Mickey Abbott on *Seinfeld*.

Pop Culture References: Robbins quotes from Shakespeare's *A Midsummer Night's Dream*. Nick thinks that Brass sounded a bit like Jack Lord, the actor who played Steve McGarrett on *Hawaii Five-0*. He must have seen reruns! Melanie Grace quotes from Carson McCullers.

Mistakes Really Can Be Fatal: Warrick says that they lost a CSI two years earlier because the crime scene wasn't cleared properly. He might be trying to justify things to himself, but Holly Gribbs was killed by the perpetrator returning to the scene, rather than not going in the first place.

Notes: An attempt to have continuity to 00, 'Pilot', as Warrick gets angry over the crime scene not being cleared properly (but see **Mistakes**).

The signing conversation at the end, after greetings, goes roughly as follows:

Student: Where are you going?

Grissom: I'm taking a course on lip-speaking (lip reading).

Student: I think I should tell the teacher you're a troublemaker.

Grissom: (Shakes his head) No (laughing).

Student: I'll see you around.

Overall: An enjoyable episode which isn't afraid to tackle 'class' issues. A vulnerable Catherine is a novelty as well.

50
Abra-Cadaver

US Air Date: 31 October 2002 17.3/27
UK Air Date: 25 February 2003

Written by: Anthony E. Zuiker & Danny Cannon
Directed by: Danny Cannon
Guest Cast: Tom Noonan (Zephyr Dillinger), Lawrence Monoson (Toby Arcane), Salvator Xuereb (Keith Castle), Jennifer Sky (Matilda), Tushka Bergen (Samantha Dean), John Sklaroff (Punky Dillinger), Esteban Powell (Band member), Jack McGee (Band Manager), Catherine Grace (Orlando Wile), Sven Holmberg (Bassist), Blumes Tracy (Gus Kenyon)

Teaser One-liner: 'I can understand why he doesn't want to reveal his trick . . . but would he like to explain this blood?'
The Cases: A magic trick goes wrong on stage as The Amazing Zephyr somehow manages to lose a volunteer from the audience. She came up, entered his Chamber of Doom, which was filled with gas obscuring her from view, and then swords were run through it. She should have reappeared in her seat, but she didn't. Grissom wonders about the blood on the swords. The swords may be blunt, but the blood is real. Zephyr claims to know nothing.

Grissom, Warrick and Sara talk to Punky Dillinger, the stagehand, who operates the trick and makes Grissom disappear – in reality sending him down a chute to the floor beneath the stage. Dillinger says that he turned his back for a second and the volunteer had gone. The CSIs find a blood trail leading backstage and down to an alleyway. They find more blood there and a tyre track. Sara gets a print from the stage door. It's Dillinger's and it matches a print Warrick found in the Chamber. Dillinger claims that he wanted to know how the trick worked so one night climbed inside the Chamber. Greg confirms that the blood in the Chamber matches the blood found in the basement, but not that found in the alleyway. That blood was animal and also contained Thorazine, an animal tranquilliser.

Archie Johnson goes through some photos taken by tourists at the time of the incident, and spots Toby Arcane, aka Freak Man, as an audience member. Arcane is a more visceral magician who initially denies going to Zephyr's show but later admits it, although he decries Zephyr's working methods.

Greg runs the blood DNA through the CODIS missing persons database and comes up with Zoë Clein. Her last known address is deserted. Sara notes that none of Zoë's clothes has gone. Warrick finds blood in the fridge, while Grissom discovers a hidden panel in the wall which goes down to a hidden room. Here he finds blueprints for the Chamber of Doom. Sara and Warrick join him and find a photo of Zoë with an older man and young Zephyr, who is carrying a baby in his arms. It's titled 'The Clein Magical Tour'. They hear a noise and find Zephyr's assistant Matilda, who says she came to speak with Zoë, who is the best inventor in the business. Matilda wants to buy one of her inventions so she can set up by herself. Matilda's car matches the tyre track that Warrick found behind the stage. Inside her car are a black panther, some blood and used syringes. Matilda explains that her cat Sadie cut her leg on the car tailgate, hence the blood and the sedative.

Zephyr is premiering a new trick. The CSIs go along to watch, and see Zephyr attempt to make himself disappear. He enters the Chamber, it fills with smoke, but then it bursts into flames. The CSIs check the Chamber, and the trap door has been nailed shut in a manner similar to one of Arcane's tricks. Doc Robbins performs an autopsy on Zephyr – he died from swallowing fire. He also discovers that Zephyr had little skin pockets surgically created inside his mouth. Toby Arcane denies killing Zephyr, and shows Sara and Warrick the secrets of his tricks to prove it.

Grissom gets the CSIs to look into everything about Zephyr and his team. They discover that Zephyr and Dillinger are father and son. Grissom prints the corpse – it's Dillinger, not Zephyr. Grissom returns to Zoë Clein's hidden room and finds a further hidden room. Zephyr is there, and admits to Grissom that the 'woman' who entered the cabinet to disappear was Zephyr himself with Dillinger acting as Zephyr on stage, thus keeping the details of the trick secret. Zephyr then killed his son and tried to frame Toby Arcane for the murder. He won't tell Grissom how he did that – and when he is being taken away by the police, he is able to regurgitate a key, presumably for the handcuffs.

Nick and Catherine are investigating the death of Gus Kenyon, lead singer of rock group Pekinpah. It looks as if he overdosed on heroin, but the CSIs wonder why there is still some heroin in the syringe, and no vomit on the floor. The tourniquet has been applied back to front, and there's an odd black mark on Kenyon's right index finger. There's also an empty bottle of whiskey.

Doc Robbins tells Catherine that Kenyon had loads of bourbon in his system, but no heroin. He was killed by an air bubble to the heart but would have been unconscious from the alcohol before his heart stopped. The black mark is printing ink.

Nick talks to the surviving band members. The whole band had been clean for six years. Kenyon had suffered from depression after cleaning up, and the band knew that he had wanted to get out of the band for some time. Greg passes some material on the band to Catherine and casually mentions he knew they were breaking up. All the songs were written by Kenyon, so he would be the only one benefiting after the band split up. Catherine returns to the tour bus and finds a destroyed cellphone and a copy of the telephone directory, with a smudge by the name Samantha Dean. Nick finds heroin inside the guitarist's CD player. Greg shows Nick and Catherine a clip from an MTV show of Gus Kenyon saying that a 'Best of Pekinpah' CD will only happen over his dead body. The album is now being planned by Keith Castle, the guitarist. Nick interrogates Castle, who admits that he tried to give some heroin to Kenyon the previous night, but Kenyon wouldn't take it.

Catherine speaks with Samantha Dean, who denies receiving a call from Kenyon. She also meets Samantha's nine-year-old son Brandon, who is wearing expensive sunglasses. Catherine then finds a photo of Samantha with

Kenyon backstage. There's material on Kenyon's ring that could be from Samantha's front door.

Samantha is a registered nurse, with access to needles. Confronted with the evidence, she tells them that Kenyon had threatened to have Brandon taken from her. She went to the tour bus, saw Kenyon with Castle's heroin, and killed him to save her son from becoming part of Kenyon's world.
Personal Notes: Lindsey is now nine years old.
The Wit and Wisdom of Gil Grissom: 'Magic is fun, Jim, but it's not real. The woman is somewhere.'

'That's the conflict of magic – the burden of knowledge versus the mystique of wonder.'

'My livelihood is dispelling lies and finding the truth.'

'Magicians of Zephyr's calibre belong to a very secluded society. They barnstorm from city to city ... no contact with the outside world, no association with other magicians. They're like ghosts with skin.'

' "Abracadabra". That's a cabalistic charm said to be made up from three Hebrew words meaning, father, son and the holy spirit. You're the father who took his son's life, so that you could disappear and become the holy spirit?'
Classic Dialogue: Samantha Dean: 'You're a mother. What would you be willing to do to save the life of your child?' Catherine: 'I think that I'd rather have my daughter know a bad father than no father at all.'
Fantastic Voyages: We follow the progress of the air bubble as it makes its journey to Gus Kenyon's heart to kill him. We monitor the sword as it enters the Chamber of Doom and passes through skin, and then see Zephyr drowning in fire from the inside.
The Usual Suspects: Tom Noonan (Zephyr) played Francis Dollarhyde opposite William Petersen in *Manhunter*. Tushka Bergen (Samantha Dean) was Alice Hastings in the most recent remake of *Journey to the Centre of the Earth*. Jennifer Sky (Matilda) was the titular *Cleopatra 2525*, and played Amarice on *Xena, Warrior Princess*.
Pop Culture References: Greg refers to actress Thora Birch. Unsurprisingly, there are mentions of Harry Houdini.

Notes: This episode is set on and after 6 November 2002 (Warrick's print envelope).

Overall: There are some suitably spooky moments as Grissom, Warrick and Sara explore the Clein residence, but why did they have to finish the episode with the hokey old 'magician has the key to get out' routine? Great to see William Petersen and Tom Noonan in some scenes together.

51
The Execution of Catherine Willows

US Air Date: 7 November 2002 17.2/26
UK Air Date: 4 March 2003

Written by: Carol Mendelsohn & Ann Donahue
Directed by: Kenneth Fink
Guest Cast: Beth Grant (Sally Roth),
Wade Andrew Williams (Mr Reston), Wayne Pere (Painter),
Viola Davis (Ms Campbell), David Lee Smith (Cody Lewis),
Victor Bevine (John Mathers), Phe Caplan (Charlene Roth),
John Goodwin (Psychiatrist), Nikki Danielle Moore (Debbie)

Teaser One-liner: 'It's just about evidence. It's not up to you whether he lives or dies. Case has no face.'

The Case: John Mathers, the first person who is to be executed based on Catherine Willows' CSI work, is given a last-minute stay of execution so that some pubic hairs can be checked for DNA at the Department of Justice lab in Norfolk, Virginia. He was responsible for murdering three co-eds at Western Las Vegas University fifteen years earlier, with the strongest evidence for number three, Charlene Roth. The DA only proceeded with that indictment.

Seventeen-year-old Debbie Reston didn't turn up for work, and her father is found unconscious in a blood-soaked T-shirt. He claims he was in a bar fight. The main part of the house is filthy, but Debbie's bedroom is clean, with two big locks on the door. Her bedroom even has a kitchen. Debbie was a martial arts black belt. Grissom spots blood on a towel. He and Nick find a shovel in the backyard and a toolshed containing a Glock which has been tampered with, and then discover a stack of guns under the floorboards. Nick checks for density changes beneath the ground and finds something two and a half feet down. It's the body of an animal. Reston claims that his daughter is ashamed of him. The blood on Reston was his own, and the blood on the towel is Debbie's, although it could be from an innocuous injury.

Meanwhile Catherine and Warrick re-examine the three murders which took place fifteen years ago. She gives the trash bag in which Charlene was found to Jacqui Franco, the prints technician who is back working nights. Charlene Roth's parents are concerned that Mathers might be exonerated. O'Riley calls Catherine to a copycat killing of Charlene's death – a body dumped in a garbage bag. She processes the new corpse and finds a bug in the hair and some black fibres. She's been dead for at least twelve hours.

The cases coincide. The corpse is Debbie Reston. She was a Western LVU student, like the rest of Mathers' victims. Doc Robbins explains that the killer is familiar with the minutiae of the previous cases. The only difference is that Debbie has defensive wounds on her hands, with some glass still left in them. There's blue paint on it that hasn't yet dried.

Warrick and Sara retrace Debbie's steps across the University campus from where she parked to where her lecture was. There's wet blue paint on the metal rails. They surmise that Debbie got her hands dirty, and went to wash them. Her killer was waiting. They find an empty light socket, and some other glass which Warrick takes for comparison. In the Mathers cases, the CSIs didn't know why there was blue paint on the victims' hands. How did this copycat know? Warrick finds Debbie's wallet and Catherine comes across a bug like the one she found on Debbie. They also find some polarised glass, and surmise that Debbie fought back.

Jacqui has had no luck with the trash bag from the old case, but gets a partial print from Debbie's last resting place. Sara finds that the fibres Catherine found on Debbie come from a Chevy, while Warrick is able to work out the lens prescription of the glasses worn by her attacker.

The Mathers report returns from Norfolk – the hairs from Charlene Roth are from Mathers.

On the new case, the paint is oil-based, meaning it stayed wet longer, but it matches the other paint on the campus. There's also some badger hairs in the sample of paint that Grissom checks – badger hair brushes are sold in the campus shop.

Greg discovers that a hair found on Debbie's wrists comes from Janet Kent, the very first victim fifteen years earlier. Grissom tests the paint found on the victims, and all bar that found on Charlene are the same. John Mathers was the copycat killer.

The Dean of the Art School points the finger at Cody Lewis, who was around at the time of the original deaths, and returned to the University in September. Brass discovers that he dated Janet Kent, one of the murdered girls, and he paints pictures of bound girls. His car matches the description they have, but it's clean and his prints don't match the partial print found on the garbage bag. As Catherine goes to witness Mathers' execution, Grissom and Brass reluctantly concede that they aren't getting anywhere.

Personal Notes: Two people have been executed based on Grissom's testimony. Catherine attends Mathers' execution. She drinks vanilla ice soy blended latte. Brass keeps a bottle of Scotch in his desk drawer, which he offers Grissom.

Techniques: Jacqui uses vacuum metal deposition to get a print off the plastic garbage bag.

The Wit and Wisdom of Gil Grissom: 'With the exception of the termite queen, the cicada is the longest-living insect. Spends seventeen years dormant underground and then the cicada nymph emerges and sheds its skin.'

'I don't believe in luck. My only real purpose is to be smarter than the bad guys to find the evidence that they didn't know they left behind and make sense of it all.'

Classic Dialogue: Nick: 'People are pigs.' Grissom: 'Don't insult the pigs, Nick. They're actually very clean.'

Grissom: 'As adults they flit around for about five weeks of activity in the hot sun and then they die.' Catherine: 'They spend their whole lives waiting for the end.' Grissom: 'Not unlike death row.'

Fantastic Voyages: We follow the liquid being prepared for the execution, then entering the bloodstream, and making the heart slow to a halt. We go right inside the DNA on the hairs being examined. We watch the particles being moved around inside the fuming machine to stick to the prints inside the bag.

Notes: The Mathers trial took place around 3 March 1987.

Overall: Criticised for its graphic portrayal of the execution scenes, this episode stands out for exactly that reason, particularly to audiences in countries or even states that don't have a death penalty. There are times in this series when it might all seem like a game that the CSIs are playing, but it isn't – people's lives are quite literally on the line.

52
Fight Night

US Air Date: 14 November 2002 18.3/28
UK Air Date: 11 March 2003

Written by: Andrew Lipsitz & Naren Shankar
Directed by: Richard J. Lewis
Guest Cast: Roma Maffia (Adelle Cross), Khalil Kain (Jerome Anderson),
Greg Serano (Javier Molina), Jennifer Aspen (Mrs Vicky Ramsey),
Ron Canada (Gerry Barone), Richard Biggs (Attorney),
Geoffrey Rivas (Detective Sam Vega), Ricky Aiello,
Ryan Cutrona (Cut Man), Marty Rackham (Ramsey),
Terry Bozeman (Lewis), Gary Carlos Cervantes (Molina's Chief Trainer),
Dawn Marie Church (Jewellery Store Manager),
Pete Cunningham (LaRoi Steele), Rick Fitzgerald (Randy James),
Charley Rossman (Officer Beltram),
Robert Paul Lewis (Nevada Gaming Commissioner)

Teaser One-liner: 'If death occurs during commission of a felony, that's a murder.'

The Cases: LaRoi Steele is killed in the boxing ring during a fight with Javier Molina. Five hours before the start, the odds changed dramatically against Steele, leading to a felony investigation. Sara and Warrick check the fight gloves and the ring while Grissom and Brass talk to the referee. All he saw was Steele getting a heavy beating.

Grissom talks to Adelle Cross, the fight promoter, and finds mercury in the locker room. Molina says he didn't want Steele to die, and would have stopped if the referee had stopped the match. Sara finds mercury inside Molina's hand wraps.

Steele died from being punched too much – but there was also a sedative in his system. Brass talks to the referee, whose cousin made a big bet on Molina. The referee asks if he's accusing him of keeping the fight going and thus killing Steele.

The mercury comes from a Mexican folk remedy for a chronic stomach condition that Molina suffers from. His gloves have sweat and inorganic salts on them, but the swab from Steele's corner shows the sedative. The CSIs examine Steele's second's bag and find the sedative. However, the prints on the bottle belong to Gerry Barone, Steele's manager. Barone admits he was trying to save Steele from himself – Steele had slowed down and Molina was going to defeat him. The videos of the pre-fight conference and the fight itself corroborate that.

Robbins discovers that Steele was struck with a very powerful blow, which could not have been achieved with normal boxing gloves. Greg has checked the gloves on his own initiative, and discovers that they are not the gloves that killed Steele. Adelle Cross admits that she didn't actually see Molina put the gloves on as she should have done.

Warrick tests gloves loaded with mercury, and they are capable of hitting at the right power. Molina's urine tests positive for mercury, and he eventually admits that he was responsible – he wanted the edge.

A gang member is found shot dead in the street between two cars. Catherine finds a shell case and a gun; Detective

Vega finds a weapon. There's a third gun inside the car but none of the bullets matches the guns found, but all come from the same gun. There's something on one of the bullets that Catherine takes to Trace.

Bobby runs the shell case against IBIS. The same gun was used in a murder two years ago; the suspect was Tiny Tim Fontaine, a member of the Snakebacks. Fontaine has 'gone', although there's still one Snakeback around, Jerome Anderson, who has a burn on his neck possibly formed by the shell casing ejecting. Vega and Catherine get a warrant to check Jerome Anderson for DNA matching. As Catherine brings in Anderson's clothes, Vega announces the discovery of Fontaine's body with a calling card from the 10th Street Vandals. A Snakeback killed a Vandal, so a Vandal killed a Snakeback.

Nick is left to work solo on a smash-and-grab at a diamond store, and finds some blood inside a broken jewellery display case. The manager provides a list of stolen items, including a ring that had been brought in as surety by the Ramsays, a couple who borrowed a necklace to wear at the fight and now won't return it until they get their ring. Nick asks O'Riley to check hospitals for anyone with a forearm laceration. Randy James is duly arrested. However, Mr Ramsay says that the ring Nick has found isn't theirs. Nick does some tests on it and then tells Mrs Ramsay that he knows that she switched the diamond in her ring for moissanite. He refuses to say he made a mistake.

Personal Notes: During Grissom's first year as a criminalist, he thought that boxing would be a good place to observe live bloodspatter. Sara doesn't like dealing with saliva. Warrick knows a lot about boxing. Nick enjoys watching wildlife documentaries, including *Animal Planet*.

The Wit and Wisdom of Gil Grissom: 'A heavyweight can land a punch at a thousand pounds per square inch. The energy of the punch is transferred through the cerebrospinal fluid compressing the brain against the skull temporarily disrupting neural activity.'

Classic Dialogue: Robbins: 'Massive soft tissue damage, severe facial fractures. Are they letting guys go at each other with clubs these days?' Grissom: 'Only on cable.'

Grissom: 'It's called an uppercut.' Robbins: 'You say tomato and I say cause of death.'

Catherine: 'Do you mind if I ask how The Man got the burn mark on his neck?' Jerome Anderson: 'Well, all the ladies say that The Man is hot. I guess I must have just burned myself and forgot all about it.'

Nick to Grissom: 'How come when you talk about bugs everyone says you're a genius, but when I talk about birds everyone says I watch too much television?'

Grissom: 'For most CSIs, fashion is irrelevant.' Catherine: 'Speak for yourself. The only thing between me and a wardrobe like this is a few extra zeros on my paycheque.'

Fantastic Voyages: We see the effects on the brain when it's punched, and then what happens when a vertebral artery is broken. We also see the mercury permeating through the glove.

The Usual Suspects: Ron Canada (Gerry Barone) was Judge Orrin Bell on *Murder One*. Richard Biggs (Jerome's Attorney) played Dr Stephen Franklin on *Babylon 5*, and is Clayton Boudreaux on *The Guiding Light*.

Pop Culture References: There are numerous references to other fighters and their managers: Sonny Liston, Cassius Clay, Felix Trinidad, Ray Mancini, Don King. Nick gets some of his information from watching *Animal Planet*.

Mistakes Really Can Be Fatal: Nick's complaint about working solo wasn't that he wasn't allowed to work on his own, as this episode implies – from the very start in **00**, 'Pilot', he flew solo on ordinary cases – but that he wasn't allowed to work a dead body case alone. Here he's surprised at being given an apparently routine hold-up.

Notes: The episode begins on 9 November 2002 – the date of the fight. There are numerous little twists throughout the episode: a fantastic gag with the precredits music starting up but being interrupted by Grissom's pager; Warrick and Sara casually pass someone who might be

Nick's suspect. A lot of this episode was filmed on location
a mere three weeks before transmission.

Overall: Barring Nick's out-of-character reaction, this is a
good episode showcasing different facets of the team, with
some sparkling dialogue. The fight scenes are well shot,
and there's an energy to the episode that some lack.

53
Snuff

US Air Date: 21 November 2002 16.2/24
UK Air Date: 18 March 2003

Written by: Ann Donahue & Bob Harris
Directed by: Kenneth Fink
Guest Cast: Tyler Christopher (Billy Rattison),
Sam Hennings (Pete Banson), Niecy Nash (Snuff Film Manager),
Sal Lopez (Enrique Vasquez), Stephen Spacek (Pete Banson),
William Mapother (Douglas Sampson),
Meredith Giangrande (Susan Hodap), Blair Williamson (Randy Traschel)

Teaser One-liner: 'It's not fake blood. It's human. That
was a murder . . . on 16 mm.'

The Cases: A film processor is sent a snuff film that she
thinks could be real. When Grissom and Catherine watch
it, the arterial spray from the woman's throat confirms it.
Detective Sulik checks the private mail depot to which the
order was to be returned, but it's a cash-only place. Archie
gets a digitised picture of the dead woman which Sulik
takes to missing persons.

Sara checks the film and identifies the stock, but
Catherine tells her it won't help. Warrick and Archie check
the film for any identifying marks, either on the people, or
in the background. They spot the Stratosphere Tower so
Archie can pinpoint the location. It's an old hotel in
receivership. Warrick, Sara and Catherine identify the
specific room, but the furniture has been removed, and the
room repainted. That doesn't prevent the ALS from seeing
the arterial spray. There's a void which could be a face.

Sulik talks to the security guard and Catherine sees a mole on his neck which matches the man's in the film. The guard admits he had sex with the girl, but she was alive when he left. He didn't say anything later about the blood because he didn't want to lose his job. The video confirms the guard's story – he is shorter than the killer. Sara points out that there might be more information on the negative.

Sara finds the negative and they realise that a lamp has been moved out of the room. It might have some prints on it. Once they find it they test the lamp for saliva, which leads them to Douglas Sampson, who did three years for sexual assault and battery. He's a pornographer now, and the security guard recognises him but, without the evidence, Sampson tells Catherine and Sulik to get lost. Warrick checks his car by the side of the road, and finds mud from a specific area. Later, Sulik's men find the body there, wrapped in a curtain. Robbins identifies her as Susan Hodap, killed by a slicing stab. He agrees to boil the skeleton to check for serration marks, and informs Catherine and Sara that Susan was HIV positive. Although Sampson denies having sex with Susan, Catherine and Sara know that he is HIV positive, from the same strain as Susan – he got it when her blood hit his eyes, proving he was there.

A dead body with fire ants flying out of it is found in a toolbox. Brass knows that fire ants can kill animals, and Grissom points out that although they can kill people, they need to learn how to put the corpse in a box and dump him in a ditch. The body has been eaten down to the bone.

Robbins estimates the man has been dead at least a year. There are multiple fractures to both clavicles, and two wounds on his back. Grissom finds a pupa case that will help establish an entomological timeline – it indicates the man has been dead approximately nineteen months. Nick finds some carbon steel at the bottom of the box. With some mathematical calculation, he works out that it's a spur.

Teri Miller comes to help Grissom identify the deceased, and spots a dung beetle that had been missed before the skull was cleansed. Teri builds the face, realising that the victim had Down's Syndrome. Brass sends out a fax to the local Down's Syndrome organisations and comes up with a name – Randy Traschel, who disappeared around seventeen months previously, and worked at the Las Vegas Ranch. The manager, Pete Banson, recognises Traschel's picture and says he suddenly disappeared. Enrique, Traschel's replacement, is wearing spurs, and there's a tooth missing from them that matches the piece found in the box. Enrique picked them up from a place where cowboys chuck their unwanted gear, and Banson reckons they might belong to Billy Rattison. Rattison has a new toolbox and he's angry when he's asked about 'that damn retard'. He says he was away during March 2000, nineteen months earlier, the time of death according to the pupae.

Analysing the rust level of oxidation shows that the spur has been in the toolbox since May 2000 – seventeen months earlier. The ants were wrong, missing persons was right. That brings Rattison back into the frame. Grissom looks at the marks on Traschel's back again and then asks Banson about any bulls he has at the ranch. There's only one old one, but when they search Rattison's new toolbox, they find a mounted set of bull horns of the right diameter to make the marks, which test positive for blood. They used to be on the front of Rattison's truck and Traschel was thrown onto them when he antagonised Rattison.

Personal Notes: Grissom has never ridden a horse, only a roller coaster. Catherine worked on a case, breaking a porno ring using teenage girls, a couple of years earlier (in an unseen case during the period of Season One, presumably). Teri Miller has married a teacher.

Techniques: Nick uses phenolphthalein to test for blood.

The Wit and Wisdom of Gil Grissom: 'I've got to see a woman about a face.'

'By the way, the definition of the word "retard" is "to hinder" or "to hold someone back". I think your life is about to become "retarded".'

Classic Dialogue: Robbins: 'And how does an entomologist feel about putting ants to death?' Grissom: 'I view them as martyrs in a scientist's holy war.'

Sara: 'How does somebody cross the line where killing a woman is a turn-on?' Catherine: 'Oh, I don't think snuff-makers cross a line, I think they start on the other side of it.'

Grissom: 'I heard you were married. Hopefully not to a criminalist.' Teri: 'You think I'm stupid? He's a teacher.'

Catherine: 'You killed her.' Sara: 'I guess she killed you back.'

Fantastic Voyages: We see the right clavicle clean up and then break. We watch the effect of a short end of film. We see Susan's blood entering Sampson's eyes.

The Usual Suspects: Tyler Christopher (Billy Rattison) plays Nikolas Cassidine on *General Hospital*. Larry Clarke debuts as Detective Sulik, having played Detective Morris LaMotte on *Law and Order*. Pamela Gidley returns for her last appearance to date as Teri Miller.

Notes: This episode was broadcast in the US with a warning about adult content.

Overall: An unpleasant subject that gets a fair treatment from the CSI team, and good to see Grissom playing to his strengths as an entomologist, but being prepared to accept that the ants got it wrong.

54
Blood Lust

US Air Date: 5 December 2002 18.0/27
UK Air Date: 25 March 2003

Written by: Josh Berman & Carol Mendelsohn
Directed by: Charlie Correll
Guest Cast: Michele Green (Jan Branson), Gina Phillips (Raina Krell),
James MacDonald (Jonathan Ruark), Michael Welch (Todd Branson),
Brandon Mauro, Candace Edwards (Nurse),
Anjul Nigam (Rajeeb Khandewahl), Bryan Friday (Rick Midgen),
Matthew Kaminsky (Stewart Bradley), David Meunier (Barry Lawrence),
Tim Mikulecky (Claude Allen), Mary Jo Mrochinski (Ms Karpell),
Victoria Reiniger (Judy), Eric Ritter (Graham Cooper),
William Winter (Joey Gillman)

Teaser One-liner: 'His insides are on the outside.'
The Case: Rajeeb Khandewahl, a taxi driver, drives into a young boy who has staggered out in front of him. A group of bikers extract revenge and beat him up. The young boy's viscera are exposed, which is very unusual for a traffic accident. The woman passenger in the cab confirms that Khandewahl hit the boy, went out to check him, then came back to radio for help before being dragged out and beaten up. The bikers Joey Gillman, Barry Lawrence and Claude Allen are proud of attacking this non-American, and making a citizen's arrest. Brass points out that what they were doing was illegal. Grissom photographs them and takes DNA swabs.

Grissom goes to the hospital where Khandewahl is in a critical condition. Doc Robbins finds no signs of a hit and run. The boy died of multiple rib fractures – he was run over by the taxi – but he had been stabbed some time earlier.

Grissom and Sara follow a blood trail to a basketball court in Haskell Park where they find droplets and cast-off, indicating the primary crime scene.

Jan Branson identifies her 14-year-old son Todd. She doesn't know of any enemies of Todd, although they moved down from Portland nine months earlier because she's on the run from her ex-husband who threatened to kill her and her sons. He rang them a couple of days ago, and Jan was preparing to run again.

Sara lets the sniffer dogs go to work, while Grissom checks the crime scene with a metal detector. He finds a gun; the dogs find another dead body.

There is gunshot residue on Todd's jacket and burned skin on the gun from where an inexperienced shooter's palm got caught on the cylinder gap as the gun fired. It won't help for DNA, but perspiration found on the weapon might. The second body has a knife wound on its palm, a bullet in the left ventricle and a fragment in a knee. He also has a dislocated shoulder which occurred after death. The bullet seems designed to fragment on impact. It matches the gun found at the scene, which is registered to

Jonathan Ruark – Jan Branson's ex-husband. Jan identifies the second corpse as Stewart Bradley, her boyfriend.

Sara finds some grooves in the dirt and tries to work out a physical connection between the stabbing and the shooting.

Brass interrogates Ruark. He says he hasn't come near Jan, and claims not to know about either Todd or Bradley's deaths. He says he was in Taos, New Mexico, and has a hotel receipt to prove it. Grissom looks at his hands, and asks Brass to come up with a holding charge. He then carries out an experiment using first Sara and then Judy, a secretary who is smaller than Sara, to try to drag Warrick across the floor. When the smaller girl tries, Warrick's shoulder is badly pulled because she has to keep stopping and starting. Jan Branson is about the same size as Judy. Maybe she is responsible.

However, when Brass and Grissom visit her, her hands are clean, but her other son Eric has a burn mark. He claims he burned his hand on an iron, but then changes his story to say that he followed Todd to the park, where he saw him argue with Stewart Bradley. Eric tried to stop Todd firing, and so he only hit Bradley's knee; Bradley then stabbed Todd, and Todd fired again, killing Bradley. But his story doesn't match the evidence – Eric was the shooter. He believed Bradley was making his mother move house – he didn't know she was moving because of Ruark – and didn't want to move again. Jan admits that Eric must have borrowed her gun without her knowledge. Bradley had only started carrying a knife because Jan had told him about the threat from Ruark; Todd was stabbed by it in the commotion.

Khandewahl has died, so the investigation becomes a murder enquiry. Greg processes the DNA from Khandewahl's clothing and matches it to the different suspects – only six of the twelve men left evidence. It's down to Brass and his men to try to get evidence against the other six.

Personal Notes: Grissom claims he was on a date at the start of the episode. Sara is attending a forensic anthropology seminar. She won't tell Grissom her weight. Warrick weighs 195 lbs (give or take a doughnut!). It's supposed to be Lindsey's ninth birthday on the date of this episode.

Techniques: Sara uses a new technique to match perspiration from a gun barrel, as described in a recent Australian paper.

The Wit and Wisdom of Gil Grissom: 'Fiction is often more compelling.'

'Emerson once said, "The mob is man voluntarily descending to the nature of the beast." The beast is up for murder.'

Classic Dialogue: Grissom: 'Greg, this is your DNA lab. You are the master. We serve you.' Greg: 'Well, your stuff just moved to the top of the pile.'

Grissom: 'OK, Doc, tell me something I don't know.' Robbins: 'OK. In fourth grade, I dropped out of karate class because a kid half my size made me cry.'

Grissom: 'Warrick, would you lie down on the floor?' Warrick: 'I don't get paid enough to play dead.'

Grissom: 'Unfortunately, physical evidence is limited by human action.' Brass: 'Well, nothing's absolute, Gil – even forensics.'

Fantastic Voyages: We see the effects of a car hitting a person and the relevant bones breaking, and how it doesn't apply in this case. We follow a bullet as it goes through clothes and skin and shatters when it hits bone.

The Usual Suspects: Michael Welch (Todd Branson) played Artim in *Star Trek: Insurrection*. Michele Green (Jan Branson) was Abbie Perkins on *LA Law*.

Pop Culture References: Grissom uses Gene Rayburn, the host of quiz show *The Match Game*, as a point of reference for Greg, and Greg quotes its catchphrase. Brass refers to the movie *Sleeping With The Enemy*, and mockingly calls Jonathan Ruark a Gumby, from *Monty Python*.

Mistakes Really Can Be Fatal: Screwy continuity again – Catherine revealed that Lindsey was already nine in **50**, 'Abra-Cadaver' set in November. This episode is clearly dated 2 December.

Greg says Catherine is working on a no-suspect rape, and is pressing for the evidence from him; but according to the conversation between her and Sara, she's on two days leave, taking Lindsey and friends to Circus Circus.

Overall: There's a growing reliance between Grissom and Sara that is communicated as much through looks as by dialogue, which gives an extra focus to an episode that is light on the primary cast. Removing three of them for most of the episode tightens the show up, and at least we get to see Catherine and Warrick. Nick is missing entirely. From interviews at the time, it's clear the production schedule was getting very hectic and the cast were shooting more than one episode simultaneously.

55
High and Low

US Air Date: 12 December 2002 16.1/25
UK Air Date: 8 April 2003

Written by: Eli Talbert & Naren Shankar
Directed by: Richard J. Lewis
Guest Cast: Richard Burgi (Rick Weston), Michael Trucco (Fred Dacks), Colleen Porch (T), Cynthia Preston (Waitress), Sal Landi (Frank Kraft), Philip McNiven, Cooper Thornton (Ned Bookman), Catherine MacNeal (Grissom's Doctor), Dennis Cockrum (Roger Edmonds), Justice Coleman (Jake), Jeremy Jimenez (Tim), Carl Paoli (Jimmy Maurer), Rain Denise Wilson (Female Employee)

Teaser One-liner: 'It's never the fall that kills you.'

The Cases: A body falls out of the sky in front of two roller bladers. At the top of the building beside which he was found, Grissom finds a lot of blood mess, from high velocity splatter. There are no casings or bullets to be found. Warrick finds some specks on the victim's trouser hem. The finger bones have burst through the skin eliminating prints, but dental records may assist with identification. He also had a tattoo. Nick finds a crack pipe which might have been used to hit the victim.

Warrick takes the photo of the tattoo to CSI technician Leah, who recognises the artist from his signature – it's a psychiatrist who also does tattoos. The doctor recognises the tattoo as belonging to Jimmy Maurer – it's a tattoo of Icarus, the Greek who flew too close to the sun. The doctor has a drug conviction for crack cocaine.

Maurer died of suffocation. However, there are no ligature marks or other signs of forcible strangulation. His brain was still inside his head when he died; he fell from a much higher point than the top of the building – and simply hit the side on his way down. But, according to Air Traffic Control, there were no planes in the area at the time.

The specks on Maurer's trousers come from pinion pine pollen, found at elevations over 4,500 ft such as Mount Potosi so Nick and Warrick visit a paragliding instructor based at the mountain. Rick Weston says that Maurer was cocky, and that sometimes he needed a long walk back to base as a lesson.

Warrick and Nick check Maurer's truck, which he left at the paragliding base. They find a paragliding canopy ripped to shreds, and a note under the wipers saying, 'Guess you can fly with anything. Find me when you get back, T' and a phone number. The T is a photographer, who has numerous photos of Maurer – a show-off. Someone had messed with his kit the day before but he was still determined to fly. T shows Nick a photo of Maurer and Fred Dacks, another paraglider who Maurer didn't get along with, so Warrick and Nick visit Dacks at the store where they both worked. Dacks says he wouldn't waste his time flying with Maurer, although he admits that they did leave around the same time the previous day. Nick picks up a sleeping bag that Dacks was touching. DNA from the sleeping bag and the shredded canopy match.

The CSIs need to find the rig that Maurer was using, so work out a rough area where it might be. Luckily, it's spotted by a traffic unit. The harness is Maurer's, but the rig belongs to the Potosi Glide Centre – although Weston had not told them that he had lent Maurer any equipment.

The lines seem to have been cut. Weston says that Dacks wanted to teach Maurer a lesson, so he agreed to give Maurer the training rig, which was big and slow. However, Nick discovers that the lines simply frayed. Maurer presumably had passed out and so toppled out of the rig when the lines gave way. But why didn't he use his oxygen if he had got so high?

They check Maurer's altimeter, and it's out by 2,000 feet. They find Dacks' fingerprints inside the meter. He knew Maurer would chase him no matter how high he went and, with a faulty gauge, Maurer would have gone higher than was safe, while Dacks would have got one up on him.

Catherine and O'Riley investigate the gunshot death of Roger Edmonds, found beside his car outside a bar. He was shot at close range but there are no bullet holes in the car. They find some blood and hair on the front licence plate.

The waitress who witnessed the shooting recalls an argument then a loud blast. The killer drove off in a pickup with a camper top. She tells them that Edmonds had been drinking Jack Daniels rather than his usual draft beer. Catherine finds a shell casing for a .50 calibre bullet, and Greg discovers that the blood and hair on the licence plate are animal, not human. Edmonds had bought a gun matching the bullet but drunk he would have been easy to disarm.

The pickup has been reported stolen from a Ned Bookman, who was one of Edmonds' neighbours. It's found, and it contains mulberries; Edmonds' house has a mulberry tree. Bookman says that another neighbour, Frank Kraft, borrowed his truck. Kraft has a number of complaints against him from his neighbours and there are odd grooves on his front lawn leading up to the tree. Kraft has a massive bruise on his chin but refuses to talk without a warrant.

Bookman tells O'Riley that Kraft and Edmonds have a bad history. Kraft's dog was tied up in the yard constantly barking, and Catherine thinks Edmonds may have dealt with that. She then starts to take branches off Edmonds' mulberry tree, which has been mutilated, for comparison with the items found in the truck. They match, and Kraft admits that everything escalated between him and Edmonds, after he cut down Edmonds' tree, and Edmonds killed his dog. They argued, and the gun went off. The gun is found at Kraft's house.

Personal Notes: Grissom's hearing loss starts to affect him, so he goes for a hearing test. It's starting to deteriorate, and the doctor thinks it's time to consider surgery. Grissom won't confide in Catherine, but investigates otosclerosis on the net. Catherine never wears perfume to work. Warrick knows his Greek mythology well enough to recognise the tattoos on Dacks' arm as the three Furies. Nick starts to learn to paraglide as a result of the case. Sara is confined to the lab because she's maxed out on overtime for the month. Brass has been to Honduras and seen the raining of fish.

Classic Dialogue: Greg: 'Luck is for those without skill.' Catherine: 'Spoken like a man who's never hit a jackpot.'

Catherine: 'That's a hell of a bruise you've got on your chin, Mr Kraft. How did you get that?' Frank Kraft: 'I sent away for it. You want one of your own?'

Fantastic Voyages: Very unusually, none.

The Usual Suspects: Richard Burgi (Richard Weston) played James Ellison, the central character in the long-running detective series *The Sentinel*. Cynthia Preston (the waitress) was Olivia Hume on *Total Recall 2070*.

Pop Culture References: Catherine refers to the neighbourly Mr Rogers from the long-running American educational series for children.

Mistakes Really Can Be Fatal: Catherine refers to Roger Edmonds as Roger Mitchell, the character's original name. O'Riley tells Catherine that the pickup was reported stolen, but Bookman's reaction when he opens his garage is that he didn't know it was gone, and no one else would have reported it.

Overall: Plot holes and half the characters missing this time don't add up to a good episode. Some nice moments, but overall completely missable but for the slight advancement in Grissom's hearing subplot.

56
Recipe for Murder

US Air Date: 9 January 2003 15.5/24
UK Air Date: 15 April 2003

Written by: Anthony E. Zuiker & Ann Donahue
Directed by: Richard J. Lewis & J. Miller Tobin
Guest Cast: Daniel Hagen (John Damon),
Marita Geraghty (Jane Damon), Robert Mailhouse (Les Dutton),
Kimberly Huie (Layla Creighton), Darren Pettie (Ross Halpo),
Chad Lindberg (Brody), Perrey Reeves (Linda's Neighbour),
Cameron Mathison (Danny Pasquale), Lori Rom (Hostess),
Scott MacDonald (Harold Haskins), Pat Asanti (Shop Foreman),
Dar Dixon (Chef Petrov Samsko), Iva Hasperger (Linda Damon)

Teaser One-liner: 'I'm going to need a hand.'
The Cases: A human hand is found sticking out of a meat
grinder in a meat packaging plant. Grissom and Catherine
believe that the only reason that it didn't join the rest of
the body was that the ulna was too strong to be ground
down. There's no point checking for blood, since, given the
location, it's everywhere. Catherine dismantles the meat
grinder as Grissom checks the surrounding area, and finds
an out-of-place earplug.

Robbins examines the arm. The palm has scar tissue
which might be an occupational hazard, and the tips of the
fingers are well worn. Fingerprints identify him as Petrov
Samsko, a chef at the five-star Debreff Restaurant.

The CSIs think the murder happened at the restaurant
because Samsko still had food under his fingernails.
Grissom finds chefs' jackets at Debreff with bloodspatter
on and a waitress uniform belonging to Stephanie with
blood on the back of her shirt. Owner Les Dutton asks if
they can wait till after the rush. As they wait impatiently,
Grissom notices a blackish V-shaped stain on one of the
booth walls. Dutton says the candles were probably put
too close to the wall, although Grissom thinks it's too big
for a candle. When they eventually start asking questions,
the kitchen staff aren't co-operative. Sous chef Ross Halpo
explains the blood on his jacket as being his own – he was

cut by Samsko because he used Samsko's knife. The chef's tradition there is 'maximum spillage' if you're cut – hence the blood on everyone else.

Nick and Catherine process the kitchen and find semen and cocaine. Grissom finds a blood clot by a drain, with sand around it. They take the chefs' knives for processing, and Catherine finds an odd red stain on one of them.

Grissom checks the owner's log, which includes a note about burns to a Danny Pasquale. He finds a gueridon, used for tableside cooking, which is not meant to be used because of the danger. Pasquale was injured when Samsko made a café diablo on a gueridon for him, but he never pressed charges. Pasquale is questioned and Brass and Grissom see a 'fight bite' on his hand, from a human.

The bacterial DNA from Samsko's mouth and Pasquale's wound match. However, he denies murder. The DNA from the earplug produces another suspect – Harold Haskins, a deliveryman for the meat packaging company, who is out on parole. He admits that he ground the body for Ross Halpo to pay back $3,000 he owed for cocaine. Halpo admits he's a dealer, but not a killer. Grissom finds some woollen fibres above the stove.

The red stain is nail polish. It matches the type used by one of the hostesses. The wool comes from an expensive suit, and it has Samsko's blood on it. The hostess says that it's not her knife so she wouldn't touch it.

Grissom finds some sand in the handle of Ross's knife. He tells Ross Halpo that he knows that he filleted Samsko and broke his knife handle while doing so. Catherine informs Dutton that she knows he was protecting his restaurant's reputation, so got Halpo to dispose of the body while he got rid of his bloody woollen suit. The hostess confesses that she killed boyfriend Samsko when she caught him making out with one of the female chefs.

Sara, Warrick and Detective Sulick investigate the apparent suicide of 23-year-old Linda Damon. Her wallet is empty. Preliminary indications are that she cut her wrist and bled out. She's on her bed, rather than in the bath as might be expected from a female suicide. Sara finds a straight-edged razor. Warrick notices that she's been moved about two feet and Hank, who's the EMT attending, says he didn't move her. There is a stained blouse in the closet and bloody footprints near the bed.

Linda's father John found the body and lets Warrick know that Linda's boyfriend Brody Jones was a gambler. Linda's injuries are consistent with a self-inflicted wound, although there are no hesitation cuts. Doc Robbins finds some minute pieces of safety glass in her hair.

New CSI Trace technician David Hodges tells Sara that the glass comes from a car windshield of a 2002 model. Linda's car windshield is intact but one of her neighbours' cars has recently had a replacement. She says that Linda was responsible, but there was no point giving her the bill – she wouldn't pay for that or anything else she'd destroyed in the complex. When Linda was depressed, she would throw furniture in the pool, and had accused the neighbour of talking about her.

Linda had been prescribed lithium – she was a rapid-cycler manic depressive. However, when she was up she didn't think she needed the lithium, so didn't take it and rapidly deteriorated again to a point where she did need it.

Brody Jones is tracked down, trying to fathom the patterns of the slot machines. He has blood on his shirt sleeve. He admits going to Linda's apartment, and borrowing some money from her wallet. He claims he then saw her with her wrists slit on the bed. He moved her and tried to revive her, but wasn't able to do anything. Warrick realises that Jones is also on lithium.

The tox screen on Linda shows no lithium in her system, but a large dose of valium. With that amount inside her, she couldn't have fought off an attacker with a razor. Jane Damon has a prescription for valium, but denies drugging her daughter. When Greg rings to say that the blouse stain comes from male tears, John Damon admits that he was responsible but he only intended to make it look like a suicide attempt. The only way to get psychological help for someone is if they hurt themselves, but when he heard

Jones at the door, he panicked, and it was too late to save Linda.

Personal Notes: Sara refers to Hank as 'babe' in front of Warrick and Detective Sulik. Nick has been to a conference outside Vegas.

Techniques: Grissom uses Lansberry's Ridge Builder to plump out the ridges temporarily on the hand's worn-away prints.

The Wit and Wisdom of Gil Grissom: 'Haven't these people ever heard of HIV?'

'Japanese call it singing sand. If you walk on certain beaches in Japan it'll make a musical sound.'

Classic Dialogue: Grissom: 'You know about meat grinders?' Catherine: 'Well, everything's pretty much plumbing. Male into female parts. Righty tighty, lefty loosey.'

Nick: 'Fresh off an aeroplane from a conference, and bam – I got seminal fluid.' Catherine: 'Lucky you.'

Greg: 'So, then I should just stop trying to impress you.' Grissom: 'That would impress me.'

Warrick: 'Reminds me of what my grandmother said a long time ago. I would never believe her.' Sara: 'What's that?' Warrick: 'Crazy people make even sane people act crazy.'

Fantastic Voyages: We see the small hesitation cuts made by potential suicides.

Pop Culture References: The Smiths' album *Meat is Murder*. Brass and Grissom both quote from Shakespeare's *Julius Caesar*.

Real-life Inspirations: Marg Helgenberger spent part of her time while she was at college working at a meat-packaging factory.

Overall: Definitely not an episode to watch while you're eating (not that many of them are!). The thematic counterpointing of the two plots and Daniel Hagen's performance as John Damon set this one apart from the other episodes.

57
Got Murder?

US Air Date: 16 January 2003 17.6/26
UK Air Date: 22 April 2003

Written by: Sarah Goldfinger
Directed by: Kenneth Fink
Guest Cast: Michael O'Keefe (Mr Easton),
Evan Rachel Wood (Nora Easton), Joey Slotnick (Marty Gibson),
Allison Smith (Nanci Linden), Terry Bozeman (Lewis),
Rebecca Boyd (Amy Ennis/Kelly Easton), Candace Edwards (Nurse),
Marc Lynn (Snake handler), Joel McKinnon Miller (Clyde Hinton),
David Starzyk (Fred Stearns), Colton James (Charlie Easton),
Joe Ochman (Man #2), Jules Sylvester (Jake)

Teaser One-liner: 'Quoth the raven, "only this ... and nothing more." '

The Cases: Birdwatchers see a raven carrying a human eye. Grissom and Catherine retrieve it from the nest – the iris is still blue, so the body has been dead for less than 48 hours. The nest also contains some foil, a leaf, a feather, some plastic and some ground limestone. All Robbins can tell Grissom from the eye is that the victim wasn't dehydrated or diabetic.

At a landfill site near where the bird might have found limestone, Catherine, Nick and Sara find a severed leg, a torso – and a head, missing an eye. The body has been mutilated by the bulldozers. Doc Robbins thinks that blunt force trauma might be the cause of death. The limb removal was after death. The corpse has an episiotomy scar, and she's had an implant – an artificial spinal disc which Robbins is able to identify as belonging to Amy Ennis of Austin, Texas. Sara and Nick go through the rubbish found near the corpse, including a frying pan, a negative home pregnancy test and a lot of frozen peas. They identify an area from the addresses on items.

Five of the rubbish bins in Storm Cloud Lane contain bloodstains, two of which are human, and one of which contained the body. Its owner, Daniel Easton, the divorced father of Charlie and Nora, denies any knowledge of the body or of an Amy Ennis.

Amy is the registered owner of a car found at the Tangiers hotel inside which Sara finds a black nightie in a suitcase. The prints in the car come back positive for a Kelly Easton registered at the same address as Daniel Easton. Easton says that his wife left him five years earlier, and he was suspected of her murder at the time. Sara finds a pair of lacy panties in the Easton's bedroom and Easton admits that Kelly came back a month earlier and they made love.

Catherine finds hairs in the bed, and Nick sees that the son, Charlie, has a notebook filled with words like 'pain' and 'hate'. Charlie isn't distressed at his mother's death and Nora says she thought she was dead anyway. She says her father couldn't have had a girlfriend. Catherine discovers a diamond tennis bracelet hidden in Nora's room. Sara checks the kitchen and finds a space where a frying pan should be while Nick comes across hairs sandwiched between some frozen peas in the freezer. They realise that Kelly had been frozen.

Easton is brought in for questioning because he has been preparing the paperwork to declare his wife legally dead, at which point he benefits from a life insurance policy. He denies killing her.

The hair in the father's bed is Nora's. She says that her father gave her the bracelet as a gift for looking after 'everything'. She says that her father loves her, and Catherine notes that she's lactating – she appears to be pregnant. Catherine accuses Easton of incest and murder, but he is shocked and says he bought the bracelet for his wife.

Examination reveals that Nora isn't pregnant. She's a virgin, and has a pseudo-pregnancy. The bracelet has her mother's DNA on it, and her shirt has both hers and her mother's blood on it. She denies the murder even though it's clear she was responsible; she'll plead insanity.

Fred Stearns, a car salesman, drops dead at work from an apparent heart attack. David Phillips starts to open him up on the autopsy table, and discovers he's still bleeding. The man is still alive.

Stearns has an organic poison in his blood. He has a gastric ulcer which may have been how the poison got into his system. His colleagues are surprised to learn that he's not dead. Marty Gibson is very pushy, Clyde Hinton is a practical joker. Warrick and Grissom take samples from the two salesmen, but leave when they learn that Stearns has died again. Warrick finds some reptilian skin on Marty Gibson's coat; the poison that killed Stearns was snake venom. The CSIs note that Gibson has put mice down on his business expenses, and he admits that he keeps snakes as a hobby.

Veterinarian Jessie Menken explains to Grissom that Gibson could have milked the snake for toxin and put it in Stearns' coffee. With a stomach ulcer, that would have killed him, after first sending him into total paralysis.

However, the venom doesn't match Gibson's snakes – at least the ones that he showed Grissom. The receptionist, Nanci, calls for help – he persuaded her to look after one for him but it has got out of control. Nanci tells Grissom that Marty had been living on hand-outs at work before Stearns' death. He's arrested for murder.

The Wit and Wisdom of Gil Grissom: 'Ravens, like eagles, have been known to travel thirty miles from roost to feeding ground.'

'Ravens are incredibly intelligent. They have a brain capacity comparable to dolphins.'

'A coincidence is a scientific anomaly.'

Classic Dialogue: Catherine: 'Heard you got to be a superhero today.' Robbins: 'I consider myself a superhero every day.'

Warrick: 'I hear David's resurrecting the dead now.' Grissom: 'Yeah, our little miracle worker.'

Marty: 'If you handle them correctly, snakes are harmless. I know what I'm doing.' Grissom: 'Yeah, that's what we're afraid of.'

Fantastic Voyages: We see the needle penetrating the salesman's heart and getting it going again. We see a spinal disc in operation. We follow David Phillips' explanation of how mucosa works in an ordinary stomach, and one with an ulcer. We see the path of the endocrine system in Nora's head illuminated.

The Usual Suspects: Evan Rachel Wood (Nora) played Chloe Waters on crime series *Profiler*. Michael O'Keefe (Daniel Easton) was Fred for three years on *Roseanne*. Joey Slotnick (Marty Gibson) played CIA Agent Steven Haladki on *Alias*. Allison Smith (Nanci) was Max London, star of the short-lived *Spy Game*, and Mallory O'Brien on *The West Wing*.

Pop Culture References: Grissom quotes Edgar Allan Poe.

Mistakes Really Can Be Fatal: The odds of finding the right landfill site and the body within the time they take is nigh on impossible. Add in all the clues that are around the body, and it's a bit surprising that Catherine didn't deduce what had happened instantly!

Why didn't Grissom and Warrick look at the commission board on the wall when they went in? It shows that Marty has considerably less sales than either Clyde or Fred, giving him an immediate motive.

Overall: Dreadful. Obvious clues are overlooked, and there's a very distasteful flashback to Daniel and his daughter Nora in bed which can't even be justified by having actually occurred. This season's episode to avoid.

58
Random Acts of Violence

US Air Date: 30 January 2003 16.6/24
UK Air Date: 29 April 2003

Written by: Danny Cannon & Naren Shankar
Directed by: Danny Cannon
Guest Cast: Keith David (Matt Phelps),
Dwayne L. Barnes (Gene Jaycobs), Melissa Marsala (Serena),
Maury Sterling (Mr Molyneaux), Kevin Chapman (Hugo Karlin),
David Packer (Todd Benton), Jim Rash (Tyrel Constantine),
Tom Virtue (Doctor), Simon Rhee (Garrett Kwan),
Barry Sigismondi (Police Officer)

Teaser One-liner: 'I want this case.'

The Cases: Matt Phelps' young daughter Aimee is the inadvertent victim of a drive-by shooting. It's in the area where Warrick grew up and Matt Phelps runs the recreation centre that Warrick used to belong to. A black teen, Jason Gilbert, was also shot. Phelps' house was broken into about a week earlier, and all his awards and medals were stolen.

Warrick processes the scene and finds silver paint transfer from a SUV on a mailbox that was knocked down. A contemporary of Warrick's, Gene Jaycobs, is arrested brandishing a weapon in a bar, boasting that he's already killed that night. Warrick swabs his hands for GSR.

The bullet that killed Aimee severed her spinal column and matches the gun that Jaycobs was carrying. Jaycobs claims he found the gun in an alleyway but Warrick doesn't believe him. He and Grissom find a lot of stolen electronic equipment in Jaycobs' house. His car has a dent in the right place, but there's no visible paint transfer from the mailbox.

Matt Phelps tells Warrick that there have been break-ins at the centre, and their minivan was stolen. He just wants five minutes alone with Jaycobs. When Warrick hears that Jaycobs has an alibi, Phelps accompanies him back to the Police Department. The DA doesn't want to file charges but Phelps can't understand why Jaycobs is being released.

Warrick finds Matt Phelps' missing trophies in Jaycobs' car but, after an argument with Grissom, he's taken off the case. Grissom goes to where Jaycobs says he found the gun and meets officers investigating a burglary nearby. At the scene, there's a railing bent back, as if hit by something thrown with force. Grissom finds a bullet with a dent in it, which he passes to Jacqui to process for a print.

Warrick gets Jaycobs' address and goes there to tell him that they're going to nail him for murder. The next day, Jaycobs is found badly beaten up. Brass finds out that the DA's office passed the address to Warrick, but Warrick denies beating Jaycobs up and Grissom gives him the job of finding out who did. There's an indentation in Jaycobs' injury that's easily identifiable, leading Warrick to Matt Phelps. Reluctantly he has his mentor arrested.

The centre's missing minivan is found, and Warrick finds bullet casings in the back. There's blue paint transfer from the mailbox, and a lollipop stick in the van. The print on the bullet matches Tyrel Constantine, a fifteen-year-old local boy, as does saliva from the stick. Phelps says that he threw Tyrel out of the centre for smoking weed, and Tyrel admits that he only wanted to scare Phelps. Aimee and Jason Gilbert were unexpected victims. Warrick realises that he handled the case badly and goes to watch as the recreation centre is closed.

Nick and Vega investigate the death of supervisor Garrett Kwan at Hypertrix, an internet service provider. He was found in the server farm, a bank of computers in the middle of the work area, which has restricted access. He's been dead between five and seven hours from apparent blunt force trauma and there were only three other people near. Nick talks to all three who say they were working hard and didn't see anything.

Kwan was killed with a roughly rectangular object, possibly made of black plastic. Nick finds an email with a picture of one of the employees, Serena, on Kwan's Palm Pilot, and Vega discovers that Kwan was suing her for sexual harassment. She claims that it was spurious.

Greg confirms the plastic is in common use. Archie Johnson finds a fantasy role-playing game on the hard drive in which the other workers decapitate Kwan. Anders Molyneaux says he put Kwan in the game because he was annoyed at him for nearly getting him fired – somehow Kwan knew that he wasn't always working. Kwan was running a program that checked everyone's computer usage. However, all three suspects were hard at work at the time of death. Nick examines the scene of the crime again, and looks in the air vent where he spots some possible transfer. Hugo Karlin, the maintenance man, admits that the hammer fell from his belt and killed Kwan. He then tried to cover it up.

Personal Notes: According to Gene Jaycobs, Warrick constantly had a book in his hand at school. Warrick used to go to Matt Phelps' recreation centre. Phelps proved to be a good moral influence on Warrick.

The Wit and Wisdom of Gil Grissom: 'The job, Warrick, is to process evidence. Objectively, and without prejudice.'

Classic Dialogue: Serena: 'You know, they confiscated all my murder weapons when I left Microsoft, so I don't know if you'll find anything.'

Brass: 'They're going to put Jaycobs in protective custody to avoid repercussions in the community. Where are we going to put Warrick?'

Nick: 'You know a lot about this stuff, don't you?' Archie: 'Mm-hmm.' Nick: 'You got to get a girlfriend.' Archie: 'You first.'

Greg: 'All work and no play make Greg a dull boy . . .' Grissom: 'All play and no work make Greg an unemployed boy.'

Warrick: 'I blew it.' Grissom: 'Yeah. But you're not the one who's paying for it.'

Fantastic Voyages: We see the bullet hitting the wall in Aimee's room and disintegrating. We go inside Garrett Kwan's head to see the damage from the wound.

The Usual Suspects: Keith David (Matt Phelps) played Frank in John Carpenter's *They Live* and is the voice of Spawn in the animated series.

Pop Culture References: Archie knows all about the different incarnations of *Star Trek*, and he's a *Farscape* fan.

Overall: A boys-only show that shines the spotlight on both Warrick and Nick, and provides a solid hour of drama. It's a little surprising that Warrick doesn't get a reprimand for obtaining Jaycobs' address illicitly, but maybe that happens offscreen!

59
One Hit Wonder

US Air Date: 6 February 2003 15.6/22
UK Air Date: 6 May 2003

Written by: Corey Miller
Directed by: Felix Enriquez Alcala
Guest Cast: Elizabeth Mitchell (Melissa Winters),
Devon Gummersall (Taylor Reed), Leslie Grossman (Wendy),
Joseph Mazzello (Justin Lamond), Jeff Kober (Roger Wilder),
Rick Worthy (Dr Stewart), Chad Morgan (Joanne Crook),
Joe Michael Burke, Frank Novak (Judge)

Teaser One-liner: 'Somebody was watching this girl.'
The Cases: A man tries to attack two women in their
apartments. He fails to get into Doreen Bainbridge's
bedroom because there's a treadmill in the way, but
succeeds next door, masturbating on top of Joanne Crook
and leaving semen in her hair. Grissom finds smudges on
the glass door and knows that the girls were being
watched. Catherine persuades Joanne to let her process the
scene. Warrick takes a cast of a shoe print outside the
apartments. Nick finds crusted semen outside the window.

The semen is in fact pre-ejaculate, so there is no sperm
in it. Grissom has checked for Peeping Toms in the area,
and there have been a number. The incidents are escala-
ting, and Catherine and Grissom know that the next stage
could be rape and murder. The semen from outside
another window has sperm in, but there's no trace in
CODIS. It does have a low sperm count, possibly caused
by excess masturbation.

The shoe is a size eight, and the print matches Justin
Lamond, a pool boy at the Tangiers Hotel. Brass and
Catherine find him in a shopping mall, spying on the girls
with a camera hidden in his shoe and a bag. Unfortunately
his shoe size is wrong for the rapist, although Brass arrests
him for his voyeuristic practices.

Warrick finds some yellow maintenance paint in the
footprint, which Catherine discusses with the Department
of Transport before learning that Grissom has identified
the sorts of apartment that their perpetrator prefers. They
realise that there are a great number of potential victims in
the area.

The attacker makes his next move within this area – and
rapes a woman. Grissom sends Catherine to the scene on

her own. The victim, Susie Spiegel, says that the attacker wore a condom. Wendy, a member of the public, grabs Taylor Reed, who is skulking in the bushes.

Catherine talks to Reed, who says he was looking for an apartment. His shoe size is about right, and Catherine persuades him that if he genuinely is not the rapist, he should file charges against Wendy. He does so, which means that Wendy can be processed and, reluctantly, she agrees.

Reed's DNA from Wendy matches that taken from a burglary five months earlier. The CSI team go out to investigate the burglary site – and find Reed there. He was able to take over the apartment from the previous tenant, who moved out because of the burglary. Suspicious of Reed's appearance, Catherine searches the apartment and discovers a bound woman. Reed is the rapist.

Sara visits her wheelchair-bound friend DA Melissa Winters, who announces that she'll be dead shortly. Melissa tells Sara about the burglary in which her husband was killed that left her with a bullet which has now started meandering towards her brain. The doctors need to clip the artery in her neck, but the operation is high risk. Doc Robbins confirms that the Traumatic Basilar Artery Aneurysm procedure is a 90 per cent risk. However, Melissa is one of the lucky 10 per cent and survives.

Sara asks the surgeon if she can have the bullet, and reopens the Winters case. The exit wounds in Mr Winters' back have an abrasion ring, which doesn't tally with Melissa's story. The bullet matches a gun used by Roger Wilder in a robbery six months ago. Wilder was sent to jail by Melissa, and she was shot only three weeks after he was released. However, he claims that he only went to her apartment to see her reaction when he walked in, found she was out, so trashed the place, and stole the gun.

Sara checks through the photos from the crime scene, and realises that there are discrepancies and that Melissa lied to her. She faces Melissa with the evidence knowing that she shot her husband, but he was able to get the gun and fire back at her. Wilder then came along later and stole the gun. Melissa confesses and says she wanted Sara to deal with the case after she had died on the operating table.

Personal Notes: Grissom's hearing problems continue, and he misunderstands Catherine. He sends her to deal with a case, rather than risk mishearing. Sara has an older brother.

Techniques: Bobby Dawson uses enzymatic detergent to clean up the bullet, then a sonar cleaner to get rid of the last traces of tissue.

The Wit and Wisdom of Gil Grissom: 'The best intentions are fraught with disappointment.'

Classic Dialogue: Nick: 'There are two CSIs you never want investigating your murder – the one on his first week, and the one on his last.'

Fantastic Voyages: We follow the bullet going through Melissa's skin and muscle, and then lodging; we also follow the surgeons as they try to remove it. We examine the wiring for Justin's hidden camera. We see the tissue growing around Melissa's bullet. We look closely at the shoe print outside the apartment.

The Usual Suspects: Elizabeth Mitchell (Melissa Winters) played Dr Kim Legaspi on *ER*. Devon Gummersall (Taylor Reed) was Sean deLuca on *Roswell*. Joseph Mazzello (Justin Lamond) appeared as little Tim in the first two *Jurassic Park* films. Chad Morgan (Joanne Crook) played Becky Clarke on *Taken*.

Pop Culture References: Brass sarcastically refers to Justin Lamond as a young Kubrick, and to another woman as Xena.

Notes: This episode is set in early February 2003 (6 September 2002 was five months earlier).

Overall: A good episode that links the police procedural work with the CSI's endeavours, showing the synergy between the two that is more close to life than is often shown on the series. Jorja Fox is also given some great opportunities as she realises that once again one of her idols has feet of clay.

60
Lady Heather's Box

US Air Date: 13 February 2002 (90 minutes) 16.7/25
UK Air Date: 13 May 2003 (80 minutes)

Teleplay by: Carol Mendelsohn & Andrew Lipsitz and Naren Shankar &
Eli Talbert
Story by: Anthony E. Zuiker & Ann Donahue and Josh Berman & Bob
Harris
Directed by: Richard J. Lewis
Guest Cast: Melinda Clarke (Lady Heather),
Michael Riley (Steven McCormick), Amy Pietz (Rebecca McCormick),
Elizabeth Berkley (Foam Dancer), Pauley Perrette (Candeece),
Samuel Ball (Kiner), Alimi Ballard (Sound Engineer), Benjamin Benítez,
Kata Dobó (Chloe Samms), David Fogg (Lord Create DJ),
Tomiko Fraser (Tall Party Girl), Rib Hillis (Croix Richards),
P.B. Hutton (Teacher), Sandra McCoy (Hot Chick), Rick Pasqualone

Teaser One-liner: 'It's amazing how the sight of blood can
clear a room.'
The Cases: The dead body of Trey Buchman is found at a
foam dance. He has a puncture wound, and his wallet is
full of money. The CSIs search his hotel room, and they
find handcuffs, a long dark hair and a champagne glass
with pussycat-pink lipstick.

Buchman had no intoxicants in him, and Doc Robbins
doesn't know what caused the puncture wound, although
it was blunt. Warrick and Grissom find a stiletto heel
among the items taken from the scene which tests positive
for blood. Grissom tests the shoe on all the women from
the VIP list until they find their person. The foam dancer
says that she didn't know what happened, just that she felt
something soft under her heel. She knew Buchman and
wouldn't have killed him. Grissom takes some of her hair.
Buchman also has some sort of bite on his shoulder. The
'bite' is in fact a mark left by an injector used to put insulin
into Buchman's system.

Catherine and Nick visit the scene of a homicide
involving a very smelly and long-dead body. She finds a
frequently used passport, cash, and designer clothing

belonging to Croix Richards. When Doc Robbins carries out an autopsy on him, he finds the end of a needle up Richards' nose.

Buchman had booked two hotel rooms – one at the Sphere which the CSIs have checked, and one at the Tangiers. Warrick and Grissom check it out and find Rebecca McCormick, a scantily clad lady, waiting there expectantly. When she realises who the CSIs are, she claims she's never done anything like this before.

Nick examines Richards' laptop and finds notes of women's names, hotels and times. He was a gigolo. Grissom realises that Buchman was, too, and both men have been injected. Grissom and Nick are working on the same case.

Further checks on the laptop lead Grissom and Brass back to Lady Heather's Domain (see **30**, 'Slaves of Las Vegas'). Lady Heather has now expanded onto the web and she admits that both Buchman and Richards worked as part of her voyeuristic business. The CSIs cross reference the two gigolos' clients and Rebecca McCormick's name turns up. Grissom and Catherine visit her and her husband, who says that he hired Croix Richards to dominate his wife. However, he doesn't know about her relationship with Buchman.

The hair from Buchman's room at the Sphere matches Rebecca McCormick's, at least visually. Lady Heather tells Grissom that McCormick came to her three years earlier in a state of confusion, and she enabled him to be dominant. She was concerned about him bringing Rebecca into it, because she didn't understand what she was after. Lady Heather also reveals she's diabetic, and uses a pressure syringe. Grissom gets a warrant to check it out.

Warrick and Brass interrogate Rebecca and tell her that they know she slept with Buchman. She also took out an identical amount of money to the cash found in Richards' room, and used to work for a pharmaceutical company selling synthetic insulin. Lady Heather's insulin is non-synthetic, which matches that injected into the victims, but she points out that anyone could have stolen it. Grissom checks her insulin bottles and gets Greg to process them immediately. But an extra problem presents itself – Rebecca McCormick is found by her husband, strangled. Grissom finds a piece of feather in Rebecca's neck, which reminds him of Chloe Samms, a submissive that he saw at Lady Heather's. Lady Heather says Chloe quit the day before.

Chloe is arrested, and DNA from the top of Lady Heather's injector matches hers. She says that she killed Buchman and Richards for Steven McCormick. McCormick says that he didn't ask her to, but Grissom explains that McCormick has never understood that the submissive is the one in charge of the relationship. She's the one who decides when or if to say stop.

Eddie arrives late for Lindsey's school play, and he and Catherine start arguing. This ruins the night for Lindsey, and she decides she wants to go home with her father.

As Catherine is processing the Richards crime scene, her phone rings a couple of times but the signal cuts out. When it rings again, it's Lindsey, frightened and alone. She says that there's water in the car and she can't get out.

Catherine follows Lindsey's rough directions. She finds her trapped in the car in the middle of a river and manages to rescue her. There's no sign of Eddie. Lindsey says a pink-haired woman had been driving, trying to get Eddie to hospital. The woman got out, then her father fell out and didn't come back. When the car is brought out of the water, Sara has to dissuade Catherine from touching the drugs that they find inside.

Sara and Vega try to question Lindsey but she constantly looks to Catherine for approval before she answers, worried she'll get her father into trouble. Catherine eventually leaves the room. Lindsey reveals that her father took her to a meeting and left her in the car alone. Eddie met up with someone he knew – possibly his girlfriend – and then, according to Lindsey, they ran to the car, with her father holding his stomach.

Eddie's body is found in a drainage tunnel by the water. Leah tells Sara that the drugs in Eddie's car are GHB with food colouring – either a date-rape drug or a plain party drink, depending on how it's used. Sara checks Eddie's car and finds a CD cover colour proof of the pink-haired woman – Candeece. She and Vega go to the recording studio named on it, where the owner tells them that Candeece's manager was Eddie Willows. He says that Eddie was trying to make Candeece into a star, but that she was very highly strung. The previous night they had been trying to lay down a track, but she got out of line, so the sound engineer went home.

Candeece claims she didn't see Eddie the previous night but Sara and Vega know she had her wrist treated after an air bag injury. She then admits she was there, and says Eddie had been shot, so they were going to the hospital. When they hit the water, she tried to get Eddie out but failed, so she left. She had no time for Lindsey. Catherine, who has been listening to the interrogation, enters the room and threatens Candeece. Sara drags Catherine out and sends her to look after Lindsey.

Archie goes through the tapes from Candeece's sessions at the studio, and isolates some gunfire, and then a car pulling away. Vega discovers that Candeece rang Eddie five times that night, but her final call was to a drug dealer named Kiner. Sara finds drugs at Kiner's house identical to the ones in Eddie's car, and he admits taking drugs out to the studio to Candeece. Eddie was there, a fight took place – about Candeece's drug use – and Candeece shot Eddie. However, Candeece says that Kiner shot Eddie. With no evidence to prove the case, all Sara can do is prosecute Candeece for child endangerment, and Kiner for possession for sale.

Personal Notes: Grissom's relationship with Lady Heather takes on further complexities when she deduces that he is having hearing problems. At the end of the episode, he's clearly contemplating taking the relationship further. Warrick has been to a foam party. Ellie Brass is now twenty.

Techniques: Doc Robbins processes the 'bite' by dipping the slide containing a cross section of the bite marks in a container of Haematoxylin, then he puts the slide in Acid Alcohol 1 per cent, then in a container of Eosin.

Sara uses a SensIR Technology machine to analyse the drugs she finds in Kiner's garage.

Classic Dialogue: Brass: 'Ever been to a foam party?' Grissom: 'What do you think?'

Lady Heather: 'Voyeurism in a Brave New World.' Grissom: 'What would Aldous Huxley say?' Lady Heather: 'Well, if his credit card were valid, he could say anything he wanted at $3.95 per minute.'

Robbins: 'Catherine, you can't say goodbye in an autopsy room.'

Lady Heather: 'I could help you, Mr Brass . . . with your inadequacy.' Brass: 'You know, I'd like that, Lady H. It's tough being me. I'd like to feel more secure in my role as a homicide detective.'

Grissom: 'I'd like to come in.' Lady Heather: 'Of course you would. Say the magic word.' Brass: 'Warrant?'

Fantastic Voyages: We travel as the weapon that was used on Trey Buchman goes inside his neck, and also inside the injector as it puts insulin into his system. We see a needle going into Croix Richards' nose and breaking off.

The Usual Suspects: Melinda Clarke returns as Lady Heather. Elizabeth Berkeley (the foam dancer) was the star of the movie *Showgirls*. Pauley Perrette (Candeece) played Alice on *Special Unit 2*. Alimi Ballard (the sound engineer) played Herbal Thought on the first season of *Dark Angel*.

Pop Culture References: Sara disdainfully calls Warrick Superfly. Lady Heather quotes from Yeats' 'A Prayer for my Daughter'.

Notes: This was *CSI*'s first ninety-minute episode, giving CBS its first Thursday night sweeps victory in a decade. Director Richard J. Lewis described Lady Heather as 'provocative, in so far that if any character transmogrified Grissom it would be Lady Heather. She was the fuse of the bomb that would light his personal life. And that was the main reason [for bringing her back].' This was deliberately designed to be 'a more emotionally based episode where characters explore new realms, instead of process science and the case itself.' CBS even put up a real Lady Heather's Domain for a few days which linked to the main site.

Overall: A 'sweeps' episode that focuses on Grissom and Catherine but ensures that everyone has something to do. The flirting between Grissom and Lady Heather adds a personal element to the case, and it's a shame to say goodbye to Eddie Willows. Of all the producers, it seems that Danny Cannon is the only one not credited!

61
Lucky Strike

US Air Date: 20 February 2003 17.0/25
UK Air Date: 20 May 2003

Written by: Eli Talbert & Anthony E. Zuiker
Directed by: Kenneth Fink
Guest Cast: Dwayne Adway (Tavian Tombs),
Tracy Lynn Middendorf (Bridget Willis), Leslie Silva (Nanny),
Mahershalalhashbaz Ali (Security Guard),
Cameron Daddo (Casino Representative), Sam Jaeger (Bellman),
Christina Christian (Kenisha James), Jimm Giannini (Joe),
Loren Lazerine (Alex James), Alexandra Victoria Lee (Josie)

Teaser One-liner: 'I don't much care where he was going. I want to know where he's been.'

The Cases: A car is chased through Los Angeles. The driver, Alex James, gets out when the police stop him, but then collapses with a wooden stake embedded in the top of his head. The corpse is filthy, and there are specks under his nails, and a .38 Special in the car. Doc Robbins says that the pressure from the stake kept James alive, but removing it would probably have killed him.

The specks are faeces, possibly from a bat. The wood is Douglas fir with some sparkly mineral in it. Grissom, Nick and Detective Lockwood go to James' business premises. They find an old slot machine, buckshot pellets, a melting furnace, some jewellery and a bathtub with dirty water in it. Lockwood also finds pieces of gold jewellery, and pawn tickets. There are maps on the wall, and Grissom discovers bloodspatter and a bullet hole in one of them. Nick finds the medium calibre bullet. But who has been shot?

The bullet matches the gun found in the car. The sparkles on the stake include arsenic and cyanide, used to extract gold. Checking the county records, Lockwood discovers that Alex James regularly sold the same mine over and over again, most recently to a Joe McPherson, who is currently missing. Nick and Grissom travel to the mine and find bats and gold. They also find a buckshot casing and deduce that James was salting the mine with gold, using the gun to fire it into the wall. Further inside the mine, the CSIs come across pieces of wood resembling the stake in James' head, and McPherson's body – he's been shot with a .38. From the evidence of fuse line and TNT that they find, Grissom believes that James was trying to hide the body but misjudged the explosion, and was hit by a piece of wood.

Catherine and Warrick are called to a kidnapping. A ransom note has been left demanding $5m for the return of Isaiah, the five-year-old son of basketball player Tavian Tombs. They meet the star, his girlfriend Kenisha, and his other two sons. Brass is talking to the nanny, who's Tavian's sister. She was taking Isaiah, and his brothers Jason and Tramelle to the carnival, and Isaiah disappeared from the roundabout. Tombs is determined to pay the ransom and the casino lends him the money.

Warrick processes the envelope the ransom demand came in. There's an odd smell which he captures with the Evidence Vacuum Sweeper, and he is then able to get some prints off it. The prints are useless, but the liquid extraction picked up menthol and nicotine.

The ransom drop is a bust – Tombs' security chief was hanging around and was probably spotted by the kidnappers. Isaiah's body is found shortly afterwards. Robbins finds foam around the mouth and extensive bruising. There are rope and dog hairs on Isaiah's clothes. He still has pill casings in his stomach, from an animal tranquilliser. Unfortunately, he died from them. Catherine, Warrick and Brass visit the dog kennels three blocks from where Isaiah was found. They find a child's sneaker, a piece of rope, and some tranquillisers. Isaiah was tied up, and then tranquillised.

The bellman at the hotel has been trying to cash a gold chip. He says he picked it up after an argument between Tombs and a woman, who was shouting that Tombs is a lousy father to Tramelle. The hotel manager identifies the woman as Bridget Willis. Bridget explains that she has two children, but Tombs is the father only of Tramelle, and he won't have anything to do with Tramelle's sister Josie. While Tramelle was with Tombs she took the little girl out, instead, to the Forum Shops where she bought her a bear as consolation.

Brass finds the dead body of local resident Jacob Price. Brass tells Tombs that he thinks he's responsible for Price's death as revenge for killing Isaiah. Tombs agrees he would have done it if he'd known, but he didn't.

At the kennels, Catherine finds some white stuffing which could have come from a stuffed bear at the Forum Shops. She checks similar stuffing and it matches. At Bridget's the CSIs find only Tramelle. His mother has taken Josie, leaving him for his father. Catherine believes that Bridget carried out the kidnapping to try to get money out of Tombs, since he was only paying her minimal child support. When Price killed Isaiah, she killed him, and then left Tramelle for his father as redemption.

Personal Notes: Warrick isn't ready to deal with another murdered child so soon after **58**, 'Random Acts of Violence'.

The Wit and Wisdom of Gil Grissom: 'Death: The cheapest show in Vegas.'

Classic Dialogue: Tavian Tombs: 'It's my note, my kid, my show.' Warrick: 'Look, I've seen you take out three guys on the glass and still finish. I'm not here to bang boards with you. I'm here to do my job.'

Nick: 'Who puts the bat gates in?' Grissom: 'Batman.'

Worst 'As You Know': Grissom to Lockwood: 'This guy's got a piece of wood sticking out of his head.' Er, yes, Lockwood found him and called Grissom!

Fantastic Voyages: We see the stake embedding in Alex James' brain, and the pills making their way down to Isaiah's stomach.

The Usual Suspects: Christina Christian (Kenisha) was one of the finalists in the first *American Idol* contest. Alexandra Victoria Lee (Josie) played Young Buffy at the end of the fifth season. Tracy Lynn Middendorf (Bridget Willis) was Carla Matheson in the second year of *24*. Leslie Silva (the nanny) was Sarah Forbes on the all-too short-lived series *Odyssey 5*.

Pop Culture References: *Nosferatu*.

Overall: Instead of working backwards from a solution, this time it seems as though the creators thought of the most compelling tag sequence they could, and then had to work out how to get out of it. The rest of the episode simply doesn't live up to the moment when James is found.

62
Crash and Burn

US Air Date: 13 March 2003 17.4/26
UK Air Date: 27 May 2003

Written by: Josh Berman
Directed by: Richard J. Lewis
Guest Cast: Jonathan Tucker (Peter Arnz), Jeremy Roberts (Mr Arnz),
Wallace Langham (David Hodges), Dahlia Salem (Elaine Alcott),
Christopher Gorham (Corey), Kevin Richardson (Fred Lychalk),
James Sutorius (Silmont Health Insurance Rep),
Kim Gillingham (Vanessa Arnz), Sandra Lee Gimpel (Diane Lambert),
Lagleder (Firefighter), Christopher Leps (Bartender)

Teaser One-liner: 'I think happy hour's over.'

The Cases: A car roars down a street and into the glass window of a restaurant where Sara's boyfriend Hank Peddigrew is dining. The old woman driving the car is still alive, but two people are killed and four are critically injured. Hank himself sustains a broken wrist. The manager gives Sara a seating plan. She and Catherine look at the car: it's an old Jaguar but there's a new GPS system in it. Sara visits the driver, Diane Lambert, in hospital, but she's still being treated. She meets Diane's grandson,

Corey, who says he can't understand why his grandmother was in Vegas. She won a Jaguar playing the slot machines, and he gave her the GPS because she kept getting lost.

Catherine and Warrick check the road and see a red-light camera and some fresh motor oil. They also find brake marks. Warrick learns from the red-light camera that Diane sped through the intersection at 52 mph. Her car is fine though. Diane Lambert dies and Robbins' autopsy reveals that her head impacted the steering wheel causing a severed middle meningeal artery. But there is nothing physiological to explain the crash.

Sara checks the GPS memory, and Diane was going exactly where she wanted to go. Greg reveals that Diane was high on cannabis. However, she wasn't legally impaired. She was taking cannabis to help slow down her glaucoma, but Robbins is insistent that her sight was adequate to drive. Warrick and Sara eliminate glare from the restaurant's windows as a contributory factor. Catherine duplicates the crash on the computers, and it shows that Diane accelerated into the building. Her blood shows high epinephrine levels and low acetylcholine – the same as kamikaze pilots.

Catherine checks out the seating chart and asks Sara who Elaine Alcott is – she was sitting with Hank. Sara recalls seeing them together at the hospital and says they're friends. Twelve of the thirty-six people in the restaurant worked for the same employer, local medical insurers Sillmont Healthcare, including three of the five people sitting in the window. Catherine and Sara wonder if someone in the restaurant might have been the target. Elaine Alcott doesn't recognise a photo of Diane, but Sara notices a photo of Elaine and Hank together. Elaine explains innocently that Hank is her boyfriend and he's about to take her to Tahiti.

Diane put her financial affairs in order shortly before she died. She also made numerous calls to one number – Sillmont Healthcare at 16 South Meadows Lane. The restaurant was at 16 North Meadows Lane. Catherine and Sara discover that Diane had cancer, which had been in remission, but had returned and needed immediate aggressive treatment. The insurance company were dragging their feet, and Diane Lambert was running out of time.

Diane didn't have an email address, which makes Sara wonder how technologically knowledgeable she was and whether she could use the GPS tracker on her own. Corey's fingerprints are all over the machine but he denies setting the destination, thereby being an accessory to murder. The CSIs believe that Diane committed suicide so Corey could benefit from a big insurance policy she had taken out to put him through college. Unfortunately, since it was suicide, the payment won't be made.

Grissom joins Nick and Lockwood at the site of a gas leak where the dead body of Vanessa Arnz has been reported. She died of gas poisoning, but her husband, who was in bed with her, is alive. He says that he woke up and felt dizzy, checked his wife, found she was dead, called 911 then passed out. Their teenage son Peter says he knows nothing about what happened.

Nick and Lockwood check the CO levels in the house, and they're too high. They find some activated charcoal in the chimney, which has a busted damper. Vanessa died of CO poisoning. She had high nicotine levels and had taken some sleeping pills. But Mr Arnz's CO level was much lower, even though he has the same high nicotine levels.

Grissom and Nick visit the Arnz's store and discover that Peter Arnz wants to be a scientist. Mr Arnz admits drugging his wife's ice cream to get her to stop nagging him. He packed up smoking three weeks earlier, and says he'd asked his son to fix the damper.

Grissom checks Peter Arnz's fish tank, and finds that there's no charcoal in the filter. Peter says he didn't fix the damper even though he said he had. Nick and Grissom explain to him that the CO levels should have been the same in both his parents but, because his father had stopped smoking, his was lower. Peter was planning to kill them both because they wouldn't let him go to Princeton University.

Personal Notes: Warrick has been called in by Internal Affairs (although we're not told why). Nick and tech Hodges don't get along at all. Sara discovers that Hank has another girlfriend, Elaine Alcott, and they split up very quietly. She and Catherine go for a beer.

Lockwood's father is a fireman who gave Lockwood's children fire detectors as Christmas presents.

Techniques: Nick uses a Nighthawk Carbon Monoxide Alarm to check the CO levels.

The Wit and Wisdom of Gil Grissom: 'Isaac Asimov – one of my favourite writers. "If knowledge can create problems, then it is not through ignorance that we will solve them." '

'You made a basic scientific mistake, Peter. You stopped observing the human element because you thought it was inferior.'

'Science isn't about the gratification, Peter. It's about the truth.'

Classic Dialogue: Grissom: 'So why is she dead and he's alive?' Nick (to deputy coroner Phillips): 'You know, Dave, when I was a CSI-1, I would've tried to answer that, but now I know "where" before "why".'

Grissom: 'I just got a page from James Watson.' Nick: 'And I got one from Francis Crick. What's going on, Greg?'

Fantastic Voyages: We see Vanessa's skin turn pink as she inhales the gas. We follow the effects of the impact to Diane Lambert's head after she hits the steering wheel.

The Usual Suspects: Christopher Gorham (Corey) played Neil Taggart on *Odyssey 5* and is the star of new series *Jake 2.0*. Jeremy Roberts (Mr Arnz) had already appeared on *CSI: Miami* as Sam Carter in **M15**, 'Dead Woman Walking'.

Notes: This episode is set on and after 5 March 2003 (the red-light camera read out).

Overall: The relationship with Hank didn't seem to be going anywhere, so it's good that that is taken out of the way. Jorja Fox gives a great performance as the distracted Sara.

63
Precious Metal

US Air Date: 3 April 2003 16.6/25
UK Air Date: 3 June 2003

Written by: Naren Shankar & Andrew Lipsitz
Directed by: Deran Sarafian
Guest Cast: Katherine La Nasa (Ginger), Matt Winston (Brian Kelso),
Garret Dillahunt (Luke), Matt DeCaro (Coin dealer),
Blake Adams (Willy Reddington), Sarah Lancaster (Mrs Mercer),
Chris Crotty (Bouncer), Wiley M. Pickett (Christian Cutler),
Pippi Boecher (Rider)

Teaser One-liner: 'We've got evidence. Signed, sealed and delivered.'

The Cases: Two quad-bikers find a chemical waste barrel with a body inside that has started to get adipocere. Opening the container carefully in the autopsy room, Robbins finds a ring among the liquified remains.

Robbins tells Catherine that the temporal bone was hit very hard – in the same way one would chop a log. The leg has been cut through by something fast and powerful. Sara tries to match the ring, while Nick processes the barrel. DNA identifies the victim as Christian Cutler. The ring comes from a mechanical engineering honour society. Nick identifies the warehouse from where the barrel came, but when they get there there's a robot rumble going on. They speak to the organiser, Ginger, who says that the last time she saw Cutler was six weeks earlier when his robot Smash-n-Burn devastated the opposition, destroying other robots including Hammer of God.

Nick and Sara dismantle and test the various robots, finding blood. They then check their cutting edges. Cutler's blood is found on three different robots, but none of them match the marks on the body. Nick and Brass visit Cutler's partner, Brian Kelso, who buys and sells parts, no matter what their condition. He says he wasn't worried about Cutler's disappearance, as he often went on the road to do pyrotechnic shows. Nick and Catherine visit the warehouse where Kelso works, which has loads of work stations for people to work on their machines. They find Smash-n-Burn's missing parts. It has a spinning weapon which could match the marks. Nick also finds a rust stain that matches the chemical waste barrel. While Nick finds blood on the floor, Catherine discovers a broken press-on nail under which are scrapings from Cutler's skin.

The warehouse belongs to Ginger. She says that Cutler tried it on with her the day before the big competition, and she scratched him but she denies killing Cutler with his machine.

Cutler isn't listed with the Mechanical Engineering Society but Kelso is. Kelso breaks down and admits that he was testing Smash-n-Burn out and it went mad, killing Cutler. He was scared so he didn't report it. He didn't want to lose his wife or daughter so he tried to hide things. Nick and Sara attempt to recreate the accident, but the remote won't work. The transmitter has been switched: Kelso wasn't controlling the robot when it killed Cutler. Catherine thinks that Kelso is covering for Ginger.

Nick and Sara return to the scene and investigate further. Hammer of God's owner, Luke, is missing a transmitter from his collection of the right frequency to have controlled Smash-n-Burn. The receiver in Cutler's robot has Luke's DNA on it. He admits that, in revenge for being beaten in the contest, he made Smash-n-Burn kill Cutler and then manipulated Kelso to hide the body.

Grissom and Warrick are investigating a case of a body that got mislaid and wasn't processed, so they can't go back to the crime scene. The deceased was found eleven days earlier in a pile of rubbish in an alley. There are scars on his lower legs, and he suffered a blunt force trauma to the head. Going through the deceased's effects, Grissom finds something yellow on the belt. Once he's identified, Grissom and Vega visit his wife Mrs Mercer. According to her, he had gone off to climb El Capitan, and she had visited her sister, but when she returned, his climbing gear was still in the house. Grissom and Warrick check the Mercers' house and find blood and a shoe print. There's also blood on the edge of an empty wooden box and on the base of a heavy figurine. Warrick tests the figurine with amido black, and finds Mrs Mercer's fingerprints on it. She says that she moved it. She also tells them that the empty box contained a coin collection.

Small-time thief Willy Reddington tries to use Mercer's credit card, and claims that Mercer said he could. He eventually admits that he took the wallet from the body. None of the evidence found can be linked to Reddington.

Greg discovers that the yellow substance on the belt is sulphur, used by coin collectors. Mercer's cellphone records show that he called Jones Collectibles, owned by a small-time fence. Grissom sends Greg in to check the place out and Greg realises that Jones is not on the level. Jones claims that he buys all his coins legitimately, and volunteers to help the CSIs when they call. In his car they find sulphur, and blood belonging to Mercer. He had called Jones to arrange for him to view the collection, but Jones went to steal them. Mercer caught him in the act, so he had to be killed.

Personal Notes: Grissom used to work in Minneapolis. Nick asks Sara for a date on behalf of a friend of his. Greg is a numismatist. As well as everything else. He also hints to Grissom that he might like to work out in the field, which he knows would mean a pay cut. Doc Robbins chops wood for relaxation.

Techniques: Nick uses Magnaflux Magnetic Particle Test Equipment. He pours some black powder to completely cover the object he's testing. When the machine is turned on, the black powder embeds itself into the etching. Warrick uses amido black to bring up the fingerprints.

Classic Dialogue: Catherine: 'Metal weapons, money, competition, testosterone.' Brass: 'We got a roomful of murder suspects.'

Ginger: 'Using the thing that he built to destroy the thing that the other guy built. It's a basic male drive.' Catherine: 'That kind of puts that whole weapons of mass destruction thing into perspective.'

Ginger: 'Listen, I let the geeks fantasise about me. And most of them are harmless, happy to stare and then go home and spank the monkey like good little college boys.'

Grissom: 'So, let's see, you surf, you scuba dive, you're into latex ... you like fashion models and Marilyn Manson. And you also have a coin collection.' Greg: 'Weird, huh?' Grissom: 'Well ... I raise cockroaches.'

Fantastic Voyages: We watch the fats of the body slowly turning to adipocere and becoming a soap mummy, which then liquifies.

The Usual Suspects: Matt Winston (Brian Kelso) plays the enigmatic crewman Daniels on *Enterprise*.

Pop Culture References: *Back to the Future*.

Overall: The start of a bad trend at the end of this season to give too much weight to the MacGuffin surrounding the plot. We see too much *Robot Wars* here, just as there's far too much bad comic material in **65**, 'Last Laugh'. It's good that someone has recognised that Greg has accumulated a great number of hobbies over the past three years.

64
A Night at the Movies

US Air Date: 10 April 2003 16.6/25
UK Air Date: 10 June 2003

Teleplay by: Danny Cannon & Anthony E. Zuiker
Story by: Carol Mendelsohn
Directed by: Matt Earl Beesley
Guest Cast: Charlie Hofheimer (Kevin McCallum),
Cyia Batten (Kelly Goodson), Megan Ward (Audrey Hilden),
Finn Carter (Mrs McCallum), Peter Dobson (Anthony Haines),
Kevin Christy (Witness), Todd Giebenhain (Usher), Knate Gwaltney (JJ),
Eric Marquette (Earl), Mathew Scollon (Zachary),
Erik Smith (Timmy McCallum)

Teaser One-liner: 'They were watching the movie.'
The Cases: A man irritates other patrons of the last art house left in Vegas when his cellphone keeps ringing. It's not his fault: he's dead. Gus Sugarman, a dentist, has a single puncture wound to the base of his skull. Robbins believes a small weapon was used. There are abrasions on the victim's neck from where a necklace or something

similar might have been ripped. Catherine drops her torch and when she tracks where it has rolled to, finds the murder weapon – a screwdriver. A witness tells them that a redheaded woman got up just before the gunfight in the movie.

Archie obtains Sugarman's phone records. He made a phone call to Audrey Hilden just before the movie, and then she rang him three times in a row after his death. Audrey claims she was meant to have accompanied him to the movie. She let her answerphone screen the call that Sugarman tried to make to her, and then rang him later three times because she wanted to apologise, expecting to get his voicemail. Grissom notes a schedule for the Wonderland art house cinema on her wall.

Brass discovers that Audrey filed a malpractice suit against Sugarman for molesting her under anaesthesia. He countersued, so she backed down. The blood on the screwdriver belongs to Sugarman, and Jacqui has found a palmprint from leather gloves.

The cinema usher says a redhead made a phone call from the payphone in the lobby halfway through the movie. She was wearing gloves, and she threw something in the rubbish before leaving. The cleaning crew are already starting to clean up, and one of them has retrieved the gloves for her own use. Grissom buys them from her.

The woman's phone call was to Audrey at 11.25. Audrey then rang Sugarman a minute later. Brass, Grissom and Catherine go to ask Audrey about the call but find her hanging in her living room. Grissom finds a chain on the floor. Checking her body, Grissom thinks she was strangled then hanged. There are carpet fibres in her heels. Grissom notices that the movie schedule is missing from Audrey's noticeboard, and finds it down the toilet.

The paper has something written above an advert for Hitchcock's Strangers on a Train, in which two strangers agree to kill the other one's hated person, but one of them reneges. There's also a note: Sphere E4-117. It's a parking space allotted to Anthony Haines, a sleazy show boss. He denies knowing Audrey, and says he's never been to the

Art House Movie Theatre. Grissom spots the same Wonderland schedule on a make-up area belonging to dancer Kelly Goodson. She says she likes old movies, but doesn't know *Strangers on a Train*. She wears a red wig but says she never gets an evening off.

Kelly had filed a sexual harassment suit against Haines. She and Audrey liked the same movies, they had the same problem and they used the same lawyers. Grissom has taken Kelly's special foot lotion and discovers there's transfer on the murder weapons. Grissom and Catherine tell Kelly that it *was* a remake of *Strangers on a Train*. Kelly killed Sugarman for Audrey, and Audrey called his cellphone to confirm that it was true. However, Audrey had no intention of killing Haines, so Kelly killed her. The evidence from her foot lotion on the murder weapons proves it.

Nick, Warrick and Sara join O'Riley at a warehouse which is riddled with bullet holes, with the body of 15-year-old Timmy McCallum lying in the middle. Nick processes the bullet holes, while Warrick collects beer bottles. Sara checks the tyre treadmarks outside, and finds footprints. She sees a long bamboo pole on a roof which she also brings in. Warrick finds some small pieces of glass mixed with black plastic. There's a small hole in the ceiling, and 109 bullet holes.

Timmy had been badly beaten, possibly with a baseball bat, and killed by a single gunshot to the chest. The angle is 25 degrees, which makes no sense, as the roof was higher – a 45-degree angle. Timmy also has scabbing abrasions on his elbows, back and kneecaps. The shoe prints show that five people walked in, but only four people ran out. Sara believes the bamboo is important.

Greg finds five different DNA donors on the beer bottles, two of whom are related: the victim and, probably, his brother. Warrick talks to Mrs McCallum and her only other son, Kevin. Kevin denies driving Timmy to the warehouse in the family minivan, but admits buying him some beer to take there. To explain his DNA he claims he had a sip before giving Timmy the twelve-pack.

Hodges in Trace finds spiral gouges on the bamboo pole, and indicates that the glass Warrick found came from a camera lens. The McCallums' van matches the tyre tracks. Inside the van is a beer carton and some blood. Kevin is interrogated and Nick spots a bloodstain on his elbow which comes from a bullet graze. When Kevin removes his shirt, he's as badly beaten as his brother was.

Sara has processed the trajectories of all 109 bullets – and they all come from one uniform area, the shape of the pole. Nick brings in the closed-circuit footage from the store, which shows Kevin, Timmy and three other boys buying the beer together.

The other kids are located. JJ and Earl are both as bruised as the McCallums. The final kid, Zachary, tells O'Riley that they were messing around with a gun they found, and a bullet shot his camera lens out. Kevin finally admits that the boys were all trying to outdo each other by thinking of extreme activities – they tried speedway surfing (riding on the front of a car as it speeds), standing in front of someone whacking golf balls at their naked bodies, and finally Bamboo Russian roulette. They put the bamboo pole down from the ceiling, and set the gun going down it. The trigger would catch at some point and fire the bullet. Unfortunately, Timmy was shot in the chest. Kevin didn't want to get into trouble so he didn't call an ambulance.

Personal Notes: Grissom and Doc Robbins are both old movie buffs. Grissom says he prefers silent movies.

The Wit and Wisdom of Gil Grissom: 'I'm with the crime lab. I'm a professional snoop.'

Classic Dialogue: Brass: 'Thursday night is noir night. The poor sap was slumped over like a sack of potatoes, oozing blood like a broken bottle of ketchup.'

Witness: 'If you ask me, anybody who leaves their phone on in a movie deserves to get stabbed in the head.' Brass: 'That's why nobody asked you.'

Warrick: 'Why don't you stand up and take off your shirt.' Kevin McCallum: 'Don't you guys need a warrant for that?' O'Riley: 'We get a warrant, and we're going to strip you down to nothing, then ask you to bend over. Choose.'

Fantastic Voyages: Once again, none.

The Usual Suspects: Megan Ward (Audrey Hilden) played Kelly Stevens on *Boomtown*. Cyia Batten (Kelly Goodson) was Tora Ziyal in fourth-season episodes of *Star Trek: Deep Space 9*. Finn Carter (Mrs McCallum) appeared with Marg Helgenberger on *China Beach*.

Pop Culture References: Film references include *Baraka*, *Koyaanisqatsi*, *The Dirty Dozen* and *The Guns of Navarone*. Nick calls himself Dennis Rodman because he's going to need the basketball player's reach to get to the bullet holes. Quentin Tarantino gets a brief mention.

Mistakes Really Can Be Fatal: The episode is set on the date it first aired: 10 April 2003, according to the cellphone records, but 2 April according to the liquor store camera footage.

Overall: It might be acknowledged, but did they really need to repeat the plot of *Strangers on a Train* right the way through? For a show that relies on twists in the evidence, it can sometimes be horribly predictable.

65
Last Laugh

US Air Date: 24 April 2003 16.2/24
UK Air Date: 17 June 2003

Teleplay by: Bob Harris & Anthony E. Zuiker
Story by: Bob Harris & Carol Mendelsohn
Directed by: Richard J. Lewis
Guest Cast: Bobcat Goldthwait (Michael Borland),
Jeffrey Ross (Dougie Max), Gilbert Gottfried (Comic),
Bryan Callen (Bartender), Alan Blumenfeld (Club Owner),
Jeff Perry (George Stark), Tom Gallop (Stark's Attorney),
Sandra Purpuro (Waitress), Maggie Wheeler (Female Comic),
Larry Thomas (Convenience Store Clerk), Molly Weber (Shelley Stark)

Teaser One-liner: 'Hey, you hear the one about the comedian who died onstage? Literally.'

The Cases: At the Comedy Hole club, comedian Michael Borland is dying on stage, the act he's warming up for, TV star Dougie Max, is rehearsing his act while a waitress is doing something for him in the alleyway outside. Alan, the club owner, reassures Max that he's still the headline act, before Max goes on stage – and literally dies, apparently from a heart attack. Alan tells Brass that any of the acts might have wanted to kill to get Max's spot on stage.

Grissom checks the water bottles beside the stage while Catherine finds some Spam and cocaine in the green room. She checks everyone's wallets, and finds cocaine on the edge of a waitress' credit card, the same girl who was with Max in the alley. Robbins finds cocaine in Max's blood. The waitress pleads guilty to possession, and says that she used to put some cocaine on Max's foreskin before the show so that he would go on stage frustrated, which gave him an edge.

However, the cocaine didn't kill Max. He died of naratriptamine poisoning – a new migraine medication. Grissom and Catherine find that the poison was in the Innoko water that Max was drinking on stage. Greg checks for other impurities in the bottle.

At the club Grissom and Catherine and see the manager use a red light to signal the end of an act's chance on stage. They talk to the bartender, ignoring Michael Borland, who is complaining about the quality of the coffee compared with his own home brew. The bartender says that Max's water bottles came from a private stash that no one but he and Max could get to, but he's instantly proved wrong by one of the comedians who is behind the bar. The CSIs take all the water for testing.

A kid drops dead at a convenience store the other side of Vegas after drinking from a bottle of Innoko water. Although the bartender is using naratriptamine for his migraines, it seems that the problem is more widespread. Innoko water is pulled off the shelves. The poison in both Max's and the kid's water is naratriptamine, and both have the same trace impurities. Catherine discovers that the drug is on the inside of the bottle cap. The CSIs need to take the caps off the 40,000 bottles of water that have been recalled but Grissom bypasses this and discovers that both tainted bottles came from the same batch lot – which is the one that was at the Comedy Store. Someone planted a tainted bottle in the store.

Naratriptamine comes in tablet form and would need to be ground up to be put into the solution. Greg finds traces of caffeine in the water. There is a coffee grinder in the green room at the club, which Grissom takes. He sees the last picture taken of Max, and notes that the red signal light is on, which is odd for the headline act. There's blood near the switch and the bartender admits that he pulled the switch to distract Max, but that was all.

The caffeine is from Kopi Luwak coffee, the most expensive coffee in the world. It's traced back to Michael Borland who admits killing both Max and the kid.

Brass spots George Stark, the widow of apparent accident victim Shelley Stark, living it up on the town, and asks Nick to reinvestigate the case. He explains that Stark was devastated by his wife's supposed accident, but he's now learned that Stark demanded an insurance payout on the day of her death.

Nick and Sara look through the photos from the accident scene. Doc Robbins did an abbreviated autopsy and found that she'd drowned in the bath, having hit her head on the back of the bath, pulling the towel rail down with her. They visit Stark, who has gutted and refurbished the bathroom so the CSIs go over to the model home, which is identical to the way things were. Sara tries to duplicate the accident, but she can't pull the towel rail from the wall. Nick can only manage it with a great deal of effort. It's clear that Stark was lying.

Doc Robbins is livid that his autopsy is being questioned, but eventually calms down and permits an exhumation of Shelley Stark. He and Nick discover bruising on her body that wasn't apparent at the original autopsy but was accentuated by the embalming process. There are also bruises, in a hand shape, on her face.

Stark is brought in, and Brass points out that when he was first questioned he said that his wife 'was' his life, rather than 'is', which is unusual that soon after death. He and Nick explain the new evidence to Stark and his lawyer, although the lawyer dismisses it as just theories. However, it's enough for the insurance company, who repossess Stark's fancy new car, and want the money back. Nick and Brass promise Stark that there will be further action.

The Wit and Wisdom of Gil Grissom: 'When was the last time a comedian died of natural causes?'

'Laughter is an involuntary motor response triggered by survival issues: Food, sex, body functions . . . death.'

Classic Dialogue: Catherine: 'What are you looking for?' Grissom: 'A punchline?'

Brass: 'I'm chasing something that Gil Grissom isn't interested in – a hunch.'

Catherine: 'I don't have to run any tests. You cannot absorb enough cocaine through your penis to OD.' Grissom: 'Cite your source.' Catherine: 'I don't have a source.' Grissom: 'That's why we did the tests.' Catherine: 'Whatever.'

David Phillips (looking at coffin): 'Doc, I'm not quite sure how to proceed. First exhumation.' Robbins: 'Well, it's very simple. You will open it up.' Nick: 'Now, if she grabs you, use your free hand and hold her down, OK?'

Borland: 'I didn't think you were going to get the joke.' Grissom: 'Oh, I got it. It just wasn't funny.'

The Usual Suspects: Bryan Callen (the bartender) was prisoner #97C638 Coushaine in *Oz*. Bobcat Goldthwait (Michael Borland) is a genuine stand-up comic. Maggie Wheeler (the female comic) plays Janice on *Friends*.

Pop Culture References: Brass talks about Grissom going 'Cousteau' on him, referring to famous French underwater explorer Jacques Cousteau. Robbins and Grissom play a game of *Jeopardy*.

Mistakes Really Can Be Fatal: According to Greg's naratriptamine readings, Dougie Max died on 23 April; the photo of him says it was 24 April.

Notes: Finding a piece of chocolate, Catherine wonders if it's another case of death by chocolate (see **46**, 'Revenge is Best Served Cold').

Overall: Some much needed scope is added with this episode. This season we've hardly seen Ecklie, nor have we seen the Sheriff or anyone else superior to Grissom, and it's good to be reminded that the Crime Lab is not a little entity functioning in a vacuum. There's too much padding in the club though.

66
Forever

US Air Date: 1 May 2003 14.6/22
UK Air Date: 24 June 2003

Written by: Sarah Goldfinger
Directed by: David Grossman
Guest Cast: Lee Garlington (Mrs Frommer),
Patrick Fabian (Rhone Confer), Elaine Hendrix (Harper Fitzgerald),
Susan Walters (Merrit), Jonathan Slavin (Jason Banks),
Michael Mantell (Dr Stevens), Olivia Friedman (Alyssa),
Lisa Wilhoit (Teen), Arielle Kebbel (Blonde teen),
Kate Houston (Girl #1), Michael Lawson (Toby Wellstone),
Keith MacKechnie (Co-Pilot), Cheryl McWilliams (Mrs Confer),
Jill Noel (Jill Frommer)

Teaser One-liner: 'First witness, first suspect.'

The Cases: A plane carrying a group of high rollers lands at Las Vegas – in its hold is a horse, High Folly, next to the body of a Lori Hutchins who was High Folly's chaperone on trips. She didn't use the emergency call button. Catherine talks to the steward, Jason Banks, who says he had visited her about three hours earlier and she was worried about the horse, but that was normal.

High Folly herself is in mandatory quarantine. In the stall Grissom finds some blood spots and a small pair of scissors with some hair on them as well as a tranquilliser dart and rifle. Catherine checks out the rest of the cargo hold, and uncovers some brown material, as well as another dart. Nick finds a shoeprint that Catherine identifies as a J.P. Tod's driving loafer. They then process the plane cabin, which shows the effects of the party. Apart from cigarette ends, and a used condom, they find bloody towels in the wastebin. The blood on the towels comes from Lori and someone else.

The horse's owner, Merritt, wants to visit her animal, but she's prevented from doing so because it's in quarantine. Grissom and Catherine meet Dr Stevens, High Folly's vet, who assists them with taking some samples from the horse, and explains that High Folly was prone to serious uterine infections. He adds that you wouldn't use a tranquilliser gun on a horse – the impact energy would produce an adrenaline response. There are some stitches from the most recent attempt to keep her bacteria-free by sealing her up and Catherine finds something between the horse's teeth which Stevens doesn't recognise.

Lori's corpse shows signs of trampling, but Robbins also finds evidence of torphine, a very powerful tranquilliser. She has a shoulder bruise with a pin prick the right size for the tranquilliser dart. Harper Fitzgerald, the plane's owner, is a match for the shoe print found in the hold, and she claims that she went to try to bribe Lori to leave Merritt and come and work for her.

There are three prints on the handrail leading down to the cargo bay: Harper Fitzgerald, Jason Banks and Rhone Confer, who used to be a concierge at the Orpheus. The brown shavings prove to be from a cigar, probably Cuban, the sort of thing you'd go to a concierge to find. Confer admits going down to the hold, but he kept his mouth shut about what he saw.

Catherine and Grissom hurry over to the quarantine area when they learn High Folly has died. Dr Stevens tried to save her but she was too infected. Grissom wonders whether Lori had used the suture scissors that he found in the hold to try to help High Folly during the flight but Stevens doesn't think she would have done. Jessie Menken performs a necropsy on the horse and finds a bag of uncut diamonds. Dr Stevens has left town very rapidly and in his office Grissom and Catherine find signs of diamond workings. There were more pouches within High Folly but Stevens took what he could get and ran. The diamonds are conflict diamonds and Catherine calculates that there are four more bags around.

The second DNA on the bloody towels belongs to Jason Banks who says that Lori gave them to him to dispose of. Trace finds elements of lentils and carrots in with the diamonds – the lentils are used to protect them – and Grissom deduces that Lori packed the diamonds, after feeding High Folly with carrots. Stevens is traced to the Cayman Islands, but they don't believe that he has the diamonds. When Catherine learns that Rhone's full name is Kinsey-Confer, she becomes suspicious and asks Brass to check out Kinsey Diamonds, where they find the diamonds. Lori changed her mind when she saw High Folly in pain and was going to remove the diamonds, but Confer wouldn't let her, put a dart in her shoulder and then let her be killed by High Folly's 1400 lbs coming down on her.

Sara and Warrick accompany Lockwood to the body of a teenage boy found in Death Valley dressed in formal wear. They find a substance that might be bird mess beside the body, and the boy's wallet identifies him as Toby Wellstone. He's got a transdermal patch of fetanyl on his hand, indicating a deliberate overdose. There are some wheeled tracks nearby but no other indication of how he got there.

No one claims Toby's body and Sara discovers that he was in seven foster homes in seven years. Doc Robbins says that he ate a large hamburger meal, then applied the fetanyl patch. He also took a cisapride pill, which stopped him from going into reflux, and therefore kept the toxins down. He had tried to kill himself at least twice previously.

Another body is found in Death Valley, just outside LVPD's jurisdiction. This girl is wearing a prom dress, which is too big for her. There's the same white substance as found near Toby, and she also has a transdermal patch. But how did she get half a mile away from Toby?

Sara notices the girl's dress is handmade. Her stomach contents are the same as Toby's and the toxic drug ratios are the same. Toby's prints are on the girl's patch and vice versa. She's identified as Jill Frommer, whose mother comes in to identify the body. She claims to know little to nothing about her daughter's life. Toby had been fostered by her and her husband, but he had to leave after her husband died of cancer. However, Jill and Toby hooked up again after Toby was abused at a foster home, and he returned to live with the Frommers. She knew the teenagers were involved romantically.

Warrick and Sara question Jill's school contemporaries and discover that she had few friends. The teenagers say the prom dress belongs to Alyssa Jamison, who works at a hospital as a volunteer. She confirms she gave Jill the dress, but didn't give her the drugs.

The white substance is baby spittle, from Toby and Jill's baby. A search of Death Valley fails to find him, but when Lockwood, Sara and Warrick visit Mrs Frommer again, they find the patches and the pills, Mr Frommer's medication during his chemotherapy. They also find the baby. They surmise that Mrs Frommer encouraged Toby and Jill to commit suicide, and she says that they were beyond saving. However, Jill changed her mind and tried to follow her mother, who was pushing the baby in its pushchair back to her car. Sara and Warrick know they have little chance of securing a murder conviction.

Personal Notes: Grissom read all the James Bond novels when he was a boy. Catherine's engagement ring came from Kinsey Diamonds so, naturally, since it was bought by Eddie, she might be suspicious that it was a little extra-legal.

The Wit and Wisdom of Gil Grissom: 'Did you know that the term 'carat' comes from the Mediterranean Carob Tree, whose seeds were used for centuries as a standard of measurement?' (Catherine didn't.)

Classic Dialogue: Catherine: 'I may shop the outlets . . . but I read *Vogue*.'

Sara: 'Deathbed . . . casket-ready. Laying in the Hell's Gate section of Death Valley.'

Mrs Frommer: 'I'm this baby's only chance.' Sara: 'Lady, you are out of chances.'

Nick: 'Ski instructor, massuese – geez! Is there anyone not on Harper's payroll?' Catherine: 'Well, you met her. Would you be her friend for free?'

Fantastic Voyages: We see Toby's stomach acids being calmed by the cisapride tablet. We travel inside High Folly to see her uterine wall attacking a strange object within the womb.

The Usual Suspects: Elaine Hendrix (Harper Fitzgerald) was Kristen Martin on *The Chronicle*.

Pop Culture References: *Mr Ed*; Ian Fleming; Shakespeare's *Richard III*.

Mistakes Really Can Be Fatal: Why didn't Jill's autopsy show she had had a baby?

Notes: The case is set on and around 30 April 2003.

Overall: An intriguing episode with some nicely handled red herrings – although Catherine's memory of her engagement ring does come as a bolt from the blue. The last stand-alone episode of the season doesn't disappoint.

67
Play with Fire

US Air Date: 8 May 2003 15.9/24
UK Air Date: 1 July 2003

Written by: Naren Shankar & Andrew Lipsitz
Directed by: Kenneth Fink
Guest Cast: Raymond Cruz (Miguel Durado),
Bob Gunton (Director Robert Carvallo), Max Martini (Jason Kent),
Luis Antonio Ramos (Jesus Cardenas), Rebecca McFarland (Attorney),
Olivia Rosewood (Alison Carpenter), Josh Jacobson (Boy),
Danielle Panabaker (Girl)

Teaser One-liner: 'The killer's still on her.'
The Cases: Two youngsters looking for a place to make love find the body of a woman in the announcers' box at

their high school football stadium. Alison Carpenter has been strangled. There are defensive wounds on her hands and blood on her leg where she hit the door. Grissom realises that the crime only occurred less than an hour earlier, and the CSIs speedily print the body, finding a partial print on the ankle.

Nick and Sara process Alison's rental car. There's a ripped-up pair of panties in the back, and evidence of sex in the backseat. Sara finds a pack of medication and a small chip of something ceramic. Robbins confirms that Alison was strangled by someone just using their right hand. There's vaginal clock indications of rough sex rather than rape. Alison had asked for a week off work some time before. Oddly, she has brought a tape recorder with her to her motel room.

Hodges analyses the items: the medication is methadone, and the 'ceramic' comes from a dental crown. Greg discovers that the semen inside Alison belonged to Jason Kent, a convicted murderer, nicknamed The Circle Killer. He has just been released from prison. Brass arrests him, and Grissom finds some skin still on his nail clippers from where he tried to clear the evidence. However, all the evidence is destroyed in an explosion in the DNA lab.

Kent's attorney doesn't want to co-operate, knowing that she'll be able to have a field day with any evidence following the explosion. Kent, however, passes over his false teeth, and Brass sees a chip in the crown.

Alison's microcassettes are recordings of her conversations with Jason Kent about his life. On the last tape, Kent sounds concerned and says that whatever's bugging him isn't about Jesus Cardenas, before asking her to switch the recorder off. Cardenas turns out to be another prisoner at the same correctional facility from which Kent was recently released. Alison visited both men, Kent thirteen times and, on the last two occasions, Cardenas as well. On the times she saw Cardenas, the surveillance tapes show that they had sex.

Sara and Nick interview Cardenas, who explains that Kent used Alison to pay back a debt.

The partial print from Alison's ankle matches Miguel Durado, a member of the same gang as Cardenas. Sara accompanies the raid arresting Durado, and is overzealous, getting him herself rather than letting the officers do it.

Durado has human bite marks on his head, from headbutting Kent. He says he was simply there to collect the money Kent owed. Grissom and Brass face Kent with their supposition that he killed Alison because she refused to have sex with Durado to pay off Kent's remaining debt, but all they have as evidence after the explosion in the lab is the fact that his handspan is the right width. They know that he is going to walk.

Catherine and Warrick aren't able to check a container of green liquid into the evidence vault, so they put it in the fumer for storage overnight. The next day, Greg is seriously injured in an explosion that devastates the Chemical/DNA lab. Sara is also caught by the blast. Grissom's superior, Director Robert Carvallo, demands answers and Grissom puts Catherine in charge of the investigation.

Catherine and Warrick ask Greg about what he can remember before the explosion. He recalls a smell of burning plastic, but that's all. Catherine discovers that the hotplate had been left on inside the fume hood. David Hodges was the last person known to use the hot plate, but he reacts indignantly to the idea that he was responsible.

When Catherine finds the remains of the green liquid container she placed under the hood, she realises that she is responsible. Catherine and Grissom tell the Director what happened. He doesn't accept Catherine's apology and suspends her for five days unpaid. She goes to tell Greg what happened.

Personal Notes: Grissom has been holding back Catherine's reports and getting her to rewrite at least one. He finally realises that it is the people who are important, rather than the lab. He calls Sara 'Honey' after the explosion. Sara eventually summons up the courage to ask Grissom to dinner, and when he says no, warns him that it might be too late by the time he makes his mind up.

After the explosion she becomes a little reckless. Lindsey has been fighting at school.

Techniques: The CSIs hastily improvise a cyanoacrylate fuming chamber over Alison's body.

The Wit and Wisdom of Gil Grissom: 'Well, if you can't kill the one you want, kill the one you're with.'

Classic Dialogue: Grissom: 'His nails, her DNA, traces of the booth, et cetera.' Greg: 'Killer, victim, location.' Grissom: 'Holy trinity, Greg.'

Nick:'I think for some freaks, killing's a turn-on, you know?'

Catherine (on being asked why she didn't follow procedure): 'Because there's 24 hours in the day and I'm pulling sixteen for the county, spending three pretending to sleep and the other five lying to my daughter that everything's going to be all right.'

Director Carvallo: 'It's not your job to protect your people. It's to protect the integrity of this lab.' Grissom: 'Without the people, there is no lab.'

Grissom: 'I don't know what to do about this.' Sara: 'I do. You know, by the time you figure it out, you really could be too late.'

Fantastic Voyages: We look inside the joint that Jason Kent was caught smoking.

The Usual Suspects: Max Martini (Jason Kent) played Agent Steve Goodrich on year 2 of *24*. Luis Antonio Ramos (Jesus Cardenas) was Miguel Dias on *Early Edition*. Raymond Cruz (Miguel Durado) appeared as Stephano alongside Gary Dourdan in *Alien Resurrection*.

Mistakes Really Can Be Fatal: Grissom has a flashback to something he didn't actually see – the tattoo on Cardenas' neck.

Notes: Director Carvallo refers back to the events of **47**, 'The Accused Is Entitled', and Grissom points out that Haviland was convicted.

Check out the visitor lists that Nick has sent – both Kent and Cardenas have received visits from a number of familiar names to *CSI* viewers, including Rick Culpepper, Brad Kendall, Melissa Marlowe and Jimmy Tadero!

Overall: The start of what is effectively a two-parter to finish the third year reminds the audience of the human factor involved in the Crime Lab. The strength of the relationships that have been forged between the characters, and also between the viewers and the characters, is demonstrated.

68
Inside the Box

US Air Date: 15 May 2003 15.4/24
UK Air Date: 8 July 2003

Written by: Carol Mendelsohn & Anthony E. Zuiker
Directed by: Danny Cannon
Guest Cast: Scott Wilson (Sam Braun),
Michael Shamus Wiles (Rob Rubio), David Selburg (Bank Manager),
Emilio Rivera (Robber), Christie Lynn Smith (Jimmy's Mother),
Jimmy 'Jax' Pinchak (Jimmy), Lawrence McNeall III (Bank Robber #2),
Scott DeFoe (SWAT Leader)

Teaser One-liner: 'There is no right time to kill a cop.'
The Case: Detective Lockwood is killed during a bank raid in which the robbers were after one specific safe deposit box from the vault. As the robbers escape, the police are kept from following by covering fire. Grissom notices that the shots have all come from outside. Warrick checks the security cameras, which were covered in a black substance. Sara and Grissom process the vault and find an electric blasting cap with leg wires feeding into the grommet, and the detonator. Nick checks the police radio car that was shot at when it arrived, searching for any part of the bullet.

The getaway car has been found; the driver has nearly been decapitated. Robbins gets the bullet out of Lockwood, and Nick finds a bullet in the police car. The black substance is camouflage cream – and there's an eyelash in it.

The getaway driver is identified as Larry Whiting, who was a valet at the Rampart Hotel, one of Sam Braun's concerns. With his criminal record, Whiting shouldn't have been able to get the job, so Grissom sends Catherine to ask Braun about it, despite her personal relationship with him. Sam Braun says his human resources people shouldn't have given Whiting the job, but Catherine doesn't believe he didn't know. She points out that one of the cocktail waitresses at the Whiskey Town was killed a year previously, and now Whiting has died – both Braun's employees. Braun isn't worried about adverse publicity, and Catherine warns him that she'll be following the case through. Warrick and Brass check Whiting's house and find two $5,000 stacks from the Rampart, presumably the pay off for the driving.

Bobby Dawson suggests that the shooter had military training and Nick traces the shots to a building across the street. Sara replaces all the boxes in the vault, and it's clear that Box 729 was the target. The box belonged to Benny Murdock – another of Braun's employees. Murdock died a couple of weeks earlier from a brain aneurysm. Catherine asks Braun about a falling out between him and Murdock but he avoids the question, and just says they made their peace. Grissom notices a framed photo of the opening of the Rampart with the usual ceremonial ribbon.

Catherine asks Greg if he knows what 'off the record' means, and sighs when he says he does. Grissom realises that there is a print available of one of the robbers when the CSI team start discussing how fortune cookies are made. It turns out to be Robert Rubio, who worked at the Rampart. Rubio's house is raided and they find box 729 inside a barbecue. Inside is some silk fabric, and a couple of dried drops of blood.

Three of the bank robbers meet Sam Braun out in the desert and, shortly afterwards, they're being processed by the CSI team. One of the robbers is female, and they find a scarf identical to the material found in the box and they were killed by the same gun that killed Lockwood. One of the blood spots from the box belongs to Vivian Verona, the dead cocktail waitress. Grissom looks at a photo of Verona in which she's wearing the scarf that was found at the crime scene; she wasn't wearing it when she was killed.

Grissom deduces that she was killed with a pair of scissors, which were wrapped in the scarf, and computer enhancement shows the letters R – p – r – t on it. Catherine goes to confront Sam Braun on her own because Grissom is heading for his surgery.

Rubio is arrested but won't give evidence against Braun. Braun tells Catherine that Benny Murdock killed Verona because she was cheating on him with Braun. Catherine doesn't believe him and tells him that she tested her own DNA against the unknown blood sample, and there were seven alleles in common. Braun killed Verona because he was jealous of the time she spent with Murdock. Murdock covered for him but had kept the evidence as an insurance policy.

Personal Notes: Grissom's hearing deteriorates increasingly during this episode. He eventually goes for a second opinion to Doc Robbins, who tells him to go for surgery immediately. At the end of the episode, he is being wheeled in for the operation after receiving a good luck hug from Catherine. Catherine has served her unpaid suspension (see **67**, 'Play with Fire'). She realises that Grissom is having hearing problems before he finally admits it to her. Greg is back at work (incredibly quickly) but still shaking from the effects of the explosion (see **67**, 'Play With Fire'). Detective Cyrus Lockwood was 34.

The Wit and Wisdom of Gil Grissom: 'Do you ever wonder how the fortune gets inside the cookie?'

Classic Dialogue: Catherine: 'How long have we known each other?' Grissom: 'In days, months, or years?' Catherine: 'I'm serious here.'

Brass: 'So, here's the deal. You give up your boss, you get to spend the rest of your life in a jail cell, not on death row.' Rubio: 'I'll take death row. I'll live longer.'

Catherine: 'I think that we're past playing games, Sam. I need the truth.' Sam Braun: 'You sure about that?'

Sam Braun: 'Do you really think I could murder someone?' Catherine: 'Science tells me that you did. So, yes, I do. It's just such a lousy way to find out that you're my father.'

Fantastic Voyages: We follow the electrical current going to the receiver on the explosives.

Mistakes Really Can Be Fatal: Catherine says that the cocktail waitress' death was 'last year' but Greg says it was nearly two years ago.

Overall: Season Three goes out with a bang, with an explosive action sequence at the start of the episode, followed by 'revelations' galore. That Sam Braun is Catherine's father isn't that much of a shock, and it can't really have shocked her either. It was a brave move to demonstrate Grissom's increasing deafness by tuning out the audio for sequences that he can't hear, but anyone coming in cold to this episode based on the heavy publicity that it received in the States might have wondered if *CSI* is always this inaudible!

CSI: MIAMI – Season One

Regular Cast:

David Caruso (Horatio Caine)
Emily Procter (Calleigh Duquesne)
Khandi Alexander (Alexx Woods)
Adam Rodriguez (Eric Delko)
Rory Cochrane (Tim Speedle)
Kim Delaney (Megan Donner 01–10)

Michael McGrady (CSI technician Peter 01, 11)
Alex Paez (Detective Martin Puig 02, 07)
Wanda de Jesus (Detective Adell Sevilla 03, 05, 07–13, 17)
Diane Mizota (CSI technician Jade Horowitz 06, 10)
Josh Stamberg(CSI Tech 06, 11)
Michael Whaley (Detective Bernstein 06, 11, 14, 15, 20–22)
Damien Perkins (CSI technician Damon Wyatt 10, 14)
Daniel Betances (Police officer 13, 16)
Salli Richardson Whitfield (CSI technician Laura 13, 14, 16, 18, 19)
Rex Linn (Detective Frank Tripp 16, 18, 20–23)
Holt McCallany (Detective John Hagen 17, 19, 23, 24)
Sofia Milos (Detective Yelina Salas 17–19, 21, 24)
Stephen Tobolowsky (Don, District Attorney 17, 23)
Brian Poth (CSI technician Tyler Jenson 19, 21)
Stephen Mendel (CSI technician Jon 21)
Troy Winbush (CSI technician Welch 21, 23)

M1
Golden Parachute

US Air Date: 23 September 2002 14.9/24
UK Air Date: 1 February 2003

Written by: Steven Maeda
Directed by: Joe Chappelle
Guest Cast: Sam Anderson (Scott Sommer),
Anne Betancourt (Mrs Colucci), Michael Canavan (Detective Delacroix),
Julie Dretzin (Christina Colucci), Biff Henderson (Man at Beach),
David Labiosa (Senor Esparza), Tim Sampson (Jim Tigerfish),
Elayn Taylor (Nurse), Bhetty Waldron,
Emil Lawrence (NTSB Technician), William Haze (Handsome Agent),
Bobby Robinson (Pilot Stunt Double)

Teaser One-liner: 'We don't need him. We've got the whole story right here.'

The Case: A private jet crashes in the Everglades. Horatio and Delko discover that Flight 906 from Miami to Washington, DC, crashed shortly after take-off with two pilots and six passengers on board. Delko spots one of the pilots but the man dies shortly after he reaches him.

Megan identifies the site as a Level Two biohazard and she and Horatio wonder whether a bomb might be responsible. However, it seems unlikely, since there is no gas washing or pitting, and no thinning of metal or thermal effect. The crime scene is going to degrade very quickly, as the river is moving at around four feet per hour.

Working from a mobile lab, Alexx indicates that the injuries to the dead passengers are consistent with catastrophic blunt force trauma. The pilot, however, has a small entry wound in the upper torso. Calleigh thinks this could come from either a .32 or a .38, and starts searching for the bullet.

Detective Delacroix questions Jim Tigerfish, who witnessed the crash, but he says he and his fishing partner didn't go near the site. Speedle is very dubious, and doesn't think that Tigerfish is simply a fisherman.

The fuel injector looks as though it has been worn down but given a new serial number so it could be sold as new.

Horatio also finds an empty briefcase with the initials CMC on it. A check of the belts on the recovered seats indicates that one of the passengers was not in their seat at the time of impact, and since they were so close to take-off, everyone should have been buckled in.

Scott Sommer, the registered owner of the plane and a local insurance boss, is discovered alive and is taken to hospital in a coma. There's no friction burn on his chest, which means he was standing up. The case is complicated when the CSIs are called to another body, which has been found five miles away. It's a woman in an expensive business suit who's clearly fallen from a great height. Since there was only one woman on board, the CSIs can identify her as Christina Maria Colucci, Sommer's senior accountant and the owner of the briefcase. There are no friction burns on her chest either, and none on her lower torso. Alexx's tox screen shows that she had been drinking heavily, and was taking Prozac. Horatio spots three small circular indentations on her hand. He visits her mother, who confirms that the briefcase belonged to her daughter, and that she used to take Prozac for depression when she was at college.

Sommer's company was in trouble and he and his senior staff had been summoned to appear before the Securities Exchange Commission to explain themselves.

Calleigh discovers that the bayonet locking pins holding the aircraft door shut are scored, which might indicate sabotage. She matches the striations to the tools used by Sommer's engineer, who explains that he had had to make the wrong-sized pin fit. Negligence is ruled out when Horatio realises that the plane had not reached a sufficient altitude for depressurisation to have happened. The door must have been opened from the inside.

Scott Sommer wakes, and becomes increasingly agitated by Horatio and Megan's questioning. He says that he was seated when the door opened, and doesn't know what happened. He then claims that he didn't want to hurt Christina's reputation, but she had been acting strangely and drinking heavily. She jumped from the plane before anyone could stop her. He doesn't know anything about a gunshot. With bad grace, he submits to DNA sampling and fingerprinting.

Megan processes a hair sample from Christina, which shows that three months earlier there was a huge spike of Dialudid, a painkiller, which probably indicates that she tried to commit suicide. Horatio thinks it's more likely to be murder, since he believes that Christina was going to blow the whistle to the SEC. The CSIs fume the door and find both Christina's and Sommer's prints on it. The only way that the prints make sense is if Sommer forced Christina out of the door. Before they can question him about it, Sommer checks himself out of hospital.

Delko has not been able to locate the plane's black box flight recorder, but Speedle thinks that the 'fishermen' might have a more lucrative catch than normal. He's right, and CSI technician Peter processes the information found inside. Four minutes into the flight, the pilots heard a noise from the cabin, saw that one of the exit lights had gone on, and then one of the engines lost power. Processing the tape further reveals a seventeen-second gap between the door opening, and Christina's final scream.

The pilot's injury turns out to be not from a bullet at all, but from one of the plane's rivets. Delko finds a red fibre on one of the engine's fan blades. Speedle checks Christina's apartment, which clearly shows that she intended to come home a day later. There are no indications of suicide.

Walking through the events, Horatio realises that the fire extinguisher is not where it should be – and its top could have caused the three circles they found on Christina. The accountant opened the door accidentally, and then tried to hang on to the door frame. Sommer battered at her with the fire extinguisher, and as she fell to Earth, her red shoe was sucked into the engine, causing it to blow. Sommer's prints are all over the fire extinguisher, but when the police go to arrest him, he has escaped justice by hanging himself. Christina had FedExed documents to the SEC before getting on the plane – Sommer was finished, despite murdering her.

Personal Notes: Megan Donner returns to CSI after taking six months off following the death of her husband. She used to be the boss of the unit, and has some difficulties with accepting that Horatio is the new boss. Eric Delko didn't know the circumstances of Megan's absence.

Techniques: Calleigh uses a colposcope, more often employed in covert surveillance, to examine the plane's door. She also uses mikrosil to make a cast of the pilot's breastbone to get the exact shape of the 'bullet'.

The Wit and Wisdom of Horatio Caine: 'Means, motive, all they needed was an opportunity.'

Classic Dialogue: Horatio: 'Do you think you can find it?' Calleigh: 'Does Elvis wear a white jump-suit?'

Megan: 'The problem with the obvious, Tim, is it can make you overlook the evidence.' Horatio: 'A woman was murdered on that plane.' Megan: 'That's a hunch talking. Where is the evidence?'

Delko: 'I guess I saved the wrong guy.' Horatio: 'No such thing, brother, not here.'

Fantastic Voyages: We see the 'bullet' wound in the pilot's torso.

The Usual Suspects: Kim Delaney (Megan Donner) played Detective Diane Russell on *NYPD Blue*. Emily Procter (Calleigh Duquesne) was Ainsley Hayes on *The West Wing*. Adam Rodriguez (Eric Delko) played Jesse Ramirez on *Roswell*. Khandi Alexander (Alexx Woods) was Jackie Robbins on *ER*. Rory Cochrane (Tim Speedle) appeared with Jeff Goldblum in *Fathers and Sons*. All bar Kim Delaney, of course, guest starred with David Caruso in **CSI 44**, 'Cross-Jurisdictions'.

Sam Anderson (Scott Sommer) played Holland Manners on *Angel*. Anne Betancourt (Mrs Colucci) was Principal Stevens on *Buffy*.

Real-life Inspirations: Two cases inspired this episode. Elisabeth Mathilde Otto jumped to her death from a corporate plane in December 2000. According to the *Miami Herald*, the episode was also based on the incident of a ValuJet crashing in 1996 in the Everglades.

Mistakes Really Can Be Fatal: Where do you begin? This episode was ripped apart on transmission for its failings. The chances of a shoe causing the jet engine to blow up are low – they've survived birds hitting them before now – and the odds of a rivet popping out during the brief descent, going through the windshield of the aircraft and getting the pilot are almost impossible. Black boxes can't simply be opened up by on the spot CSIs and processed.

Overall: You might be able to argue that the mistakes are OK and covered by the catch-all description of dramatic licence, but there's a borderline between that and implausibility and this episode crosses it at the same speed that the plane hit the Everglades. It's ironic that the original *CSI* produced an equally weak episode to lead out the season. Megan Donner's role seems to be almost as a very senior Greg Sanders, who'd still like to be boss – she certainly doesn't make that much impact here.

M2
Losing Face

US Air Date: 30 September 2002 13.2/22
UK Air Date: 8 February 2003

Written by: Gwendolyn Parker & Steven Maeda
Directed by: Joe Chappelle
Guest Cast: Seth Adkins (Conner), Lou Beatty Jr (Al Humphries),
Candy Ann Brown (Felicia), Magali Caicedo (Lauriana),
Mercedes Colon (Katrina Cabera), Jessica Ferrarone (Julisa),
Tony Noakes (Police Commander), Conor O'Farrell (Charlie Berenger),
Joe Renteria (Aurelio Moreno), Liz Alvarado (Lauriana),
Bill Jacobson (Bomb Tech)

Teaser One-liner: 'That's not the way you taught us, big man.'

The Case: The Bomb Squad is called in when Julisa Moreno finds her husband Aurelio inside a necklace bomb. Since Horatio used to be a member of the bomb squad, he goes down to the scene, and meets up with his former mentor, Al Humphries, one of the senior Miami-Dade specialists. Unfortunately Humphries is killed as he tries to defuse the bomb.

Despite his friendship with the victim, Horatio takes the case and tells Megan that the device contained a high explosive. The blast and fragment pattern indicate that the majority of the explosive was packed at the front. There are three types of bomb damage present: fragmentation from the container, the thermal effect from the liberation of gasses, and blast pressure from the shock front. Because of the negative vacuum caused during the explosion, most of the bomb's components have been sucked back into the room.

The CSIs find what's left of the ransom note and some plastic fragments. Horatio locates Humphries' wedding ring, which he later returns to the widow despite Megan's objections. Calleigh finds some white fabric caught in the window frame of the maid's room. It was the maid's regular day off, so the bomber clearly knew Moreno's routine. Despite the flash burn and bloodspatter on the note, the demand for $50,000 is clearly visible, a trifling sum for someone as obviously wealthy as Moreno.

Alexx carries out an autopsy on Moreno, and finds avulsive destruction of the face and frontal calvarium, as well as thermal damage of the epidermis. There was chloroform in his system, which is how the bomber could fit him with the explosive collar.

Horatio notices a pinhole in the casing of the explosive device, and Megan confirms that the bomb casing tests positive for TATP (triacetone triperoxid). The explosive was homemade and very sensitive. Speedle reports that whoever made the bomb knew what he was doing as there are numerous alternate paths within it. Horatio points out that they are still missing the action switch, and realises that the emergency personnel might have taken evidence away on the heels of their boots. Inside one is a small, partially melted, electronic photocell.

Calleigh identifies the white fabric as machine-made Flanders mesh pattern, size 10, 32-count Pella Linen, or expensive French lace. The vast majority of users of such fabric would be women. Delko checks the ransom note and finds that although the ink is quite standard, the paper is made of Bagasse pulp, sugar-cane fibre, which is imported primarily from Colombia by Aurelio Moreno. Delko has also discovered similar bombings taking place in Bogotá, Colombia.

Delko visits Miami Port Customs to check out the paper that is currently impounded and speaks with the agent-in-charge, Charlie Berenger, who tells him that Moreno is currently under investigation by the Counter-Smuggling Task Force. Berenger shares his file on Moreno with Delko – Moreno has another wife, Lauriana, in Bogota, who arrived in Miami a week earlier.

Horatio pieces together the bomb, and then he and Megan question the two Moreno wives separately. Both wear the same kinds of wedding rings and watches, and Julisa wears an expensive French lace blouse. They both submit to DNA swabs in the interests of ruling out cross-contamination. Megan observes them as they wait by the elevator to leave, but they seem oblivious to each other.

The DNA samples reveal that Julisa's hands are clean, but Lauriana has trace elements of TATP. Megan points out to Horatio that Lauriana wears nail polish and has dyed hair, the trace elements from which are the same as TATP. She is concerned that Horatio is getting obsessed with getting justice for Humphries and, as a result, making errors.

The CSIs are called over to a second necklace bomb victim, Maura Burgos, a Colombian antiques dealer. Horatio takes over the scene and instructs the bomb technician how to disarm the device, using the knowledge that he gained from piecing together the first bomb. When the seam is opened, the bomb is a dud, filled with sand. Horatio is concerned that there is another bomb nearby, but nothing seems out of place in the house.

However, Horatio spots a young boy on a BMX bicycle waiting at the nearby intersection, with a very large parcel in the bike's carrier. Taking an Electronic Counter Measures machine with him to block a radio detonation signal, Horatio questions the boy, who says he was told that he could have the bike if he waited at that corner for someone to meet him. Horatio gets him safely into the hands of Megan, who combs his hair for any trace evidence, finding a long, brown, adult hair. The bomb squad then disarm the power source, leaving Horatio with an unused device to examine.

Horatio deduces that the targets are the Bomb Squad – the decoy bomb lured the Squad into the area, and the boy's position was exactly right to cause the most damage to them. Horatio tries to determine the bomber's unique signature. The bomb is made from some counterfeit parts, and there are traces of chlordane – an insecticide used in coffee-growing countries – on it. Horatio believes that their bomber is a show off. The hair doesn't provide any DNA, but Megan discovers some adhesive on the end of it, and realises that it came from a wig, some of which use French lace in their manufacture.

All the clues lead back to the Customs Impound Warehouse, and Horatio immediately recognises Charlie Berenger's name. He is a former Bomb Squad member fired four years earlier. Horatio enters the warehouse, where he meets Berenger wearing another necklace bomb. Berenger is simply after revenge, and took advantage of the Colombian connection to throw the Squad off the scent. He challenges Horatio to disarm the bomb, which the CSI does in one swift movement, removing the toothpick that Berenger is chewing and placing it within the small hole he spotted on the first device. The bomb is immediately rendered powerless, and Berenger is arrested.

Personal Notes: Al Humphries was Horatio Caine's mentor when he worked in the Bomb Squad. He has a strong enough relationship with the family to be able to tell Al's children about their father's death, and he risks serious penalties by taking evidence from the crime scene and returning it to the widow. Horatio never encountered a female bomber when he was in the Squad. Megan's husband Sean was a cop who died when a suicide jumper pulled him along for the ride. Megan worked the case initially, but couldn't cope.

The Wit and Wisdom of Horatio Caine: 'For a bomb to do its job, it needs three components. It needs a power source, it needs an action switch and it needs an explosive load.'

'Bombers are ego-driven. They make bombs to gain control, get revenge, sow terror.'

Classic Dialogue: Megan: 'How can anyone go anywhere with you running roughshod over the evidence? Can't you see this isn't about you finding out what happened to Al?'

Worst 'As You Know': Megan tells Horatio about how her husband died and how she decided to process the case herself. Given that he must have been around, he must know all this.

Megan also tells the bomb technician what an electronic countermeasures device does. Presumably just in case she's forgotten in the relief at not being blown up!

Fantastic Voyages: We see Moreno's lungs bursting and the organs liquifying as a result of the bomb.

The Usual Suspects: Lou Beatty Jr (Al Humphries) played Rudy Richards on *Dynasty*. Jessica Ferrarone (Julisa) went on to play Angela Lupo on *NYPD Blue*.

Pop Culture References: David Letterman and his Top 10 lists at the start of his chat show. Maura Burgos sings Stevie Wonder songs to keep her spirits up.

Mistakes Really Can Be Fatal: How long has Horatio been a CSI rather than a member of Bomb Squad? He was obviously at Bomb Squad four years earlier when Charlie Berenger left, yet he was senior enough at CSI to take over when Megan took the leave of absence after her husband's death.

Are we meant to believe that because Al Humphries died that Bomb Squad is disorganised enough to just let Horatio come in and blithely organise a bomb disposal?

And why does Berenger put a bomb round his own neck? Is he meant to be so far gone that he'd rather that Horatio be blown up than survive himself?

Notes: The trailer for this episode shows Horatio Caine screaming loudly when Al is killed. The final version cuts away from him as he realises what's happened, and goes straight to the titles.

Overall: Establishing Horatio's credentials as a man of action compared to Grissom's coldly logical thinker is all very well, but there are too many plotholes in this for it to stand up to close scrutiny.

M3
Wet Foot/Dry Foot

US Air Date: 7 October 2002 12.1/19
UK Air Date: 15 February 2003

Written by: Eddie Guerra
Directed by: Tucker Gates
Guest Cast: Fernanda Andrade (Elena De Soto),
Ismael 'East' Carlo (Basilio), Don Creech (Captain Bob),
Alma Delfina (Estella De Soto), Steve DuMouchel (Captain),
Tony Perez (Mr De Soto), Christopher Perez (Pedro De Soto),
Wayne Lopez (Marin Diaz)

Teaser One-liner: 'You find human body parts in a shark. Is that murder?'
The Case: A right arm and part of the connected torso are found inside a ten-foot mako shark. There's a bullet hole with a small fragment in the front shoulder area, with gunshot residue around it. The boat captain who found it has an illegal GPS system, and tells Horatio and Detective Salinas the exact position of the find, fourteen miles southeast of Miami.

The arm and torso weigh 28 lbs, 7 oz. The body part has gynecomastia, which generally would mean that it was female, but males with alcoholism or endrogen deficiency could also fit the pattern. From the stippling and the GSR, Alexx tells Horatio that the shot was fired at close range. Since mako sharks eat only live prey, dermal ecchymosis around the teeth marks and haemorrhagic capillaries in the deltoid muscle confirm that the victim was still alive when attacked by the shark. Alexx removes another bullet from the body and Calleigh finds raised land markings on it, which means it probably came from a Colt .45.

Horatio and Delko recognise a tattoo on the forearm as a symbol of the Cuban resistance movement and surmise that the victim was probably trying to escape by sea from Cuba to start a new life in the USA.

A storm-damaged boat is found abandoned on the shore, and the CSIs process it. There are deeply embedded rear tyre tracks near the scene, and one of the tyres has pattern baldness. There's a bullet in the fibreglass transom and blood all over the vinyl seats, as well as an empty asthmatic inhaler, a rosary and some books in Spanish. On a corkboard there's a sodden handwritten note which Speedle photographs in the hope of deciphering it at the lab. The boat is missing its Hull Identification Number (HIN), making it impossible to trace.

The bullets from the body and the boat match, as does the blood. Although that is male, tissue on the bullet found on the boat is female. Speedle manages to clean up the HIN sufficiently to be able to work on it in the lab. Horatio and Delko discover that the boat has a hollow hull, capable of carrying up to 500 kg of material. They find cocaine on the interior walls. The HIN identifies the boat's owner, 'Captain Bob' Morton and Speedle checks the videotapes of the harbour for any sign of him.

A young woman's body is found, floating in a Russian-made lifebelt. She was shot near the femoral artery, and bled out within thirty minutes. A tourniquet was made from the lifebelt ropes and tied around her leg but clearly had no effect. She has no sunburn, so she wasn't drifting alive for long. She has a medallion round her neck showing the patron saint of Cuba; these are often sent as good luck charms by Cuban-American families to those about to make the perilous trip. The work on the medallion is intricate enough that Horatio can get Basilio, a contact of his within the Cuban-American community, to identify the senders as Joe and Estella De Soto. They recognise the medallion but refuse to say anything. The De Soto's nephew Pedro refuses to speak to them either, but when Megan tells Estella that she lost her husband recently, the woman breaks down and explains that the girl was her niece, Elena.

Alexx finds a synthetic-based material in the wound on Elena's leg, which doesn't match her clothing. It does, however, match the shirt the torso was wearing, and therefore might have been transferred from the bullet, if the shark victim was shot first. She also has a high level of an anti-asthmatic drug in her system. The epithelials on the tourniquet indicate that it was tied by one of Elena's family members, probably her brother. The bullet in her leg matches the bullet in the male torso and the boat. Speedle notes that a rental truck driver sat watching the boat slipway for over six hours without taking a break. The truck tyres are bald.

Horatio and Megan get a warrant to speak to Pedro De Soto. While Salinas keeps Pedro out of the way, they process the room, finding a Colt .45 hidden inside the vacuum cleaner bag, which Calleigh confirms is the gun they are searching for.

Speedle and Delko find the rental truck, and discover linear bloodstains with small crystalline reflections, indicating that the material wrapping the cocaine was exposed to blood on the boat.

Calleigh and Horatio surmise that when the storm rose, the captain had the option of getting rid of his cocaine or his human cargo to save the boat, and forced everyone into the water at gunpoint; the torso in the shark was one of the emigrés. The Colt belongs to Captain Bob. Pedro De Soto admits that he was able to get the Colt off Captain Bob before he and his sister ended up in the water. When they saw a Coastguard boat coming near, Pedro shot his sister, since if the Coastguard gave her medical assistance, she could claim asylum. Unfortunately, the boat turned around before seeing them and Elena bled to death.

Personal Notes: Horatio Caine is 45 years old. Megan goes – or at least used to go – shark fishing. She is still giving orders to Tim Speedle, although he questions her authority. Delko asks if he can stay at Calleigh's place (on the couch!), while Horatio is causing disturbance in the Cuban-American community. He made the dangerous trip across from Cuba inside his mother's belly.

Techniques: Horatio tests for cocaine with cobalt thiocyanate.

The Wit and Wisdom of Horatio Caine: 'Are you going to rebut everything I'm saying? Excellent!'
Classic Dialogue: Speedle: 'It's unclear if I'm working for him or I'm working for *you*.' Megan: 'You work for the victim.'

Megan: 'Families in Miami send them to their relatives as a good-luck piece for the journey.' Horatio: 'And that ninety miles of open ocean will take that luck away from you in two seconds.'
Fantastic Voyages: We see the bullet firing and entering a woman, the drill going through the fake hull, and a close-up of the bullet leaving the Colt and getting the striation pattern on it.
The Usual Suspects: Tony Perez (Mr De Soto) played Officer Mike Perez in *Hill Street Blues*.
Pop Culture References: Horatio quotes from Cuban freedom fighter Ramon Grau.
Overall: We've had the Everglades, we've seen the Colombians, so the Cubans are the logical next iconic image of Miami. This tries a little too hard but is an entertaining hour.

M4
Just One Kiss

US Air Date: 14 October 2002 12.7/20
UK Air Date: 22 February 2003

Written by: Laurie McCarthy & Matt Witten
Directed by: Scott Brazil
Guest Cast: Jamie Brown (Jane Renshaw),
David Denman (Tyler Hamilton), Joe Duer (Estevan),
Tom Everett (Ryan Cutler), Jeremy Garrett (Varnette),
Kevin Kilner (Drake Hamilton), Erik King (Detective Fenwick)

Teaser One-liner: 'The evidence, as always, will speak for itself.'
The Case: A man is found murdered on the beach; near him, dragged into the water and left for dead is a girl, severely beaten and raped. It looks as if the man was

running away from the scene when he was killed. His throat has been slashed by a jagged object, and Alexx's preliminary findings on the scene indicate that he also suffered multiple blunt force blows to the head. He died around midnight from exsanguination. There's a burn mark on his cheek, and the ash and a brown substance from around the burn are taken for examination. The CSIs find black hair and blood on the support beam of a nearby lifeguard stand, and long blonde hair on a crumpled blanket. Speedle sifts through the sand around the crime scene and finds a piece of sharp green glass. Delko finds the small nosepiece from a pair of glasses in the sand, which tests positive for blood.

Megan visits the female victim, Jane Renshaw. SART examination shows that she has had semi-violent sex recently, and has received a grade 3 concussion. She has no memory of the last twelve hours, and keeps asking about her boyfriend Paul Varnette. She doesn't want to have any sort of oral examination done, but Megan persuades her to agree to a DNA swab, and discovers that Jane wears braces. In the metal screw is a 3 mm strip of skin.

Alexx conducts an autopsy on the man, and finds a shard of glass inside the wound in his neck similar to the piece that Speedle found. From the lime peel under the fingernails and the dermatitis on his arms, Alexx deduces that the victim may have been a bartender. Since Jane said her boyfriend had a desk job, this clearly isn't Varnette.

The boyfriend claims that he hasn't seen Jane since 11 p.m. the previous evening. They had been at a party at the Hamiltons' house, and he got very drunk, passed out, and has just woken up in the guesthouse. He doesn't recognise a photo of the deceased. He gladly gives a DNA sample, but points out that he and Jane had rough sex the day before which might account for some of her bruising. Horatio is concerned by Varnette's relationship with the Hamiltons, and decides to keep a close eye on him.

Calleigh and Horatio visit the Hamiltons' beach house. The family are Miami 'royalty', and there's a very polite but obvious hostility between the paterfamilias, Drake

Hamilton, and Horatio. Drake admits that there was a party there the night before, but it was thrown by his nephew Tyler. He doesn't recognise the picture of the victim, and isn't prepared to let Horatio inspect the guesthouse without a warrant.

The victim is identified as Estevan Ordonez, a Guatemalan immigrant. The green glass carries Paul Varnette's fingerprints, and the sperm inside Jane match the timeframe Varnette gave for when they had sex. The burn on Ordonez's cheek comes from the same brand of tobacco and cigar that Paul Varnette smokes. However, the skin in Jane's braces isn't Varnette's – it's someone else's penile tissue.

The Hamiltons send their attorney to 'help' Varnette, but Horatio continues to pile the pressure on him. He notices that Varnette is wearing a very expensive watch, and the young man admits that he was given it as a gift by Tyler Hamilton in return for his permission to kiss Jane. Varnette claims that she agreed, and he then tried to make it up to her by opening a bottle of champagne and suggesting they take a quiet walk. She refused, so he stayed at the party and got drunk. Against the advice of the Hamiltons' lawyer, he hands over the watch.

There are three sets of DNA on it. One is Varnette's and of the other two, one matches the penile tissue, and the other is a from a close relative of that man. Faced with this, Drake Hamilton agrees to let Tyler be interviewed. Tyler says he and Jane had consensual sex on the beach, and he didn't see Ordonez at the scene. Drake Hamilton will still not allow anything to be inspected without a warrant.

Calleigh and Horatio discover a trail of blood on the public beach leading up to the Hamiltons' house. When they prove it belongs to Ordonez, they get a warrant, but by the time they get back to the beach, the guesthouse has been burnt down. However, the remains include pieces of burned fabric, a scorched zip and three Cuban cigars inside a humidor initialled T.A.H. The zip matches photos of Tyler taken at the party, and there are fragments of the murder weapon glass in it. The cigars match the ash on Ordonez's face, and one of them has sand on the end.

The CSIs think Tyler was infuriated when Jane chose to go off with the bartender rather than with him, and so he followed them to the beach, murdering Ordonez and raping Jane. However, he doesn't wear glasses, and the bloodspatter on the nosepiece ties it directly to the murder. Drake Hamilton, however, does wear glasses. Against his attorney's advice, he admits to Horatio that he heard a scream out on the beach and found Tyler in the middle of a sexual assault and attempted murder. He therefore finished the job, and told Tyler to burn his clothing, in a vain attempt to save his family from another scandal.

Paul Varnette tries to patch things up with Jane, but she won't have anything more to do with him.

Personal Notes: In July 1987, when Horatio was still only a CSI-1, he processed a car crash in which Drake Hamilton was involved, although Hamilton was able to produce an alibi and escape possible charges. This is the first time that Horatio has returned to the Hamiltons' house.

The Wit and Wisdom of Horatio Caine: 'If you buy into this, the Hamiltons will hang you out to dry in two seconds.'

'Did you know your entire genetic code is stored in a single cell?'

Classic Dialogue: Calleigh: 'Hamilton men, try as they might, cannot hide their zippers.'

Drake Hamilton: 'You said our entire genetic make up is in one cell. How do we escape that?' Horatio: 'Your family? You stop procreating.'

Fantastic Voyages: We go inside Estevan Ordonez's jugular to see the odd-shaped wound.

The Usual Suspects: Kevin Kilner (Drake Hamilton) was William Boone, the original lead character in *Earth: Final Conflict*. David Denman (Tyler Hamilton) has regularly appeared as Skip on *Angel*. Erik King (Detective Fenwick) played Prisoner #00D718 Moses Deyell on *Oz*. Jamie Brown (Jane Renshaw) is Connie Riesler on *The Shield*. Tom Everett (Attorney Ryan Cutler) was Jack Doherty on *Air Force One*, alongside *CSI*'s Paul Guilfoyle.

Real-life Inspirations: The main case is apparently based on a pair of Miami teenagers who were kidnapped off Ocean Beach in Miami in April 2002. The case in which Horatio failed to nail Hamilton, in 1987, is obviously inspired by the death of Mary Jo Kopechne at Chappaquidick, which put paid to Teddy Kennedy's presidential aspirations.

Overall: The Kennedy parallels are clear enough without Horatio's little story at the end of the episode. The first *CSI: Miami* episode to feel like it's not trying to compete with its older brother, and to tell a story on its own terms.

M5
Ashes to Ashes

US Air Date: 21 October 2002 12.4/20
UK Air Date: 1 March 2003

Written by: Mark Israel
Directed by: Bryan Spicer
Guest Cast: Lisa Arning (Lisa Valdez), Raja Fenske (Cameron),
Marina Gonzalez Palmier (Rebecca Montero),
Mark Sivertsen (Jeffrey Douglas), Al White (Father Carlos),
Bernard White, Ruth Zalduondo (Mrs Medina),
Johnny Michaels (Emilio Medina), Marcia Jeffries (Ms Clara Denize)

Teaser One-liner: 'Who would want to kill a priest?'
The Cases: Father Carlos doesn't appear for Sunday morning mass, and is found dead in a pool of blood in the church vestry. The last time he was seen by the housekeeper was 8.15 the previous evening. Megan and Speedle process the room, finding a partial print on the coffee table. Alexx establishes that the time of death was between 9 p.m. and midnight. Horatio notes a bullet in the wall with some blood around it. Fr Carlos has two bullet wounds, meaning there were three shots, but only two casings can be found. Speedle finds two separate shoeprints; the left sole is far more worn than the right. There are two glasses, one with alcohol, one without, but with lip balm on the rim. Alexx finds a condom in Fr Carlos' pocket.

Megan discovers blood in the holy water in the body of the church, and surmises that the killer blessed him- or herself. Alexx gets a .223 bullet from Fr Carlos' body; it's a homemade bullet cast from hot lead, fired from a hunting rifle, and matching the bullet from the wall. It's also the cause of *two* of Fr Carlos' injuries, passing through him and then re-entering in his leg. The lip balm is commonly worn by skateboarders, and Speedle wonders whether there might be a link between a young skate- boarder and the priest, possibly giving a motive.

Calleigh and Megan can't understand why Fr Carlos lay bleeding for about ten seconds by the wall before walking to his killer. Speedle identifies the shoeprints as coming from DVs, worn by skateboarders. They decide to question the altar boys. They get them all to gum a piece of glass, then show the soles of their feet. It leads them to Cameron Medina. Megan, Calleigh and Speedle search his home, and find the lip balm, a rifle, DNA evidence and shots of Cameron skateboarding. Megan uncovers evidence of domestic violence, and Cameron's mother says she doesn't know where her husband is. Megan then talks to Cameron separately, and tells him she knows from the lip balm that he was at Fr Carlos' home. He admits it, but says he was at the Ollie Oop skating park at the time Fr Carlos died. When Megan asks if Fr Carlos hurt him, Cameron just says that that's between him and God now. The photos Megan found were taken at the park at the time of the murder, clearing Cameron; however, the gunpowder found at the house matches the gun used to kill Fr Carlos.

The rifle that killed Fr Carlos isn't among those found at the Medinas' home. Calleigh wonders if Cameron's father killed Fr Carlos for molesting his son. Calleigh and Megan visit Medina's workplace, and discover he's not been seen since the end of the previous week. Inside his truck they find a bloody pipe wrench, dried blood on the steering wheel and an empty rifle rack.

The blood on the steering wheel is Fr Carlos', and the brains on the pipe wrench belong to Emilio Medina. They take sniffer dogs to the Medinas, and find Cameron's blood-soaked clothing buried in the dirt outside. A hair in the truck belongs to Mrs Medina; she claims she killed her husband, but Megan points out that the forensic evidence is clear that Cameron did it, protecting her. The two of them then dragged the body to the river. Megan believes that Cameron needed to speak to someone about the murder, so went to Fr Carlos. Fr Carlos wanted to go to the police, so Mrs Medina went back and killed him to prevent him, firing once to warn him, and then again.

Cameron is the crucifer at Fr Carlos' funeral before being taken away by Detective Sevilla.

A burned out SUV, stolen two weeks earlier in Georgia, is found with a woman's corpse inside. Delko finds an empty bottle of expensive cognac nearby, a handbag that has no ID in it, and a suitcase.

The woman has no broken bones, and there is soot in her lungs, so she was alive during the fire. Extracting the stomach contents, Alexx finds a four-carat diamond ring. The tox screen shows negative for alcohol, but she had a high amount of Demerol and folic acid in her system, so she was probably pregnant. Checking out the SUV, Horatio finds a cork with no glass attached to it, and Delko spots that the fuel line is intact. Horatio believes that the fire began in the rear seat, and travelled forward to the front; someone did not want the mother and child to be identified. Alexx takes some foetal recovery tissue to try to identify the father from his half of the DNA.

The woman's dress was covered in cognac, but the glass was covered with chemicals that would cause an exothermic reaction – a Molotov cocktail. There's also a name engraved on the diamonds in the ring, which leads them to the ring's purchaser, Jeffrey Douglas. He says he bought it for Lisa Marie Valdez around eleven weeks earlier. He last saw Lisa about three weeks after that. Horatio deduces that Lisa read more into the gift of the diamond ring than Douglas meant. Douglas agrees and admits that he broke off the relationship. Horatio breaks the news of Lisa's death, and Douglas is horrified by the corpse photo.

Horatio and Delko find a lump of charred rubber in the SUV, which, when it's cut into, smells of strawberries. Horatio sends Delko to Artie's Adult Playground to find out who bought a strawberry-scented rubber teddy. According to Artie, Douglas bought the rubber teddy only three days earlier. However, there's no physical evidence linking Douglas to the crime scene and, very reluctantly, Delko and Horatio agree that he will probably get away with murder.

Horatio tells Douglas that he believes him to be the father, and that Douglas killed Lisa and his daughter. Horatio has had Jerome create a computer reconstruction of the little girl as she would look aged two, and promises Douglas that he will haunt him on the girl's birthday every year.

Personal Notes: Megan's uncle is a Jesuit priest. Alexx is never happy to deal with recovering foetal tissue.

Techniques: Not exactly a forensic technique, but Horatio asks the composite artist to prepare a likeness of what Lisa and Douglas' child would have looked like.

The Wit and Wisdom of Horatio Caine: 'So, he's going to get away with it? That's what you're telling me – he's going to get away with it. He's going to crawl under that rock that he slithered out from, because he's killed the only person that knows the truth.'

'Know this, my friend: every year, on this child's birthday, I am going to haunt you. I am going to be all over you until I get what I need to put you in jail.'

Classic Dialogue: Delko: 'You paste the potassium chloride and the sugar to the label, then you pour sulphuric acid and gasoline into the bottle. And when the bottle breaks, you serve up a Molotov cocktail.'

Horatio: 'What do you get when you cross strawberries with rubber?' Delko: 'A guaranteed good time.'

Fantastic Voyages: We follow the bullet going into the priest's shoulder, and travel inside Lisa's lungs to see the smoke inhalation.

Mistakes Really Can Be Fatal: Horatio Caine threatens to harass a suspect in front of the suspect's lawyer – and nothing happens about it?

Notes: This episode is set on and after Sunday 27 October 2002. There are in-joke references to David Caruso's film *Cold Around The Heart* when Delko asks whether Horatio was a jewel thief in another life, and to his series *NYPD Blue* when he says that he caught them.

Overall: Managing to avoid the cliché of priestly sexual abuse of an altar boy, this episode serves up a few surprises, and Horatio's righteous anger at the end of the episode contrasts neatly with the 'it's not my place' attitude of Fr Carlos. Horatio's case against Douglas is weak, and you can't see Grissom going within ten yards of it!

M6
Broken

US Air Date: 28 October 2002 12.2/20
UK Air Date: 8 March 2003

Written by: Ildy Modrovich & Laurence Walsh
Directed by: Deran Sarafian
Guest Cast: Philip Bolden (Bryan Woods), Vic Chao (Asian Reporter),
Tanya Memme (Female Reporter), William O'Leary (Stuart Otis),
Angelo Perez (Latino Employee), Grace Phillips (Mrs Chrighton),
Austin Priester (Preppy Black Guy), Channon Roe (Brad Repkin),
Bob Rumnock (Store Manager), Kevin Sizemore (Uniform Cop),
Rachel Rogers, Tanya Memme (Female Reporter),
Suzette Craft (Black Reporter), Ambrosia Kelley (Jamie Woods)

Teaser One-liner: 'This place is a buffet for these creeps.'
The Case: Five-year-old Ruth Chrighton is murdered at a children's indoor fun park. As soon as her mother raises the alarm, the security gates are sealed, and the scene is locked down. Ruth was killed in a restroom; her hair has been cut, and she was dressed in a boy's T-shirt, which suggests that the killer was planning to take her away from the park rather than kill her there. Horatio finds some glitter on the floor, and tells Speedle to keep an eye out for anyone with it. The clothing put over Ruth is old, and there are latent blood patterns on it, probably from the

killer's previous victims. The bathroom lock is broken, but there's a cone indicating that the room is out of use.

Speedle and Delko process the parents and children within the park to see if there are any likely suspects. One man starts to make a fuss about being processed, but is forced to wait when Speedle finds glitter on his shirt.

Alexx finds facial oedema and petechial haemorrhaging, indicating a high level of venous pressure consistent with asphyxia. Ruth's lips are purple-blue, but turquoise on the inner lip rim and tongue. The body isn't bruised, but her underwear has been taken. There are no erythema or ruptured capillaries around her mouth, so it seems unlikely she was strangled or smothered. The blue tinge on Ruth's lips comes from blue candy floss, and there's a fingerprint in a candy floss mark on her neck which Megan prints.

Horatio retraces Ruth's last steps as seen on the centre's video cameras, and they realise that the killer knew the range of the cameras, since he was able to stay out of view the whole time. However, that means he walked in the dust, and they are able to get a muddy foot print.

Unable to get a match from AFIS for the fingerprint, Megan notices that it is odd: it looks as if it might be a cross-section of several different fingers. Only four people at the park refuse to give their prints, including the man who made a fuss. Calleigh covers her hand in ridge lifter, shakes the man's hand then contrives to get him to pick up a clipboard, getting the print.

Alexx discovers Ruth suffered broken ribs on her right side, which punctured her lungs, filling them with blood. Megan and Alexx wonder if Ruth died from positional asphyxia, but when the tox screen shows that Ruth had a barbiturate sedative and also an antihistamine in her system, they realise she went into anaphylactic shock. Whoever broke her ribs was trying to revive her, not kill her.

As the lab processes some half-eaten blue candy floss Calleigh has found, Horatio talks to the man who made a fuss, who has been identified as Brad Repkin, a sex offender on parole. He has two suitcases in his car, one of which is a little girl's, but he claims that he was only checking the place out to see if he could bring his daughter there. He is cleared of the murder charge when Calleigh finds him on camera masturbating at the time of the killing.

Megan and Speedle are bemused by the prints, and eventually realise that the killer has skinned his own fingers, cut up the fingerprints, and regrafted them onto different fingers. They cut up the new prints into their component constituents and create a new print.

The shoe prints include a pair of loafers which are worn by someone for whom they are too large. The service entrance isn't barred, but requires a pass code, only known to six employees and the manager. The glitter on Ruth's body comes from the facility's uniforms, and the manager admits that he leaves the code for the service entrance on his desk in plain view. They realise that the killer left that way, and check the footprints found near the entrance, revealing soil containing rare butterfly eggs only found in the Biscayne National Park.

AFIS has a match for the reconstituted print – Stewart Otis. There's a house registered to William and Margaret Otis near the park, and the CSIs raid it, finding scores of tapes of child pornography, a bloodstained playroom, and uniforms from various children's parks. Delko finds a collection of milk cartons with pictures of missing children on them, and Horatio realises it's a sick set of headstones for the unmarked graves in the back yard.

The CSIs exhume five bodies, one of whom is very recent. A blue substance is found on this victim's under-wear but it doesn't contain the barbiturates that the killer used to quieten Ruth. Speedle realises that the sugar crystals have not yet been heated, indicating that the paedophile makes the candy floss.

Stewart Otis is arrested, and claims that Ruth was flirting with him, then ruined everything by dying.

Personal Notes: Alexx has two young children.

The Wit and Wisdom of Horatio Caine: 'This animal provided us with a mountain of evidence and we will not sleep until we've been all the way through it, because beneath that mountain lies his grave.'

Classic Dialogue: Megan: 'If it was the alarms, we could have a fish in the net.' Horatio: 'Not a fish – a shark.'

Alexx: 'I want to talk to you guys about bad people . . .'

Fantastic Voyages: We see how the pressure of the rib breaking can puncture the lung, and how fingerprints might be changed by cuts or chemicals.

The Usual Suspects: Diane Mizota (CSI Trace tech Jade Horowitz) was Fook Mi in *Austin Powers in Goldmember*.

Pop Culture References: Not really pop culture as such, but Speedle refers to Megan's Law, by which paedophiles in the States have to register so local communities know they are there.

Real-life Inspirations: Sadly, too many real cases are similar to this.

Mistakes Really Can Be Fatal: At the end of a case in which he's arrested someone for loitering near children, bachelor Horatio goes and sits in a park watching children. As sad an indictment as that may be on our society, it's not the wisest of things he could have done!

Overall: As harrowing in its own way as CSI 18, 'Gentle, Gentle', full marks to the producers for not shying away from vocalising the reasons that paedophiles give for their offences. In his brief performance, William O'Leary is every bit as menacing as Steve Buscemi's child molester in *Con Air*.

M7
Breathless

US Air Date: 4 November 2002 12.1/19
UK Air Date: 15 March 2003

Written by: Steven Maeda & Gwendolyn Parker
Directed by: Charlie Correll
Guest Cast: Liza Del Mundo (Claire Heitmann),

Chris Payne Gilbert (Carson Cassidy), Richard Gross (Gardener),
Tom Jourden (Mark Tupper), Jamie Luner (Nikki Olson),
Bobby Nish (Brian Fan), Ion Overman (Sophia),
Lou Richards (Lawyer), Sarah Rafferty (Melissa),
Baron Rogers (Noel Peach), Michael Irby (Ignatio Paez),
Laura Leigh Hughes (Lisa Tupper), Brian Wade (Other Lap Dancer),
Kris Jeffrey (Adam Cassidy)

Teaser One-liner: 'I guess we can't rule out exposure.'

The Cases: A male lap dancer is found dead in Melissa Starr's rose garden the morning after a party. Noel Peach died somewhere between 5 and 7 a.m. but there's no obvious wound on his body. The CSIs notice that he has some white crystals on his lip, and a dried substance, possibly semen, on his genitals. Under his thigh there's a torn condom wrapper. On his chest are a number of different-coloured long hairs, while between the folds of the sheets that he's been tangled in, there are six dead mosquitoes. Since mosquitoes are attracted by circulating blood and the CO that comes from breathing, they must have bitten him while he was alive, and might have ingested any toxic substance in his system.

The previous night was a 'cupcake' party, a chance for women to celebrate their sexuality. Peach had been hired as harmless entertainment. Although sex is not necessarily the end result of these parties, the women questioned indicate that it wasn't unusual either.

Alexx's autopsy reveals that Peach's heart stopped, but the tox screen shows no common drug. The white crystals come from harmless pearl dust, and there's no sign that he had a reaction to them. The substance on the genitals is semen, from sexual activity shortly before he died, and there is a small vaginal contribution which eluded the condom. The mosquitoes are dried out, indicating that they died from something they ate. Horatio asks for DNA contributions from all six women at the party, but Claire Heitmann admits that she had sex with Peach around 2 a.m. without a condom.

Horatio spots a small oval mark on Peach's chest. Alexx finds an injection site on Peach's thigh, but nothing in his medical records indicates that he required injections. There's no sign of the most common poisons (strychnine, arsenic and cyanide), which leaves the CSIs chasing an unknown substance which has probably dissipated within Peach's body. They therefore return to Melissa's house to look for possible poisons.

Their search turns up torn underwear belonging to Nikki Olson, with one of Peach's pubic hairs inside. Her bra clasp matches the oval mark on his chest. Horatio also finds a spring-loaded injector pen, used to treat allergies. The prints on that also belong to Olson. She is brought in for questioning, and says that she is allergic to bee stings and carries the pen with epinephrine in, for emergencies. When Peach drank a 'pearl shooter', he feared a reaction because he was allergic to shellfish, so she injected him. She also admits that she paid Peach to put on her underwear.

When Speedle finds yellow chalk dust on the condom wrapper, teacher Sophia Ananova comes into the frame. Detective Sevila finds a strip of condoms in Sophia's handbag which matches the wrapper found under Peach's body, but Sophia strongly denies having sex with him. Horatio notes her very nervous movements, and she admits that she is using nicotine patches since she has recently quit smoking. Horatio runs a test using cockroaches and nicotine to work out its toxicity, and discovers that only three to four patches' worth of nicotine could kill an adult male. Trace analysis confirms that Peach died of nicotine poisoning.

The CSIs search Peach's body for any sign of adhesive from a patch, and also swab the body for nicotine sulphate. The latter proves that Peach absorbed the nicotine through his penis. However, Sophia's box of patches is virtually full and she wouldn't have had time to distil the nicotine from them. The other potential source of nicotine is the insecticide used by the gardener on the rose bushes. Peach's phone records indicate that he called Melissa Starr 107 times, and while Horatio questions her about her relationship with Peach, the CSIs process the rose bushes and find a used condom. Melissa claims that

Peach didn't understand her 'rules' for the relationship, and couldn't understand that she wanted to terminate it. Eventually, she put a lethal dose of the insecticide in a condom, and had sex with him one last time. The nicotine entered his system and killed him.

Megan and Delko are called by Detective Puig to a dead body on a yacht. Lisa and Mark Tupper say that an unknown man climbed onto their boat seven miles from shore and died on deck instantly. He has a single stab wound in his stomach. Although it looks as if he bled out, there is no blood on deck, although phenolphthalein shows that it has been cleaned up. Delko finds blood and hair on a marine torch in the main cabin. He accidentally sneezes on it but fails to mention that to Megan until much later.

None of the knives from the boat carries blood, although the hair on the torch is from the deceased. Lisa Tupper admits that she hit the intruder when she saw him bending over her husband.

That, however, was not the cause of death. The man died from liver injury. His organs are peculiar in size – the spleen is a fifth smaller than normal, while the lungs and heart are a fifth larger than normal. Inside the wound is a barrel sponge microorganism that is only found a minimum of fifty feet below the surface. Delko surmises that the man is a free diver, someone who goes deep-sea diving without the help of breathing apparatus. The water pressure alters the shape of the organs. The sport has an inherent danger of oxygen starvation, which can lead to delusional behaviour. On the morning the man died, there was a free-diving competition.

Megan, Speedle and Puig visit the marina where it was held, and meet Carson Cassidy, who identifies the picture of the victim as his missing brother Adam. The CSIs confiscate the knives and spear guns from the dive house, and find human tissue on one of the guns belonging to Ignacio Paez, a Cuban diver, who denies all knowledge of the incident. Megan notices that he has difficulty hearing her questions, and checks his ears, to find that his eardrum has been ruptured by the water pressure. He could not have dived to the depths at which Adam Cassidy's wound was caused.

The tissue from the gun doesn't belong to Adam Cassidy, which means it's not the murder weapon. Delko dives to the ocean floor at the site of the diving contest and recovers a blue tang dive knife with an inscription on it, '1998 Blue Water Meet – Champion', indicating it belonged to Carson Cassidy. There are flecks of blood concealed on the knife tang. During questioning, Megan asks Carson to remove his shirt, revealing a wound in his side. She deduces that the Cassidy brothers had a struggle underwater while both were suffering from hypoxia and acting irrationally. Adam fired at Carson, who responded by knifing him.

Personal Notes: This is the first case that Megan and Delko have worked together, confirming the theory that he joined CSI very shortly before **CSI 44**, 'Cross-Jurisdictions'.

The Wit and Wisdom of Horatio Caine: 'Our friend here wasn't the predator. He was the prey.'

'When people get stimulated, they get territorial. That's human nature, and that can be dangerous.'

'Nicotine is one of the most toxic of all poisons. More lethal than cyanide or cobra venom, believe it or not.'

Classic Dialogue: Alexx: 'Nicotine was introduced through the penile tissue. It gives a whole new meaning to the term "members only".'

Carson Cassidy: 'It's a trip down to primal instinct.' Megan: 'Killing your brother – it doesn't get more primal than that.'

Fantastic Voyages: We see the poison metabolising inside Peach's body, the drink going down his throat, and the effects of nicotine on him. We see Adam's organs contracting from the pressure, and the water breaching Paez's eardrum.

The Usual Suspects: Chris Payne Gilbert (Carson Cassidy) played Peter Berglund, the scuba-diving Scandinavian SEAL in **CSI 48**, 'Let The Seller Beware'. Richard Gross (the gardener) played Logger Dave on *Malcolm in the*

Middle. Jamie Luner (Nikki Olsen) was Rachel Burke on *Profiler*.

Real-life Inspirations: Possibly inadvertently, Sophia Ananova echoes Bill Clinton's denial concerning his relationship with Monica Lewinsky: 'I did not have sex with that man.'

Overall: Kim Delaney seems very uncomfortable leading the investigation – either Megan's very nervous or she's just not quite with it. We've already had one 'hen party go wrong' episode (see **CSI 13**, 'To Halve and To Hold') – not one of the original series' finest plotlines, and equally underwhelming here.

M8
Slaughterhouse

US Air Date: 11 November 2002 13.3/22
UK Air Date: 22 March 2003

Written by: Laurie McCarthy
Directed by: Dick Pearce
Guest Cast: Thomas Curtis (Timmy Caplin),
Calvin DeVault (Luke Caplin), Denice Duff (Mrs Caplin's Sister),
Tom Hughes (Paramedic), Ingrid Koopman (Stephanie Caplin),
David Moreland (O.R. Doctor), Albie Selznick (Jason Caplin),
Isabella Bleu Corton/Nicolette Alexis Corton (Erin)

Teaser One-liner: 'The blood had to come from somewhere, didn't it? My guess is that someone close to this child is either dead or dying.'

The Case: A two-year-old girl is found wandering down the road, her clothing covered in human blood. Since she is only sunburned down one side of her face, she was walking in a straight line, and Horatio retraces her steps by car, looking for the crime scene. The other CSIs process her clothing and find soil on the feet from an area being resodded, and four separate blood sources, three of them male.

The crime scene is located – the house of the Caplin family. Mother Stephanie is dead on the settee, part of her head blown off. Her sixteen-year-old son, Luke has been shot, and lies on the living room floor, with the body of his six-week-old baby brother Max underneath him. In a side bedroom, nine-year-old Tim is slumped over his computer, shot in the back. The father, Jason Caplin, is still alive and mutters something about his son before passing out and being taken to hospital. There's no sign of an intruder.

The time of the deaths is between 11 a.m. and 1 p.m. Everyone except Stephanie was shot in the back, and her injuries could have been self-inflicted. There is bloodspatter on the muzzle of the gun on the floor between her and her husband, which could have been used by either of them. Alexx discovers that Timmy had a fever when he died; he was shot from a distance, since the pellets have started to disperse.

Although Timmy's room is tidy, the parents' room is a dreadful mess. Jason Caplin's clothes are pressed and folded, but Stephanie's are thrown everywhere. The CSIs find long brown hairs on the bed sheets, which aren't Stephanie's, and there's a picture of an attractive brunette among the family photos. The baby's cot is in the bedroom with the parents, indicating that they probably didn't get much sleep, and there's also an unused bottle of antidepressants prescribed for Stephanie three weeks earlier.

The kitchen is also in a bad state. The microwave contains a baby's bottle, and the rubbish bin is full of fast food refuse. There's a lunch bag on the side with burgers and fries, one of which is partly eaten.

Her footprints show that the toddler, Erin, stood next to Luke as he bled out. The gunsafe in the garage is open, and there are two shotguns inside with room for more. Horatio notes a strong smell of ammonia. In the living room, he also notices that Stephanie seemed relaxed, with her socks off. The police discover that Jason Caplin received a call at work at 11.45 and left for home, obviously upset.

The autopsy reveals that Luke was shot in the shoulder and at the base of the skull. He exhibits visible signs of stress, with a gastric ulcer, ground teeth and bitten nails. The gun lies within Stephanie's reach, which is sufficient to have pulled the trigger on herself. She died instantly, as did Timmy.

The brown hairs belong to the brunette from the photo, Stephanie's sister Audrey. She says that Jason did nothing to help, and she was trying to help her sister. Her hairs got in the bed when she cuddled her sister.

Calleigh finds Timmy's prints on the baby's bottle, and Stephanie's on the gunsafe. Delko and Speedle find a bloody blanket in the kennel outside the house which was used for Erin. Calleigh and Horatio reconstruct Stephanie's 'suicide' and realise that she was lying down at the time of death, making suicide unlikely. The blanket has only Stephanie's blood on it, and has no soil on it, meaning that Erin was carried across there when only Stephanie had been shot. Only Luke and Jason have soil on their shoes. Speedle finds transfer blood from Stephanie on Luke's trousers in the shape of Erin's shoes – he took his sister outside after their mother's death. The blood on the baby comes from Luke, Stephanie and Jason, but his father's blood is gravitational spatter, indicating that he was standing over the baby while he was bleeding.

Jason Caplin recovers consciousness and tells Detective Sevilla that he came home because his wife was at the end of her tether, hinting that she might have been threatening the children's lives. He says he got in, saw his son covered in blood then felt a hot pain in his back. He is released from hospital and reunited with Erin. However, the CSIs believe that he killed Stephanie and Timmy, but was surprised by Luke, who hid Erin in the kennel, then came back for Max. He took the shotgun from his father and shot him, then picked up the baby. However, Jason got the gun back and killed them both. When confronted, Caplin claims that it all happened in a moment of insanity.

The CSIs establish that he used ammonia to clean his prints off the gunsafe. He then called his wife and, they presume, asked her to check the safe, thereby putting her prints on it. Any indication of premeditation will destroy his defence, which is Post Partum Psychosis by Proxy.

Personal Notes: Delko reveals his full surname to Speedle as Delektorsky; he has three older sisters.

The Wit and Wisdom of Horatio Caine: 'Your average adult has been clocked at two-and-a-half to three miles per hour, but to my knowledge, no toddler has ever been road-tested.'

Classic Dialogue: Audrey: 'All I wanted was my sister's happiness.' Sevilla: 'Well, that goal can get you into trouble.'

Fantastic Voyages: We see the bloodspatter hitting the muzzle, and the pellets firing into Timmy's back. We also see Luke's gastric ulcer at work, and the grinding of his teeth.

The Usual Suspects: Albie Selznick (Jason Caplin) played Hugh Young, the attorney boyfriend in **CSI 20**, 'Justice Is Served'.

Mistakes Really Can Be Fatal: The shots of the baby lying under Luke's body are, all too obviously, of a doll.

Overall: Again, *CSI: Miami* takes a *CSI* situation (see **06**, 'Blood Drops') and gives it a fresh spin. Some gruesome shots (the family members lined up for autopsy) match a depressing but well-acted script. Megan Donner has so little to do that Kim Delaney probably didn't work more than one day on the episode!

M9
Kill Zone

US Air Date: 18 November 2002 11.4/18
UK Air Date: 29 March 2003

Written by: Lois Johnson & Mark Israel
Directed by: Daniel Attias
Guest Cast: Nancy Duerr (Reporter #1), Shawn Elliott (Ray Santoya),
Eddie Fernandez (Jason Groves), Markus Flanagan (Sniper Expert),
Claudette James (Mary Franklin), David Renaud (Lou Blake),
Rafael Sardina (Gustavo Santoya), Kaye Wade (Dorothy Lawrence),
Nelson Perez (Christopher Harwood), Kathleen Corso (Reporter #2)

Teaser One-liner: 'An alpaca herdsman in Peru knows more about our case than we do.'

The Case: Three members of the public are killed, each with a single gunshot to the head, during the morning rush hour. Each receives a wound in the 'kill zone' between the eyes. Despite the scores of people around, no one saw a shooter, and only one shot was heard.

Calleigh finds the bullet from one of the victims, Mary Franklin, which has shattered into three pieces but seems to be a .223. The autopsy on all three victims shows that the bullets entered them from above. The shots could not have been taken at ground level. The bullets themselves have no striations: they are sabots encased in plastic, which prevents them from being matched to a specific weapon.

At the same time as the sniper-shooting, an elderly tourist on a tour bus at the intersection was shot through the head. However, that bullet was a 9 mm, and entered Dorothy Lawrence from beneath.

Horatio and Calleigh recreate the crime scene using dummies and laser tips, which show where the bullets came from. The result points to the Inter Continental Hotel, 650 yards away. The suspect must be a professional marksman, trained by either the police force or the military, and probably by the best marksmen, the Marine Corps. The CSIs go to the rooftop, where they find the sniper's nest. He has taped the stairwell door shut, and then taken up position on top of the ventilator shaft to get the best view. They discover some burlap ribbons which come from a homemade camouflage suit, sand and urine.

The 9 mm bullet has traces of government-issued blue paint on it. Speedle creates a 3D animated model of the scene and, turning 180 degrees, reveals that behind the tour bus was an ATM. Speedle is already working through the videotapes from the ATM camera along with all the other surveillance cameras around the crime scene.

Horatio and Calleigh discover that the residue on the rooftop door came from electrical tape, and there are very small plant needles within the burlap, which come from Japanese Black Pine, used to create bonsai trees. To learn more about snipers, they visit an old boyfriend of Calleigh who runs a firing range.

Megan and Sevilla visit Ray Santoya, who withdrew money from the ATM at the time of the shooting. He is clearly nervous and says he can't help. Megan and Speedle process the video from the ATM, and discover that Santoya was talking to someone wearing a jacket with the Nuevitas baseball team logo on it. Megan and Sevilla return to Santoya's house, and meet his son Gustavo, who is wearing a jacket with the logo on, which tests positive for GSR. Although Ray Santoya tries to claim his son was nowhere near, Gustavo admits that he fired his gun at a car full of gang members who, he thought, were doing the shooting. His bullet ricocheted and hit Dorothy Lawrence.

The sniper strikes again during the evening rush hour, killing a Miami-Dade College professor. He was shot at a 19.4-degree angle, and Calleigh uses a chronograph and a gelatine block to recreate the shot, estimating that the sniper was 975 yards away. Horatio has analysed the sand and discovered that it is coral with traces of jet fuel in it. In the only one abandoned coral quarry near Miami International airport, there is evidence of the sniper's preparations – a flag to indicate the wind speed, a small shed for cover, and two poles that have been used as targets as well as some bullets from the sand around the poles. Calleigh is able to identify the sniper from a fingerprint on the pole: Christopher Harwood, ex-Marine Special Corps.

Harwood's home is filled with rifles and bonsai trees. He has kept a meticulous record of every shot that he has fired, and Horatio finds a card bearing that morning's date, with some sticky residue on the back. As Speedle has been unable to find a link between the victims, Horatio realises that the sniper chooses sites, not victims.

Only one building still uses the RT 600 adhesive, found on Harwood's card, on its roof, and it has a clear line of sight to a shopping area. Assuming that the sniper won't fire unless he is certain of a kill, Horatio gets Delko to hover in the helicopter to vary the wind pattern, and then clears the area while a SWAT team, accompanied by Calleigh, arrest the sniper.

Personal Notes: Calleigh's mother still lives in Louisiana. She used to date a sniper with whom she is still friendly.

Delko's father lives with at least one of his sisters, and works downtown in the sniper's target area.

The Wit and Wisdom of Horatio Caine: 'Three dead before the morning rush hour is over. Who knows what the day will bring us?'

'You put a human being at the end of the barrel of your weapon, and you become God.'

Classic Dialogue: Horatio: 'So what do you get when a six-foot-tall man lays down with a three-foot-long rifle?' Calleigh: 'Hot flashes. But that's just me.'

Harwood: 'Don't you want to know why?' Horatio 'You just killed four innocent people. You're evil. You enjoy death. I hope you enjoy your own.'

Fantastic Voyages: We see the bullet's entry causing the brain to stop functioning; the sabot-encased bullet coming out of the gun and losing its jacket; the GSR cone being formed; the path of the bullet at the firing range.

Pop Culture References: References to indiscriminate sniper Charles Whitman (1 August 1966). Horatio quotes from Bob Dylan. Speedle mentions betonanything.com.

Real-life Inspirations: Although any link was strenuously denied at the time, this episode coincided with the Beltway Sniper killings in Washington, DC. As happened with M22, 'Tinder Box', which also could be seen to be dealing with recent events, the producers stated that the episode was already in production before the incident happened. Certainly consideration was given to postponing the episode if the Beltway killers hadn't been apprehended.

Mistakes Really Can Be Fatal: How did the press find out about the sabot-jacketed bullet?

Overall: 'You're evil.' That's Horatio's summation of the sniper he's been tracking. There's no debate about his motive, or any attempt at three-dimensionality. What has been a fair episode up till then takes a sharp downwards turn at the end, leaving a bad taste in the mouth.

M10
A Horrible Mind

US Air Date: 25 November 2002 12.4/20
UK Air Date: 5 April 2003

Written by: Ildy Modrovich & Laurence Walsh
Directed by: Greg Yaitanes
Guest Cast: Jesse Corti (Student), Vicki Davis (Teresa),
Josh Kemble (Doug Reid), Ian Reed Kesler (Ned Sante),
Heather McComb (Ginny Taylor), Diane Mizota (Jade Horowitz),
Paolo Seganti (Lorenzo Castanotto), Christina Souza (Caroline Lorente),
Aaron D. Spears (Playing Jerry),
Eduardo Yáñez (Colombian Interrogator),
Lenny von Dohlen (Professor Metzger), Ian Reed Kesler (Ned Sante),
Randy Hunter Johnson (Safety Diver)

Teaser One-liner: 'It's not a suicide!'
The Cases: Adam Metzger, Professor of Cultural Anthropology at Carbrera University, is found hanging from a rusted pulley, bound hand and foot, in a state park. Horatio rules out suicide – there are too many signs of violence on the body. A search of the area reveals the mutilated body of a Dalmatian dog, as well as some fabric and blood on a nearby bush.

Metzger's eyes have been glued open, and he has retinal burns normally indicative of snowblindness. There are sixty-two wounds on his body, but none hit a major artery – he didn't bleed to death, he asphyxiated. Alexx estimates that he was being tortured for four to six hours.

The knot binding the professor is a military type, and the DNA on the fabric isn't his. Thirteen different weapons were used to torture Metzger, including a taser or electroshock baton to his scrotum. Horatio wonders whether this might be the result of cult activity.

The faculty dean informs Horatio that although his students worshipped Metzger, he was not popular with the other faculty members or the parents, because of his teaching methods. He believed students should learn from real-life situations, not just books, and this term he has been teaching a course about 'The Evil of Mankind;

Violence Through the Ages'. Horatio takes swabs from each of his thirteen students. The DNA from the fabric belongs to Ned Sante, who admits that he had threatened to kill Metzger, but wouldn't actually harm him.

Horatio and Speedle go to process Metzger's home, and are surprised to find some of the students, including Ginny Taylor and Teresa Watson, going through his papers. They claim that Metzger had given them keys and that they often did chores for him. The CSIs find a collection of torture implements and a mass of shredded documents. They are all taken for processing, which shows that the torture devices were used on a dog, but not on Metzger.

The Dalmatian contains a microchip, showing he belonged to Ginny Taylor. She says he ran away three weeks earlier, and she is horrified when she learns how he died. She claims not to know who killed Metzger, but reveals that he had sufficient influence over her to get her to kiss his shoes.

The rope used to bind Metzger is a Colombian bamboo, and the CSIs bring in Efrain Barbosa, a former Colombian interrogator whom Metzger had invited to lecture to his students. Although he can't be Metzger's torturer, because his flexor tendons have been severed leaving him unable to pick anything up, Barbosa explains the dynamics of the relationship between the torturer and his victim.

The CSIs return to Metzger's house to print his computer, but it's been wiped clean. Horatio realises that Metzger was tortured with standard office equipment – staple removers, tacks and pencils. There is latent blood all over his desk. Metzger's 'snowblindness' came from being made to stare into the photocopier, and inside the copier they find a woollen fibre. Only one of the suspects wears woollen sweaters in Miami's heat – Teresa Watson, who has a taser, disguised as a cellphone, in her bag.

The shredded documents relate to the 'Teresa Project'. Metzger's subject wasn't the dog, it was Teresa, whom he tortured and humiliated. She finally snapped and tortured Metzger, leaving him to strangle himself on the rope.

* * *

Megan, Delko and Detective Sevilla discover a bloated body in the trunk of a car found in the canal. It is noted that the car hasn't skidded into the canal. Unfortunately, the body explodes before it can be properly examined. The remains are fluroroscoped and photographed, and there's a circular fracture of the cranial vault.

Delko processes the car interior, which has been completely emptied. There's an adhesive square on the dashboard but nothing on it. Megan goes through the trunk and finds some clothing and crumpled paper. She also discovers the car's ignition key, and scratches that indicate the victim was alive when the car hit the water. The autopsy confirms that he drowned.

The car is registered to Lorenzo Castanotto, who says his car was stolen and that he doesn't recognise the deceased. On his desk, though, is a hula girl figurine whose base matches the adhesive square.

The victim is identified as Doug Reid, who was reported missing the day after Castanotto's girlfriend Caroline Lorente reported his car stolen. She says Reid had no enemies, and can't think why he was killed. She provides a photo of him wearing a shirt from Reed Metal, the same place as Castanotto works.

Delko tries to confirm the identification by matching earplugs, found in Reid's work locker, with the corpse. The crumpled paper is a travel brochure for Aruba, where Lorente says Reid was going to take her, and a note saying 'Bus 15 to FR' with Castanotto's address on the back.

Sevilla and Delko believe that Castanotto and Reid were planning on dumping the car to claim the insurance since Castanotto had removed his favourite figurine. They point out to Castanotto that insurance fraud carries a much lower penalty than murder and he admits that he and Reid were carrying out a fraud. However, he wasn't responsible for Reid's death as he has an alibi. Delko and Sevilla are surprised to see Caroline Lorente entering with a bottle of champagne.

Delko surmises that Reid wanted the insurance money to use for a holiday. He and Megan recreate the scene and realise that when he reached inside the trunk to find a CD before the car could go into the water, he hit his head on an obtruding screw. Reid fell in, the trunk slammed shut, and he was carried into the water when the bank of the canal gave way.

Personal Notes: Calleigh speaks fluent Colombian Spanish. Delko used to work for Underwater Rescue. Bernstein has been a police officer for sixteen years.

Classic Dialogue: Delko: 'I've got my glass slipper, now where's my Cinderella?'

Barbosa: 'It is not what you do to people – it is what you get them to do for you.'

Teresa: 'Had I known that I was a test ... I wouldn't have snapped. But I'm happy he's dead.' Horatio: 'After six hours of torture, I bet he is, too.'

Fantastic Voyages: We go into the retina and see the effect of a burn; we watch the process of a scab healing, and we see Metzger's flesh cave in as the sharp point enters.

The Usual Suspects: Heather McComb (Ginny Taylor) played Frances Malone on *Profiler*.

Pop Culture References: Neil Diamond's 'Sweet Caroline'.

Real-life Inspirations: The college professor was based on a real Californian high school teacher who exerted an unhealthy influence over his students when he taught them about Nazis in 1967. The 1981 TV movie *The Wave* was based on the same case.

Overall: Blink and you miss her – Kim Delaney's final appearance as Megan Donner fails to ignite the screen, and she's only seen briefly. The show copes admirably without her, with what were presumably her lines being given to assorted technicians, Sevilla, and even, briefly, Horatio.

M11
Camp Fear

US Air Date: 16 December 2002 11.9/19
UK Air Date: 12 April 2003

Written by: Eddie Guerra & Steven Maeda
Directed by: Deran Sarafian

Guest Cast: Mark Adair-Rios (Ruben Alazar),
Blair Brown (Dara's Mother), Jeff D'Agostino (Timmy Diehl),
Eddie Daniels (Carol Tedman), Natalie Farrey (Amy),
Erika Flores (Cadet Julie Morales), Rosie Malek-Yonan (Receptionist),
Melissa Paull (Devin DiMari), Josh Stamberg,
Danica Stewart (Dara Winters),
Amber Tamblyn (Sr Cadet Valerie Barreiro),
Tony Todd (Sergeant Marcus Cawdrey), Steven N. Rider (Willie Stango),
Zasu (Janet)

Teaser One-liner: 'We are in search of a crime scene.'

The Cases: The body of a teenage girl, covered in small
welts that might be insect bites, is found near a rural road.
Alexx notes that the girl has well-kept nails but her hair
has been chopped off very roughly. Double lividity is
apparent, indicating that she didn't die where she was
found, but was moved there. Horatio and Calleigh find
tyre tracks near the dump site, which come from an ATV.

The girl died between 3 and 5 a.m. There was blunt force
trauma to the right aspect of the forehead, and the blood
loss from that could have led to endotoxic shock. There's
minor tearing around the vaginal opening, and she is
wearing a contraceptive diaphragm with two sets of
fingerprints – her own and an unidentified set. Although
she smells of beer, there is none in her system. Her blood
wasn't clotting and, inside the mucus in her nose and
throat, Alexx spots some golden material which turns out
to be pollen. The tyre tracks come from 650 series ATVs,
and there is an invisible laundry mark 'Pharos B-2' on her
shirt.

Pharos is the nearby juvenile girls' detention centre. The
camp commander Sgt Marcus Cawdrey doesn't recognise
a photo of the girl, but the laundry mark means the shirt
comes from Barracks 2. The Senior Cadet in Barracks 2,
Valerie Barreiro, helps the CSIs to find the girl who is
missing one of her three issued shirts. She is Julie Morales.
Inside her locker are hair clippings of the same colour as
the victim. Horatio finds a white crystalline substance on
the floor of the barracks which turns out to be salt, and
also notes a red stain later confirmed as blood, on
Cawdrey's trousers.

The girl is identified by her mother as Dara Winters, a fifteen-year-old teenage model. She last saw her daughter at 8 p.m. the previous evening, and doesn't recognise Julie Morales' name.

The tyre tracks match one of the camp's ATVs, which are only used by camp staff and senior inmates. Luminol reveals human blood on the ATV, which also contains the same pollen – from the rare Lignum vitae tree – that was found in Dara's nose.

Cawdrey cannot explain how Dara's blood came to be on his trousers, and gladly gives a DNA sample. Horatio believes him, and surmises that he might have got the blood on him through passive transfer from the blood-stained ATV.

Forensic palynology reveals that Lignum vitae grow within fifty feet of a small pond on the perimeter of the Pharos camp grounds, nearly three miles from the dump site. There are ATV tracks present that are deeper on departing the site than those caused by arrival. There's also clotted blood on a tree root. Calleigh finds Dara's clothing in the water, and needs some salt to remove the leeches from her skin.

The beer covering Dara would have attracted the leeches, whose saliva allows blood to flow more freely. Dara had lost about half her blood.

The Barracks 2 girls are all checked for leech bites, and Valerie Barreiro has some. She says she found Dara and Julie drinking beer together the previous night, and escorted Dara off the premises, after accidentally spilling some beer on her. The next morning she found her body by the pond and drove it away, because she didn't want to get into trouble for not reporting Dora's presence in the first place. She then removed the leeches from her leg using salt.

Julie tells Calleigh that Dara hated her mother, who was pushing her to be a model and to get involved sexually with people. The reason Julie (or Louise, as she is known to both Dara and her mother) was sent to the camp was because she assaulted her mother. Dara chopped off her own hair to try to ruin her looks.

Calleigh finds Lignum vitae pollen in Mrs Winters' car, and she eventually confesses that she knew that Dara would run to Julie after the fight they had had over the diaphragm, so she followed her. They met, argued again, and Dara ran into the night. Unfortunately, she tripped and fell into the pond where the leeches drained her.

Speedle and Delko investigate the death of Willie Stango at his trailer at the marina. The skin around his nose and mouth is burned. There are no signs of forced entry, but there is a milk carton and a cellphone nearby showing that Stango missed a large number of calls. Alexx finds that Stango has partial-thickness burns to the lips, tongue and oral mucosa, and his stomach lining is inflamed. Swelling in the lungs and the release of oedema fluid mean that heat from the burns cut off his airway. He had gasoline in his system, with some sodium trace elements, possibly from salt water contamination.

Stango owned a small boat which was overloaded with gasoline containers and lengths of hose. The CSIs deduce that he was siphoning ultra-high octane fuel from the big boats. Gas chromatography confirms that the gas that killed him was high-end fuel, not available domestically.

Seventy-four of Stango's calls came from one person, Timothy Diehl aka Motor, who has a jet ski that needs the ultra-high octane fuel to run properly. Testing it, the CSIs discover that the fuel he is using has been cut with ordinary gasoline, and surmise that Diehl killed Stango because he was cheating him. But Diehl says that none of his calls was answered, except when he withheld his number, and then the line went dead. The CSIs deduce that the electrical spark from the cellphone's lithium battery ignited the fumes from the fuel that Stango had within his system and that the fire killed him.

Personal Notes: Horatio nearly resigned on one occasion, and from the way he looks at a picture of the late Raymond Caine, presumably his brother, there's some connection between Raymond and the resignation. Megan Donner resigns from CSI because work reminds her too

much of her husband's death. She leaves a message for
Horatio asking him not to try to contact her again.

The Wit and Wisdom of Horatio Caine: '[Lignum vitae:]
The hardest wood in the world. The US Navy almost
wiped them out during World War II using them for
propeller pins.'

'I told you that I would figure out who did this, didn't I?'

Classic Dialogue: Delko: 'You have any idea yet what
killed our guy?' Speedle: 'He had gas ... gasoline, to be
more precise, all the way down to his stomach lining.'

Julie Morales: 'Her mom always told her, "No choir girl
ever made the A-list."'

Fantastic Voyages: We look inside the mucus found in
Dara's nose, and spot the pollen. We see a leech at work.
We follow the progress of the gasoline down Stango's
throat, and then see it set alight.

The Usual Suspects: Blair Brown (Dara's mother) appears
with Nicole Kidman in *Dogville*. Danica Stewart (Dara
Winters) was a teenage girl in **CSI 30**, 'Slaves of Las
Vegas'. Tony Todd has appeared in numerous cult series,
and is probably best known as The Candyman.

Pop Culture References: The 'Got Milk' advertising campaign.

Mistakes Really Can Be Fatal: Horatio refers to the dead
girl as Jane Doe at the pond crime scene long after he and
Calleigh have been calling her Dara.

Notes: The title sequence is re-edited to remove Kim
Delaney, adding in extra sequences from recent episodes.

Overall: Put Grissom and Catherine in place of Horatio
and Calleigh, and Nick and Warrick for Speedle and
Delko, and this script would work just as well. A good,
competent hour of television. Sorry, Kim who?

M12
Entrance Wound

US Air Date: 6 January 2003 11.6/19
UK Air Date: 19 April 2003

Written by: Laurie McCarthy & Gwendolyn Parker
Directed by: David Grossman
Guest Cast: Sarah Aldrich (Mrs Judson), Todd Eckert (Michael Gotti),
Patricia Forte (Grandma), Janie Liszewski (Susan McCleary),
Tim Quill (Werner Roebling), Saxon Trainor (Officer Saxon),
Bree Michael Warner (Girlfriend), Cameron Watson (Leo Bastille),
Belinda Waymouth (Greta Roebling), Carlton Wilborn (Brian Davidson),
Kirk B.R. Woller (Detective Christian Brunner),
D.B. Woodside (Cole Judson), Xavier Lynch (Malcolm Davidson)

Teaser One-liner: 'Typical maid service – scrub the surfaces. Scrubbed the surfaces but left a dead body under the bed.'

The Cases: The body of local prostitute Susan McCleary is found underneath a hotel bed. She died between 7 and 9 p.m. the previous evening, and was stabbed repeatedly in the chest, abdomen and thighs with a slim, sharp weapon. There are no visible bloodstains on the sheets or under the bed, but there has been blood on the wall beside the bed. The body smells of cardamom, a spice used in curries and soap. The hotel confirms that the previous occupant removed the soap, hand towels and flannel. There's a ring of blood around the bath, and discarded women's clothing in a dumpster behind the hotel.

Alexx discovers that Susan was stabbed, after some initial hesitation, 23 times – most of them deep wounds. She died from exsanguination after the aorta was cut – the aorta bleeds into the chest cavity, hence the lack of external blood. There is adhesive residue around her wrists, ankles and mouth, but no sign of sexual assault.

The bathroom sink has been purged with drain cleaner, removing all DNA evidence. There's minor bloodspatter on the bed, and an unidentified mould in the middle of the bedspread which isn't from anything in the room.

Horatio gets a print off a man's belt from the hotel room, and it matches Cole Judson, who has a record for a knife assault on a woman. Judson's landlord, Leo Bastille, says that Judson is a wealthy man who relaxes by helping with repairs to the complex. Judson is arrested in front of his wife and two stepchildren. The CSIs find knives, an ice pick and scissors which might match the wounds, and

mould on the shower curtain. Wendy Judson can't believe
her husband is capable of this, but she didn't know about
his record. She says he was at his weekly Wednesday
evening sales meeting. However, his firm says that he never
works late on a Wednesday, and Judson admits that he just
takes some time for himself. He claims that his record is
the result of him taking the rap for his girlfriend.

Horatio further examines the print from the belt and
discovers that it was originally left in oil, and then the
blood was applied later. Judson may have been framed. He
therefore decides to test the DNA within the mould to try
to identify a single host colony.

Judson says that his wife's ex-husband, Michael Gotti,
was caught in the apartment a week earlier, and when
Gotti is asked about this, he says that he was looking for
anything he could use against Judson. However, he has a
solid alibi for the time of death. Horatio therefore starts to
query the time of death, and discovers that some orchids
in the room have been subjected to intense cold. If the
room had been intensively air conditioned and then
reheated, the time of death would seem to be earlier than
it really was. The electrical company confirms that there
was a spike in usage between 9 p.m. and midnight.

Horatio wonders how Gotti could have known about
Judson's record, and gets Speedle to ask checking agencies.
Leo Bastille, the landlord, had registered a full search
against Judson, but when his wife is asked about this, she
says that they only check credit histories. When Horatio
spots forensic textbooks on the bookshelves, he investigates further and, in the Bastilles' bathroom, finds a bar of
cardamom soap, which Ellen Bastille says her husband
brought home earlier in the week. She tells Horatio that
Bastille has started acting strangely, getting her to lie
absolutely still in the bathtub while he washes her. She
confirms that he was at home for dinner on Wednesday,
but left just before 9 p.m. after receiving a call from a
tenant, although she doesn't recall hearing the phone.
Horatio searches the appartment and finds a can of putty
with Judson's fingerprints inside, as well as epoxy from

where Bastille made the impression of the prints. Bastille is arrested and admits the murder and framing Judson.

Detective Sevilla brings Calleigh and Delko in to help investigate the shooting of a German tourist at a gas station. A masked man shot Greta Roebling's husband Werner after approaching the car from her side. Roebling ran into the gas station, but the shooter pursued and killed him. The CSIs process the car, and find a vivid orange smear on the rear view mirror. There is bloodspatter, but no bullet in the car.

There only seems to be one bullet wound to Roebling's head: the entrance wound is behind his ear, and it may have exited through his mouth. There is an odd bloody print near the body, and a white truck in the garage with high velocity spatter on it. However, the angles don't correlate between the wound and the truck. The print probably comes from the odd gloves that the murderer was wearing, as seen on the surveillance tapes. Alexx discovers that Roebling was shot twice: the second bullet went into his mouth and came to rest in his throat. That would explain the considerable splattering of blood, since there are more than forty veins or arteries in that area.

The bullet matches a gun used in a robbery and the CSIs visit the convicted robber, juvenile Malcolm Davidson, who is now in the care of his grandmother. They find the glove, which has been washed. However, Davidson's epithelials are on it, as are Roebling's blood, and lipstick matching the smudge on the rear view mirror, which they think comes from Davidson's grandmother. Davidson must therefore have been inside the car at some point prior to the murder.

The CSIs conclude that the shooting was not random. They obtain prints and an impression of Mrs Roebling's lipstick in a clandestine fashion, and review the security camera footage. They realise that she ducked too quickly when the gun was pointed into the car: she must have known it was coming. They also discover a link between the lipstick and Davidson's older brother Brian: both came from Germany. Brian Davidson admits he was in Stuttgart with the ballet company but, after losing his job, he took on private ballet clients, including Greta Roebling. Although both claim that they weren't serious about the proposed murder, they admit separately that Mrs Roebling hired Brian to kill her husband, and he passed the job on to his younger brother.

Personal Notes: Horatio doesn't have much time for Detective Brunner.

The Wit and Wisdom of Horatio Caine: 'How about the joy of just taking a life? That's always good.'

Classic Dialogue: Calleigh: 'It's bad enough when you're in that awkward stage between boy and cold-blooded killer, but it's even worse when Grandma's kiss links you to the scene.'

Horatio: 'How many things do you think we'll overlook in the course of a career?' Speedle: 'You? Less than anyone I know. And me, fewer because of it.'

Fantastic Voyages: We see the aorta being cut and bleeding out. We follow the drain cleaner at work. We examine the print being manufactured, and see the orchid cells dying. We watch the bullet coming into Werner Roebling's mouth, hitting his teeth, and the resultant mess filling his mouth with blood.

The Usual Suspects: Bree Michael Warner (the girlfriend) played Anna on *Haunted*. Kirk B.R. Woller (Detective Christian Brunner) was a Prison Guard in **CSI 34**, 'You've Got Male'. D.B. Woodside (Cole Judson) is the most recent Principal of Sunnydale High, Robin Wood, on *Buffy*.

Real-life Inspirations: Horatio mentions a study carried out by a criminalist from Taos about transferring fingerpints that would have sparked this episode.

Overall: The series is really starting to find its feet now. The methods may not be the same as in Las Vegas, but this is as entertaining.

M13
Bunk

US Air Date: 27 January 2003 11.2/18
UK Air Date: 26 April 2003

Written by: Elizabeth Devine
Directed by: Charles Correll
Guest Cast: Wil Albert (Leo Klein), Daniel Betances (First Officer),
Mary Boss (Betty Rosen), Barbara Eve Harris (Wilmont's Lawyer),
Pat Healy, Hans Hernke (Beach Boy), Dawn Lewis (Instructor),
Claire Malis (Adele Alonzo), Howard Mann (Marty Gaines),
Betty McGuire (Pearl Abrams), D.W. Moffett (Dr Wilmont),
Toby Moore (Gregory Kimble),
Victoria Gabrielle Platt (Beverly Caldwell),
Quinn K. Redeker (Herb Rines), Victor Rivers (Keith Sewell),
Al Rodrigo (Dante, State's Attorney), Aaron Seville (Rudy Caldwell)

Teaser One-liner: 'There's no telling what's in there. We'd better figure it out, and we'd better get it contained before more people die.'
The Cases: When a man is killed by accidental exposure to some toxic fumes after chasing his cat into a neighbouring house, the CSIs are called in to deal with the situation. Horatio and Speedle don fully enclosed breathing suits and find that the kitchen sink is filled with various glasses and flasks. There is a chemical residue all over them, and Horatio uses a Drager tube to detect an incredibly high concentration of nitric acid, eighteen times the lethal level. Getting Sevilla to evacuate a one-block radius in case of explosion, the CSIs carefully remove the glasses from the sink until the reading falls to a very safe level. They then process the kitchen, finding a used latex glove over the sink.

The landlord, Dr James Wilmont, explains that he and two other dermatologists have an investment group, Diamond Sun. He says the house has been vacant for six months, and is flippant about his responsibilities for what goes on there. Speedle tries to determine what drug was being made, but the components don't make sense for any recognised narcotic. Horatio realises that if formic acid had been used instead of nitric, the lab would have been producing Ecstasy. It's possible that pills containing the wrong drug are on the street.

The latex glove produces a print for Gregory Kimble, who has a chemical burn on his upper lip. His shirt also has traces of the same chemical components found at the lab. Although he claims not to have a regular income, he is driving a brand new car. Unfortunately, because Kimble hadn't managed to create Ecstasy and therefore wasn't producing a drug prohibited by Florida state law, the state attorney orders his release. Horatio is angered by this, and follows Kimble to another of the Diamond Sun properties, where he is unloading drugs from his car. He and Sevilla tell Kimble that although he may be getting a fancy car as his reward, the doctors are making a fortune from their work.

The false 'Ecstasy' pills claim the life of a nineteen-year-old student, and one of the undissolved pills from his stomach has the Diamond Sun logo on it. Horatio, Speedle and Sevilla return to the Diamond Sun property and find Kimble stabbed in the chest in his car. It appears, from the angle of the wounds, that he was stabbed by someone sitting in the passenger seat, and thermal imaging shows that that person had a bandage on his upper back. Wilmont had earlier said that one of his colleagues had recently removed a carcinoma from his back.

Under questioning, Wilmont hands over the knife that he carried for protection, and its hilt matches the bruising around Kimble's stab wounds. Without the knife as evidence, he would have been arrested only for the drugs; now, Horatio has him for murder.

The bloodied body of 81-year-old Betty Rosen is found by her sister Pearl. There is blood on the walls and floor of the apartment they shared at a retirement community. She died around 2 a.m., although the attack occurred earlier. Her skull has been fractured by blunt force trauma. The bedroom window has been broken, and the plants beneath it trampled, and there is bloodspatter on the bedside table and on the couch. Delko finds a piece of paper in a pool of blood which he puts aside for drying.

Alexx's autopsy shows that Betty survived for some hours after her injuries. She has Cumadin, a blood thinner, in her system, accounting for the amount of blood. She was in the late stages of Alzheimer's Disease, but it is hard to tell whether or not she has been sexually assaulted.

Pearl stayed with friends the night her sister died. Betty was very popular, and couldn't keep a secret. Everyone knew she would be alone. The SART kit indicates that Betty was assaulted by someone who had had a vasectomy about eight to twelve hours previously.

The broken window carries the prints of Keith Sewell, a paroled rapist who is a gardener for the retirement community. However, Sewell says that he regularly had to replace the glass as Betty believed she needed to break it in order to sneak out behind her parents' back to meet her boyfriend. The apartment manager confirms this, and says that Betty had numerous boyfriends. Herb Rines is proved to be the person with whom Betty had intercourse the night she died, but he left her at 9 p.m. and his alibi is confirmed. One of the other residents, Marty Gaines, used to date Betty, but she ended the relationship.

The now-dry letter is from Betty's lawyer, confirming an amendment to her will. They string her movements based on the blood patterns, and realise that she fell and hit her head on a granite countertop and then staggered back to her bedroom, leaving pools of blood as she went, banging into furniture along the way. Her death was accidental, and all her money has been left to Pearl, who herself is beginning to show signs of Alzheimer's.

Personal Notes: Horatio's brother Raymond C. Caine died on 15 March 1993, aged 24, according to his grave. Horatio taunts Dante, the State Attorney, that releasing someone and then having to send a sympathy card to a widow would be déjà vu, and Dante takes that to be a reference to Raymond's death. At the end of the episode, Horatio goes to the grave. Speedle is dating a girl called Pam, whom Horatio knows about. Delko's grandmother is still alive. He knows Laura, the technician who spent a year at Quantico (see **Mistakes** below).

Techniques: Horatio and Speedle use a new XRF machine to analyse the chemicals within Kimble's shirt. Speedle uses a thermal-imaging camera to measure the body heat of the various people in Kimble's van.

The Wit and Wisdom of Horatio Caine: 'Like my old man says, "You didn't have a backup, you didn't have a plan." '

'For me, it is all about the victims, especially the ones who die too young, too soon.'

Fantastic Voyages: We look out from the Ecstasy victim's stomach and we see the knife going into Kimble's skin. We also observe the neurofibrillary tangles that signify Alzheimer's Disease.

The Usual Suspects: Quinn K. Redeker (Herb Rines) appeared in most of the 70s detective shows, and is the co-writer of the Oscar-winning movie *The Deer Hunter*.

Mistakes Really Can Be Fatal: Why isn't the hazardous materials team called in to the clandestine drug lab?

Delko welcomes Laura back after her year at Quantico, but according to **M01**, 'Golden Parachute', he didn't know Megan Donner, the former CSI boss before she took her six-months leave from March 2002. Either he knew Laura from his other police department work or his history is being rewritten.

Overall: The second reference in successive episodes to Horatio's brother – with Megan gone, a new angle has to be thought of to make Caine 'interesting', apparently. At this point, the show doesn't need it.

M14
Forced Entry

US Air Date: 3 February 2003 20.0/19
UK Air Date: 3 May 2003

Written by: Mark Israel & Lois Johnson
Directed by: Artie Mandelberg

Guest Cast: Michael Bergin (Thomas Carpenter),
Casey Biggs (Michael Guerro), Ski Carr (Victor Eli),
Caitlin Dulany (Erin Murphy), Dominic Fumusa (Vincent Graziano),
Chris Mulkey (Leonard Murphy), Ruben Pla (Benito Ramon),
Sandra Thigpen (Detective Riboul),
Oscar Orlando Torres (Officer Torres),
Eduardo Verástegui (Jarod Parker)

Teaser One-liner: 'No signs of forced entry . . .'
The Cases: A man has been found face down spreadeagled
on his bed, his robe pushed up around his thighs, and his
mouth gagged. His hands and feet have been taped to the
bedstead, and there's blood on the pillow. There's an
untouched collection of expensive watches, and no sign of
struggle, disturbance or forced entry. An expensive suit has
been laid out on the bed.

Alexx checks the body and finds severe anal trauma, and
lacerations in the distal portion of the rectum. He died
around 11 p.m. Speedle finds several hairs in the bed, and
there's a metallic brown substance in the gash on his head.
The police find several conflicting sets of identification: the
Porsche outside is registered to Richard Lee Hauschild, the
house belongs to Deveraux Jones, but his watch is
engraved to Zack Kelsey.

During the full autopsy, Alexx establishes the cause of
death as suffocation – a piece of fabric was stuffed into his
mouth. The tape covering his mouth was cut, rather than
torn. Alexx adds that the victim was sodomised violently
with a foreign object, resulting in spleen and colon
damage. The victim has had a tattoo removed, which
Alexx raises by using a butane torch to melt the skin to
reveal the still-tattooed layers underneath.

The tattoo matches one worn by a recently released
robber, Danny Blue, who is questioned, and admits that
the dead man is his partner, Thomas Carpenter. He served
five years for their joint crimes, and admits that he was at
Carpenter's home a few days earlier hoping for compensa-
tion for not betraying his partner. Carpenter refused to
help him, and kicked Blue out after telling him that he had
been working on a foolproof scam for about a year.

Horatio returns to the crime scene and examines the items there, most of which have been stolen. A big crystal vase is inscribed to Erin from Leonard. Blue's hair doesn't match those found in the bed, and Speedle reports that comparison of the head and rectum wounds shows that they contained rust probably from a corroded iron pipe.

One of the items found was reported stolen three weeks earlier by Judy Johnson, who was sodomised by the thief after he had wrapped electrical tape around her hands, ankles and mouth so Carpenter was killed by someone using his own MO against him. Judy Johnson committed suicide a week after the attack, so Horatio talks to her husband, Dean Johnson, who is furious that the police are concerned over Carpenter's death. He denies being involved. Horatio learns that there are three other victims who have been robbed and sodomised by Carpenter, all of whom left Miami. Johnson's alibi is not conclusive but Speedle confirms that the Johnsons' scissors weren't used to cut the tape found on Carpenter's body.

There are ten different outlets that stock the fabric that choked Carpenter, one of which belongs to Leonard and Erin Murphy. The vase that was found with those names on at the crime scene was never reported missing. At Murphy Home Furnishings, Horatio spots Carpenter's name in the guest book. Their workshop uses scissors like those used to cut the tape, and there are lengths of rusty pipe stacked against the wall.

Erin Murphy doesn't recognise Carpenter's picture and denies being raped or burgled. She says their vase wasn't stolen, it was smashed accidentally by her husband while she was overseas. Horatio realises that perhaps Erin wasn't raped, but her husband was. Under questioning, Leonard Murphy admits that he thought he could deal with the rape until Carpenter came in to buy fabric. He persuaded Carpenter to give his name and address and then went to administer his own form of justice.

A crematorium owner, Benito Ramon, has been found with his head crushed on the floor of his crematorium.

Nearby is a box containing numerous gold fillings. There's also a handbag on the floor, belonging to Michelle Carter and behind the crematorium is a pile of uncremated corpses.

Alexx suspects that Ramon's death was caused by internal haemorrhaging to the brain. A bloody smear on the wall probably marks where his head was crushed. Michelle Carter was reported missing two weeks earlier but her description doesn't match any of the bodies found outside. Delko notes that there is a body still in the cremation oven, but bones will provide only mitrochondrial DNA, showing the maternal lineage though the teeth might be identifiable. There's also blood inside the oven, which can't be from the body, but might be from Ramon, who has ash on his face.

However, the skull from the oven is from a sixty-year-old, not from Michelle. Ramon is clutching something in his right hand, and Alexx severs his hand and heats it to release the rigor mortis. It turns out to be a VIP medallion for an expensive nightclub called Canvas. The owners, Michael Guerro and Jarod Parker, deny any knowledge of Ramon or Michelle. They each wear a large ring with a C in diamonds in the middle. They confirm that the medallion is for VIPs, but won't reveal a list of who they are.

Michelle's body is found buried in the ground underneath the mound of corpses. There are blotches of fluorescent paint on her skin, like that used at Club Canvas. At the club, the CSIs take paint chippings off the wall, and the club's legal counsel, Vincent Graziano, produces a copy of the VIP list. Ramon is on it. Parker has lied on both counts, but claims he just wanted the police to go away.

Michelle was strangled and, under ultraviolet light, there's a C-shaped bruise on her cheek. Calleigh and Delko collect the rings from Guerro and Parker. Guerro admits that Michelle worked at the club, but says she had started to work elsewhere. However, the rings have no blood, epithelials or crematorium ash on them.

Calleigh discovers that three rings were made. Graziano denies that the third ring is his, but the CSIs have a photo of all three men wearing them. Michelle's blood is in the ring. Graziano is secretly the majority owner of the club, and needed it to be a success. He was furious that Michelle was drawing clients away, so strangled her. He then promised Ramon a VIP membership in return for him cremating Michelle. When he brought the medallion over, he found the pile of bodies, the broken cremation chamber and Michelle's items unburned. He therefore killed Ramon in a fit of rage.

Personal Notes: Both Calleigh and Delko have been to the expensive Canvas nightclub. Calleigh has a tattoo.

Techniques: Alexx microwaves Ramon's hand (over Calleigh's objections) to release the medallion.

Classic Dialogue: Bernstein: 'Mother and daughter team selling Girl Scout cookies. Found the door open, saw the blood and called 911.' Horatio: 'Well, there's got to be a badge for that,'

Horatio: 'So someone used his own MO on him, didn't they?' Bernstein: 'It makes for poetic justice.'

Speedle: 'We can nail a grieving husband for killing his wife's rapist. That's good. I think the guy deserves a medal, don't you?'

Calleigh: 'Diamonds are a girl's best friend, and a suspect's worst enemy.'

Calleigh: 'You may be a lawyer, but I'm a CSI. A damn good one.'

Fantastic Voyages: We see the fibres being made.

The Usual Suspects: Casey Biggs (Michael Guerro) played Damar on *Star Trek: Deep Space 9*. Sandra Thigpen (Detective Riboul) was Driscoll's attorney in **CSI 32**, 'Ellie'.

Real-life Inspirations: A pile of over 300 corpses was found on the premises of a crematorium in Atlanta.

Overall: Horatio's behaviour to Dean Johnson is unpleasant to watch, and you can fully agree with the man's reactions. At least the episode didn't show the whole murder scene for once!

M15
Dead Woman Walking

US Air Date: 10 February 2003 11.5/18
UK Air Date: 10 May 2003

Written by: Ildy Modrovich & Laurence Walsh
Directed by: Jeannot Szwarc
Guest Cast: Adam Baldwin (De Soto), Greg Crooks (Carl Aspen),
John Getz (George Risher), Eddie Jemison (Parker Boyd),
Stevie Johnson (Radiation Man #2), Jeremy Roberts (Sam Carter),
Karen Sillas (Belle King), Rachel Singer (Janet Carter),
Maria Teresa Rangel

Teaser One-liner: 'Junkie or not, somebody killed this
man.'

The Case: A dead body is found with a syringe beside it.
Horatio doesn't believe it was an overdose – there's no
foam around the mouth, and the syringe is too big. The
body is identified as that of Carl Aspen, who has a long
record for possession, assault and battery. He has lacerations to his face and lips, and a couple of torn nails.
Underneath the body is a pile of damp money, totalling
$203. Alexx sets the time of death as 4 to 6 a.m. A chewed
pencil is also found at the scene.

Aspen's neck has been snapped. When Alexx checks his
nails, she finds the flesh on the top of his hands has been
eaten away. It wasn't obvious at the scene – which rules
out a chemical burn – and it doesn't look like parasite
activity. It's radiation and the lab is evacuated. The
radiation management team neutralise Aspen, and its
leader, De Soto, tells Horatio that the material could have
been injected by syringe. The money is also radioactive
from iodine-131, luckily at the end of its half life.

The pencil bears the name of Belle King, an attorney.
When the CSIs visit her, they find that she is a radioactive source, with levels ten times higher than those
found at the lab. Belle is being killed by iodine radiation,
and has less than a week to live. Horatio breaks the news
and asks if she has any enemies. She does – she has been
suing a power plant for plume contamination, and Risher

Pharmaceuticals over toxic waste contamination. Speedle checks Belle's office and finds a drawer containing seven rolls of film and a camera.

De Soto confirms that Belle's home, including her chickens, is clean. She has received hate mail from a Sam Carter, who promises to kill her if she contacts them again. Carter's oldest son had just died when he wrote it, but Belle says everything is OK now, and Carter's wife Janet sends fresh orange juice as a thank-you. Calleigh checks the orange juice with sulphur, and it confirms iodine content. The Carters deny trying to kill Belle; they were angry because Belle had turned down an earlier settlement of their case. Horatio checks the juice jug and finds a small hole where it's been injected, clearing the Carters.

Delko has been processing the $203 found with Carl Aspen's body, and has uncovered impressions from a credit card pressed against one of the bills. It correlates to George Risher, CEO of Risher Pharmaceuticals, whose office is three blocks from the crime scene. The radioactive isotopes are kept about twenty feet from the door, and there's a new lock on the facility where freezer burns indicate that the old lock was frozen with freon and snapped off.

Risher claims that there was a break-in, but he failed to report it because they hadn't completed the inventory yet. Horatio asks if this was going to include some syringes of iodine-131, and tells Risher that he knows it would be convenient if Belle disappeared.

Calleigh has found a footprint in chicken dung in the facility. The film Speedle found shows Risher's lab, and he wonders if Belle took the photos and an isotope, either to analyse it, or to kill herself and make herself a martyr. Horatio disagrees and goes to check Belle's shoes, which don't show anything. Belle tells him that she has someone working for her, but won't say who.

An examination of the photos reveals that they were taken by an insider, since the lock hadn't been broken. Belle still refuses to name him. There aren't any prints on the camera, but it is set up for use by a long-sighted person, and Belle is short-sighted. The Risher records are checked for long-sighted employees, and Horatio gets a DNA sample from under Aspen's now-deradiated fingernails. It matches Parker Boyd, the receptionist at Risher, who hastily deletes a file of photos of Belle from his computer when the police arrive. Boyd is arrested and admits that he tried to kill Belle because she spurned his attentions. He also killed Aspen when Aspen tried to mug him. If Belle was dead, he could forget about her. Horatio gets the evidence that Belle needs and tells her before she dies that he will help finish her work.

Personal Notes: Delko is concerned about his exposure to the radiation, and gets stress-related nosebleeds.

The Wit and Wisdom of Horatio Caine: 'Eric, your genius knows no bounds.'

Classic Dialogue: Delko: 'The guy says my exposure was equal to what a pilot gets on a flight to Paris.' Calleigh: 'Well, next time, take the trip to Paris. It'll be easier on all of us.'

Belle King: 'If you keep interrupting me, I'm never going to get through my list of enemies.'

Belle: 'Do you know Horatio was the first CSI?' Horatio: 'He was . . . the what?' Belle: 'In *Hamlet*, when Hamlet was poisoned and dying, he asked his best friend Horatio to tell the world.'

Fantastic Voyages: We see the radiation working at the subatomic level on Aspen's flesh, and the radiation particles around his hand. We also watch the different versions of radiation affecting Delko, and what the radiation has done to Belle King.

The Usual Suspects: Adam Baldwin (De Soto) was Jayne Cobb, pilot of the *Firefly*. John Getz (George Risher) was art owner and unpopular father Richard Ziegler in **CSI 09**, 'Sex, Lies and Larvae'. Eddie Jemison appeared in **CSI 40**, 'Chasing the Bus'. Jeremy Roberts (Sam Carter) was the demon Kakistos on *Buffy*. Karen Sillas (Belle King) appeared with *CSI*'s William Petersen in *Peter Benchley's The Beast*.

Mistakes Really Can Be Fatal: Why isn't anyone looking after Belle once her condition has been diagnosed? If the Carters were so grateful to her, you'd think they might.

Overall: After the unsympathetic Horatio of **M14**, 'Forced Entry', it's good to see him empathising with the victims again. It was the strength that set him apart from Gil Grissom in **CSI 44**, 'Cross-Jurisdictions', and it would be a mistake to lose – or indeed, overuse – it.

M16
Evidence of Things Unseen

US Air Date: 17 February 2003 11.5/18
UK Air Date: 17 May 2003

Written by: David Black
Directed by: Joe Chappelle
Guest Cast: Tomas Arana (Seth Davis), Shelby Fenner (Amy Cannon),
Boris Lee Krutonog (Vadim), Pavel Lychnikoff (Victor Ratsch),
J.C. MacKenzie (Eduardo Infante), David Sutcliffe (Rick Breck),
Pamela Warren (Stripper)

Teaser One-liner: 'Poised to see paradise.'
The Case: A man is found slumped against the glass booth in a peepshow. He looks Eastern European, and has two knife wounds in his back, although there are three knife strikes through the door. Calleigh saws away a portion of the door, and she and Horatio deduce that the weapon was an eight-inch serrated blade, with the strike wider at the top than the bottom – probably a hunting knife. There is also what looks like a new peephole in the door. In among the mess of bodily fluids in the booth, Delko finds a black hair which isn't human. There are at least twenty more of these on the body.

The first strike punctured the victim's lung, while the second clipped the fifth vertebra and severed the spinal cord. Calleigh believes that the knife was one used by the military and Horatio estimates that the killer was six feet tall and right-handed. He talks to the stripper the victim was watching. She denies having seen him before.

The hair Delko found comes from a higher primate, so the CSIs search for somewhere an Eastern European could have access to an ape. Delko talks to Vadim Slonim, one of the ape-keepers at the zoo, while Horatio learns that their victim is Victor Ratsch, the night custodian, and Slonim's cousin. The two men used to fight regularly.

Slonim is questioned and says that he's not seen Ratsch for a couple of days. He claims that neither of them would go to a peepshow. Ratsch always dumped extra work on him and the scratches on his face are from Ratsch, who left Slonim to feed the lions while he went to a business meeting.

The stripper is killed in a hit-and-run incident. Alexx finds she was a drug addict. There is an odd imprint on her thigh, which also has a fragment of some non-safety glass embedded in it. Detective Tripp talks to the peepshow's owner about the stripper, and he points him towards her husband Rick Breck. Horatio and Tripp visit Breck on his houseboat, who tells them that he and Amy were married less than a year, and don't have a car, which is why she was walking home. He claims that she left him a message the night before, but he erased it. Horatio takes the answering machine for testing. He believes that this is a murder, but Tripp thinks it's a simple hit-and-run.

The shard of glass comes from a Mercedes S-class vehicle, and Amy's message indicates that her husband had got some drugs for them to use, and that there was someone called Ace near her when she called, with whom she had made some sort of deal. When Horatio goes back to ask Breck about this, he finds him dead in the water.

The water in Breck's lungs isn't from the marina or city water, but there are chemicals in it. Horatio deduces that Breck was drowned in his own toilet. Calleigh discovers more ape hair, and a digital camera showing Breck and Amy in various sexual positions. She processes the floor nearby for any ejaculate and finds multiple residues of semen by the bed, and many different samples around the boat. It seems as if Amy brought her work home. Horatio finds the markings from a chair positioned by the bed. Delko comes across the knife hidden in a false panel in the bathroom. It shows Breck's fingerprints.

Speedle finds elephant dung on the piece of glass in Amy's leg, and asks Horatio about a clicking noise that he's found in the background on the answerphone tape. Horatio and Tripp speak to the zoo manager, Eduardo Infante, who owns an S-class Mercedes which has disappeared. He claims not to know who Amy is.

Infante is recognised by the peepshow owner who says that Amy was one of his regular clients. The Mercedes, which is tracked down using its theft-deterrent device, has a cracked headlight with blood smears. DNA from its steering wheel comes from two donors – the person who stained the boat carpet, and a minor donor.

Tripp and Horatio interrogate Infante, and he eventually admits that he went to Amy's boat. She and Breck were blackmailing him, so he hired Ratsch to frighten them off. However, he denies involvement in their murder.

The minor donor is peepshow owner, Seth Davis. As he listens to Horatio's theory, he starts to make a clicking noise with his jaw. Horatio believes that Davis was angry that Amy wasn't cutting him in on her blackmail scheme, so killed her and Breck. The clicking noise places Amy in Infante's stolen car.

Personal Notes: Delko speaks fluent Russian.

Techniques: Speedle uses a spectrogram to map the microscopic magnetic fields across the erased section of the answerphone tape to recreate what was there.

The Wit and Wisdom of Horatio Caine: 'There's your cause of death. Lights out, my friend.'

'Let's go talk to the other Russian, the cousin, before he chokes on a Twizzler.'

'Tomorrow is what you make of it.'

Classic Dialogue: Amy: 'My whole life's a crime scene. When are you going to arrest whoever's responsible for me having this crappy job in this crappy town?'

Fantastic Voyages: We watch the knife slipping into the victim, puncturing the left lung and filling it with blood, and then severing the spinal cord. We see the toilet water flooding Breck's lungs.

The Usual Suspects: Tomas Arana (Seth Davis) was Vice Admiral Fletcher in *Pearl Harbor*. Shelby Fenner (Amy Cannon) was the missing co-ed Paige Rycoff in **CSI 24**,

'Chaos Theory'. J.C. MacKenzie (Mr Infante) played a character called Normal on *Dark Angel* and was Arnold Spivak on *Murder One*. David Sutcliffe (Rick Breck) was Christopher Hayden on *The Gilmore Girls*.

Overall: A bit confusing once the deaths start piling up, and crucial evidence (Davis' TMJ syndrome isn't noticeable when he's being questioned by the police earlier in the episode) arrives at the last minute. Not one of the stronger episodes, with a lot of gory flashbacks.

M17
Simple Man

US Air Date: 24 February 2003 12.4/20
UK Air Date: 24 May 2003

Written by: Steven Maeda
Directed by: Greg Yaitanes
Guest Cast: Jessica Diz (Bonita Cruz), Mel Fair (Reporter #1),
Paula Garcés (Carmen Abregon),
Elliott Grey (Well-Manicured Attorney), Jodi Knotts (Miss Talbot),
Elizabeth Peña (Mercedes Escalante), Stan Sellers (Judge Arce),
Richard Yniguez (Lorenzo Escalante), José Zúñiga (Carl Galaz),
Gennia Ambatielos (Reporter #2), Ken Garcia (File Clerk),
Jenna Chevigny (Reporter #4), John J. Dalesandro (Reporter #3)

Teaser One-liner: 'We better find out before we send an innocent man to jail for murder.'
The Case: Horatio is waiting to give evidence in the trial of Lorenzo Escalante, the husband of a prominent Miami councilwoman, for the murder of his housekeeper Abby Sandoval. However, Speedle has news of another victim murdered in the same way – a young, pretty Latina has been killed with a single shot to the left temple, at close range. There are mint leaves in her stomach, which Alexx is sure tox will confirm came from a Mojito. Reluctantly, Horatio has to withdraw his evidence.

Alexx performs a hasty autopsy and tells Horatio that this is a mirror of Abby's death except that Abby had glass in her wound track and the new corpse doesn't. This might be because Abby was shot in her car, whereas the new victim was found by the roadside. Calleigh believes the bullet is probably a Golden Talon, and agrees to compare it with Abby's.

Escalante's legal team try to get the case thrown out. The DA pressurises Horatio to follow through with his testimony, but Horatio needs to be sure that Escalante is the culprit. They never found the gun, although Escalante had admitted getting rough with the maid, and his DNA was under her fingernails. Horatio heads to the crime scene and, from the lack of blood, deduces that this wasn't where the girl was killed. He and Detective Sevilla follow a trail back to a canal, in which there's a submerged car. The car is extracted from the water – the driver's window has been hit by a bullet. A handbag identifies the victim as Bonita Cruz, who lived in the same neighbourhood as Abby Sandoval. Delko spots a bullet casing. He throws a gun-sized rock as far as he can, and Horatio designates the area in-between as the search grid for the gun.

Speedle finds fifty woollen fibres on Bonita's dress that match the fibres found on Abby Sandoval, which link her to Escalante. Inside Bonita's handbag is a very wet advert for domestic cleaners from the Cuban language press. They find the complete ads at the newspaper's office: Bonita circled one that paid considerably more than the others. The number in the ad is for a prepaid cellphone which doesn't answer. The ad was mailed in, and the newspaper has kept the envelope, which reveals a postal code matching Councilwoman Escalante's office complex.

At the office, Horatio and Sevilla talk to Carl Galaz, the councilwoman's special assistant. They need to know who had access to the machines, and want to take them for processing. The councilwoman overrides her assistant and gives them permission. Galaz writes out a list of employees on his legal pad, and gives it to Horatio. The CSI realises that Escalante was expecting them, and Sevilla admits that she gave her old schoolfriend Mercedes the heads-up.

Calleigh is supposed to be processing rounds from a major shooting on the Causeway for Detective Hagen, but is performing the Sandoval/Cruz bullet comparison instead. She can't match the bullets from Abby and Bonita, since Bonita's has been smashed up. However, she can test-fire the pistol that Delko has found in the river with them. That misfires, so she cannibalises a gun from the gun vault to make it work. The test-fires match. Unfortunately, that means that Escalante walks free.

Horatio agrees with Speedle that there might be two killers, the second one knowing all the details of the first murder. Alexx informs Horatio that the bullet which killed Bonita did not shatter the passenger window, and the second bullet is found in the car. The only reason that Bonita didn't have glass in her wound was because her window was already down when she was shot, so the killer had to wind the window up to shoot through it.

Sevilla brings in Carmen Abregon, who, like Bonita, answered the ad for domestic cleaners. She met the advertiser, but had a bad feeling about him because he was wearing gloves and ordered her a Mojito when he agreed to hire her. Her description matches Carl Galaz. The CSIs process the list of employees that he provided to see if there's anything hidden in the indentations on the page.

Galaz is arrested and still has the disposable cellphone in his briefcase; he's been unwilling to give up the $7 credit remaining. Galaz insists he is responsible for both murders, even though Horatio is convinced he is covering up for Lorenzo. Mercedes Escalante thanks Horatio for his work, but he points out that he's not finished yet. Speedle has found a marking BBQ 7A 3D in Lorenzo Escalante's writing in the latent impressions on Galaz's list, as well as Galaz's list of what he had to do to commit the murders. The marking refers to a brick near the barbeque at the Escalante's, behind which Horatio and Sevilla find a box of Golden Talon bullets. Escalante is rearrested.

Calleigh finally completes the analysis for Hagen but learns that he had to let the suspect go. He then killed someone else. Calleigh's time working for Horatio cost that person his life.

Personal Notes: Horatio has an as-yet-unexplained relationship with a detective called Yelina, who is connected to Horatio's late brother Raymond – she thinks about him every day.

Delko used to play right field for the University of Miami Hurricanes baseball team.

Techniques: Horatio and Speedle use a video spectral comparator to identify the newsprint.

The Wit and Wisdom of Horatio Caine: 'There's a flag on the play, Don. I can't testify today.'

'Seven dollars in exchange for the rest of your life.'

Classic Dialogue: Don, the attorney:'You want to know what I really like? I like smoking a Montecristo Number Two after winning a slam-dunk case. Now, your grandma wouldn't be trying to screw me out of a good cigar.'

Detective Hagen: 'I know you look up to the guy. I'm just saying, it's a hell of a lonely road he's walking.' Calleigh: 'Well, that's why I'm walking it with him.'

Horatio: 'Tell him what he's won, Adell.' Sevilla: 'It's a new kind of membership – gated estate, private room, high security . . .' Horatio: 'And here's the best part – it's for life.'

The Usual Suspects: Elliott Grey (Well-Manicured Attorney) played Winston Barger's attorney in **CSI 03**, 'Pledging Mr Johnson'. Elizabeth Peña (Mercedes Escalante) was Bibi Corrales on Latino boxing drama *Resurrection Boulevard*. Stan Sellers (Judge Arce) was the Bank Manager in **CSI 36**, 'The Finger'.

Overall: Horatio's beginning to make enemies, but his team clearly will stick up for him. Some great scenes between Elizabeth Peña and David Caruso make you not notice that there are no *CSI* trademark flashbacks at all in this episode.

M18
Dispo Day

US Air Date: 10 March 2003 12.9/21
UK Air Date: 31 May 2003

Teleplay by: Elizabeth Devine
Story by: Ildy Modrovich & Laurence Walsh
Directed by: David Grossman
Guest Cast: Julie Ann Emery (Lynn Martell), Tad Griffith (SWAT #1),
Thomas Robinson Harper (SWAT #2), Ken Kerman (Bob Stokes),
Carlos Lacamara (Dr Guillermo Santoyo),
Don McManus (Enrique Rayas/Erik Riden/Nedir Kire),
John Meier (Cesar Rubio), Maximo Morrone (Paul Tomassi),
Annika Peterson (Polygraph Tester), Larry Rippenkroeger (Sam Laskey),
Troy Robinson (Lester Cassidy), Mic Rodgers (Jeff Macher),
Michael Runyard (Sgt Hollis), Nick Searcy (Jack Seeger),
Tim Trella (Mike Tooley), Oakley Lehman (Horatio Stunt Double),
Bob Brown (Speedle Stunt Double),
Anne Ellis (Lynn Martell Stunt Double)

Teaser One-liner: 'Rescue! Get me rescue right now!'
The Case: Horatio and Speedle, along with a SWAT team,
are accompanying a batch of drugs being taken for
disposal at an industrial incinerator. The convoy is hi-
jacked when a fake funeral procession accompanied by
'policemen' is hit by a station wagon thereby blocking the
convoy. In the ensuing shoot-out, Speedle's weapon
doesn't fire, and he is shot in the chest; the officer with him
is killed. Horatio manages to shoot two of the robbers, one
fatally, knock out the tyre of their getaway van and
attempt to rescue the mother and child in the station
wagon.

The robber Horatio shot looks as if he has a prison-
gained physique. Calleigh discovers that the bullets are
Death Talons, which haven't been commercially available
since 1997. Horatio is questioned by TV reporter Enrique
Rayas, who asks him about parallels with his brother's
death two years earlier. Horatio ignores him and goes to
help the processing of the abandoned getaway van. Of the
drugs that were inside, only the cocaine is missing, for
which the CSIs assume the robbers had a buyer. Speedle's
Kevlar armour has saved him and he finds the robbers'
fake police uniforms in the truck. They were stolen from a
dry cleaners not long after Horatio decided which day
would be Dispo Day. There's a trail of blood leading to
where the getaway car is presumed to have been, and it's
clear the robber was seriously injured from an extremity.

Jack Seeger from Internal Affairs makes CSI his first port of call in the investigation into what went wrong. He intends polygraphing everyone.

Horatio finds a Death Talon in the station wagon but there's no mess in the car, strange given that it's being used by a toddler. Horatio also recollects that the woman, Lynn Martell, screamed about 'the' baby, rather than 'my' baby. She admits that it isn't her baby, and Tripp points out she's been in three serious accidents in fifteen months. It all points to insurance fraud, and Lynn admits she was going to be paid $5,000 to hit the hearse. She won't give the doctor's name who organised the fraud until it's pointed out to her that the bullet that hit her shoulder was actually meant to kill her.

Tripp and Horatio visit Dr Guillermo Santoyo and, after Horatio finds a wound dressing and a police-issued bullet in his rubbish, he eventually admits that he treated Lester Cassidy for a gunshot wound. Santoyo overheard Cassidy's fellow robbers saying that they would dump him at the Hialeah Hotel. Cassidy is found there, bleeding to death, and gives Horatio the name Nedir Kire before he dies.

Two robbers whose prints were found on the uniforms were on the same prison floor as Lester Cassidy, along with the two dead men. However, there's no trace of a Nedir Kire. Calleigh has processed the 122 bullets and casings found at the site, and tells Horatio that the shot fired at Lynn Martell came from across the street.

Calleigh has checked Speedle's gun and finds it's filthy, which is why it didn't fire. When he walks out of the polygraph test he gets a lecture from her on cleaning his gun. Horatio asks his brother's widow, Yelina, whether the name Nedir Kire means anything to her or her Task Force, but it doesn't.

Calleigh finds another bullet in the alleyway near the scene, and she and Tripp look inside Tomassi Stone and Marble. Calleigh searches for bullets, wiping her nose with her arm as she does so, and eventually finds one in some marble tiles. When she returns for her polygraph, she is extremely nervy, and tests positive for cocaine. Seeger believes that this makes her the mole, but Horatio is sure she's been dosed. The bullet found at Tomassi tests positive for cocaine, and the owner, Paul Tomassi, eventually admits that he makes fake tiles with cocaine. When the tiles are dissolved to release the cocaine, there are small pieces of red evidence tape inside them, proving they are from the stolen convoy.

Horatio realises that Nedir Kire is Erik Riden spelt backwards, and he and Delko discover that Erik Riden was a journalist who changed his name to Enrique Rayas when he came to Miami. On the news story Rayas broadcast from the hijack scene, the CSIs notice black spots on his shirt, which turns out to be GSR. The owner of the incinerator admits that he told Rayas about the disposal. Rayas says that he masterminded the hijack so he could be first on the scene and get tremendous ratings from the national coverage.

Personal Notes: Horatio's brother Raymond was killed in the line of duty two years earlier. Yelina is his widow, and now runs a Task Force. Speedle is lackadaisical about his gun cleaning; Horatio gives him a cleaning kit as a belated birthday present. Delko admits that he has recently lied to someone who loves and trusts him, not connected to his job. Detective Frank Tripp has three children.

The Wit and Wisdom of Horatio Caine: 'There are no secrets in Miami. Only useful information.'

'In this case, the lack of evidence is the evidence.'

'Did you know Florida has the highest percentage of unlicensed doctors in the US?'

'You guys couldn't find your ass with both hands. Now, you should be thanking her. If it's what I think, she just cracked the case.'

Classic Dialogue: Tripp: 'Saw your friend out front. Guy thinks he's Tom Brokaw.' Horatio: 'If he's Tom Brokaw, I'm Elliott Ness.'

Calleigh: 'So, you gonna shave before you go to IAB?' Speedle: 'It's a polygraph test, not a portrait.'

Calleigh: 'Do you always work on Sundays?' Paul Tomassi: 'Only when I am expecting a visit from an angel.' Calleigh: 'You might think I'm the devil in just a second.'

Fantastic Voyages: We see the interior of the polygraph and its workings, the interior of Speedle's gun, and follow the bullet being fired at Lynn Martell.

The Usual Suspects: Don McManus (Enrique Rayas) was Lee Michaelson on *Murder One*. Nick Searcy (Jack Seeger) was Deputy Ben Healey on *American Gothic*. The vast majority of the rest of the cast are credited stuntmen!

Pop Culture References: Newsman Tom Brokaw and 'Untouchable' Elliot Ness.

Mistakes Really Can Be Fatal: If Ray was killed two years ago, how come his grave says 1993?

Overall: Horatio Caine isn't above squeezing the mortal wound of a dying man to get information – Dirty Harry seems to have wandered into the wrong show. That apart, this is an action-packed episode that shows that the CSI team's loyalty goes both ways. But why did Raymond's death have to be changed from 1993 to 2001 so quickly?

M19
Double Cap

US Air Date: 31 March 2003 11.4/19
UK Air Date: 7 June 2003

Written by: Marc Dube
Directed by: Joe Chappelle
Guest Cast: Jodi Carlisle (Waitress), Anne De Salvo (Mrs Cusack),
Jack Guzman (Hugo), John Heard (Calleigh's Father),
Tom Hillmann (Special Agent Sackheim),
Rif Hutton (US Deputy Marshal Ardine), Michael Lopez (Ricardo),
Laurie O'Brien, Kathleen Rose Perkins (Communications Tech),
Al Sapienza (James Fukes), Steve Saucedo (Undercover Detective),
Nestor Serrano (Edward Hinkle),
Noa Tishby (Gloria Tynan/Gina Cusack)

Teaser One-liner: 'Who would risk a murder like this in front of all these people in broad daylight?'

The Case: A woman is found dead beside a hotel pool, shot in the back of the head from close range some time after 2.30 p.m. She's carrying an expensive bag and wears a large, oval, cut-emerald ring. There are no casings around, and Alexx thinks this might be an execution.

The victim is Gloria Tynan, who checks into the penthouse every Tuesday with an unknown man and always pays cash, although she has only $10 left on her when she dies. Speedle and Delko process the penthouse, where the bed appears unused. Speedle finds some pornography, and Delko lifts a fresh, partial print. Calleigh discovers Gloria's watch on one of the hotel staff's wrist but he is just a petty thief.

The autopsy reveals a 'double tap' shooting, the mark of a professional killer. There are rubbery black straps found around the wound. Calleigh takes the bullets for processing. The video records from the hotel show Gloria going down to the pool, and although her cabana is hidden from view, she can be seen asking the attendant for a phone, even though she has a cellphone of her own.

Horatio runs Gloria's fingerprints through AFIS and finds that they've been flagged by federal authorities. Horatio realises that Gloria was probably under federal protection. The bullets found in her have two sets of striations, indicating they went through a silencer – not the ordinary kind, but one specially created and capped off with a black neoprene washer, which produced the black straps. Similar bullets were found after a robbery in Uleta, investigated by Horatio's sister-in-law Yelina Salas. She tells Horatio that two suspects in ski masks terrorised customers at a bank. One of them had a mole on his neck and a security guard was killed with a double tap.

According to the information Delko has found, Gloria kept a low profile. She went to court only when there was a noise complaint about her dog, and she drove an average economy car. She reported the theft of her wallet six months earlier from her place of work, a boat tour company, which turns out to be owned by the father of narcotics detective Jeff Gabler – but no one was caught.

Speedle discovers that Gloria used the landline at the hotel to ring an address in Coconut Grove. Horatio and Hagen head over there and Patricia Cusack tells them that she doesn't know any Gloria Tynan. However, she recognises the photo as her daughter Gina, whom she hasn't seen for over a year, although she paid for her mother to move to Miami three months earlier. Gina was seeing a married man in Pennsylvania, who persuaded Patricia to wear a ring like the one Gina had. Horatio asks for the ring's gift box, and she confirms that Gina called her every Tuesday. Horatio notes that Mrs Cusack uses a cordless phone.

Outside the house, Horatio spots US Federal Marshals parked watching the house. Gina was the mistress of a man in the Witness Protection Programme. She was moved to Miami to be near him, but broke protocol by bringing her mother down from Philadelphia. The Marshals weren't aware of the cordless phone, since they knew there was a secure landline in the house.

The prints from the box and the bedroom match Edward Hinkle, who also has a Federal tag. FBI agent Sackheim tells Horatio that Hinkle is a vital witness against a major drugs gang, but Horatio is concerned about the murder during the robbery in Uleta. Sackheim denies any knowledge of this, but Hinkle's driver's licence photo shows a mole on his neck. Hinkle has now disappeared, and Horatio demands a meeting with his wife, Mary, who is extremely displeased to discover that her husband's mistress was also brought down in the protection programme. Her husband has a large amount of cash, although she doesn't know where. She occasionally sneaks some from his wallet, which she hands over to Horatio.

From the video tapes, Speedle has established that the killer disguised himself as a poolside attendant who didn't react with the customers in the prescribed manner. He went from cabana to cabana dispensing towels, except when he came to Gina's, where the towel count stayed the same. Calleigh returns to the hotel and checks the dirty towels for GSR, and on the one that tests positive finds a hair. This matches James Fukes, an ex-convict with a record for armed robbery in Philadelphia. However, his 'known associates' file has been wiped clean.

Horatio deduces that Fukes and Hinkle carried out a robbery in Pennsylvania and Hinkle kept the proceeds. Fukes has tracked him down, and killed Gina as a warning. Delko explains that there is a trace of chrysanthemum on the bills in the wallet Mary handed over, as well as some synthetic soap. Since the particular brand is used on cruise ships and other tour boats, Horatio deduces that Gina kept the money at her job at the tour company. Chances are that Hinkle has gone to collect it, and will be returning to Miami later that evening. The CSIs arrange for Hinkle to be arrested, but Sackheim intervenes. Horatio and Sackheim agree that Hinkle can be returned to the protection programme if he gives them Fukes.

Fukes realises that Hinkle is trying to set him up when he calls, and hangs up before his location can be traced. However, Hinkle says that Fukes loves horse racing, and he is duly arrested at the racecourse. He is about to be put into the system for trial for the crime in Uleta when Sackheim arrives and explains that Fukes' attorney has made an offer for his client to give evidence against an alleged hit man, and Washington has agreed. Despite Horatio's objections, Fukes is released and presumably placed in the Witness Protection Programme. The Hinkles are also moved on.

Personal Notes: Calleigh's father calls her Lamb Chop; he has a major drink problem. He lives in Miami (although we know from **M09**, 'Kill Zone' that her mother lives in Louisiana). From the photos on her desk, it appears Yelina and Raymond had a child.

The Wit and Wisdom of Horatio Caine: 'You know what they say – you lie down with the devil, you wake up in hell.'

Classic Dialogue: Fukes: 'There's ten thousand guns like that out there. You're not going to be able to prove a thing.' Horatio: 'Very dumb thing to say to a CSI.'

Fantastic Voyages: None.

The Usual Suspects: Tom Hillman recreates the role of Agent Dennis Sackheim from **CSI 44**, 'Cross-Jurisdictions'. Rif Hutton plays Lt Comdr Mattoni on *JAG*. Al

Sapienza played Logan's Attorney and partner in crime in **CSI 36**, 'The Finger'. Nestor Serrano (Edward Hinkle) was Captain Bruno Dante on *Witchblade*.

Mistakes Really Can Be Fatal: Calleigh says the crime Yelina investigated took place four years ago; Yelina says it was eighteen months.

The CSIs wonder why Gloria didn't use her cellphone to make the call. Cellphone calls cost. Local calls from landlines at many hotels don't.

Notes: Intriguing similarities between this and the first CSI novel, *Double Dealer*, in which Grissom tracks a Federally protected murderer, who is being monitored by FBI Agent Rick Culpepper. In the book, though, Grissom gets his man.

Overall: Nice to see Dennis Sackheim back – the relationship between him and Horatio in **CSI 44**, 'Cross-Jurisdictions' was one of the potential strengths of the series, and it's been wasted up until now. However, the rest of the episode isn't up to much, and the subplot with Calleigh's father is obviously leading somewhere.

M20
Grave Young Men

US Air Date: 14 April 2003 10.3/17
UK Air Date: 14 June 2003

Written by: Lois Johnson
Directed by: Peter Markle
Guest Cast: Robert Alan Beuth (Principal Roland),
Dayton Callie (Adams), Chad Gordon (Mark Hubbard),
Whip Hubley (Nick Gordon), Aaron Paul (Ben Gordon),
Chris Penn (Pete Wilton), Ta'sia Sherel (DNA Tech),
Rena Sofer (Alison), Hayden Tank (Raymond Caine Jr)

Teaser One-liner: 'So you're not interested in the kid unless he's dead?'

The Cases: Horatio is asked for help by an ex-convict. Peter Wilton's son Jeff has disappeared after going to school three days earlier. Since it was Horatio who arrested

Peter, he knows that the CSI will actively pursue the case. Horatio checks with Detective Tripp, but he hasn't had time to deal with it.

Horatio and Delko search Jeff's room and find a magazine about guns hidden inside a newspaper, a container of oil that could be used to clean firearms, and a T-shirt with the logo Four-Twenty Boyz on it. Horatio thinks that might refer to 4.20, the time high school children get home to experiment with drugs. They also find a stash of drugs, and a conical smudge on the window sill that could be caused by firearms use. A tree in the backyard is riddled with bullets, and is cut down and taken for processing.

Calleigh finds hundreds of bullets in the tree, including over two hundred that were hidden from view by the tree's growth indicating training rather than target practice. Peter Wilton claims not to know anything about his son's activities, but they violate the terms of his parole, so he's returned to jail. In Jeff's locker, Delko finds another gun magazine, and a pair of sneakers encrusted with dirt.

One of the bullets is matched to a gun owned by Nick Gordon, which was used to shoot out a scoreboard at Jeff's high school. The school says the perpetrator was Gordon's son Ben, along with another boy whose name they won't divulge, but Calleigh thinks that they were hinting at Jeff Wilton. The Gordons come into the CSI lab where Ben exhibits a morbid interest in the corpses. Nick Gordon appears to have little control over his son, who's blatantly smoking in front of him though Horatio gets him to stub the cigarette out. Ben admits that he likes guns, but if he fired one, it wouldn't be at a tree, but at whoever killed Jeff. Horatio asks how he knows Jeff is dead, but Ben says it's because Jeff would otherwise have rung him.

Delko finds some man-made Mastico in the dirt on Jeff's sneakers, which is used to repair headstones. Redeemer Cemetery is within walking distance of the high school and there Detective Tripp and Horatio find the body of another teenager, Mark Hubbard. Alexx confirms that this body has been moved. The primary scene is a mausoleum with high velocity bloodspatter and a bullet. Reconstructing the murder, the CSIs realise that there was a third person present as well as the murderer and Hubbard.

The CSIs process a baseball bat bag and a cigarette found in the mausoleum, and find that Ben Gordon is one of the three smokers. The bag has been used to transport rifles. The Gordons are questioned again, and the father tries to blame Jeff for the crimes. He says that his son goes to the cemetery in the mornings, and Horatio suggests to Ben that he knows what he was up to. The bag is also marked Four-Twenty, which Ben explains refers to Adolf Hitler's birthday, rather than a drug-taking time. Horatio realises that the boys are intending to carry out a massacre at their school. Ben says that he and Hubbard backed out of it so Jeff shot Hubbard and threatened him. Horatio deduces that Jeff is going to start the massacre at 4.20 p.m. during a school assembly. He races to the school, which is evacuated. Jeff shoots up the building but Horatio persuades him to give himself up.

Alexx examines the dead body of Charles Maxfield, whose girlfriend says they made love the night before and when she woke up he was dead. Alison Roufow flirts with Bernstein, but transfers her attention to Speedle when she is told that he is, effectively, in charge. Alexx tells him that the deceased ran marathons and may have had an enlarged heart. It's possible that he was smothered, since it's very hard to distinguish accident from homicide. She also finds dual lividity – the man was turned over from his stomach. Speedle takes swabs from beneath Alison's fingernails, and notices marks on her chest which he proceeds to photograph.

Alison visits Speedle at work, on her way to another modelling job. She says that she turned Maxfield over just before she called the paramedics. Speedle tells her that isn't right, and she then claims she turned him over during the night when he got too close. Speedle notes that she's admitting that he was dead in the middle of the night.

Speedle tests the pillows from Maxfield's bed, and informs Bernstein that they are down pillows, which retain more air. It would take some time to suffocate someone, which might explain the scratches on Alison's chest. Bernstein explains that Maxfield was about to marry someone else, who wasn't aware of Alison.

Speedle analyses the pillow further and finds a facial impression. He challenges Alison, who says that she did press his face into the pillow but it was to help him orgasm. The tox screens on Maxfield show he was three times over the legal limit, and incapable of making love. Speedle finds indentations in the pillow impression that match the jewellery Alison is wearing. She eventually admits her crime.

Personal Notes: Calleigh had just started working at CSI when Raymond Caine was killed. Raymond and Yelina's son is Ray junior. According to Calleigh, Raymond was an undercover narcotics detective who 'might have been dirty'.

The Wit and Wisdom of Horatio Caine: 'Kids make excellent criminals – they're sneaky.'

Classic Dialogue: Alexx:'Honey, that amount of alcohol would impede an elephant's sexual performance.'

Fantastic Voyages: We see the process of suffocation, and dual lividity with the blood settling. We see the bullet entering Mark Hubbard's head.

The Usual Suspects: Whip Hubley (Nick Gordon) played Brian Hawkins in the sequels to *Tales of the City*, and appeared with *CSI*'s Marg Helgenberger in *Species*. Aaron Paul (Ben Gordon) played the temple-visiting Peter Hutchins Jr in **CSI 39**, 'Felonious Monk'. Chris Penn (Pete Wilton) was Nice Guy Eddie Cabot in *Reservoir Dogs*. Rena Sofer (Alison) was Grace Hall on *The Chronicle*.

Pop Culture references: *Vanity Fair*.

Real-life Inspirations: The Columbine massacre.

Overall: The Alison Roufow subplot almost feels like a plotline planned for Nick Stokes that has been transferred over to Speedle. Otherwise, it's not one of the more inspired episodes.

M21
Spring Break

US Air Date: 28 April 2003 11.6/19
UK Air Date: 21 June 2003

Written by: Stephen Maeda
Directed by: Deran Sarafian
Guest Cast:Eric Dearborn (Brandon), Maggie Grace (Amy Gorman),
Brian Gross (Matt), Brandon Johnson (Trey Hanson),
Adam Kaufman (Ted), Sean Maher (Carson),
Laurel Marlantes (Rachel Moon), Michelle Morgan (Tiffany),
Wesley A. Ramsey (Kip), Stephen Reed (College Guy #1),
Riley Smith (Jack), Lauren Stamile (Marie), Tyson Turrou (Creepy Guy)

Teaser One-liner: 'Should have been the time of her life, Alexx, instead of the end of it.'

The Cases: The body of a young bikini-clad woman is found on the beach with her neck broken. Nearby are several oil patches, indicating that a number of cars had parked there. Alexx finds at least seven bite marks on the girl's inner thigh, all of which are avulsed, which suggests a predator. She swabs for semen, and confirms that the girl was sexually assaulted after death.

Speedle finds a Michigan driver's licence with the dead girl's photo on it buried in the sand near where the girl was found. It turns out to be a very good forgery, and its real owner Rachel Moon identifies the girl as her dorm mate Tiffany Heitzenrader. Her sister flies down to pick up her body.

The rapist is Carson Mackie, who has a record for statutory rape. He is in Miami filming a sleazy amateur Spring Break film called 'Babes on Break'. He found the girl on the beach, and believing she had just passed out, had sex with her. The forensic dentist tries to match a cast of Mackie's teeth to the bites on Tiffany's thighs but, while there are similarities, there are not enough concordant points to make a positive match. Mackie is only charged with necrophilia.

There have been three other cases similar to Tiffany's around Florida, combining a beach, broken neck and bite

marks, all of them at Spring Break destinations. Amy
Gorman is the fifth victim, but she's still alive. She was at
a tequila party, got drunk, went onto the beach to be ill,
and passed out. She woke up and found a man on top of
her, biting her. She kicked him as hard as she could and
ran. She has some bite marks on her abdomen and her
thigh, although the abdominal bites are from a game.
Unfortunately the bite marks aren't clear enough to use.

Speedle finds a memory stick from a digital camcorder
near the area where Amy was assaulted, and it shows both
Amy and Tiffany, and has a recording of Carson Mackie's
voice. However, they can tell from the girls' eyelines that
the camcorder wasn't being used by Mackie's crew, but by
someone else, who accidentally wipes the lens with his
finger, allowing the CSI technicians to gain a print.

This matches Kip Miller, who has parking tickets for all
the dates and times that the women were murdered.
Unfortunately his teeth don't match the bites either, and
Horatio asks Amy if he can take photos of the bites now
that the bruising has gone down. She reluctantly agrees,
and Miller matches the bites in all but two respects.
Horatio realises that Miller must wear temporary crowns,
and removes them – at which point the bite matches Amy's
thigh. Although there is insufficient evidence to arrest him
for murder, Miller is arrested for the assault.

The body of another Spring Break student is found lying
in the bottom of a pool, wearing only a pair of swimming
trunks. The death was comparatively recent, as the body
hasn't risen to the surface. Delko retrieves it and notes that
there is no foam around the boy's mouth and nose, so he
didn't drown. The body has a number of bruises and
scratches on it, and his swimming trunks are on back-to-
front.

He's identified as Trey Hanson and the cause of death
was an aneurysm. There is perimortem bruising on his
scalp that might have caused the aneurysm, although the
other marks are old. Hanson's three room-mates claim that
they've not seen him since the previous evening. When the

lab confirms Trey had a high amount of cannabis in his body, the room is searched and their clothing confiscated. Calleigh finds marijuana in the toilet cistern, and Delko finds a white-flecked bong hidden under the settee.

All four students used the bong, according to the DNA analysis, and the white flecks are from Hanson's vomit. The students claim that they had a 'Bong Olympics' – who could hold the smoke in their lungs for the longest – and Hanson threw up as a result. They then jumped into the pool to clear their heads. However, it's clear from the state of Hanson's feet that he was dragged to the roof, rather than walking of his own volition. The students confess that they were teamed for the Bong Olympics and Hanson was forced to go on for longer than he wanted, leading to the aneurysm. They then panicked, and dressed him in his swimming trunks the wrong way round before dragging him to the roof and jumping into the pool with him.

Personal Notes: Yelina has started working near Horatio's lab.

Fantastic Voyages: We see the bruise forming into a bite mark on Amy's flesh. We see the aneurysm blowing inside Trey's brain, and later see the oxygen deprivation leading to that.

The Usual Suspects: Adam Kaufman (Ted) was Buffy's college lover Parker Abrams. Sean Maher (Carson) was Dr Simon Tam on *Firefly*. Troy Winbush who debuts as Welch in this episode played Denny on *The Cosby Show*.

Pop Culture References: There's a throwaway mention of Federico Fellini.

Mistakes Really Can Be Fatal: How come Kip Miller didn't have legal representation during his questioning?

Trey's body is face up when Delko dives in to get him in the reconstruction, he lands face down.

Overall: A little too unnecessarily sleazy at times – the 'Babes on Break' motif is pushed to the limit and beyond – with not particularly inspired dialogue (hence the lack of quotes above!).

M22
Tinder Box

US Air Date: 5 May 2003 9.7/15
UK Air Date: 28 June 2003

Written by: Corey Miller
Directed by: Charlie Correll
Guest Cast: Robert Beltran (Ojeda), Ben Browder (Danny),
Natalia Cigliuti (Toni), Richard Edson (Haid), Lisa Gerber (Veronica),
Jaclyn Guitterez (Connie Wilkes), Craig Kvinsland (Johnny Brosnan),
John F. O'Donohue (Jameson), Heather Salmon (Blood Bank Nurse),
William Lee Scott (DJ)

Teaser One-liner: 'This building will be our witness.'
The Case: A fire breaks out at Club Descent at which
Speedle and Delko are partying. Sparks from a pyrotechnic
display seem to ignite the curtains behind DJ Scorpius, and
the clubbers desperately try to escape. However, two of the
doors are chained shut. The emergency back door isn't
closed, so Speedle leads people out through it.

There was a compliance question on the soundproofing,
so that's an immediate target for the CSIs. The sniffer dogs
are unable to find any evidence of an accelerant. Scorpius
didn't have a permit for his pyrotechnics.

The club's owner, Quentin Haid, says he chained the
doors to stop people sneaking in, and claims that $15,000
has been taken from his safe. The only other person with
a key is the barman, Johnny Brosnan, who is among those
unaccounted for. The safe is taken for fingerprinting.

Horatio and Alexx are briefly called off the case by
Detective Tripp to assist Judge Ojeda. Jill Susan, a
prostitute who regularly visits him, came by at 11.30. She
had driven her own car rather than coming by cab, as
usual. Ojeda noted that Jill had been disorientated and
agitated when she arrived, and asked to take a shower. He
then heard a noise, and found her collapsed. Alexx finds
no sign of semen or defence wounds; Jill has a frontal skull
fracture. There's bloody mucus on the wall and on the
showertap. Her clothes smell of smoke, and Alexx finds
soot in her throat. On her wrist is the Club Descent stamp.

She clearly was in the fire, and died belatedly from smoke inhalation, bringing the total dead to sixteen.

Susan's car is registered to Haid, and the car is impounded. When the CSIs check Haid's employee list, he has 33 cocktail waitresses: he is clearly managing prostitutes. Haid even made Jill go to an appointment immediately after the fire.

A girl that Delko was dancing with at the club is one of the victims, and Alexx explains that she died from breathing in superheated air. She also had broken ribs as a result of pressure from the panicked crowd. He talks to Danny Maxwell, the club's bouncer, who assisted Delko with bringing people out of the club, and was the first on the scene with a fire extinguisher. Maxwell says that Haid couldn't care less about the club.

Speed and Calleigh process the evidence on the scene, and deduce that the curtains behind DJ Scorpius ignited high up, burned, then dropped to the floor. They also find the remnants of a tape recorder. Calleigh isolates the microphone track from the tape, and they can hear the distinctive sound of an accelerant igniting. Speedle finds that the curtains were soaked in rum.

Scorpius is brought in and denies any involvement with the fire. His sparklers burn for eight seconds at a height of ten feet. They are so non-dangerous that you can put your hand in them. He admits that he kicked over one of the sparklers to try to stop the fire, but it only succeeded in making the blaze worse.

Haid had been served with a notice to deal with the soundproofing a month earlier, and a fortnight later had produced receipts displaying the renovation. However, the soundproofing wasn't tested again.

Scorpius' story is confirmed on the site, and Speedle notices a pour pattern on the floor. He, Calleigh and Horatio follow this back to the storeroom at the back of the club, which has a different burn pattern from the rest of the building. Underneath some debris, they find the bartender's body, with a large bloodstain on the front. He has been stabbed many times, with the incisions surrounded by contusions. Alexx believes that the piece of glass found in one of the wounds comes from an amber bottle. However, there is no smoke in Brosnan's nose, probably ruling him out as the arsonist.

Quentin Haid has been desperately trying to release his car from impoundment, and when he is allowed to, immediately opens the trunk and reveals $30,000 in a safe hidden in the spare tyre. Horatio and Tripp arrest him, since it's clear he removed the money long before the fire.

Speedle searches for the bottle, and notices that the weighted back door through which he escaped does not close properly. Someone must have exited from the club through that door on the night of the fire, and if it was the bartender's killer, there's a good chance he has left blood. Although the blood from the door will be useless, he recalls that he used his shirt sleeve to open it. He retrieves his shirt from the trash and the bloodstain is tested, but the DNA doesn't match anyone registered on CODIS.

The CSIs learn that Danny Maxwell has been turned down three times by the Miami-Dade Rescue Squad. Delko finds it hard to believe that Maxwell is guilty, since he helped to try to put the blaze out, but he might have been trying to be a hero. He obtains a sample of Maxwell's blood from a used plaster, after the bouncer gives blood, and it matches the blood on Speedle's shirt. He is interrogated and eventually admits that he did want to be a hero. He was meant to be a fireman, like two generations of his family before him, and he just wanted to stand out. The bartender caught him in the act, so he killed him, and the fire burned much faster than he had anticipated, leading to the deaths.

Calleigh tests the soundproofing at the club, and discovers that, although it had been replaced, Haid had painted over it. Haid's insurance company are very interested by the news, since it will invalidate a claim he has filed. The Fire Marshal wants to resign over the incident, but Horatio persuades him that there is nothing he could have done about it.

Personal Notes: Speedle and Delko go clubbing together.

The Wit and Wisdom of Horatio Caine: 'Every time we eliminate a suspect, another one pops up.'

'You've gained his trust – now use it.'

Fantastic Voyages: We see the effects of inhaling super-heated air, scorching the airways, and we observe the inside of the DJ's sparkler device. We also see the magnetic particles on the tape passing the head.

The Usual Suspects: Ben Browder (Danny) plays John Crichton on *Farscape*. Robert Beltran (Ojeda) was Chakotay on *Star Trek: Voyager*. John F. O'Donohue (Jameson) was the transplant donee Carl Mercer in **CSI 33**, 'Organ Grinder'.

Pop Culture References: DJ Scorpius is probably named after the villain on *Farscape*.

Real-life Inspirations: Although this episode was already in the planning stages before the events, there are strong resemblances to the fire at a Rhode Island nightclub in February 2003. As a result, the CBS Rhode Island affiliate refused to air the episode, and broadcast highlights from a benefit concert for the fire's victims instead.

Overall: The fire sequences at the beginning seem to go on too long, but given the amount of evidence that Speedle and Delko need to have seen for themselves for the case to be cracked, it's not too surprising. Whether we needed all the flashbacks mid-episode, when the evidence is being processed, is another thing altogether. But good to see Ben Browder back in action.

M23
Freaks and Tweaks

US Air Date: 12 May 2003 11.6/19
UK Air Date: 5 July 2003

Written by: Elizabeth Devine & John Haynes
Directed by: Deran Sarafian
Guest Cast: John Bentley (Officer German),
Chopper Bernet (Dennis Harmon), Clayne Crawford (Chaz),
Allen DiGioia (Medical Examiner), Sean Douglas (Officer Lyle),

Debrah Farentino (Julie Harmon), Patrick Flueger (Brad Kenner),
Craig Gellis (Hairy Tweaker), Mark Harelik (Valenta),
S.E. Perry (SWAT Leader), Billy Rieck (Tommy Lee Harkins),
Azura Skye (Susie Barnham)

Teaser One-liner: 'Once a meth head starts something, there's no off-button.'

The Cases: The CSIs are called out to a barn in the country where a twenty-five-year-old Caucasian male bound with duct tape has been found dead. The barn is a meth-amphetamine lab, and there are numerous disassembled pieces of electronic apparatus around. As they're searching the barn, Delko trips a circuit, and the barn blows up, although everyone has time to get clear.

The bomb was formed from dynamite helped by gasoline on a time delay. Delko comes across pieces of a guitar; Speedle finds a capacitor. The duct tape from the victim's wrists is sent for analysis and Alexx digs some wood out of the victim's head, which has haemorrhagic tissue on it, indicating that he was alive when it was applied with some force. The victim also had liver disease, which would have killed him within a year. Horatio determines the wood is probably from a pool cue. Tripp discovers that the barn's owner is Judith Lindeman, who rents to their victim, Darwin Capshaw, a small-time drug dealer, whose closest associate is Tommy Lee Harkins. He is brought in, and is found to be drugged up to his eyeballs on meth, with blood on his shirt. He claims that Capshaw was beaten up by another drug-addict tweaker, Chaz, because he complained about Chaz's music, and asks if Chaz has killed the girl.

A charred document reveals a cellphone number for Chaz. The cellphone is tracked down using GPS to a meth party, and Chaz is identified by the calluses on his left hand caused by his guitar playing. Chaz's trailer is full of assorted notebooks about his drug habit, one of them with comments about a 'Tin Man playing both sides'. Horatio asks for a copy of the book before it's given to the narcotics division. He finds a bomb-making kit in the next room. There's an empty kennel outside, which is masking the entrance to a basement, inside which they find Susie

Barnham, who is petrified of Chaz. Susie is a meth head, and says Horatio reminds her of someone. She agrees to give evidence if she can get out of town to try to clean up. She admits that she saw Chaz beat Capshaw to death.

Inside Chaz's car, Speedle and Delko find disposable cameras and some duct tape. Although the ends are cut, so they can't be matched to Capshaw's bindings, Chaz wrote his name on the side of the reel. Unfortunately, the murder and kidnapping cases are both compromised by a letter Susie sends to Chaz promising to get her revenge. The DA recalls that Raymond Caine was part of the unit who were after Chaz (see **Personal Notes**), but Horatio says that is classified information. However, without further evidence, Chaz will be set free.

Horatio realises that Chaz used the capacitor from a disposable camera, along with the guitar wire, to build the explosive that blew up the barn. Chaz is charged with the attempted murder of the employees who checked out the barn, and goads Horatio by saying that it was Raymond who taught him how to make bathtub meth. Horatio sees Susie on to a bus home, and she tells him that Raymond only pretended to take the drugs.

Calleigh and Detective Hagen investigate the death of a family man who has been shot in the heart at close range. A wallet was found in a nearby trash can with cash and credit cards. Calleigh finds a used bullet and an unspent bullet in the back of the victim's SUV. When she looks at the corpse's face, she realises she recognises him – Alexx's next-door neighbour Dennis Harmon. Alexx comforts Dennis' wife Julie, who can't think why anyone would kill him.

The unspent bullet produces a fingerprint matching Brad Kenner, a security man at the docks. He claims that the gun isn't his, but belongs to Julie Harmon, who told him to kill her husband. Alexx is furious when she hears this, and Calleigh suggests that she should no longer be involved with the case. Julie admits knowing Kenner, since she is his ophthalmologist, and says she gave the gun to him. She admits they had an affair for four months until she broke it off, but denies telling him to kill her husband.

The tox report on Dennis Harmon shows he has a high level of eyedrops. His wife says she prescribed them to help with his migraines. The drops made his vision blurry, so he wouldn't have seen his killer. Julie claims that he took the drops in response to a sudden headache. Calleigh can't prove that Julie deliberately gave him the eyedrops to blur his eyesight so, with equivocal evidence, she walks free.

Julie asks Alexx for forgiveness, but Alexx is furious that Julie put Alexx's kids at risk, since Dennis often took them out. If Kenner had chosen a different day to remove his rival, the children could be dead.

Personal Notes: One of Calleigh's parents is a lawyer. The drug addict Chaz claims to have known Raymond Caine, who he says was a meth head; another meth head, Susie Barnham, says she knew he was a narcotics officer because he only pretended to take the drugs.

Techniques: The QD technician uses parylene polymer in a vacuum-sealed isolation cell to harden the fragment of paper, which means it can be analysed without causing further damage. He then uses infrared light to read the charred ink.

The Wit and Wisdom of Horatio Caine: 'This comes under the heading of "No crime scene is ever safe," huh?'

'Physical evidence, my friend, is always better than an eyewitness.'

Classic Dialogue: Alexx: 'Why would she lie to me? To my face! Why would she have me sit there and tell her kids their daddy passed, like she had no idea why? My *friend*! To my face!'

Fantastic Voyages: The difference between a bullet firing and not firing. We see the wood hitting the bound body's head. We observe eyedrops entering the blood stream.

The Usual Suspects: Clayne Crawford (Chaz) played a student in **CSI 24**, 'Chaos Theory'. Debrah Farentino (Julie Harmon) played Molly Anderson on *Stephen King's Storm of the Century*. Mark Harelik (Valenta) was Ben Hildebrand in *Jurassic Park III*. Azura Skye (Susie) played Potential Cassie Newton in *Buffy*.

Overall: Was he or wasn't he? Hopefully by the time the next Raymond Caine episode comes around, the producers will have sorted out the story. Bits and pieces are all very well, but if they can't form a coherent whole that doesn't involve time travel, there's not a lot of point. Full marks to Khandi Alexander and Emily Procter for their confrontation scene – the ladies' best work in the series.

M24
Body Count

US Air Date: 19 May 2003 12.0/19 (75 mins)
UK Air Date: 12 July 2003 (65 mins)

Teleplay by: Ildy Modrovich & Laurence Walsh
Story by: Stephen Maeda
Directed by: Joe Chapelle
Guest Cast: Scott Adsit (Izzy), Kenny Alexander (Randall Kaye),
Tessa Allen (Emma Kaye), Cristos Andrew (Inmate #1),
Don Brunner (Burly CO), Maurice Compte (Guillermo),
John Eddins (Dan Clarkson), Troy Evans (Butch),
Stacy Haiduk (Mrs Kaye), Tomiko Martinez (Female Tech),
Geoff Meed (Hank Kerner), William O'Leary (Stewart Otis),
James Pickens Jr (Prison Warden), Cisco Reyes (Joe Aviar),
Saafir (Mega-G), D.B. Sweeney (Simon Bishop),
Charles A. Tamburro (Bryce Kaye), Aisha Tyler (Janet)

Teaser One-liner: 'This murder is a decoy. We have an escape in progress!'
The Case: A murder at the Miami Detention Centre brings Horatio out to investigate. The suspects aren't wearing the right identity bands and, as the prisoners are being checked, a helicopter lands, and three prisoners race out to it. Despite the guards and Horatio firing, they make their escape.

Many of the prisoners have switched their bracelets around, making it difficult to identify the escapees. One is eventually identified as Hank Kerner, a carjacker and murderer. The helicopter is found abandoned, with two dead bodies in it: the pilot Bryce Kaye and his brother Randall, a hit-and-run stockbroker and one of the escapees.

Speedle and Delko process Kaye's cell. There are photos of his daughter Emma, and they find an embroidery hoop hidden within a mattress. They also note a spark plug in the cell which has been used to break into the maintenance tunnel behind the toilet. Delko follows the tunnel and finds the prisoners' exit point to the yard.

Kerner's handiwork is soon found – a young mother is killed at a traffic intersection. Detective Yelina Salas and Horatio check the traffic camera tape and identify Kerner and his companion, child murderer Stewart Otis (see **M06**, 'Broken'). With Kerner on the loose, Alexx is concerned for Calleigh's safety, as she's the CSI giving evidence against him, and there have been two hung trials already. Calleigh goes to check with the prosecutor, Janet Madrano, that their star eyewitness is safely in protection.

In the lab, Speedle and Delko find water-soluble weave stabiliser, the material used to make patches, along with red, white and blue thread. Emma Kaye's photo has been taken down regularly, and Horatio realises that Otis will go after Emma at her school. Horatio and Yelina race to the school, but it's too late: Otis has abducted her. Mrs Kaye arrives, and doesn't seem surprised that someone has her daughter – but she thinks it's her husband, not Otis. They tell her about her husband's death, and explain that Otis' interest in her daughter is not monetary.

The bullet Kerner used on the young mother matches the bullets found in the helicopter victims. She's only been killed within the last hour, so fresh roadblocks are set up to apprehend Kerner. Hagen is told that the prosecutor has been killed; Calleigh is probably Kerner's next target, but she refuses to be intimidated.

A sniffer dog tracks Emma to a dumpster behind a shopping mall, where Horatio and Delko find her abandoned uniform and clumps of her hair. Otis is following his usual pattern and has disguised Emma as a boy.

Kerner is tracked down to the apartment of Treynice, a hooker he regularly uses. Calleigh isn't happy that Hagen didn't tell her about this, and accompanies the raid. Kerner escapes but leaves a message: the figure 31 painted on a wall, referring to the police code for homicide, and the information from Treynice that he is going to pop a blonde police bitch. Calleigh processes the 'paint', which she identifies as gun lubricant. She sends a sample to Trace to get the brand overnight. Hagen elects to stand watch over her. Calleigh leaves Hagen asleep and goes to the only gunshop in Miami that sells the particular brand of gun oil. Kerner is there and, after a brief game of cat and mouse in the aisles, she arrests him.

Dawn Kaye recalls that one of the escapees wanted an RV mobile home, and Yelina tracks down the only one rented in the past 24 hours to the home of Simon Bishop, another child molester. Bishop eventually admits that he lent the van to Otis in return for photos of Emma.

Delko analyses the photos of Emma, and discovers that Simon Bishop was in the RV when they were taken. Using the Geographic Information System, he discovers that they were photographed with the Orange Bowl Stadium in the background. Horatio and Yelina go to the empty parking lot with Bishop, but the RV has gone. However, it has a leaky waste system, and they are able to track it into the countryside, where they find it abandoned. Inside there's a video greeting for Horatio; outside there are two sets of footprints and the mark of a shovel being dragged. Horatio follows the prints and finds Emma Kaye in a shallow grave, still alive.

Horatio talks to Emma who tells him that she told Otis where her six-year-old cousin Robyn goes to school. Yelina discovers that Robyn's class is on a field trip to the aquarium, where Otis is spotted in uniform about to abduct her. Seeing Horatio and Yelina, he panics and runs, taking Robyn hostage. Horatio pursues, and Otis threatens to throw Robyn over the edge of the building. Horatio fires, freeing the little girl who flees the scene, and sending Otis dangling over the edge of the building. Horatio drags him back, although Otis wants to be left to die, knowing that he will get out and reoffend. As Otis is arrested by Yelina, Horatio promises that he'll be waiting.

Personal Notes: Detective John Hagen was Ray Caine's partner.

Techniques: Delko uses the Geographic Information System database to compare the shape found in the background of the photos with the shapes of buildings in the Miami area.

The Wit and Wisdom of Horatio Caine: 'What about the accepted view that exploiting a child in any way is a felony?'

Classic Dialogue: Calleigh: 'I took a drive, got some fresh air, apprehended an escaped felon.'

  Stewart Otis: 'I will get out. It's my nature.' Horatio: 'And I'll be waiting. It's my nature.'

Fantastic Voyages: We see the spark triggering the traffic camera. We follow each of Kerner's three bullets into the brains of their victims. Finally, for this season, we see how the odours affect the sniffer dog.

The Usual Suspects: William O'Leary reprises his role as Stewart Otis from M06, 'Broken'. Troy Evans (Butch) plays Frank on *ER*. Stacy Haiduk (Mrs Kaye) played Katie Hitchcock on *seaQuest DSV*. James Pickens Jr (the Warden) was FBI Director Alvin Kersh on *The X-Files*. D.B. Sweeney (Simon Bishop) was the star of Chris Carter's short-lived *Harsh Realm*.

Pop Culture References: Treynice's pimp sarcastically calls Hagen 'Starsky'. Given his own resemblance to Huggy Bear, that's quite appropriate.

Mistakes Really Can Be Fatal: Child molesters are regarded as the lowest of the low in prison – how come Otis was locked up with a drunk driver?

Overall: William O'Leary shows his skill at playing a paedophile once more, and we see a burgeoning romance between Calleigh and Hagen, as well as the potential for one between Horatio and Yelina. The 'Calleigh in danger' subplot gives Emily Procter more to do than she's had for most of the rest of the season, and can only bode well for the new year. But poor old Cochrane and Rodriguez – they hardly made an appearance at all!